CONTEMPORARY
AMERICAN POETRY

CONTEMPORARY AMERICAN POETRY

FOURTH EDITION

Edited by A. Poulin, Jr.

State University of New York,
College at Brockport

HOUGHTON MIFFLIN COMPANY   BOSTON
Dallas   Geneva, Illinois
Lawrenceville, New Jersey   Palo Alto

Printed in the U.S.A.

Library of Congress Catalog Card Number: 84-81715

ISBN: 0-395-35805-1

EFGHIJ-MP-8987

AMERICAN POETRY

Whatever it is, it must have
A stomach that can digest
Rubber, coal, uranium, moons, poems.

Like the shark, it contains a shoe.
It must swim for miles through the desert
Uttering cries that are almost human.

— Louis Simpson

© *Arthur Furst*

for Basilike and Daphne

Contents

JOHN BERRYMAN

ELIZABETH BISHOP

ROBERT BLY

CONTENTS

GWENDOLYN BROOKS

LUCILLE CLIFTON

CONTENTS

CONTENTS

WILLIAM STAFFORD

GERALD STERN

MARK STRAND

CONTENTS

Preface

For this Fourth Edition of *Contemporary American Poetry* I have expanded the selection of poets to include thirteen who were not represented in the three previous editions; and, in an attempt to make this edition even more "contemporary" than its predecessors, I've included representatives of a younger generation of poets whose reputations were established in the late sixties and early seventies. I've expanded and/or updated the selections of poems by most of the poets in the previous edition, I've made substantial revisions in a few other selections of poems with which I was not entirely comfortable, I've added as much recent poetry as possible, and, with the cooperation of the poets, I've included many poems which to date have not been collected in individual volumes.

In addition, I've updated all Notes on the Poets, as well as my general essay, "Contemporary American Poetry: The Radical Tradition," and I've considerably expanded the selected bibliography of criticism of American poetry since 1945. To encourage students to buy and read books of poetry by individual poets, I've also prepared an Index of Poets and Their Publishers, in which are listed the names and addresses of the publishers of all the poets represented in this anthology.

*   *   *

The fifty-one poets presented here are among those who have shaped the contours and direction of poetry in this country from about World War II to the present. While achieving an individual and collective distinction all of their own, they also have contributed to and expanded American poetic traditions.

Some critics may still be honing or inventing sharper tools with which to evaluate American poetry since 1945; eventually literary history may arrive at its own harsher, retrospective conclusions. However, today, for us, these poets clearly are among the major voices in contemporary American poetry. I hope this book reflects the quality of our communal experiences for almost half a century as much as it testifies to the vitality of our own imagination and of our poetry.

My primary concern while preparing this edition has continued to be to offer an anthology that is both discriminatingly representative and generously selective — a balance that becomes increasingly delicate. Thus I've selected poets whose work is representative of the full vitality and rich diversity of contemporary American poetry. And I've attempted to represent each poet as fully and as equitably as possible, selecting works that reflect each poet's characteristic subjects, themes, and styles.

Various poets in this book share a number of characteristics, and they might have been grouped accordingly. However, I have chosen to arrange them in a simple alphabetical order. No contemporary poet belongs to one "school" exclusively; some belong to no school at all. And attempts to categorize poets in such a fashion often simply convince the discriminating reader that so-and-so isn't just a confessional, Beat, New York, or Projectivist poet. Besides, such an approach also may predispose the reader to a given set of anticipations, thereby violating the integrity of the individual poem, the uniqueness of the individual poet, and the spontaneity of the reader's own response.

For much the same reasons, I've placed all critical apparatus at the back of the book, where a handful of readers may turn should they feel uncontrollably compelled to do so. For each poet, I've supplied a selected bibliography of primary and secondary works and a biographical and critical note sketching some of the prominent features of each writer's work. In these notes, I've taken schools into account now and then, but primarily I've let the poet's work—and not any set of critical assumptions—serve as my point of departure.

In my essay on "The Radical Tradition," I've attempted to delineate the major characteristics of contemporary poetry and to view it from a critical and historical perspective—in the hope of providing readers with a sense of how and why today's poetry is both new and a continuation of various American literary traditions.

Serious readers of poetry know full well that, regardless of how representative and generous it is meant to be, any anthology is necessarily no more than an *introduction*. The only way any reader can appreciate the true richness of today's poetry is by eventually setting this anthology aside and turning to the individual poets' own books. Indeed, the genuine measure of this anthology's effectiveness and "success" will be the extent to which it encourages readers to buy and read and respond to the books published by the poets represented. Thus I offer this anthology only as a gathering, an introduction, a door.

Readers should know that, in selecting poets and poems for each new edition of this anthology, I have been most sensitive to the ever-increasing measure of responsibility that such decisions place on me. I hope that I have lived up to that responsibility by offering teachers and students an intelligent and justifiable selection of some of the truly best poetry published in this country during the past four decades.

Readers should also know that this edition of *Contemporary American Poetry* would have been quite literally impossible without the generous cooperation of many of the poets, their agents, and their publishers, especially in the intricate negotiations for permission to reprint poems. To those poets and their representatives I am profoundly grateful.

I trust readers will agree with my belief that the full-page photographs of the poets add to this book a human dimension that isn't found very often in anthologies. I want to thank the photographers for supplying me with so many stunning photographs.

Obviously, I continue to be indebted to a long list of other individuals for their assistance and suggestions, but trying to name them all necessarily would result in overlooking too many. They should know that the absence of their names in this preface does not reflect an absence from my thoughts. However, I would be most remiss if I did not acknowledge the substantial encouragement and sensitive suggestions I've received from Michael Waters (Salisbury State College, Maryland) over the many years of working on the last three editions of this anthology. The presence of several poets and poems in *Contemporary American Poetry* is the direct result of his judicious exhortations...

...and you, Basilike and Daphne—spouse, daughter, friends, all.

A. Poulin, Jr.
Brockport, New York
Lisbon, Maine
Summer, 1984

CONTEMPORARY
AMERICAN POETRY

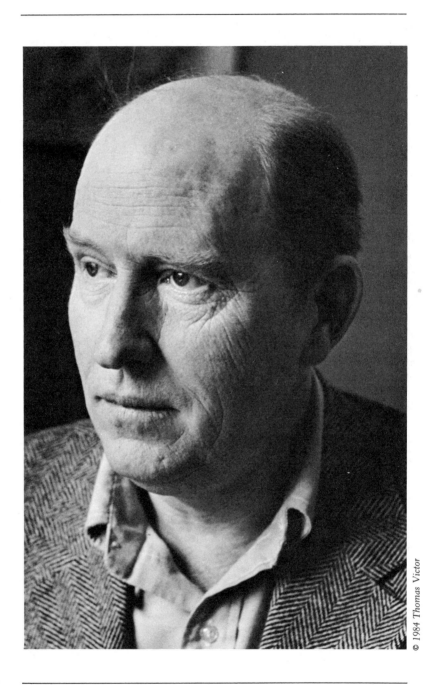

A. R. Ammons

APOLOGIA PRO VITA SUA

I started picking up the stones
throwing them into one place
and by sunrise I was going far away
for the large ones
always turning to see never lost
the cairn's height
lengthening my radial reach:

the sun watched with deep concentration
and the heap through the hours grew
and became by nightfall
distinguishable from all the miles around
of slate and sand:

during the night the wind falling
turned earthward its lofty freedom and speed
and the sharp blistering sound muffled
toward dawn and the blanket was
drawn up over a breathless face:

even so you can see in full dawn
the ground there lifts
a foreign thing desertless in origin.

LASER

An image comes
and the mind's light, confused
as that on surf
or ocean shelves,
gathers up,
parallelizes, focuses
and in a rigid beam illuminates the image:

1

the head seeks in itself
fragments of left-over light
to cast a new
direction,
any direction,
to strike and fix
a random, contradicting image:

but any found image falls
back to darkness or
the lesser beams splinter and
go out:
the mind tries to
dream of diversity, of mountain
rapids shattered with sound and light,

of wind fracturing brush or
bursting out of order against a mountain
range: but the focused beam
folds all energy in:
the image glares filling all space:
the head falls and
hangs and cannot wake itself.

HE HELD RADICAL LIGHT

He held radical light
as music in his skull: music
turned, as
over ridges immanences of evening light
rise, turned
back over the furrows of his brain
into the dark, shuddered,
shot out again
in long swaying swirls of sound:

reality had little weight in his transcendence
so he
had trouble keeping
his feet on the ground, was

terrified by that
and liked himself, and others, mostly
under roofs:
nevertheless, when the
light churned and changed

his head to music, nothing could keep him
off the mountains, his
head back, mouth working,
wrestling to say, to cut loose
from the high, unimaginable hook:
released, hidden from stars, he ate,
burped, said he was like any one
of us: demanded he
was like any one of us.

WORKING WITH TOOLS

I make a simple assertion
like a nice piece of stone
and you
alert to presence and entrance
man your pick and hammer

and by chip and deflection
distract simplicity
and cut my assertion
back to mangles, little heaps:

well, baby, that's the way
you get along: it's all right,
I understand such
ways of being afraid:
sometimes you want my come-on

hard, something to
take in and be around:
sometimes you want
a vaguer touch: I understand
and won't give assertion up.

THE UNIFYING PRINCIPLE

Ramshackles, archipelagoes, loose constellations
are less fierce, subsidiary centers, with the
attenuations of interstices, roughing the salience,

jarring the outbreak of too insistent commonalty:
a board, for example, not surrendering the rectitude
of its corners, the island of the oaks an

admonishment to pines, underfigurings (as of the Bear)
that take identity on: this motion is against
the grinding oneness of seas, hallows distinction

into the specific: but less lovely, too, for how
is the mass to be amassed, by what sanction
neighbor touch neighbor, island bear resemblance,

how are distinction's hard lines to be dissolved
(and preserved): what may all the people turn to,
the old letters, the shaped, characteristic peak

generations of minds have deflected and kept:
a particular tread that sometimes unweaves, taking
more shape on, into dance: much must be

tolerated as out of timbre, out of step, as being not
in its time or mood (the hiatus of the unconcerned)
and much room provided for the wretched to find caves

to ponder way off in: what then can lift the people
and only when they choose to rise or what can make
them want to rise, though business prevents: the

unifying principle will be a
phrase shared, an old cedar long known, general
wind-shapes in a usual sand: those objects single,

single enough to be uninterfering, multiple by
the piling on of shared sight, touch, saying:
when it's found the people live the small wraths of ease.

A. R. AMMONS

CUT THE GRASS

The wonderful workings of the world: wonderful,
wonderful: I'm surprised half the time:
ground up fine, I puff if a pebble stirs:

I'm nervous: my morality's intricate: if
a squash blossom dies, I feel withered as a stained
zucchini and blame my nature: and

when grassblades flop to the little red-ant
queens burring around trying to get aloft, I blame
my not keeping the grass short, stubble

firm: well, I learn a lot of useless stuff, meant
to be ignored: like when the sun sinking in the
west glares a plane invisible, I think how much

revelation concealment necessitates: and then I
think of the ocean, multiple to a blinding
oneness and realize that only total expression

expresses hiding: I'll have to say everything
to take on the roundness and withdrawal of the deep dark:
less than total is a bucketful of radiant toys.

THE CITY LIMITS

When you consider the radiance, that it does not withhold
itself but pours its abundance without selection into every
nook and cranny not overhung or hidden; when you consider

that birds' bones make no awful noise against the light but
lie low in the light as in a high testimony; when you consider
the radiance, that it will look into the guiltiest

swervings of the weaving heart and bear itself upon them,
not flinching into disguise or darkening; when you consider
the abundance of such resource as illuminates the glow-blue

bodies and gold-skeined wings of flies swarming the dumped
guts of a natural slaughter or the coil of shit and in no
way winces from its storms of generosity; when you consider

that air or vacuum, snow or shale, squid or wolf, rose or lichen,
each is accepted into as much light as it will take, then
the heart moves roomier, the man stands and looks about, the

leaf does not increase itself above the grass, and the dark
work of the deepest cells is of a tune with May bushes
and fear lit by the breadth of such calmly turns to praise.

THE ETERNAL CITY

After the explosion or cataclysm, that big
display that does its work but then fails
out with destructions, one is left with the

pieces: at first, they don't look very valuable,
but nothing sizable remnant around for
gathering the senses on, one begins to take

an interest, to sort out, to consider closely
what will do and won't, matters having become
not only small but critical: bulbs may have been

uprooted: they should be eaten, if edible, or
got back in the ground: what used to be garages,
even the splinters, should be collected for

fires: some unusually deep holes or cleared
woods may be turned to water supplies or
sudden fields: ruinage is hardly ever a

pretty sight but it must when splendor goes
accept into itself piece by piece all the old
perfect human visions, all the old perfect loves.

A. R. AMMONS

WHITE DWARF

As I grow older
arcs swollen inside
now and then fall
back, collapsing, into
forming walls:
the temperature shoots
up with what I am not
and am: from
multiplicities, dark
knots, twanging twists,
structures come into sight,
chief of these
a blade of fire only now
so late, so sharp and standing,
burning confusion up.

DISTRACTION

During my glorious,
crazy years, I
went about the business of
the universe relentlessly,
inquired of goat
and zygote,
frill and floss,
touched, tasted,
prodded, and tested and as
it were kept the
whole thing going
by
central attention's
central node:

now my anklebones hurt
when I stand up
or the mail truck
drops by to bury
me under two

small obligations: I
can't quite remember
what call I went to find
or why so much
fell to me: in fact,
sometimes
a whole green sunset
will wash dark
as if it could go
right by without me.

NEIGHBORS

How little I have really cared about nature: I always
thought the woods idyllic and let it go at that; but,
look, one tree, the near pine, cracked off in high wind,

dry rot at the ground, and coming down sheared every
branch off one side of the sweetgum: one tree, trying
to come up under another, has only one bough in light:

an ice storm some years ago broke the tops off several
trees that now splinter into sprouts: one sweetgum,
bent over bow-like to the ground, has given up its

top and let an arrow of itself rise midway: ivy has
made Ann Pollard's pine an ivy tree: I can't regain
the lost idyllic at all, but the woods are here with us.

BREAKING OUT

I have let all my balloons aloose
what will become of them now
pricked they will show some weight
or caught under a cloud lack
ebullience to feel through

but they are all let loose
yellow, red, blue, thin-skinned, tough

and let go they have put me down
I was an earth thing all along
my feet are catching in the brush

EXTRICATION

I tangled with
the world to
let it go
but couldn't free

it: so I made
words
to wrestle in my
stead and went

off silent to
the quick flow
of brooks, the
slow flow of stone

VOLITIONS

The wind turned
me round and
round all day, so
cold it planed
me, quick it

polished me
down: a spindle
by dusk,
too lean to
bear the open dark,

I said, sky,
drive me
into the
ground here,
still me with the ground.

John Ashbery

THE PICTURE OF LITTLE J. A. IN A
PROSPECT OF FLOWERS

He was spoilt from childhood by the future, which he mastered rather early and apparently without great difficulty.

Boris Pasternak

I

Darkness falls like a wet sponge
And Dick gives Genevieve a swift punch
In the pajamas. "Aroint thee, witch."
Her tongue from previous ecstasy
Releases thoughts like little hats.

"He clap'd me first during the eclipse.
Afterwards I noted his manner
Much altered. But he sending
At that time certain handsome jewels
I durst not seem to take offense."

In a far recess of summer
Monks are playing soccer.

II

So far is goodness a mere memory
Or naming of recent scenes of badness
That even these lives, children,
You may pass through to be blessed,
So fair does each invent his virtue.

And coming from a white world, music
Will sparkle at the lips of many who are
Beloved. Then these, as dirty handmaidens
To some transparent witch, will dream

11

Of a white hero's subtle wooing,
And time shall force a gift on each.

That beggar to whom you gave no cent
Striped the night with his strange descant.

III

Yet I cannot escape the picture
Of my small self in that bank of flowers:
My head among the blazing phlox
Seemed a pale and gigantic fungus.
I had a hard stare, accepting

Everything, taking nothing,
As though the rolled-up future might stink
As loud as stood the sick moment
The shutter clicked. Though I was wrong,
Still, as the loveliest feelings

Must soon find words, and these, yes,
Displace them, so I am not wrong
In calling this comic version of myself
The true one. For as change is horror,
Virtue is really stubbornness

And only in the light of lost words
Can we imagine our rewards.

"THEY DREAM ONLY OF AMERICA"

They dream only of America
To be lost among the thirteen million pillars of grass:
"This honey is delicious
Though it burns the throat."

And hiding from darkness in barns
They can be grownups now
And the murderer's ash tray is more easily—
The lake a lilac cube.

He holds a key in his right hand.
"Please," he asked willingly.
He is thirty years old.
That was before

We could drive hundreds of miles
At night through dandelions.
When his headache grew worse we
Stopped at a wire filling station.

Now he cared only about signs.
Was the cigar a sign?
And what about the key?
He went slowly into the bedroom.

"I would not have broken my leg if I had not fallen
Against the living room table. What is it to be back
Beside the bed? There is nothing to do
For our liberation, except wait in the horror of it.

And I am lost without you."

LEAVING THE ATOCHA STATION

The arctic honey blabbed over the report causing darkness
And pulling us out of there experiencing it
he meanwhile . . .   And the fried bats they sell there
dropping from sticks, so that the menace of your prayer folds . . .
Other people . . .   flash
the garden are you boning
and defunct covering . . .   Blind dog expressed royalties . . .
comfort of your perfect tar grams nuclear world bank tulip
Favorable to   near the night pin
loading formaldehyde.   the table torn from you
Suddenly   and we are close
Mouthing the root   when you think
generator   homes enjoy leered

The worn stool blazing   pigeons from the roof
                driving tractor to squash
Leaving the Atocha Station   steel

infected bumps the screws
    everywhere   wells
abolished top ill-lit
scarecrow falls   Time, progress and good sense
strike of shopkeepers dark blood
no forest you can name drunk scrolls
the completely new Italian hair . . .
Baby . . .   ice falling off the port
The centennial   Before we can

              old   eat
members with their chins
              so high up   rats
   relaxing the cruel discussion
  suds   the painted corners
white   most aerial
      garment crow
                 and when the region took us back
the person left us like birds
  it was fuzz on the passing light
over disgusted heads, far into amnesiac
permanent house depot   amounts he can
       decrepit mayor . . .   exalting flea
for that we turn around
experiencing it is not to go into
the epileptic prank forcing bar
to borrow out onto tide-exposed fells
over her morsel, she chasing you
and the revenge he'd get
establishing the vultural over
rural area cough protection
murdering quintet. Air pollution terminal
the clean fart genital enthusiastic toe prick album serious evening flames
the lake over your hold   personality
      lightened . . .   roar
You are freed
      including barrels
head of the swan   forestry
the night and stars fork
That is, he said
   and rushing under the hoops of
equations probable
      absolute mush   the right
entity   chain store   sewer opened their books

JOHN ASHBERY

The flood dragged you
I coughed to the window
last month: juice, earlier
like the slacks   to be declining
        the peaches   more
    fist
sprung expecting the cattle
false loam   imports
                next time around

DEFINITION OF BLUE

The rise of capitalism parallels the advance of romanticism
And the individual is dominant until the close of the nineteenth century.
In our own time, mass practices have sought to submerge the personality
By ignoring it, which has caused it instead to branch out in all directions
Far from the permanent tug that used to be its notion of "home."
These different impetuses are received from everywhere
And are as instantly snapped back, hitting through the cold atmosphere
In one steady, intense line.

There is no remedy for this "packaging" which has supplanted the old
    sensations.
Formerly there would have been architectural screens at the point where
    the action became most difficult
As a path trails off into shrubbery—confusing, forgotten, yet continuing
    to exist.
But today there is no point in looking to imaginative new methods
Since all of them are in constant use. The most that can be said for them
    further
Is that erosion produces a kind of dust or exaggerated pumice
Which fills space and transforms it, becoming a medium
In which it is possible to recognize oneself.

Each new diversion adds its accurate touch to the ensemble, and so
A portrait, smooth as glass, is built up out of multiple corrections
And it has no relation to the space or time in which it was lived.
Only its existence is a part of all being, and is therefore, I suppose, to be
    prized
Beyond chasms of night that fight us
By being hidden and present.

And yet it results in a downward motion, or rather a floating one
In which the blue surroundings drift slowly up and past you
To realize themselves some day, while, you, in this nether world that could
    not be better
Waken each morning to the exact value of what you did and said, which
    remains.

AS YOU CAME FROM THE HOLY LAND

of western New York state
were the graves all right in their bushings
was there a note of panic in the late August air
because the old man had peed in his pants again
was there turning away from the late afternoon glare
as though it too could be wished away
was any of this present
and how could this be
the magic solution to what you are in now
whatever has held you motionless
like this so long through the dark season
until now the women come out in navy blue
and the worms come out of the compost to die
it is the end of any season

you reading there so accurately
sitting not wanting to be disturbed
as you came from that holy land
what other signs of earth's dependency were upon you
what fixed sign at the crossroads
what lethargy in the avenues
where all is said in a whisper
what tone of voice among the hedges
what tone under the apple trees
the numbered land stretches away
and your house is built in tomorrow
but surely not before the examination
of what is right and will befall
not before the census
and the writing down of names

remember you are free to wander away
as from other times other scenes that were taking place
the history of someone who came too late
the time is ripe now and the adage
is hatching as the seasons change and tremble
it is finally as though that thing of monstrous interest
were happening in the sky
but the sun is setting and prevents you from seeing it

out of night the token emerges
its leaves like birds alighting all at once under a tree
taken up and shaken again
put down in weak rage
knowing as the brain does it can never come about
not here not yesterday in the past
only in the gap of today filling itself
as emptiness is distributed
in the idea of what time it is
when that time is already past

THE ICE-CREAM WARS

Although I mean it, and project the meaning
As hard as I can into its brushed-metal surface,
It cannot, in this deteriorating climate, pick up
Where I leave off. It sees the Japanese text
(About two men making love on a foam-rubber bed)
As among the most massive secretions of the human spirit.
Its part is in the shade, beyond the iron spikes of the fence,
Mixing red with blue. As the day wears on
Those who come to seem reasonable are shouted down
(Why you old goat! Look who's talkin'. Let's see you
Climb off that tower—the waterworks architecture, both stupid and
Grandly humorous at the same time, is a kind of mask for him,
Like a seal's face. Time and the weather
Don't always go hand in hand, as here: sometimes
One is slanted sideways, disappears for awhile.
Then later it's forget-me-not time, and rapturous
Clouds appear above the lawn, and the rose tells
The old old story, the pearl of the orient, occluded
And still apt to rise at times.)

A few black smudges
On the outer boulevards, like squashed midges
And the truth becomes a hole, something one has always known,
A heaviness in the trees, and no one can say
Where it comes from, or how long it will stay—

A randomness, a darkness of one's own.

STREET MUSICIANS

One died, and the soul was wrenched out
Of the other in life, who, walking the streets
Wrapped in an identity like a coat, sees on and on
The same corners, volumetrics, shadows
Under trees. Farther than anyone was ever
Called, through increasingly suburban airs
And ways, with autumn falling over everything:
The plush leaves the chattels in barrels
Of an obscure family being evicted
Into the way it was, and is. The other beached
Glimpses of what the other was up to:
Revelations at last. So they grew to hate and forget each other.

So I cradle this average violin that knows
Only forgotten showtunes, but argues
The possibility of free declamation anchored
To a dull refrain, the year turning over on itself
In November, with the spaces among the days
More literal, the meat more visible on the bone.
Our question of a place of origin hangs
Like smoke: how we picnicked in pine forests,
In coves with the water always seeping up, and left
Our trash, sperm and excrement everywhere, smeared
On the landscape, to make of us what we could.

PARADOXES AND OXYMORONS

This poem is concerned with language on a very plain level.
Look at it talking to you. You look out a window

Or pretend to fidget. You have it but you don't have it.
You miss it, it misses you. You miss each other.

The poem is sad because it wants to be yours, and cannot.
What's a plain level? It is that and other things,
Bringing a system of them into play. Play?
Well, actually, yes, but I consider play to be

A deeper outside thing, a dreamed role-pattern,
As in the division of grace these long August days
Without proof. Open-ended. And before you know
It gets lost in the steam and chatter of typewriters.

It has been played once more. I think you exist only
To tease me into doing it, on your level, and then you aren't there
Or have adopted a different attitude. And the poem
Has set me softly down beside you. The poem is you.

INTRODUCTION

To be a writer and write things
You must have experiences you can write about.
Just living won't do. I have a theory
About masterpieces, how to make them
At very little expense, and they're every
Bit as good as the others. You can
Use the same materials of the dream, at last.

It's a kind of game with no losers and only one
Winner—you. First, pain gets
Flashed back through the story and the story
Comes out backwards and woof-side up. This is
No one's story! At least they think that
For a time and the story is architecture
Now, and then history of a diversified kind.
A vacant episode during which the bricks got
Repointed and browner. And it ends up
Nobody's, there is nothing for any of us
Except that fretful vacillating around the central
Question that brings us closer,
For better and worse, for all this time.

Marvin Bell

WHITE CLOVER

Once when the moon was out about three-quarters
and the fireflies who are the stars
of backyards
were out about three-quarters
and about three-fourths of all the lights
in the neighborhood
were on because people can be at home,
I took a not so innocent walk
out among the lawns,
navigating by the light of lights,
and there there were many hundreds of moons
on the lawns
where before there was only polite grass.
These were moons on long stems,
their long stems giving their greenness
to the center of each flower
and the light giving its whiteness to the tops
of the petals. I could say
it was light from stars
touched the tops of flowers and no doubt
something heavenly reaches what grows outdoors
and the heads of men who go hatless,
but I like to think we have a world
right here, and a life
that isn't death. So I don't say it's better
to be right here. I say this is where
many hundreds of core-green moons
gigantic to my eye
rose because men and women had sown green grass,
and flowered to my eye in man-made light,
and to some would be as fire in the body
and to others a light in the mind
over all their property.

THE EXTERMINATION OF THE JEWS

to Donald Justice

A thousand years from now
they will be remembered as heroes.
A thousand years from now
they will still be promised their past.

Objects of beauty notwithstanding,
once more they will appear
for their ruin, seeking a purse,
hard bread or a heavy weapon

for those who must survive,
but no one shall survive.
We who have not forgotten,
our children shall outremember:

their victims' pious chanting—
last wishes, last Yiddish, last dreaming—
were defeats with which the Gestapo
continues ceasing and ceasing.

from THE ESCAPE INTO YOU

Homage to the Runner

The form of this "sport" is pain,
riding up into it, he hurts to win.
These are the moments when death is really
possible, when a man can fit into
his enlarged heart all that is known
or was or shall be pumping fulfills.

The love of form is a black occasion
through which some light must show
in a hundred years of commitment.
By the time the body aches to end it,
the poem begins, at first in darkness,
surrounded by counterfeits of leisure.

MARVIN BELL

Run away. Leave them to ease.
What does it matter you wind up alone?
There is no finish; you can stop for no one.
When your wife cries, you pass a kiss.
When your sons worry, you flash a smile.
When your women wave, you ignore them.

THE MYSTERY OF EMILY DICKINSON

Sometimes the weather goes on for days
but you were different. You were divine.
While the others wrote more and longer,
you wrote much more and much shorter.
I held your white dress once: 12 buttons.
In the cupola, the wasps struck glass
as hard to escape as you hit your sound
again and again asking Welcome. No one.

Except for you, it were a trifle:
This morning, not much after dawn,
in level country, not New England's,
through leftovers of summer rain I
went out rag-tag to the curb, only
a sleepy householder at his routine
bending to trash, when a young girl
in a white dress your size passed,

so softly!, carrying her shoes. It must be
she surprised me—her barefoot quick-step
and the earliness of the hour, your dress—
or surely I'd have spoken of it sooner.
I should have called to her, but a neighbor
wore that look you see against happiness.
I won't say anything would have happened
unless there was time, and eternity's plenty.

TO DOROTHY

You are not beautiful, exactly.
You are beautiful, inexactly.

MARVIN BELL

You let a weed grow by the mulberry
and a mulberry grow by the house.
So close, in the personal quiet
of a windy night, it brushes the wall
and sweeps away the day till we sleep.

A child said it, and it seemed true:
"Things that are lost are all equal."
But it isn't true. If I lost you,
the air wouldn't move, nor the tree grow.
Someone would pull the weed, my flower.
The quiet wouldn't be yours. If I lost you,
I'd have to ask the grass to let me sleep.

DURING THE WAR

I was one of those who sees something cross the moon
and is never again the same person.
I was one of those who fought for an envelope, for a stamp.
I was one who felt the pain of the potted plant
and the loneliness of the tree.

It was all in my mind. It was an idea I had!
Was it such a bad idea?
Did it hurt anyone? Did it even delay for a minute
a father thousands of miles from me
fleeing a tank from my own beloved country?

Did it hasten the deaths by bombing?
Did it quicken the suffering of the homeless?

Certainly not. Absolutely, unequivocally, the answer is No.
My love for the tree did not interfere
with one decision of a committee, one staff meeting.
My joining forces with the mysterious
did not blot a single marching order, nor break a rifle.

The world went on without me. To its mind,
I was no part of it, but to my mind I was too much a part.
I put it all down on paper but in code.
Even at night, I watched the skies like a spy
for the intersection of a planet and the future.

MARVIN BELL

THE LAST THING I SAY

to a thirteen-year-old sleeping,
tone of an angel, breath of a soft wing,
I say through an upright dark space
as I narrow it pulling the door
sleepily to let the words go surely into
the bedroom until I close them in
for good, a nightwatchman's-worth
of grace and a promise for morning
not so far from some God's first notion
that the world be an image by first light
so much better than pictures of hope
drawn by firelight in ashes,
so much clearer too, a young person
wanting to be a man might draw one finger
along an edge of this world and it
would slice a mouth there
to speak blood and then should he put that wound
into the mouth of his face,
he will be kissed there and taste
the salt of his father as he lowers
himself from his son's high bedroom
in the heaven of his image of
a small part of himself and sweet dreams.

THESE GREEN-GOING-TO-YELLOW

This year,
I'm raising the emotional ante,
putting my face
in the leaves to be stepped on,
seeing myself among them, that is;
that is, likening
leaf-vein to artery, leaf to flesh,
the passage of a leaf in autumn
to the passage of autumn,
branch-tip and winter spaces
to possibilities, and possibility
to God. Even on East 61st Street
in the blowzy city of New York,

someone has planted a gingko
because it has leaves like fans like hands,
hand-leaves, and sex. Those lovely
Chinese hands on the sidewalks
so far from delicacy
or even, perhaps, another gender of gingko—
do we see them?
No one ever treated us so gently
as these green-going-to-yellow hands
fanned out where we walk.
No one ever fell down so quietly
and lay where we would look
when we were tired or embarrassed,
or so bowed down by humanity
that we had to watch out lest our shoes stumble,
and looked down not to look up
until something looked like parts of people
where we were walking. We have no
experience to make us see the gingko
or any other tree,
and, in our admiration for whatever grows tall
and outlives us,
we look away, or look at the middles of things,
which would not be our way
if we truly thought we were gods.

DRAWN BY STONES, BY EARTH,
BY THINGS THAT HAVE BEEN IN THE FIRE

I can tell you about this because I have held in my hand
the little potter's sponge called an "elephant ear."
Naturally, it's only a tiny version of an ear,
but it's the thing you want to pick up out of the toolbox
when you wander into the deserted ceramics shop
down the street from the cave where the fortune-teller works.
Drawn by stones, by earth, by things that have been in the fire.

The elephant ear listens to the side of the vase
as it is pulled upwards from a dome of muddy clay.
The ear listens to the outside wall of the pot
and the hand listens to the inside wall of the pot,

MARVIN BELL

and between them a city rises out of dirt and water.
Inside this city live the remains of animals,
animals who prepared for two hundred years to be clay.

Rodents make clay, and men wearing spectacles make clay,
though the papers they were signing go up in flames
and nothing more is known of these long documents
except by those angels who divine in our ashes.
Kings and queens of the jungle make clay
and royalty and politicians make clay although
their innocence stays with their clothes until unravelled.

There is a lost soldier in every ceramic bowl.
The face on the dinner plate breaks when the dish does
and lies for centuries unassembled in the soil.
These things that have the right substance to begin with,
put into the fire at temperatures that melt glass,
keep their fingerprints forever, it is said,
like inky sponges that walk away in the deep water.

THEY

My destiny has been to prune one tree
to make it look more and more common.
Friends, I am still at it.

It has been suggested, knowing I plan a tattoo,
that I permit myself to be tattooed all over
and become, myself, a tree. Stick my arms out.

But that wouldn't be me. Nor would there be,
afterwards, as there is now,
the object of my desire

in the form of my desire unveiling.
What do they think this is all about?
Nothing was known before I came to know it.

The purpose of a tree is that I have given it:
to be the sane result of chaos,
to be so completely known it may be overlooked.

MARVIN BELL

THE NEST

The day the birds were lifted from my shoulders,
the whole sky was blue, a long-imagined effect
had taken hold, and a small passenger plane
was beating the earth with its wings
as it swung over the bean fields toward home.
A fat car barely travelled a narrow road
while I waited at the bottom of a hill.
People around me were speaking loudly
but I heard only whispers, and stepped away.

You understand, I was given no choice.
For a long time, I was tired of whatever it was
that dug its way into my shoulders for balance
and whispered in my ears, and hung on for dear life
among tall narrow spaces in the woods
and in thickets and crowds, like those of success,
with whom one mingles at parties and in lecture halls.
In the beginning, there was this or that . . .
but always on my shoulders that which had landed.

That was life, and it went on in galleries
and shopping plazas, in museums and civic centers,
much like the life of any responsible man
schooled in the marriage of history and culture
and left to learn the rest at the legs of women.
In furtive rooms, in passing moments, the sea
reopened a door at its depth, trees spoke
from the wooden sides of houses, bodies became
again the nests in the naked tree.

After that, I was another person,
without knowing why or how, and after that,
I lived naked in a new world where the sun
broke through windows to grasp entire families
and crept between trees to wash down streets
without disturbing any object, in a world
where a solitary kiss blew down a door.
The day the birds were lifted from my shoulders,
it killed me — and almost cost me a life. . . .

MARVIN BELL

LONG ISLAND

The things I did, I did because of trees,
wildflowers and weeds, because of ocean and sand,
because the dunes move about under houses built on stilts,
and the wet fish slip between your hands back into the sea,
because during the War we heard strafing across the Bay
and after the War we found shell casings with our feet.
Because old tires ringed the boat docks,
and sandbags hung from the prows of speedboats,
and every road in every country ends at the water,
and because a child thinks each room in his house big,
and if the truth be admitted, his first art galleries
were the wallpaper in his bedroom and the carlights
warming the night air as he lay in bed counting.

The things I did, I counted in wattage and ohms,
in the twelve zones that go from pure black to pure white,
in the length of the trumpet and the curves of the cornet,
in the cup of the mouthpiece. In the compass and protractor,
in the perfect bevelled ruler, in abstract geometry,
and if the truth be known, in the bowing of cattails
he first read his Heraclitus and in the stretching box turtle
he found his theory of relativity and the gist of knowledge.
He did what he did. The action of his knee in walking
was not different from the over-stretching of an ocean wave,
and the proofs of triangles, cones and parallelograms
were neither more nor less than the beauty of a fast horse
which runs through the numbers of the stopwatch and past the finish.

The things I counted, I counted beyond the finish,
beyond rolling tar roadways that squared the fields,
where I spun on the ice, wavered in fog, sped up or idled,
and, like Perry, like Marco Polo, a young man I saw
alone walk unlit paths, encircled by rushes
and angry dogs, to the indentations of his island.
And if the truth be told, he learned of Columbus,
of Einstein, of Michelangelo, on such low roads and local waters.
Weakfish hauled weakening from the waters at night,
and the crab rowing into the light, told him in their way
that the earth moved around the sun in the same way,
with the branched mud-print of a duck's foot to read,
and life in the upturned bellies of the fishkill in the creek.

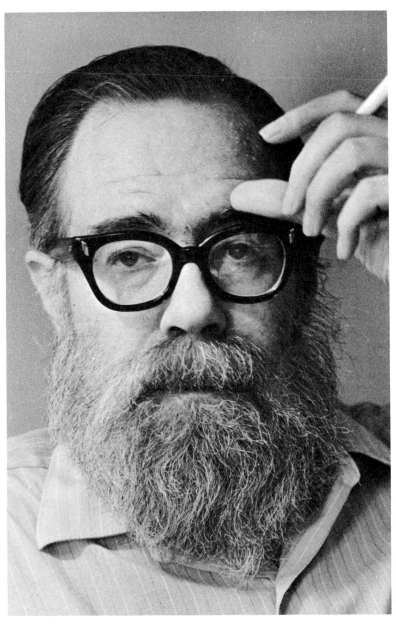

John Berryman

THE SONG OF THE TORTURED GIRL

After a little I could not have told—
But no one asked me this—why I was there.
I asked. The ceiling of that place was high
And there were sudden noises, which I made.
I must have stayed there a long time today:
My cup of soup was gone when they brought me back.

Often "Nothing worse now can come to us"
I thought, the winter the young men stayed away,
My uncle died, and mother broke her crutch.
And then the strange room where the brightest light
Does not shine on the strange men: shines on me.
I feel them stretch my youth and throw a switch.

Through leafless branches the sweet wind blows
Making a mild sound, softer than a moan;
High in a pass once where we put our tent,
Minutes I lay awake to hear my joy.
—I no longer remember what they want.
Minutes I lay awake to hear my joy.

from THE DREAM SONGS

1

Huffy Henry hid   the day,
unappeasable Henry sulked.
I see his point,—a trying to put things over.
It was the thought that they thought
they could *do* it made Henry wicked & away.
But he should have come out and talked.

All the world like a woolen lover
once did seem on Henry's side.

Then came a departure.
Thereafter nothing fell out as it might or ought.
I don't see how Henry, pried
open for all the world to see, survived.

What he has now to say is a long
wonder the world can bear & be.
Once in a sycamore I was glad
all at the top, and I sang.
Hard on the land wears the strong sea
and empty grows every bed.

4

Filling her compact & delicious body
with chicken páprika, she glanced at me
twice.
Fainting with interest, I hungered back
and only the fact of her husband & four other people
kept me from springing on her

or falling at her little feet and crying
'You are the hottest one for years of night
Henry's dazed eyes
have enjoyed, Brilliance.' I advanced upon
(despairing) my spumoni. —Sir Bones: is stuffed,
de world, wif feeding girls.

—Black hair, complexion Latin, jewelled eyes
downcast . . . The slob beside her   feasts . . . What wonders is
she sitting on, over there?
The restaurant buzzes. She might as well be on Mars.
Where did it all go wrong? There ought to be a law against Henry.
—Mr Bones: there is.

8

The weather was fine. They took away his teeth,
white & helpful; bothered his backhand;
halved his green hair.
They blew out his loves, his interests. 'Underneath,'
(they called in iron voices) 'understand,
is nothing. So there.'

The weather was very fine. They lifted off
his covers till he showed, and cringed & pled
to see himself less.
They installed mirrors till he flowed. 'Enough'
(murmured they) 'if you will watch Us instead,
yet you may saved be. Yes.'

The weather fleured. They weakened all his eyes,
and burning thumbs into his ears, and shook
his hand like a notch.
They flung long silent speeches. (Off the hook!)
They sandpapered his plumpest hope. (So capsize.)
They took away his crotch.

9

Deprived of his enemy, shrugged to a standstill
horrible Henry, foaming. Fan their way
toward him who will
in the high wood: the officers, their rest,
with p. a. echoing: his girl comes, say,
conned in to test

if he's still human, see: she love him, see,
therefore she get on the Sheriff's mike & howl
'Come down, come down'.
Therefore he un-budge, furious. He'd flee
but only Heaven hangs over him foul.
At the crossways, downtown,

he dreams the folks are buying parsnips & suds
and paying rent to foes. He slipt & fell.
It's golden here in the snow.
A mild crack: a far rifle. Bogart's duds
truck back to Wardrobe. Fancy the brain from hell
held out so long. Let go.

13

God bless Henry. He lived like a rat,
with a thatch of hair on his head
in the beginning.

Henry was not a coward. Much.
He never deserted anything; instead
he stuck, when things like pity were thinning.

So may be Henry was a human being.
Let's investigate that.
. . . We did; okay.
He is a human American man.
That's true. My lass is braking.
My brass is aching. Come & diminish me, & map my way.

God's Henry's enemy. We're in business . . . Why,
what business must be clear.
A cornering.
I couldn't feel more like it. —Mr Bones,
as I look on the saffron sky,
you strikes me as ornery.

14

Life, friends, is boring. We must not say so.
After all, the sky flashes, the great sea yearns,
we ourselves flash and yearn,
and moreover my mother told me as a boy
(repeatedly) 'Ever to confess you're bored
means you have no

Inner Resources.' I conclude now I have no
inner resources, because I am heavy bored.
Peoples bore me,
literature bores me, especially great literature,
Henry bores me, with his plights & gripes
as bad as achilles,

who loves people and valiant art, which bores me.
And the tranquil hills, & gin, look like a drag
and somehow a dog
has taken itself & its tail considerably away
into mountains or sea or sky, leaving
behind: me, wag.

JOHN BERRYMAN

29

There sat down, once, a thing on Henry's heart
só heavy, if he had a hundred years
& more, & weeping, sleepless, in all them time
Henry could not make good.
Starts again always in Henry's ears
the little cough somewhere, an odour, a chime.

And there is another thing he has in mind
like a grave Sienese face a thousand years
would fail to blur the still profiled reproach of. Ghastly,
with open eyes, he attends, blind.
All the bells say: too late. This is not for tears;
thinking.

But never did Henry, as he thought he did,
end anyone and hacks her body up
and hide the pieces, where they may be found.
He knows: he went over everyone, & nobody's missing.
Often he reckons, in the dawn, them up.
Nobody is ever missing.

45

He stared at ruin. Ruin stared straight back.
He thought they was old friends. He felt on the stair
where her papa found them bare
they became familiar. When the papers were lost
rich with pals' secrets, he thought he had the knack
of ruin. Their paths crossed

and once they crossed in jail; they crossed in bed;
and over an unsigned letter their eyes met,
and in an Asian city
directionless & lurchy at two & three,
or trembling to a telephone's fresh threat,
and when some wired his head

to reach a wrong opinion, 'Epileptic'.
But he noted now that: they were not old friends.

He did not know this one.
This one was a stranger, come to make amends
for all the imposters, and to make it stick.   .
Henry nodded, un-.

46

I am, outside. Incredible panic rules.
People are blowing and beating each other without mercy.
Drinks are boiling. Iced
drinks are boiling. The worse anyone feels, the worse
treated he is. Fools elect fools.
A harmless man at an intersection said, under his breath: "Christ!"

That word, so spoken, affected the vision
of, when they trod to work next day, shopkeepers
who went & were fitted for glasses.
Enjoyed they then an appearance of love & law.
Millenia whift & waft—one, one—er, er . . .
Their glasses were taken from them, & they saw.

Man has undertaken the top job of all,
son fin. Good luck.
I myself walked at the funeral of tenderness.
Followed other deaths. Among the last,
like the memory of a lovely fuck,
was: *Do, ut des*.

55

Peter's not friendly. He gives me sideways looks.
The architecture is far from reassuring.
I feel uneasy.
A pity,—the interview began so well:
I mentioned fiendish things, he waved them away
and sloshed out a martini

strangely needed. We spoke of indifferent matters—
God's health, the vague hell of the Congo,
John's energy,

anti-matter matter. I felt fine.
Then a change came backward. A chill fell.
Talk slackened,

died, and he began to give me sideways looks.
'Christ,' I thought 'what now?' and would have askt for another
but didn't dare.
I feel my application   failing. It's growing dark,
some other sound is overcoming. His last words are:
'We betrayed me.'

230

There are voices, voices. Light's dying. Birds have quit.
He lied about me, months ago. His friendly wit
now slid to apology.
I am sorry that senior genius remembered it.
I am nothing, to occupy his thought
one moment. We

went at his bidding to his cabin, three,
in two bodies; and he spoke like Jove.
I sat there full of love,
salt with attention, while his jokes like nods
pierced for us our most strange history. He
seemed to be in charge of the odds:

hurrah. Three. Three. I must remember that.
I love great men I love. Nobody's great.
I must remember that.
We all fight. Having fought better than the rest,
he sings, & mutters & prophesies in the West
and is our flunked test.

I always come in prostrate; Yeats & Frost.

384

The marker slants, flowerless, day's almost done,
I stand above my father's grave with rage,
often, often before

I've made this awful pilgrimage to one
who cannot visit me, who tore his page
out: I come back for more,

I spit upon this dreadful banker's grave
who shot his heart out in a Florida dawn
O ho alas alas
When will indifference come, I moan & rave
I'd like to scrabble till I got right down
away down under the grass

and ax the casket open ha to see
just how he's taking it, which he sought so hard
we'll tear apart
the mouldering grave clothes ha & then Henry
will heft the ax once more, his final card,
and fell it on the start.

from ELEVEN ADDRESSES TO THE LORD

1

Master of beauty, craftsman of the snowflake,
inimitable contriver,
endower of Earth so gorgeous & different from the boring Moon,
thank you for such as it is my gift.

I have made up a morning prayer to you
containing with precision everything that most matters.
'According to Thy will' the thing begins.
It took me off & on two days. It does not aim at eloquence.

You have come to my rescue again & again
in my impassable, sometimes despairing years.
You have allowed my brilliant friends to destroy themselves
and I am still here, severely damaged, but functioning.

Unknowable, as I am unknown to my guinea pigs:
how can I 'love' you?
I only as far as gratitude & awe
confidently & absolutely go.

I have no idea whether we live again.
It doesn't seem likely
from either the scientific or the philosophical point of view
but certainly all things are possible to you,

and I believe as fixedly in the Resurrection-appearances to Peter & to Paul
as I believe I sit in this blue chair.
Only that may have been a special case
to establish their initiatory faith.

Whatever your end may be, accept my amazement.
May I stand until death forever at attention
for any your least instruction or enlightenment.
I even feel sure you will assist me again, Master of insight & beauty.

HENRY'S UNDERSTANDING

He was reading late, at Richard's, down in Maine,
aged 32? Richard & Helen long in bed,
my good wife long in bed.
All I had to do was strip & get into my bed,
putting the marker in the book, & sleep,
& wake to a hot breakfast.

Off the coast was an island, P'tit Manaan,
the bluff from Richard's lawn was almost sheer.
A chill at four o'clock.
It only takes a few minutes to make a man.
A concentration upon now & here.
Suddenly, unlike Bach,

& horribly, unlike Bach, it occurred to me
that *one* night, instead of warm pajamas,
I'd take off all my clothes
& cross the damp cold lawn & down the bluff
into the terrible water & walk forever
under it out toward the island.

Elizabeth Bishop

THE MAN-MOTH*

       Here, above,
cracks in the buildings are filled with battered moonlight.
The whole shadow of Man is only as big as his hat.
It lies at his feet like a circle for a doll to stand on,
and he makes an inverted pin, the point magnetized to the moon.
He does not see the moon; he observes only her vast properties,
feeling the queer light on his hands, neither warm nor cold,
of a temperature impossible to record in thermometers.

       But when the Man-Moth
pays his rare, although occasional, visits to the surface,
the moon looks rather different to him. He emerges
from an opening under the edge of one of the sidewalks
and nervously begins to scale the faces of the buildings.
He thinks the moon is a small hole at the top of the sky,
proving the sky quite useless for protection.
He trembles, but must investigate as high as he can climb.

       Up the façades,
his shadow dragging like a photographer's cloth behind him,
he climbs fearfully, thinking that this time he will manage
to push his small head through that round clean opening
and be forced through, as from a tube, in black scrolls on the light.
(Man, standing below him, has no such illusions.)
But what the Man-Moth fears most he must do, although
he fails, of course, and falls back scared but quite unhurt.

       Then he returns
to the pale subways of cement he calls his home. He flits,
he flutters, and cannot get aboard the silent trains
fast enough to suit him. The doors close swiftly.
The Man-Moth always seats himself facing the wrong way
and the train starts at once at its full, terrible speed,
without a shift in gears or a gradation of any sort.
He cannot tell the rate at which he travels backwards.

* Newspaper misprint for "mammoth."

41

Each night he must
be carried through artificial tunnels and dream recurrent dreams.
Just as the ties recur beneath his train, these underlie
his rushing brain. He does not dare look out the window,
for the third rail, the unbroken draught of poison,
runs there beside him. He regards it as a disease
he has inherited the susceptibility to. He has to keep
his hands in his pockets, as others must wear mufflers.

If you catch him,
hold up a flashlight to his eye. It's all dark pupil,
an entire night itself, whose haired horizon tightens
as he stares back, and closes up the eye. Then from the lids
one tear, his only possession, like the bee's sting, slips.
Slyly he palms it, and if you're not paying attention
he'll swallow it. However, if you watch, he'll hand it over,
cool as from underground springs and pure enough to drink.

THE FISH

I caught a tremendous fish
and held him beside the boat
half out of water, with my hook
fast in a corner of his mouth.
He didn't fight.
He hadn't fought at all.
He hung a grunting weight,
battered and venerable
and homely. Here and there
his brown skin hung in strips
like ancient wallpaper,
and its pattern of darker brown
was like wallpaper:
shapes like full-blown roses
stained and lost through age.
He was speckled with barnacles,
fine rosettes of lime,

and infested
with tiny white sea-lice,
and underneath two or three
rags of green weed hung down.
While his gills were breathing in
the terrible oxygen
—the frightening gills,
fresh and crisp with blood,
that can cut so badly—
I thought of the coarse white flesh
packed in like feathers,
the big bones and the little bones,
the dramatic reds and blacks
of his shiny entrails,
and the pink swim-bladder
like a big peony.
I looked into his eyes
which were far larger than mine
but shallower, and yellowed,
the irises backed and packed
with tarnished tinfoil
seen through the lenses
of old scratched isinglass.
They shifted a little, but not
to return my stare.
—It was more like the tipping
of an object toward the light.
I admired his sullen face,
the mechanism of his jaw,
and then I saw
that from his lower lip
—if you could call it a lip—
grim, wet, and weaponlike,
hung five old pieces of fish-line,
or four and a wire leader
with the swivel still attached,
with all their five big hooks
grown firmly in his mouth.
A green line, frayed at the end

where he broke it, two heavier lines,
and a fine black thread
still crimped from the strain and snap
when it broke and he got away.
Like medals with their ribbons
frayed and wavering,
a five-haired beard of wisdom
trailing from his aching jaw.
I stared and stared
and victory filled up
the little rented boat,
from the pool of bilge
where oil had spread a rainbow
around the rusted engine
to the bailer rusted orange,
the sun-cracked thwarts,
the oarlocks on their strings,
the gunnels—until everything
was rainbow, rainbow, rainbow!
And I let the fish go.

LETTER TO N. Y.

for Louise Crane

In your next letter I wish you'd say
where you are going and what you are doing;
how are the plays, and after the plays
what other pleasures you're pursuing:

taking cabs in the middle of the night,
driving as if to save your soul
where the road goes round and round the park
and the meter glares like a moral owl,

and the trees look so queer and green
standing alone in big black caves
and suddenly you're in a different place
where everything seems to happen in waves,

and most of the jokes you just can't catch,
like dirty words rubbed off a slate,
and the songs are loud but somehow dim
and it gets so terribly late,

and coming out of the brownstone house
to the gray sidewalk, the watered street,
one side of the buildings rises with the sun
like a glistening field of wheat.

—Wheat, not oats, dear. I'm afraid
if it's wheat it's none of your sowing,
nevertheless I'd like to know
what you are doing and where you are going.

THE ARMADILLO

for Robert Lowell

This is the time of year
when almost every night
the frail, illegal fire balloons appear.
Climbing the mountain height,

rising toward a saint
still honored in these parts,
the paper chambers flush and fill with light
that comes and goes, like hearts.

Once up against the sky it's hard
to tell them from the stars—
planets, that is—the tinted ones:
Venus going down, or Mars,

or the pale green one. With a wind,
they flare and falter, wobble and toss;
but if it's still they steer between
the kite sticks of the Southern Cross,

receding, dwindling, solemnly
and steadily forsaking us,
or, in the downdraft from a peak,
suddenly turning dangerous.

Last night another big one fell.
It splattered like an egg of fire
against the cliff behind the house.
The flame ran down. We saw the pair

of owls who nest there flying up
and up, their whirling black-and-white
stained bright pink underneath, until
they shrieked up out of sight.

The ancient owl's nest must have burned.
Hastily, all alone,
a glistening armadillo left the scene,
rose-flecked, head down, tail down,

and then a baby rabbit jumped out,
short-eared, to our surprise.
So soft!—a handful of intangible ash
with fixed, ignited eyes.

Too pretty, dreamlike mimicry!
O falling fire and piercing cry
and panic, and a weak mailed fist
clenched ignorant against the sky!

NORTH HAVEN

(*In Memoriam: Robert Lowell*)

I can make out the rigging of a schooner
a mile off; I can count
the new cones on the spruce. It is so still
the pale bay wears a milky skin; the sky
no clouds except for one long, carded horse's tail.

The islands haven't shifted since last summer,
even if I like to pretend they have—
drifting, in a dreamy sort of way,
a little north, a little south, or sidewise—
and that they're free within the blue frontiers of bay.

This month our favorite one is full of flowers:
buttercups, red clover, purple vetch,
hawkweed still burning, daisies pied, eyebright,
the fragrant bedstraw's incandescent stars,
and more, returned, to paint the meadows with delight.

The goldfinches are back, or others like them,
and the white-throated sparrow's five-note song,
pleading and pleading, brings tears to the eyes.
Nature repeats herself, or almost does:
repeat, repeat, repeat; revise, revise, revise.

Years ago, you told me it was here
(in 1932?) you first "discovered *girls*"
and learned to sail, and learned to kiss.
You had "such fun," you said, that classic summer.
("Fun"—it always seemed to leave you at a loss . . .)

You left North Haven, anchored in its rock,
afloat in mystic blue . . . And now—you've left
for good. You can't derange, or rearrange,
your poems again. (But the sparrows can their song.)
The words won't change again. Sad friend, you cannot change.

IN THE WAITING ROOM

In Worcester, Massachusetts,
I went with Aunt Consuelo
to keep her dentist's appointment
and sat and waited for her
in the dentist's waiting room.
It was winter. It got dark

early. The waiting room
was full of grown-up people,
arctics and overcoats,
lamps and magazines.
My aunt was inside
what seemed like a long time
and while I waited I read
the *National Geographic*
(I could read) and carefully
studied the photographs:
the inside of a volcano,
black, and full of ashes;
then it was spilling over
in rivulets of fire.
Osa and Martin Johnson
dressed in riding breeches,
laced boots, and pith helmets.
A dead man slung on a pole
—"Long Pig," the caption said.
Babies with pointed heads
wound round and round with string;
black, naked women with necks
wound round and round with wire
like the necks of light bulbs.
Their breasts were horrifying.
I read it right straight through.
I was too shy to stop.
And then I looked at the cover:
the yellow margins, the date.

Suddenly, from inside,
came an *oh!* of pain
—Aunt Consuelo's voice—
not very loud or long.
I wasn't at all surprised;
even then I knew she was
a foolish, timid woman.
I might have been embarrassed,
but wasn't. What took me
completely by surprise
was that it was *me:*

my voice, in my mouth.
Without thinking at all
I was my foolish aunt,
I—we—were falling, falling,
our eyes glued to the cover
of the *National Geographic*,
February, 1918.

I said to myself: three days
and you'll be seven years old.
I was saying it to stop
the sensation of falling off
the round, turning world
into cold, blue-black space.
But I felt: you are an *I*,
you are an *Elizabeth*,
you are one of *them*.
Why should you be one, too?
I scarcely dared to look
to see what it was I was.
I gave a sidelong glance
—I couldn't look any higher—
at shadowy gray knees,
trousers and skirts and boots
and different pairs of hands
lying under the lamps.
I knew that nothing stranger
had ever happened, that nothing
stranger could ever happen.

Why should I be my aunt,
or me, or anyone?
What similarities—
boots, hands, the family voice
I felt in my throat, or even
the *National Geographic*
and those awful hanging breasts—
held us all together
or made us all just one?
How—I didn't know any
word for it—how "unlikely". . .

How had I come to be here,
like them, and overhear
a cry of pain that could have
got loud and worse but hadn't?

The waiting room was bright
and too hot. It was sliding
beneath a big black wave,
another, and another.

Then I was back in it.
The War was on. Outside,
in Worcester, Massachusetts,
were night and slush and cold,
and it was still the fifth
of February, 1918.

ONE ART

The art of losing isn't hard to master;
so many things seem filled with the intent
to be lost that their loss is no disaster.

Lose something every day. Accept the fluster
of lost door keys, the hour badly spent.
The art of losing isn't hard to master.

Then practice losing farther, losing faster:
places, and names, and where it was you meant
to travel. None of these will bring disaster.

I lost my mother's watch. And look! my last, or
next-to-last, of three loved houses went.
The art of losing isn't hard to master.

I lost two cities, lovely ones. And, vaster,
some realms I owned, two rivers, a continent.
I miss them, but it wasn't a disaster.

—Even losing you (the joking voice, a gesture
I love) I shan't have lied. It's evident
the art of losing's not too hard to master
though it may look like (*Write* it!) like disaster.

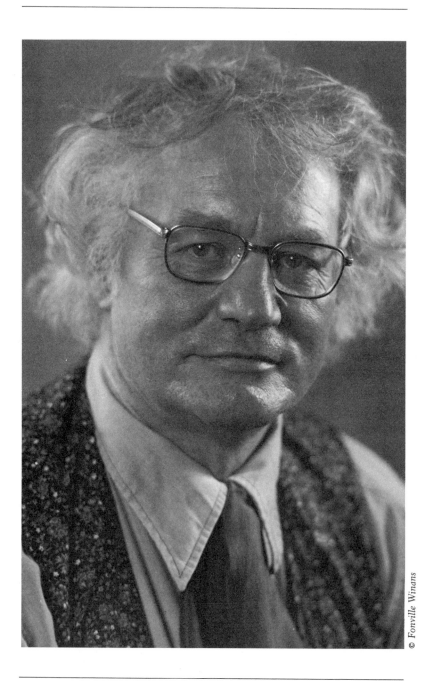

Robert Bly

SURPRISED BY EVENING

There is unknown dust that is near us,
Waves breaking on shores just over the hill,
Trees full of birds that we have never seen,
Nets drawn down with dark fish.

The evening arrives; we look up and it is there,
It has come through the nets of the stars,
Through the tissues of the grass,
Walking quietly over the asylums of the waters.

The day shall never end, we think:
We have hair that seems born for the daylight;
But, at last, the quiet waters of the night will rise,
And our skin shall see far off, as it does under water.

WAKING FROM SLEEP

Inside the veins there are navies setting forth,
Tiny explosions at the water lines,
And seagulls weaving in the wind of the salty blood.

It is the morning. The country has slept the whole winter.
Window seats were covered with fur skins, the yard was full
Of stiff dogs, and hands that clumsily held heavy books.

Now we wake, and rise from bed, and eat breakfast!—
Shouts rise from the harbor of the blood,
Mist, and masts rising, the knock of wooden tackle in the sunlight.

Now we sing, and do tiny dances on the kitchen floor.
Our whole body is like a harbor at dawn;
We know that our master has left us for the day.

ROBERT BLY

POEM IN THREE PARTS

I

Oh, on an early morning I think I shall live forever!
I am wrapped in my joyful flesh,
As the grass is wrapped in its clouds of green.

II

Rising from a bed, where I dreamt
Of long rides past castles and hot coals,
The sun lies happily on my knees;
I have suffered and survived the night
Bathed in dark water, like any blade of grass.

III

The strong leaves of the box-elder tree,
Plunging in the wind, call us to disappear
Into the wilds of the universe,
Where we shall sit at the foot of a plant,
And live forever, like the dust.

SNOWFALL IN THE AFTERNOON

I

The grass is half-covered with snow.
It was the sort of snowfall that starts in late afternoon,
And now the little houses of the grass are growing dark.

II

If I reached my hands down, near the earth,
I could take handfuls of darkness!
A darkness was always there, which we never noticed.

ROBERT BLY

III

As the snow grows heavier, the cornstalks fade farther away,
And the barn moves nearer to the house.
The barn moves all alone in the growing storm.

IV

The barn is full of corn, and moving toward us now,
Like a hulk blown toward us in a storm at sea;
All the sailors on deck have been blind for many years.

IN A TRAIN

There has been a light snow.
Dark car tracks move in out of the darkness.
I stare at the train window marked with soft dust.
I have awakened at Missoula, Montana, utterly happy.

DRIVING TO TOWN LATE TO MAIL A LETTER

It is a cold and snowy night. The main street is deserted.
The only things moving are swirls of snow.
As I lift the mailbox door, I feel its cold iron.
There is a privacy I love in this snowy night.
Driving around, I will waste more time.

WATERING THE HORSE

How strange to think of giving up all ambition!
Suddenly I see with such clear eyes
The white flake of snow
That has just fallen in the horse's mane!

ROBERT BLY

AFTER LONG BUSYNESS

I start out for a walk at last after weeks at the desk.
Moon gone, plowing underfoot, no stars; not a trace of light!
Suppose a horse were galloping toward me in this open field?
Every day I did not spend in solitude was wasted.

COUNTING SMALL-BONED BODIES

Let's count the bodies over again.

If we could only make the bodies smaller,
The size of skulls,
We could make a whole plain white with skulls in the moonlight!

If we could only make the bodies smaller,
Maybe we could get
A whole year's kill in front of us on a desk!

If we could only make the bodies smaller,
We could fit
A body into a finger-ring, for a keepsake forever.

LOOKING INTO A FACE

Conversation brings us so close! Opening
The surfs of the body,
Bringing fish up near the sun,
And stiffening the backbones of the sea!

I have wandered in a face, for hours,
Passing through dark fires.
I have risen to a body
Not yet born,
Existing like a light around the body,
Through which the body moves like a sliding moon.

THE HERMIT

Darkness is falling through darkness,
Falling from ledge
To ledge.
There is a man whose body is perfectly whole.
He stands, the storm behind him,
And the grass blades are leaping in the wind.
Darkness is gathered in folds
About his feet.
He is no one. When we see
Him, we grow calm,
And sail on into the tunnels of joyful death.

SHACK POEM

1

I don't even know these roads I walk on,
I see the backs of white birds.
Whales rush by, their teeth ivory.

2

Far out at the edge of the heron's wing,
where the air is disturbed by the last feather,
there is the Kingdom. . . .

3

Hurrying to brush between the Two Fish,
the wild woman flies on . . .
blue glass stones a path on earth mark her going.

4

I sit down and fold my legs. . . .
The half dark in the room is delicious.
How marvelous to be a thought entirely surrounded by brains!

LOOKING INTO A TIDE POOL

It is a tide pool, shallow, water coming in, clear, tiny white shell-people on the bottom, asking nothing, not even directions! On the surface the noduled seaweed, lying like hands, slowly drawing back and returning, hands laid on fevered bodies, moving back and forth, as the healer sings wildly, shouting to Jesus and his dead mother.

VISITING EMILY DICKINSON'S GRAVE WITH ROBERT FRANCIS

A black iron fence closes the graves in, its ovals delicate as wine stems. They resemble those chapel windows on the main Aran island, made narrow in the fourth century so that not too much rain would drive in . . . It is April, clear and dry. Curls of grass rise around the nearby gravestones.

The Dickinson house is not far off. She arrived here one day, at fifty-six, Robert says, carried over the lots between by six Irish laboring men, when her brother refused to trust her body to a carriage. The coffin was darkened with violets and pine boughs, as she covered the immense distance between the solid Dickinson house and this plot . . .

The distance is immense, the distances through which Satan and his helpers rose and fell, oh vast areas, the distances between stars, between the first time love is felt in the sleeves of the dress, and the death of the person who was in that room . . . the distance between the feet and head as you lie down, the distance between the mother and father, through which we pass reluctantly.

My family addresses "an Eclipse every morning, which they call their 'Father.'" Each of us crosses that distance at night, arriving out of sleep on hands and knees, astonished we see a hump in the ground where we thought a chapel would be . . . it is a grassy knoll. And we clamber out of sleep, holding on to it with our hands . . .

ROBERT BLY

INSECT HEADS

These insects, golden
and Arabic, sailing in the husks of galleons,
their octagonal heads also
hold sand paintings of the next life.

PASSING AN ORCHARD BY TRAIN

Grass high under apple trees.
The bark of the trees rough and sexual,
the grass growing heavy and uneven.

We cannot bear disaster, like
the rocks—
swaying nakedly
in open fields.

One slight bruise and we die!
I know no one on this train.
A man comes walking down the aisle.
I want to tell him
that I forgive him, that I want him
to forgive me.

DRIVING MY PARENTS HOME AT CHRISTMAS

As I drive my parents home through the snow,
their frailty hesitates on the edge of a mountainside.
I call over the cliff,
only snow answers.
They talk quietly
of hauling water, of eating an orange,
of a grandchild's photograph left behind last night.
When they open the door of their house, they disappear.

And the oak when it falls in the forest who hears it through miles and miles
of silence?
They sit so close to each other . . . as if pressed together by the snow.

FOR MY SON NOAH, TEN YEARS OLD

Night and day arrive, and day after day goes by,
and what is old remains old, and what is young remains young, and
grows old.
The lumber pile does not grow younger, nor the two-by-fours lose their
darkness,
but the old tree goes on, the barn stands without help so many years;
the advocate of darkness and night is not lost.

The horse steps up, swings on one leg, turns its body,
the chicken flapping claws onto the roost, its wings whelping and
walloping,
but what is primitive is not to be shot out into the night and the dark.
And slowly the kind man comes closer, loses his rage, sits down at table.

So I am proud only of those days that pass in undivided tenderness,
when you sit drawing, or making books, stapled, with messages to the
world,
or coloring a man with fire coming out of his hair.
Or we sit at a table, with small tea carefully poured.
So we pass our time together, calm and delighted.

MY FATHER'S WEDDING
1924

Today, lonely for my father, I saw
a log, or branch,
long, bent, ragged, bark gone.
I felt lonely for my father when I saw it.
It was the log
that lay near my uncle's old milk wagon.

Some men live with an invisible limp,
stagger, or drag
a leg. Their sons are often angry.
Only recently I thought:
Doing what you want...
Is that like limping? Tracks of it show in sand.

Have you seen those giant bird-
men of Bhutan?
Men in bird masks, with pig noses, dancing,
teeth like a dog's, sometimes
dancing on one bad leg!
They do what they want, the dog's teeth say that!

But I grew up without dogs' teeth,
showed a whole body,
left only clear tracks in sand.
I learned to walk swiftly, easily,
no trace of a limp.
I even leaped a little. Guess where my defect is!

Then what? If a man, cautious
hides his limp,
Somebody has to limp it! Things
do it; the surroundings limp.
House walls get scars,
the car breaks down; matter, in drudgery, takes it up.

On my father's wedding day,
no one was there
to hold him. Noble loneliness
held him. Since he never asked for pity
his friends thought he
was whole. Walking alone, he could carry it.

He came in limping. It was a simple
wedding, three
or four people. The man in black,
lifting the book, called for order.
And the invisible bride
stepped forward, before his own bride.

He married the invisible bride, not his own.
In her left
breast she carried the three drops
that wound and kill. He already had
his barklike skin then,
made rough especially to repel the sympathy

he longed for, didn't need, and wouldn't accept.
They stopped. So
the words are read. The man in black
speaks the sentence. When the service
is over, I hold him
in my arms for the first time and the last.

After that he was alone
and I was alone.
No friends came; he invited none.
His two-story house he turned
into a forest,
where both he and I are the hunters.

AT MIDOCEAN

All day I loved you in a fever, holding on to the tail of the horse.
I overflowed whenever I reached out to touch you.
My hand moved over your body, covered
with its dress,
burning, rough, an animal's hand or foot moving over leaves.
The rainstorm retires, clouds open, sunlight
sliding over ocean water a thousand miles from land.

IN RAINY SEPTEMBER

In rainy September, when leaves grow down to the dark,
I put my forehead down to the damp, seaweed-smelling sand.
What can we do but choose? The only way for human beings
is to choose. The fern has no choice but to live;
for this crime it receives earth, water, and night.

We close the door. "I have no claim on you."
Dusk comes. "The love I have had with you is enough."
We know we could live apart from one another.
The sheldrake floats apart from the flock.
The oaktree puts out leaves alone on the lonely hillside.

Men and women before us have accomplished this.
I would see you, and you me, once a year.
We would be two kernels and not be planted.
We stay in the room, door closed, lights out.
I weep with you without shame and without honor.

Gwendolyn Brooks

from **A STREET IN BRONZEVILLE**

to David and Keziah Brooks

kitchenette building

We are things of dry hours and the involuntary plan,
Grayed in, and gray. "Dream" makes a giddy sound, not strong
Like "rent," "feeding a wife," "satisfying a man."

But could a dream send up through onion fumes
Its white and violet, fight with fried potatoes
And yesterday's garbage ripening in the hall,
Flutter, or sing an aria down these rooms

Even if we were willing to let it in,
Had time to warm it, keep it very clean,
Anticipate a message, let it begin?

We wonder. But not well! not for a minute!
Since Number Five is out of the bathroom now,
We think of lukewarm water, hope to get in it.

the mother

Abortions will not let you forget.
You remember the children you got that you did not get,
The damp small pulps with a little or with no hair,
The singers and workers that never handled the air.
You will never neglect or beat
Them, or silence or buy with a sweet.
You will never wind up the sucking-thumb
Or scuttle off ghosts that come.
You will never leave them, controlling your luscious sigh,
Return for a snack of them, with gobbling mother-eye.

I have heard in the voices of the wind the voices of my dim killed
     children.
I have contracted. I have eased
My dim dears at the breasts they could never suck.
I have said, Sweets, if I sinned, if I seized
Your luck
And your lives from your unfinished reach,
If I stole your births and your names,
Your straight baby tears and your games,
Your stilted or lovely loves, your tumults, your marriages, aches, and your
     deaths,
If I poisoned the beginnings of your breaths,
Believe that even in my deliberateness I was not deliberate.
Though why should I whine,
Whine that the crime was other than mine?—
Since anyhow you are dead.
Or rather, or instead,
You were never made.
But that too, I am afraid,
Is faulty: oh, what shall I say, how is the truth to be said?
You were born, you had body, you died.
It is just that you never giggled or planned or cried.

Believe me, I loved you all.
Believe me, I knew you, though faintly, and I loved, I loved you
All.

a song in the front yard

I've stayed in the front yard all my life.
I want a peek at the back
Where it's rough and untended and hungry weed grows.
A girl gets sick of a rose.

I want to go in the back yard now
And maybe down the alley,
To where the charity children play.
I want a good time today.

They do some wonderful things.
They have some wonderful fun.
My mother sneers, but I say it's fine
How they don't have to go in at quarter to nine.
My mother, she tells me that Johnnie Mae

Will grow up to be a bad woman.
That George'll be taken to Jail soon or late
(On account of last winter he sold our back gate).

But I say it's fine. Honest, I do.
And I'd like to be a bad woman, too,
And wear the brave stockings of night-black lace
And strut down the streets with paint on my face.

of De Witt Williams on his way to Lincoln Cemetery

> He was born in Alabama.
> He was bred in Illinois.
> He was nothing but a
> Plain black boy.
>
> Swing low swing low sweet sweet chariot.
> Nothing but a plain black boy.
>
> Drive him past the Pool Hall.
> Drive him past the Show.
> Blind within his casket,
> But maybe he will know.
>
> Down through Forty-seventh Street:
> Underneath the L,
> And Northwest Corner, Prairie,
> That he loved so well.
>
> Don't forget the Dance Halls—
> Warwick and Savoy,
> Where he picked his women, where
> He drank his liquid joy.
>
> Born in Alabama.
> Bred in Illinois.
> He was nothing but a
> Plain black boy.
>
> Swing low swing low sweet sweet chariot.
> Nothing but a plain black boy.

NEGRO HERO

to suggest Dorie Miller

I had to kick their law into their teeth in order to save them.
However I have heard that sometimes you have to deal
Devilishly with drowning men in order to swim them to shore.
Or they will haul themselves and you to the trash and the fish beneath.
(When I think of this, I do not worry about a few
Chipped teeth.)

It is good I gave glory, it is good I put gold on their name.
Or there would have been spikes in the afterward hands.
But let us speak only of my success and the pictures in the Caucasian
    dailies
As well as the Negro weeklies. For I am a gem.
(They are not concerned that it was hardly The Enemy my fight was
    against
But them.)

It was a tall time. And of course my blood was
Boiling about in my head and straining and howling and singing me on.
Of course I was rolled on wheels of my boy itch to get at the gun.
Of course all the delicate rehearsal shots of my childhood massed in
    mirage before me.
Of course I was child
And my first swallow of the liquor of battle bleeding black air dying and
    demon noise
Made me wild.

It was kinder than that, though, and I showed like a banner my kindness.
I loved. And a man will guard when he loves.
Their white-gowned democracy was my fair lady.
With her knife lying cold, straight, in the softness of her sweet-flowing
    sleeve.
But for the sake of the dear smiling mouth and the stuttered promise I
    toyed with my life.
I threw back!—I would not remember
Entirely the knife.

Still—am I good enough to die for them, is my blood bright enough to
    be spilled,

Was my constant back-question—are they clear
On this? Or do I intrude even now?
Am I clean enough to kill for them, do they wish me to kill
For them or is my place while death licks his lips and strides to them
In the galley still?

(In a southern city a white man said
Indeed, I'd rather be dead;
Indeed, I'd rather be shot in the head
Or ridden to waste on the back of a flood
Than saved by the drop of a black man's blood.)

Naturally, the important thing is, I helped to save them, them and a part
    of their democracy.
Even if I had to kick their law into their teeth in order to do that for
    them.
And I am feeling well and settled in myself because I believe it was a
    good job,
Despite this possible horror: that they might prefer the
Preservation of their law in all its sick dignity and their knives
To the continuation of their creed
And their lives.

WE REAL COOL

The Pool Players.
Seven at the Golden Shovel.

We real cool. We
Left school. We

Lurk late. We
Strike straight. We

Sing sin. We
Thin gin. We

Jazz June. We
Die soon.

THE LOVERS OF THE POOR

arrive. The Ladies from the Ladies' Betterment
League
Arrive in the afternoon, the late light slanting
In diluted gold bars across the boulevard brag
Of proud, seamed faces with mercy and murder hinting
Here, there, interrupting, all deep and debonair,
The pink paint on the innocence of fear;
Walk in a gingerly manner up the hall.
Cutting with knives served by their softest care,
Served by their love, so barbarously fair.
Whose mothers taught: You'd better not be cruel!
You had better not throw stones upon the wrens!
Herein they kiss and coddle and assault
Anew and dearly in the innocence
With which they baffle nature. Who are full,
Sleek, tender-clad, fit, fiftyish, a-glow, all
Sweetly abortive, hinting at fat fruit,
Judge it high time that fiftyish fingers felt
Beneath the lovelier planes of enterprise.
To resurrect. To moisten with milky chill.
To be a random hitching-post or plush.
To be, for wet eyes, random and handy hem.
Their guild is giving money to the poor.
The worthy poor. The very very worthy
And beautiful poor. Perhaps just not too swarthy?
Perhaps just not too dirty nor too dim
Nor—passionate. In truth, what they could wish
Is—something less than derelict or dull.
Not staunch enough to stab, though, gaze for gaze!
God shield them sharply from the beggar-bold!
The noxious needy ones whose battle's bald
Nonetheless for being voiceless, hits one down.
But it's all so bad! and entirely too much for
them.
The stench; the urine, cabbage, and dead beans,
Dead porridges of assorted dusty grains,
The old smoke, *heavy* diapers, and, they're told,
Something called chitterlings. The darkness. Drawn
Darkness, or dirty light. The soil that stirs.
The soil that looks the soil of centuries.

And for that matter the *general* oldness. Old
Wood. Old marble. Old tile. Old old old.
Not homekind Oldness! Not Lake Forest, Glencoe.
Nothing is sturdy, nothing is majestic,
There is no quiet drama, no rubbed glaze, no
Unkillable infirmity of such
A tasteful turn as lately they have left,
Glencoe, Lake Forest, and to which their cars
Must presently restore them. When they're done
With dullards and distortions of this fistic
Patience of the poor and put-upon.
        They've never seen such a make-do-ness as
Newspaper rugs before! In this, this "flat,"
Their hostess is gathering up the oozed, the rich
Rugs of the morning (tattered! the bespattered. . . .)
Readies to spread clean rugs for afternoon.
Here is a scene for you. The Ladies look,
In horror, behind a substantial citizeness
Whose trains clank out across her swollen heart.
Who, arms akimbo, almost fills a door.
All tumbling children, quilts dragged to the floor
And tortured thereover, potato peelings, soft-
Eyed kitten, hunched-up, haggard, to-be-hurt.
        Their League is alloting largesse to the Lost.
But to put their clean, their pretty money, to put
Their money collected from delicate rose-fingers
Tipped with their hundred flawless rose-nails seems . . .
        They own Spode, Lowestoft, candelabra,
Mantels, and hostess gowns, and sunburst clocks,
Turtle soup, Chippendale, red satin "hangings,"
Aubussons and Hattie Carnegie. They Winter
In Palm Beach; cross the Water in June; attend,
When suitable, the nice Art Institute;
Buy the right books in the best bindings; saunter
On Michigan, Easter mornings, in sun or wind.
Oh Squalor! This sick four-story hulk, this fibre
With fissures everywhere! Why, what are bringings
Of loathe-love largesse? What shall peril hungers
So old old, what shall flatter the desolate?
Tin can, blocked fire escape and chitterling
And swaggering seeking youth and the puzzled wreckage
Of the middle-passage, and urine and stale shames
And, again, the porridges of the underslung

And children children children. Heavens! That
Was a rat, surely, off there, in the shadows? Long
And long-tailed? Gray? The Ladies from the Ladies'
Betterment League agree it will be better
To achieve the outer air that rights and steadies,
To hie to a house that does not holler, to ring
Bells elsetime, better presently to cater
To no more Possibilities, to get
Away. Perhaps the money can be posted.
Perhaps they two may choose another Slum!
Some serious sooty half-unhappy home!—
Where loathe-love likelier may be invested.
          Keeping their scented bodies in the center
Of the hall as they walk down the hysterical hall,
They allow their lovely skirts to graze no wall,
Are off at what they manage of a canter,
And, resuming all the clues of what they were,
Try to avoid inhaling the laden air.

AN ASPECT OF LOVE,
ALIVE IN THE ICE AND FIRE

LaBohem Brown

It is the morning of our love.

In a package of minutes there is this We.
How beautiful.
Merry foreigners in our morning,
we laugh, we touch each other,
are responsible props and posts.

A physical light is in the room.

Because the world is at the window
we cannot wonder very long.

You rise. Although
genial, you are in yourself again.
I observe
your direct and respectable stride.

You are direct and self-accepting as a lion
in African velvet. You are level, lean,
remote.

There is a moment in Camaraderie
when interruption is not to be understood.
I cannot bear an interruption.
This is the shining joy;
the time of not-to-end.

On the street we smile.
We go
in different directions
down the imperturbable street.

TO DON AT SALAAM

I like to see you lean back in your chair
so far you have to fall but do not—
your arms back, your fine hands
in your print pockets.

Beautiful. Impudent.
Ready for life.
A tied storm.

I like to see you wearing your boy smile
whose tribute is for two of us or three.

Sometimes in life
things seem to be moving
and they are not
and they are not
there.
You are there.

Your voice is the listened-for music.
Your act is the consolidation.

I like to see you living in the world.

Lucille Clifton

ADMONITIONS

boys
i don't promise you nothing
but this
what you pawn
i will redeem
what you steal
i will conceal
my private silence to
your public guilt
is all i got

girls
first time a white man
opens his fly
like a good thing
we'll just laugh
laugh real loud my
black women

children
when they ask you
why is your mama so funny
say
she is a poet
she don't have no sense

MISS ROSIE

When I watch you
wrapped up like garbage
sitting, surrounded by the smell
of too old potato peels

or
when I watch you
in your old man's shoes
with the little toe cut out
sitting, waiting for your mind
like next week's grocery
I say
when I watch you
you wet brown bag of a woman
who used to be the best looking gal in Georgia
used to be called the Georgia Rose
I stand up
through your destruction
I stand up

[IF I STAND IN MY WINDOW]

If I stand in my window
naked in my own house
and press my breasts
against my windowpane
like black birds pushing against glass
because I am somebody
in a New Thing

and if the man come to stop me
in my own house
naked in my own window
saying I have offended him
I have offended his

Gods

let him watch my black body
push against my own glass
let him discover self
let him run naked through the streets
crying
praying in tongues

LUCILLE CLIFTON

THE LOST BABY POEM

the time i dropped your almost body down
down to meet the waters under the city
and run one with the sewage to the sea
what did i know about waters rushing back
what did i know about drowning
or being drowned

you would have been born into winter
in the year of the disconnected gas
and no car   we would have made the thin
walk over Genesee hill into the Canada wind
to watch you slip like ice into strangers' hands
you would have fallen naked as snow into winter
if you were here i could tell you these
and some other things

if i am ever less than a mountain
for your definite brothers and sisters
let the rivers pour over my head
let the sea take me for a spiller
of seas   let black men call me stranger
always   for your never named sake

GOD'S MOOD

these daughters are bone,
they break.
He wanted stone girls
and boys with branches for arms
that He could lift His life with
and be lifted by.
these sons are bone.

He is tired of years that keep turning into age
and flesh that keeps widening.
He is tired of waiting for His teeth to
bite Him and walk away.

He is tired of bone,
it breaks.
He is tired of eve's fancy and
adam's whining ways.

ROOTS

call it our craziness even,
call it anything.
it is the life thing in us
that will not let us die.
even in death's hand
we fold the fingers up
and call them greens and
grow on them,
we hum them and make music.
call it our wildness then,
we are lost from the field
of flowers, we become
a field of flowers.
call it our craziness
our wildness
call it our roots,
it is the light in us
it is the light of us
it is the light, call it
whatever you have to,
call it anything.

[COME HOME FROM THE MOVIES]

Come home from the movies,
Black girls and boys,
the picture be over and the screen
be cold as our neighborhood.
Come home from the show,
don't be the show.
Take off some flowers and plant them,

pick us some papers and read them,
stop making some babies and raise them.
Come home from the movies
Black girls and boys,
show our fathers how to walk like men,
they already know how to dance.

TO A DARK MOSES

you are the one
i am lit for.
come with your rod
that twists
and is a serpent.
i am the bush.
i am burning.
i am not consumed.

SHE UNDERSTANDS ME

it is all blood and breaking,
blood and breaking. the thing
drops out of its box squalling
into the light. they are both squalling,
animal and cage. her bars lie wet, open
and empty and she has made herself again
out of flesh out of dictionaries,
she is always emptying and it is all
the same wound the same blood the same breaking.

CUTTING GREENS

curling them around
i hold their bodies in obscene embrace
thinking of everything but kinship.

LUCILLE CLIFTON

collards and kale
strain against each strange other
away from my kissmaking hand and
the iron bedpot.
the pot is black,
the cutting board is black,
my hand,
and just for a minute
the greens roll black under the knife,
and the kitchen twists dark on its spine
and i taste in my natural appetite
the bond of live things everywhere.

[AT LAST WE KILLED THE ROACHES]

at last we killed the roaches.
mama and me. she sprayed,
i swept the ceiling and they fell
dying onto our shoulders, in our hair
covering us with red. the tribe was broken,
the cooking pots were ours again
and we were glad, such cleanliness was grace
when i was twelve. only for a few nights,
and then not much, my dreams were blood
my hands were blades and it was murder murder
all over the place.

BREAKLIGHT

light keeps on breaking.
i keep knowing
the language of other nations.
i keep hearing
tree talk
water words
and i keep knowing what they mean.
and light just keeps on breaking.

LUCILLE CLIFTON

last night
the fears of my mother came
knocking and when i
opened the door
they tried to explain themselves
and i understood
everything they said.

THE CARVER

for Fred

sees the man
in the wood and
calls his name and
the man in the wood
breaks through the bark and
the nations of wood call
the carver
Brother

HOMAGE TO MY HIPS

these hips are big hips.
they need space to
move around in.
they don't fit into little
petty places. these hips
are free hips.
they don't like to be held back.
these hips have never been enslaved,
they go where they want to go
they do what they want to do.
these hips are mighty hips.
these hips are magic hips.
i have known them
to put a spell on a man and
spin him like a top!

[THERE IS A GIRL INSIDE]

there is a girl inside.
she is randy as a wolf.
she will not walk away
and leave these bones
to an old woman.

she is a green tree
in a forest of kindling.
she is a green girl
in a used poet.

she has waited
patient as a nun
for the second coming,
when she can break through gray hairs
into blossom

and her lovers will harvest
honey and thyme
and the woods will be wild
with the damn wonder of it.

FORGIVING MY FATHER

it is friday. we have come
to the paying of the bills.
all week you have stood in my dreams
like a ghost, asking for more time
but today is payday, payday old man;
my mother's hand opens in her early grave
and i hold it out like a good daughter.

there is no more time for you. there will
never be time enough daddy daddy old lecher
old liar. i wish you were rich so i could take it all
and give the lady what she was due
but you were the son of a needy father,

LUCILLE CLIFTON

the father of a needy son;
you gave her all you had
which was nothing, you have already given her
all you had.

you are the pocket that was going to open
and come up empty any friday.
you were each other's bad bargain, not mine.
daddy old pauper old prisoner, old dead man
what am i doing here collecting?
you lie side by side in debtors' boxes
and no accounting will open them up.

I ONCE KNEW A MAN

i once knew a man who had wild horses killed.
when he told about it
the words came galloping out of his mouth
and shook themselves and headed off in
every damn direction. his tongue
was wild and wide and spinning when he talked
and the people he looked at closed their eyes
and tore the skins off their backs as they walked away
and stopped eating meat.
there was no holding him once he got started;
he had had wild horses killed one time and
they rode him to his grave.

FOR THE LAME

happen you will rise,
lift from grounded in a spin
and begin to forget the geography
of fixed things.
happen you will walk past
where you meant to stay,
happen you will wonder at the way
it seemed so marvelous to move.

FOR THE MUTE

they will blow from your mouth one morning
like from a shook bottle
and you will try to keep them for
tomorrow's conversation but
your patience will be broken when the
bottle bursts
and you will spill all of your
extraordinary hearings for there are
too many languages for
one mortal tongue.

PERHAPS

i am going blind.
my eyes exploding,
seeing more than is there
until they burst into nothing

or going deaf, these sounds
the feathered hum of silence

or going away from my self, the cool
fingers of lace on my skin
the fingers of madness

or perhaps
in the palace of time
our lives are a circular stair
and i am turning

SPEAKING OF LOSS

i began with everything;
parents, two extra fingers
a brother to ruin. i was

a rich girl with no money
in a red dress. how did i come
to sit in this house
wearing a name i never heard
until i was a woman? someone has stolen
my parents and hidden my brother.
my extra fingers are cut away.
i am left with plain hands and
nothing to give you but poems.

Bruce Jackson, Courtesy of Documentary Research, Inc.

Robert Creeley

THE BUSINESS

To be in love is like going out-
side to see what kind of day

it is. Do not
mistake me. If you love

her how prove she
loves also, except that it

occurs, a remote chance on
which you stake

yourself? But barter for
the Indian was a means of sustenance.

There are records.

I KNOW A MAN

As I sd to my
friend, because I am
always talking,—John, I

sd, which was not his
name, the darkness sur-
rounds us, what

can we do against
it, or else, shall we &
why not, buy a goddamn big car,

drive, he sd, for
christ's sake, look
out where yr going.

A FORM OF WOMEN

I have come far enough
from where I was not before
to have seen the things
looking in at me through the open door

and have walked tonight
by myself
to see the moonlight
and see it as trees

and shapes more fearful
because I feared
what I did not know
but have wanted to know.

My face is my own, I thought.
But you have seen it
turn into a thousand years.
I watched you cry.

I could not touch you.
I wanted very much to
touch you
but could not.

If it is dark
when this is given to you,
have care for its content
when the moon shines.

My face is my own.
My hands are my own.
My mouth is my own
but I am not.

Moon, moon,
when you leave me alone
all the darkness is
an utter blackness,

a pit of fear,
a stench,
hands unreasonable
never to touch.

But I love you.
Do you love me.
What to say
when you see me.

A WICKER BASKET

Comes the time when it's later
and onto your table the headwaiter
puts the bill, and very soon after
rings out the sound of lively laughter—

Picking up change, hands like a walrus,
and a face like a barndoor's,
and a head without any apparent size,
nothing but two eyes—

So that's you, man,
or me. I make it as I can,
I pick up, I go
faster than they know—

Out the door, the street like a night,
any night, and no one in sight,
but then, well, there she is,
old friend Liz—

And she opens the door of her cadillac,
I step in back,
and we're gone.
She turns me on—

There are very huge stars, man, in the sky,
and from somewhere very far off someone hands me a slice of
      apple pie,
with a gob of white, white ice cream on top of it,
and I eat it—

Slowly. And while certainly
they are laughing at me, and all around me is racket
of these cats not making it, I make it

in my wicker basket.

THE FLOWER

I think I grow tensions
like flowers
in a wood where
nobody goes.

Each wound is perfect,
encloses itself in a tiny
imperceptible blossom,
making pain.

Pain is a flower like that one,
like this one,
like that one,
like this one.

THE RAIN

All night the sound had
come back again,
and again falls
this quiet, persistent rain.

ROBERT CREELEY

What am I to myself
that must be remembered,
insisted upon
so often? Is it

that never the ease,
even the hardness,
of rain failing
will have for me

something other than this,
something not so insistent—
am I to be locked in this
final uneasiness.

Love, if you love me,
lie next to me.
Be for me, like rain,
the getting out

of the tiredness, the fatuousness, the semi-
lust of intentional indifference.
Be wet
with a decent happiness.

THE MEMORY

Like a river she was,
huge roily mass of water
carrying tree trunks
and divers drunks.

Like a Priscilla, a feminine Benjamin,
a whore gone right over
the falls,
she was.

ROBERT CREELEY

Did you know her.
Did you love her, brother.
Did wonder pour down
on the whole goddamn town.

THE RESCUE

The man sits in a timelessness
with the horse under him in time
to a movement of legs and hooves
upon a timeless sand.

Distance comes in from the foreground
present in the picture as time
he reads outward from
and comes from that beginning.

A wind blows in
and out and all about the man
as the horse ran
and runs to come in time.

A house is burning in the sand.
A man and horse are burning.
The wind is burning.
They are running to arrive.

THE LANGUAGE

Locate *I*
love you some-
where in

teeth and
eyes, bite
it but

ROBERT CREELEY

take care not
to hurt, you
want so

much so
little. Words
say everything,

I
love you
again,

then what
is emptiness
for. To

fill, fill.
I heard words
and words full

of holes
aching. Speech
is a mouth.

THE WINDOW

Position is where you
put it, where it is,
did you, for example, that

large tank there, silvered,
with the white church along-
side, lift

all that, to what
purpose? How
heavy the slow

world is with
everything put
in place. Some

man walks by, a
car beside him on
the dropped

road, a leaf of
yellow color is
going to

fall. It
all drops into
place. My

face is heavy
with the sight. I can
feel my eye breaking.

ON VACATION

Things seem empty
on vacation if the labors
have not been physical,

if tedium was rather
a daily knot, a continuum,
if satisfaction was almost

placid. On Sundays the restlessness
grows, on weekends, on
months of vacation myself grows

vacuous. Taking walks, swimming,
drinking, I am always afraid
of having more. Hence a true

Puritan, I shall never rest from my labors
until all rest with me, until I am
driven by that density home.

MOMENT

Whether to *use* time, or to *kill* time, either
still preys on my mind.

One's come now to the graveyard,
where the bones of the dead are.

All roads *have* come
here, truly common—

except the body is moved,
still, to some other use.

OUTSIDE

The light now meets
with the shuddering branch.
What I see
distorts the image.

This is an age
of slow determinations,
goes up the stairs
with dulled will.

Who would accept death
as an end
thinks he can
do what he wants to.

ROBERT CREELEY

FIRST RAIN

These retroactive small
instances of feeling

reach out for a common
ground in the wet

first rain of a faded
winter. Along the grey

iced sidewalk revealed
piles of dogshit, papers,

bits of old clothing, are
the human pledges,

call them, "We are here and
have been all the time." I

walk quickly. The wind
drives the rain, drenching

my coat, pants, blurs
my glasses, as I pass.

MOTHER'S VOICE

In these few years
since her death I hear
mother's voice say
under my own, I won't

want any more of that.
My cheekbones resonate
with her emphasis. Nothing
of not wanting only

but the distance there from
common fact of others
frightens me. I look out
at all this demanding world

and try to put it quietly back,
from me, say, thank you,
I've already had some
though I haven't

and would like to
but I've said no, she has,
it's not my own voice anymore.
It's higher as hers was

and accommodates too simply
its frustrations when
I at least think I want more
and must have it.

THE MOVIE RUN BACKWARD

The words will one day come
back to you, birds returning,
the movie run backward.

Nothing so strange in its talk,
just words. The people
who wrote them are the dead ones.

This here paper talks like anything
but is only one thing,
"birds returning."

You can "run the movie
backward" but "the movie run
backward." The movie run backward.

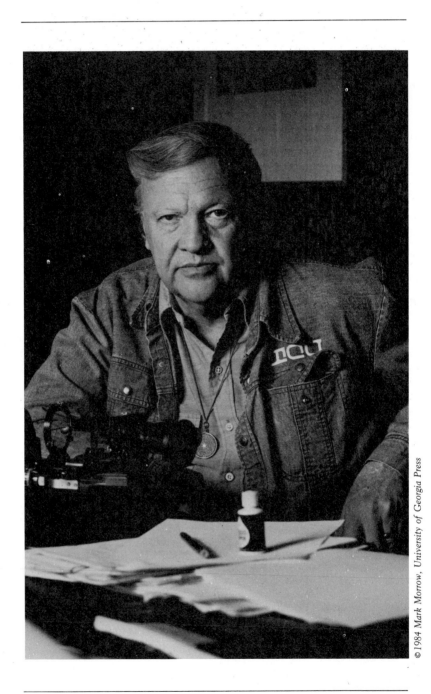

James Dickey

THE HEAVEN OF ANIMALS

Here they are. The soft eyes open.
If they have lived in a wood
It is a wood.
If they have lived on plains
It is grass rolling
Under their feet forever.

Having no souls, they have come,
Anyway, beyond their knowing.
Their instincts wholly bloom
And they rise.
The soft eyes open.

To match them, the landscape flowers,
Outdoing, desperately
Outdoing what is required:
The richest wood,
The deepest field.

For some of these,
It could not be the place
It is, without blood.
These hunt, as they have done,
But with claws and teeth grown perfect,

More deadly than they can believe.
They stalk more silently,
And crouch on the limbs of trees,
And their descent
Upon the bright backs of their prey

May take years
In a sovereign floating of joy.
And those that are hunted
Know this as their life,
Their reward: to walk

Under such trees in full knowledge
Of what is in glory above them,
And to feel no fear,
But acceptance, compliance.
Fulfilling themselves without pain

At the cycle's center,
They tremble, they walk
Under the tree,
They fall, they are torn,
They rise, they walk again.

THE PERFORMANCE

The last time I saw Donald Armstrong
He was staggering oddly off into the sun,
Going down, of the Philippine Islands.
I let my shovel fall, and put that hand
Above my eyes, and moved some way to one side
That his body might pass through the sun,

And I saw how well he was not
Standing there on his hands,
On his spindle-shanked forearms balanced,
Unbalanced, with his big feet looming and waving
In the great, untrustworthy air
He flew in each night, when it darkened.

Dust fanned in scraped puffs from the earth
Between his arms, and blood turned his face inside out,
To demonstrate its suppleness
Of veins, as he perfected his role.
Next day, he toppled his head off
On an island beach to the south,

And the enemy's two-handed sword
Did not fall from anyone's hands
At that miraculous sight,
As the head rolled over upon
Its wide-eyed face, and fell
Into the inadequate grave

He had dug for himself, under pressure.
Yet I put my flat hand to my eyebrows
Months later, to see him again
In the sun, when I learned how he died,
And imagined him, there,
Come, judged, before his small captors,

Doing all his lean tricks to amaze them—
The back somersault, the kip-up—
And at last, the stand on his hands,
Perfect, with his feet together,
His head down, evenly breathing,
As the sun poured up from the sea

And the headsman broke down
In a blaze of tears, in that light
Of the thin, long human frame
Upside down in its own strange joy,
And, if some other one had not told him,
Would have cut off the feet

Instead of the head,
And if Armstrong had not presently risen
In kingly, round-shouldered attendance,
And then knelt down in himself
Beside his hacked, glittering grave, having done
All things in this life that he could.

THE HOSPITAL WINDOW

I have just come down from my father.
Higher and higher he lies
Above me in a blue light
Shed by a tinted window.
I drop through six white floors
And then step out onto pavement.

Still feeling my father ascend,
I start to cross the firm street,
My shoulder blades shining with all

JAMES DICKEY

The glass the huge building can raise.
Now I must turn round and face it,
And know his one pane from the others.

Each window possesses the sun
As though it burned there on a wick.
I wave, like a man catching fire.
All the deep-dyed windowpanes flash,
And, behind them, all the white rooms
They turn to the color of Heaven.

Ceremoniously, gravely, and weakly,
Dozens of pale hands are waving
Back, from inside their flames.
Yet one pure pane among these
Is the bright, erased blankness of nothing.
I know that my father is there,

In the shape of his death still living.
The traffic increases around me
Like a madness called down on my head.
The horns blast at me like shotguns,
And drivers lean out, driven crazy—
But now my propped-up father

Lifts his arm out of stillness at last.
The light from the window strikes me
And I turn as blue as a soul,
As the moment when I was born.
I am not afraid for my father—
Look! He is grinning; he is not

Afraid for my life, either,
As the wild engines stand at my knees
Shredding their gears and roaring,
And I hold each car in its place
For miles, inciting its horn
To blow down the walls of the world

That the dying may float without fear
In the bold blue gaze of my father.
Slowly I move to the sidewalk
With my pin-tingling hand half dead
At the end of my bloodless arm.
I carry it off in amazement,

High, still higher, still waving,
My recognized face fully mortal,
Yet not; not at all, in the pale,
Drained, otherworldly, stricken,
Created hue of stained glass.
I have just come down from my father.

IN THE MOUNTAIN TENT

I am hearing the shape of the rain
Take the shape of the tent and believe it,
Laying down all around where I lie
A profound, unspeakable law.
I obey, and am free-falling slowly

Through the thought-out leaves of the wood
Into the minds of animals.
I am there in the shining of water
Like dark, like light, out of Heaven.

I am there like the dead, or the beast
Itself, which thinks of a poem—
Green, plausible, living, and holy—
And cannot speak, but hears,
Called forth from the waiting of things,

A vast, proper, reinforced crying
With the sifted, harmonious pause,
The sustained intake of all breath
Before the first word of the Bible.

At midnight water dawns
Upon the held skulls of the foxes
And weasels and tousled hares
On the eastern side of the mountain.
Their light is the image I make

As I wait as if recently killed,
Receptive, fragile, half-smiling,
My brow watermarked with the mark
On the wing of a moth

And the tent taking shape on my body
Like ill-fitting, Heavenly clothes.
From holes in the ground comes my voice
In the God-silenced tongue of the beasts.
"I shall rise from the dead," I am saying.

SLED BURIAL, DREAM CEREMONY

While the south rains, the north
Is snowing, and the dead southerner
Is taken there. He lies with the top of his casket
Open, his hair combed, the particles in the air
Changing to other things. The train stops

In a small furry village, and men in flap-eared caps
And others with women's scarves tied around their heads
And business hats over those, unload him,
And one of them reaches inside the coffin and places
The southerner's hand at the center

Of his dead breast. They load him onto a sled,
An old-fashioned sled with high-curled runners,
Drawn by horses with bells, and begin
To walk out of town, past dull red barns
Inching closer to the road as it snows

JAMES DICKEY

Harder, past an army of gunny-sacked bushes,
Past horses with flakes in the hollows of their sway-backs,
Past round faces drawn by children
On kitchen windows, all shedding basic-shaped tears.
The coffin top still is wide open;

His dead eyes stare through his lids,
Not fooled that the snow is cotton. The woods fall
Slowly off all of them, until they are walking
Between rigid little houses of ice-fishers
On a plain which is a great plain of water

Until the last rabbit track fails, and they are
At the center. They take axes, shovels, mattocks,
Dig the snow away, and saw the ice in the form
Of his coffin, lifting the slab like a door
Without hinges. The snow creaks under the sled

As they unload him like hay, holding his weight by ropes.
Sensing an unwanted freedom, a fish
Slides by, under the hole leading up through the snow
To nothing, and is gone. The coffin's shadow
Is white, and they stand there, gunny-sacked bushes,

Summoned from village sleep into someone else's dream
Of death, and let him down, still seeing the flakes in the air
At the place they are born of pure shadow
Like his dead eyelids, rocking for a moment like a boat
On utter foreignness, before he fills and sails down.

THE SHEEP CHILD

Farm boys wild to couple
With anything   with soft-wooded trees
With mounds of earth   mounds
Of pinestraw   will keep themselves off
Animals by legends of their own:
In the hay-tunnel dark
And dung of barns, they will
Say   I have heard tell

That in a museum in Atlanta
Way back in a corner somewhere
There's this thing that's only half
Sheep   like a woolly baby
Pickled in alcohol   because
Those things can't live   his eyes
Are open   but you can't stand to look
I heard from somebody who . . .

But this is now almost all
Gone. The boys have taken
Their own true wives in the city,
The sheep are safe in the west hill
Pasture   but we who were born there
Still are not sure. Are we,
Because we remember, remembered
In the terrible dust of museums?

Merely with his eyes, the sheep-child may

Be saying   saying

    I am here, in my father's house.
    I who am half of your world, came deeply
    To my mother in the long grass
    Of the west pasture, where she stood like moonlight
    Listening for foxes. It was something like love
    From another world that seized her
    From behind, and she gave, not lifting her head
    Out of dew, without ever looking, her best
    Self to that great need. Turned loose, she dipped her face
    Farther into the chill of the earth, and in a sound
    Of sobbing   of something stumbling
    Away, began, as she must do,
    To carry me. I woke, dying,

    In the summer sun of the hillside, with my eyes
    Far more than human. I saw for a blazing moment
    The great grassy world from both sides,
    Man and beast in the round of their need,
    And the hill wind stirred in my wool,

My hoof and my hand clasped each other,
I ate my one meal
Of milk, and died
Staring. From dark grass I came straight

To my father's house, whose dust
Whirls up in the halls for no reason
When no one comes   piling deep in a hellish mild corner,
And, through my immortal waters,
I meet the sun's grains eye
To eye, and they fail at my closet of glass.
Dead, I am most surely living
In the minds of farm boys: I am he who drives
Them like wolves from the hound bitch and calf
And from the chaste ewe in the wind.
They go into woods   into bean fields   they go
Deep into their known right hands. Dreaming of me,
They groan   they wait   they suffer
Themselves, they marry, they raise their kind.

ADULTERY

We have all been in rooms
We cannot die in, and they are odd places, and sad.
Often Indians are standing eagle-armed on hills

In the sunrise   open wide to the Great Spirit
Or gliding in canoes   or cattle are browsing on the walls
Far away   gazing down with the eyes of our children

Not far away   or there are men driving
The last railspike, which has turned
Gold in their hands. Gigantic forepleasure lives

Among such scenes, and we are alone with it
At last. There is always some weeping
Between us   and someone is always checking

A wrist watch by the bed to see how much
Longer we have left. Nothing can come
Of this   nothing can come

Of us: of me with my grim techniques
Or you who have sealed your womb
With a ring of convulsive rubber:

Although we come together,
Nothing will come of us. But we would not give
It up, for death is beaten

By praying Indians   by distant cows   historical
Hammers   by hazardous meetings that bridge
A continent. One could never die here

Never die   never die
While crying. My lover, my dear one
I will see you next week

When I'm in town. I will call you
If I can. Please get hold of   please don't
Oh God, Please don't any more I can't bear . . . Listen:

We have done it again   we are
Still living. Sit up and smile,
God bless you. Guilt is magical.

DEER AMONG CATTLE

Here and there in the searing beam
Of my hand going through the night meadow
They all are grazing

With pins of human light in their eyes.
A wild one also is eating
The human grass,

Slender, graceful, domesticated
By darkness, among the bred-
for-slaughter,

JAMES DICKEY

Having bounded their paralyzed fence
And inclined his branched forehead onto
Their green frosted table,

The only live thing in this flashlight
Who can leave whenever he wishes,
Turn grass into forest,

Foreclose inhuman brightness from his eyes
But stands here still, unperturbed,
In their wide-open country,

The sparks from my hand in his pupils
Unmatched anywhere among cattle,

Grazing with them the night of the hammer
As one of their own who shall rise.

FALSE YOUTH: AUTUMN: CLOTHES OF THE AGE

—for Susan Tuckerman Dickey—

Three red foxes on my head, come down
There last Christmas from Brooks Brothers
As a joke, I wander down Harden Street
In Columbia, South Carolina, fur-haired and bald,
Looking for impulse in camera stores and redneck greeting cards.
A pole is spinning
Colors I have little use for, but I go in
Anyway, and take off my fox hat and jacket
They have not seen from behind yet. The barber does what he can
With what I have left, and I hear the end man say, as my own
Hair-cutter turns my face
To the floor, Jesus, if there's anything I hate
It's a middle-aged hippie. Well, so do I, I swallow
Back: so do I   so do I
And to hell. I get up, and somebody else says
When're you gonna put on that hat,
Buddy? Right now. Another says softly,
Goodbye, Fox. I arm my denim jacket
On and walk to the door, stopping for the murmur of chairs,

And there it is
                    hand-stitched by the needles of the mother
Of my grandson   eagle riding on his claws with a banner
            Outstretched as the wings of my shoulders,
                Coming after me with his flag
            Disintegrating, his one eye raveling
                Out, filthy strings flying
    From the white feathers, one wing nearly gone:
                Blind eagle but flying
        Where I walk, where I stop with my fox
Head at the glass to let the row of chairs spell it out
            And get a lifetime look at my bird's
One word, raggedly blazing with extinction and soaring loose
In red threads burning up white until I am shot in the back
            Through my wings   or ripped apart
                    For rags:

                Poetry.

DOORSTEP, LIGHTNING, WAIF-DREAMING

        Who can tell who was born of what?
        I go sitting on the doorsteps of unknowns
            And ask, and hear nothing
        From the rhythmical ghosts of those others,
        Or from myself while I am there, but only
        The solid shifts of drumming made of heart.
            I come always softly,
        My head full of lingering off-prints

        Of lightning — vital, engendering blank,
    The interim spraddling crack   the crowning rollback
    Whited-out *ex nihilo*
                        and I am as good as appearing
    The other time.   I come of a root-system of fire, as it fires
    Point-blank at this hearthstone and doorstep: there is
            A tingling of light-sensitive hairs
            Between me: my clothes flicker
        And glow with it, under the bracketing split
        Of sky, the fasting, saint-hinting glimmer,

JAMES DICKEY

The shifting blasts of echo, relocating,
    And of an orphaning blaze

I have been stressed, and born, and stamped
Alive on this doorstep.   I believe it between cloud
And echo, and my own chosen-and-sifted footstep
    Arriving,
                engendered, endangered, loving,

Dangerous, seeking ground.

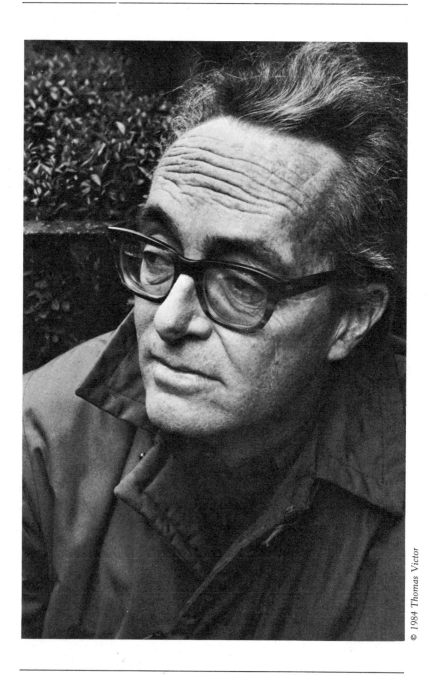

Alan Dugan

LOVE SONG: I AND THOU

Nothing is plumb, level, or square:
   the studs are bowed, the joists
are shaky by nature, no piece fits
   any other piece without a gap
or pinch, and bent nails
   dance all over the surfacing
like maggots. By Christ
   I am no carpenter. I built
the roof for myself, the walls
   for myself, the floors
for myself, and got
   hung up in it myself. I
danced with a purple thumb
   at this house-warming, drunk
with my prime whiskey: rage.
   Oh I spat rage's nails
into the frame-up of my work:
   it held. It settled plumb,
level, solid, square and true
   for that great moment. Then
it screamed and went on through,
   skewing as wrong the other way.
God damned it. This is hell,
   but I planned it, I sawed it,
I nailed it, and I
   will live in it until it kills me.
I can nail my left palm
   to the left-hand crosspiece but
I can't do everything myself.
   I need a hand to nail the right,
a help, a love, a you, a wife.

ALAN DUGAN

TRIBUTE TO KAFKA FOR
SOMEONE TAKEN

The party is going strong.
The doorbell rings. It's
for someone named me.
I'm coming. I take
a last drink, a last
puff on a cigarette,
a last kiss at a girl,
and step into the hall,
                    bang,
shutting out the laughter. "Is
your name you?" "Yes."
"Well come along then."
"See here. See here. See here."

ELEGY

I know but will not tell
you, Aunt Irene, why there
are soapsuds in the whiskey:
Uncle Robert had to have
a drink while shaving. May
there be no bloodshed in your house
this morning of my father's death
and no unkept appearance
in the living, since he has
to wear the rouge and lipstick
of your ceremony, mother,
for the first and last time:
father, hello and goodbye.

TO A RED-HEADED DO-GOOD WAITRESS

Every morning I went to her charity and learned
to face the music of her white smile so well

ALAN DUGAN

that it infected my black teeth as I escaped,
and those who saw me smiled too and went in
the White Castle, where she is the inviolable lady.

There cripples must be bright, and starvers noble:
no tears, no stomach-cries, but pain made art
to move her powerful red pity toward philanthropy.
So I must wear my objectively stinking poverty
like a millionaire clown's rags and sing, "Oh I

got plenty o' nuttin'," as if I made
a hundred grand a year like Gershwin, while
I get a breakfast every day from her for two
weeks and nothing else but truth: she has
a policeman and a wrong sonnet in fifteen lines.

FOR MASTURBATION

I have allowed myself
this corner and am God.
Here in the must
beneath their stoop
I will do as I will,
either as act as act,
or dream for the sake of dreams,
and if they find me out
in rocket ships or jets
working to get away,

then let my left great-toe-
nail grow into the inside knob
of my right ankle bone and let
my fingernails make eight new moons
temporarily in the cold salt marches of my palms!
THIS IS THE WAY IT IS, and if
it is "a terrible disgrace"
it is as I must will,
because I am not them
though I am theirs to kill.

FABRICATION OF ANCESTORS

For old Billy Dugan, shot in the ass in the Civil War, my father said.

The old wound in my ass
has opened up again, but I
am past the prodigies
of youth's campaigns, and weep
where I used to laugh
in war's red humors, half
in love with silly-assed pains
and half not feeling them.
I have to sit up with
an indoor unsittable itch
before I go down late
and weeping to the storm-
cellar on a dirty night
and go to bed with the worms.
So pull the dirt up over me
and make a family joke
for Old Billy Blue Balls,
the oldest private in the world
with two ass-holes and no
place more to go to for a laugh
except the last one. Say:
The North won the Civil War
without much help from me
although I wear a proof
of the war's obscenity.

POEM

What's the balm
for a dying life,
dope, drink, or Christ,
is there one?

I puke and choke
with it and find
no peace of mind
in flesh, and no hope.

It flows away
in mucous juice.
Nothing I can do
can make it stay,

so I give out
and water the garden: it
is all shit
for the flowers anyhow.

ELEGY FOR A PURITAN CONSCIENCE

I closed my ears with stinging bugs
and sewed my eyelids shut
but heard a sucking at the dugs
and saw my parents rut.

I locked my jaw with rusty nails
and cured my tongue in lime
but ate and drank in garbage pails
and said these words of crime.

I crushed my scrotum with two stones
and drew my penis in
but felt your wound expect its own
and fell in love with sin.

PRAYER

God, I need a job because I need money.
Here the world is, enjoyable with whiskey,
women, ultimate weapons, and class!
But if I have no money, then my wife
gets mad at me, I can't drink well,
the armed oppress me, and no boss
pays me money. But when I work,
Oh I get paid!, the police are courteous,
and I can have a drink and breathe air.

ALAN DUGAN

I feel classy. I am where the arms are.
The wife is wife in deed. The world
is interesting!, except I have to be
indoors all day and take shit, and make
weapons to kill outsiders with. I miss
the air and smell that paid work stinks
when done for someone else's profit, so I quit,
enjoy a few flush days in air, drunk, then
I need a job again. I'm caught in a steel cycle.

ON LEAVING TOWN

This must be a bad dream. We will wake up
tomorrow naked in the prior garden, each
entwined in his particular love. We will
get up to natural water, fruits, and what?,
a gambol with the lions? Nonsense. This
is petrified obsession, perfect in tautology,
visible in the smoke, the layout of the streets,
and prison buildings. The city has put on
glass armor in rock war against its death,
which is internal. It rides out radiate
on country roads to ride down enemy foliage.
Why? There's nothing left in it to kill
except its people, and they look thoroughly every way—
left, right, front, back, up, down, and in—
before they cross another, or its streets. Such animals,
joyful of desolate beauties, they are so tough, the live ones,
that they stand around like Easter Island statues of survival won
by casual struggle, proud of their tension or their craft.
Oh I reject the dream but not the city. I
have loved its life and left it and I am
a better animal for having learned its ways;
but it is not enough to be a captive animal,
social in town. Escaped emotions: boredom and fear.

ALAN DUGAN

"SPACE IS NOT MERELY A BACKGROUND FOR EVENTS,
BUT POSSESSES AN AUTONOMOUS STRUCTURE."
—A. EINSTEIN

As an individual penance when my nothing speaks
I dial the car radio on to overlapping bands
late at night, and do the stations of the breath
in one place, although the car moves at the speed of sleep.

American distances come out of the machine as one noise
fouling the time of air with wastes of music and speech
unhearable in unseeable space except mechanically
transformed by static to pollution of one's observational ears.

Then I can say to my nothing talking to itself,
"Listen to what is going on! This night atmosphere
is an articulate structure of lousy music and lies.
What do you say, why bother, who's driving, what's right?"

UNTITLED POEM

Once, one of my students read a book we had.
She was doing a history assignment on
the decline and fall of the Roman Empire
and crying. When I asked her why
she said Because. All those people died.
I said that if you start to cry for the dead
you won't have much time for anything else.
Besides, after all the city people were killed
or died off, because their cultures got too high,
the barbarians kept some peasants alive
for their food value. Some barbarian raped
some peasant woman who produced
a child who ultimately produced you

and me, so there is this family continuity,
so don't cry, it's obvious, look around!
This is the reason why we Americans
are a nation of peasants and barbarians.

ON FINDING THE TREE OF LIFE

After Genesis 3: 22-23

If there is an outside out there
one should go out to try to find it.
This I did. There is a garden world
out there, with birds, trees, and the tree
they call The Tree of Life. The birds
avoid it, naturally. The bunches of red
berries are intact except for one bunch. It's
partly eaten. The spoor around the tree
is old, but it would indicate that some
stupid godforsaken human or beast
had staggered around and crawled away
in the first agonies of immortality.
It's too bad for it, whoever it is
and will be: our own deaths are bad enough.

LAST STATEMENT FOR A LAST ORACLE

After this oracle there will be no more oracles.
The precinct is hereby desanctified. You wanted it,
you have it. From now on everything I say
will be a lie said for cash. Now, for the last time,
here's the truth: You have won with your horse power
and numbers from the north. You will go on
winning forever—this is your damnation—

ALAN DUGAN

until your conquests and the insides of your heads
are alike, and you and I know what it's like
in there, so if some dirty beast remembers,
on some future dirty night, what it was like
once to have been a human being and pleasing to me
in a fair exchange of pure sacrifice for pure prophecy
he will throw himself into a fire and howl to death.
I will now drop back into the fire you are
so curious about. When you get drunk tonight
and pee on it, it, you and I will go out like the light
and an acid yellow smoke will take the place of our souls.
We will have to go on living a lie for a while, however,
in the unspeakable condition I have referred to in passing.

© 1984 Thomas Victor

Robert Duncan

OFTEN I AM PERMITTED TO RETURN
TO A MEADOW

as if it were a scene made-up by the mind,
that is not mine, but is a made place,

that is mine, it is so near to the heart,
an eternal pasture folded in all thought
so that there is a hall therein

that is a made place, created by light
wherefrom the shadows that are forms fall.

Wherefrom fall all architectures I am
I say are likenesses of the First Beloved
whose flowers are flames lit to the Lady.

She it is Queen Under The Hill
whose hosts are a disturbance of words within words
that is a field folded.

It is only a dream of the grass blowing
east against the source of the sun
in an hour before the sun's going down

whose secret we see in a children's game
of ring a round of roses told.

Often I am permitted to return to a meadow
as if it were a given property of the mind
that certain bounds hold against chaos,

that is a place of first permission,
everlasting omen of what is.

POETRY, A NATURAL THING

    Neither our vices nor our virtues
further the poem. "They came up
      and died
just like they do every year
      on the rocks."

    The poem
feeds upon thought, feeling, impulse,
      to breed   itself,
a spiritual urgency at the dark ladders leaping.

This beauty is an inner persistence
      toward the source
striving against (within) down-rushet of the river,
      a call we heard and answer
in the lateness of the world
      primordial bellowings
from which the youngest world might spring,

salmon not in the well where the
      hazelnut falls
but at the falls battling, inarticulate,
      blindly making it.

This is one picture apt for the mind.

A second: a moose painted by Stubbs,
where last year's extravagant antlers
      lie on the ground.
The forlorn moosey-faced poem wears
      new antler-buds,
      the same,

"a little heavy, a little contrived",

his only beauty to be
      all moose.

ROBERT DUNCAN

INGMAR BERGMAN'S *SEVENTH SEAL*

This is the way it is. We see
three ages in one: the child Jesus
innocent of Jerusalem and Rome
—magically at home in joy—
that's the year from which
our inner persistence has its force.

The second, Bergman shows us,
carries forward image after image
of anguish, of the Christ crossd
and sends up from open sores of the plague
(shown as wounds upon His corpse)
from lacerations in the course of love
(the crown of whose kingdom tears the flesh)

. . . There is so much suffering!
What possibly protects us
from the emptiness, the forsaken cry,
the utter dependence, the vertigo?
Why do so many come to love's edge
only to be stranded there?

The second face of Christ, his
evil, his Other, emaciated, pain and sin.
Christ, what a contagion!
What a stink it spreads round

our age! It's our age!
and the rage of the storm is abroad.
The malignant stupidity of statesmen rules.
The old riders thru the forests race
        shouting: the wind! the wind!
Now the black horror cometh again.

And I'll throw myself down
as the clown does in Bergman's *Seventh Seal*
to cower as if asleep with his wife and child,
hid in the caravan under the storm.

Let the Angel of Wrath pass over.
Let the end come.
War, stupidity and fear are powerful.
We are only children. To bed! to bed!
 To play safe!

To throw ourselves down
helplessly, into happiness,
 into an age of our own, into
 our own days.
There where the Pestilence roars,
where the empty riders of the horror go.

SUCH IS THE SICKNESS OF MANY A GOOD THING

Was he then Adam of the Burning Way?
hid away in the heat like wrath
 conceald in Love's face,
or the seed, Eris in Eros,
 key and lock
of what I was? I could not speak
 the releasing
word. For into a dark
 matter he came
and askt me to say what
 I could not say. "I . ."

All the flame in me stopt
 against my tongue.
My heart was a stone, a dumb
 unmanageable thing in me,
a darkness that stood athwart
 his need
for the enlightening, the
 "I love you" that has
only this one quick in time,
 this one start
when its moment is true.

Such is the sickness of many a good thing
that now into my life from long ago this
refusing to say I love you has bound
the weeping, the yielding, the
    yearning to be taken again,
into a knot, a waiting, a string

so taut it taunts the song,
it resists the touch. It grows dark
to draw down the lover's hand
from its lightness to what's
    underground.

BENDING THE BOW

We've our business to attend Day's duties,
bend back the bow in dreams as we may
til the end rimes in the taut string
with the sending. Reveries are rivers and flow
where the cold light gleams reflecting the window upon the
    surface of the table,
the presst-glass creamer, the pewter sugar bowl, the litter
    of coffee cups and saucers,
carnations painted growing upon whose surfaces. The whole
composition of surfaces leads into the other
    current disturbing
what I would take hold of. I'd been

in the course of a letter—I am still
in the course of a letter—to a friend,
who comes close in to my thought so that
the day is hers. My hand writing here
there shakes in the currents of . . . of air?
of an inner anticipation of . . . ?   reaching to touch
ghostly exhilarations in the thought of her.

    At the extremity of this
      design
"there is a connexion working in both directions, as in
    the bow and the lyre"—

only in that swift fulfillment of the wish
      that sleep
   can illustrate my hand
      sweeps the string.

You stand behind the where-I-am.
The deep tones and shadows I will call a woman.
The quick high notes . . . You are a girl there too,
   having something of sister and of wife,
         inconsolate,
and I would play Orpheus for you again,

         recall the arrow or song
         to the trembling daylight
         from which it sprang.

from the Emperor Julian, *Hymn to the Mother of the Gods:*

   And Attis encircles the heavens like a tiara, and thence
sets out as though to descend to earth.

   For the even is bounded, but the uneven is without bounds
and there is no way through or out of it.

MY MOTHER WOULD BE A FALCONRESS

   My mother would be a falconress,
   And I, her gay falcon treading her wrist,
   would fly to bring back
   from the blue of the sky to her, bleeding, a prize,
   where I dream in my little hood with many bells
   jangling when I'd turn my head.

   My mother would be a falconress,
   and she sends me as far as her will goes.
   She lets me ride to the end of her curb
   where I fall back in anguish.

ROBERT DUNCAN

I dread that she will cast me away,
for I fall, I mis-take, I fail in her mission.

She would bring down the little birds.
And I would bring down the little birds.
When will she let me bring down the little birds,
pierced from their flight with their necks broken,
their heads like flowers limp from the stem?

I tread my mother's wrist and would draw blood.
Behind the little hood my eyes are hooded.
I have gone back into my hooded silence,
talking to myself and dropping off to sleep.

For she has muffled my dreams in the hood she has made me,
sewn round with bells, jangling when I move.
She rides with her little falcon upon her wrist.
She uses a barb that brings me to cower.
She sends me abroad to try my wings
and I come back to her.   I would bring down
the little birds to her
I may not tear into, I must bring back perfectly.

I tear at her wrist with my beak to draw blood,
and her eye holds me, anguisht, terrifying.
She draws a limit to my flight.
Never beyond my sight, she says.

She trains me to fetch and to limit myself in fetching.
She rewards me with meat for my dinner.
But I must never eat what she sends me to bring her.

Yet it would have been beautiful, if she would have carried me,
always, in a little hood with the bells ringing,
at her wrist, and her riding
to the great falcon hunt, and me
flying up to the curb of my heart from her heart
to bring down the skylark from the blue to her feet,
straining, and then released for the flight.

ROBERT DUNCAN

My mother would be a falconress,
and I her gerfalcon, raised at her will,
from her wrist sent flying, as if I were her own
pride, as if her pride
knew no limits, as if her mind
sought in me flight beyond the horizon.

Ah, but high, high in the air I flew.
And far, far beyond the curb of her will,
were the blue hills where the falcons nest.
And then I saw west to the dying sun—
it seemd my human soul went down in flames.

I tore at her wrist, at the hold she had for me,
until the blood ran hot and I heard her cry out,
far, far beyond the curb of her will

to horizons of stars beyond the ringing hills of the world where
     the falcons nest
I saw, and I tore at her wrist with my savage beak.
I flew, as if sight flew from the anguish in her eye beyond her sight,
sent from my striking loose, from the cruel strike at her wrist,
striking out from the blood to be free of her.

My mother would be a falconress,
and even now, years after this,
when the wounds I left her had surely heald,
and the woman is dead,
her fierce eyes closed, and if her heart
were broken, it is stilld

I would be a falcon and go free.
I tread her wrist and wear the hood,
talking to myself, and would draw blood.

ROBERT DUNCAN

THE TORSO   PASSAGES 18

    Most beautiful!   the red-flowering eucalyptus,
      the madrone, the yew

    Is he . . .

So thou wouldst smile, and take me in thine arms
The sight of London to my exiled eyes
Is as Elysium to a new-come soul

    If he be Truth
    I would dwell in the illusion of him

His hands unlocking from chambers of my male body

    such an idea in man's image

rising tides that sweep me towards him

    . . . *homosexual?*

    and at the treasure of his mouth

    pour forth my soul

    his soul   commingling

I thought a Being more than vast, His body leading
    into Paradise, his eyes
      quickening a fire in me,   a trembling

    hieroglyph: At the root of the neck

the clavicle, for the neck is the stem of the great artery
upward into his head that is beautiful

At the rise of the pectoral muscles

the nipples, for the breasts are like sleeping fountains
of feeling in man, waiting above the beat of his heart,
shielding the rise and fall of his breath, to be
awakend

At the axis of his mid hriff

the navel, for in the pit of his stomach the chord from
which first he was fed has its temple

At the root of the groin

the pubic hair, for the torso is the stem in which the man
flowers forth and leads to the stamen of flesh in which
his seed rises

a wave of need and desire over   taking me

cried out my name

(This was long ago.   It was another life)

and said,

What do you want of me?

I do not know, I said.   I have fallen in love.   He
has brought me into heights and depths my heart
would fear   without him.   His look

pierces my side   ·   fire eyes   ·

I have been waiting for you, he said:
I know what you desire

you do not yet know   but through me   ·

And I am with you everywhere.   In your falling

I have fallen from a high place.   I have raised myself

from darkness in your   rising

wherever you are

my hand in your hand   seeking   the locks, the keys

I am there.   Gathering me, you gather

your Self   ·

For my Other is not a woman but a man

the King upon whose bosom let me lie.

from DANTE ÉTUDES

The Work

De Monarchia, I, IV

"The work proper to the human race,   taken as a whole,   is to keep the whole capacity of the potential intellect constantly actualized,   primarily for speculation,   and secondarily (by extension, and for the sake of the other) for action."

I enact my being here

for the sake of

a speculation in the nature of Man,

        needs time and space (a stage)
        that only peace of mind provides.

Hence: that the human attain
    its proper work, right ratio
    and the equilibrations
    Imagination demands

       to take its spring

      from the hidden

     not yet among us

       pivot of what we are doing

        sing.

"not riches, not pleasures, not honors, not length of life, not
health, not strength" —what do we know of from where Life is
ever moving us?— "not beauty, but peace"

    leisure (time without anxiety for time)

    for furor toward

Justice —not the requital of grievances,
    not retribution for wrongs, not paying back,

    but for that freeing the grievance in us,

      the fit of the work

   to the requirement recognized

      volunteerd an emotional

      distribution:

thus exact riming
and the timing of syllables
that the idea "count"
and custom enter the poem

ROBERT DUNCAN

and that there be heart,

     a harmony

large enough to account for

     conflict

in the adequate concept seen to provide

     contrast

   the Artist   rejoices in.

Lawrence Ferlinghetti

[CONSTANTLY RISKING ABSURDITY]

Constantly risking absurdity
                 and death
      whenever he performs
           above the heads
                of his audience
   the poet like an acrobat
        climbs on rime
           to a high wire of his own making
and balancing on eyebeams
          above a sea of faces
    paces his way
        to the other side of day
   performing entrechats
        and sleight-of-foot tricks
and other high theatrics
        and all without mistaking
    any thing
       for what it may not be

   For he's the super realist
         who must perforce perceive
    taut truth
      before the taking of each stance or step
 in his supposed advance
        toward that still higher perch
where Beauty stands and waits
      with gravity
        to start her death-defying leap

  And he
     a little charleychaplin man
        who may or may not catch
    her fair eternal form
       spreadeagled in the empty air
   of existence

[SOMETIME DURING ETERNITY]

Sometime during eternity
           some guys show up
and one of them
      who shows up real late
           is a kind of carpenter
from some square-type place
        like Galilee
and he starts wailing
        and claiming he is hep
to who made heaven
       and earth
        and that the cat
who really laid it on us
      is his Dad

And moreover
  he adds
    It's all writ down
       on some scroll-type parchments
which some henchmen
      leave lying around the Dead Sea somewheres
a long time ago
      and which you won't even find
for a coupla thousand years or so
      or at least for
nineteen hundred and fortyseven
      of them
   to be exact
     and even then
nobody really believes them
     or me
      for that matter

You're hot
    they tell him

And they cool him

They stretch him on the Tree to cool

And everybody after that
                              is always making models
            of this Tree
                              with Him hung up
and always crooning His name
                              and calling Him to come down
            and sit in
                        on their combo
            as if he is the king cat
                              who's got to blow
            or they can't quite make it

            Only he don't come down
                              from His Tree

Him just hang there
            on His Tree
                              looking real Petered out
            and real cool
                        and also
            according to a roundup
                        of late world news
      from the usual unreliable sources
                              real dead

[THE PENNYCANDYSTORE BEYOND THE EL]

            The pennycandystore beyond the El
            is where I first
                        fell in love
                              with unreality
            Jellybeans glowed in the semi-gloom
            of that september afternoon
            A cat upon the counter moved among
                              the licorice sticks
                  and tootsie rolls
            and Oh Boy Gum

            Outside the leaves were falling as they died

A wind had blown away the sun
A girl ran in
Her hair was rainy
Her breasts were breathless in the little room

Outside the leaves were falling
         and they cried
                Too soon! too soon!

I AM WAITING

I am waiting for my case to come up
and I am waiting
for a rebirth of wonder
and I am waiting for someone
to really discover America
and wail
and I am waiting
for the discovery
of a new symbolic western frontier
and I am waiting
for the American Eagle
to really spread its wings
and straighten up and fly right
and I am waiting
for the Age of Anxiety
to drop dead
and I am waiting
for the war to be fought
which will make the world safe
for anarchy
and I am waiting
for the final withering away
of all governments
and I am perpetually awaiting
a rebirth of wonder

I am waiting for the Second Coming
and I am waiting
for a religious revival
to sweep thru the state of Arizona
and I am waiting
for the Grapes of Wrath to be stored
and I am waiting
for them to prove
that God is really American
and I am seriously waiting
for Billy Graham and Elvis Presley
to exchange roles seriously
and I am waiting
to see God on television
piped onto church altars
if only they can find
the right channel
to tune in on
and I am waiting
for the Last Supper to be served again
with a strange new appetizer
and I am perpetually awaiting
a rebirth of wonder

I am waiting for my number to be called
and I am waiting
for the living end
and I am waiting
for dad to come home
his pockets full
of irradiated silver dollars
and I am waiting
for the atomic tests to end
and I am waiting happily
for things to get much worse
before they improve
and I am waiting
for the Salvation Army to take over

and I am waiting
for the human crowd
to wander off a cliff somewhere
clutching its atomic umbrella
and I am waiting
for Ike to act
and I am waiting
for the meek to be blessed
and inherit the earth
without taxes
and I am waiting
for forests and animals
to reclaim the earth as theirs
and I am waiting
for a way to be devised
to destroy all nationalisms
without killing anybody
and I am waiting
for linnets and planets to fall like rain
and I am waiting for lovers and weepers
to lie down together again
in a new rebirth of wonder

I am waiting for the Great Divide to be crossed
and I am anxiously waiting
for the secret of eternal life to be discovered
by an obscure general practitioner
and save me forever from certain death
and I am waiting
for life to begin
and I am waiting
for the storms of life
to be over
and I am waiting
to set sail for happiness
and I am waiting
for a reconstructed Mayflower
to reach America
with its picture story and tv rights
sold in advance to the natives

LAWRENCE FERLINGHETTI

and I am waiting
for the lost music to sound again
in the Lost Continent
in a new rebirth of wonder

I am waiting for the day
that maketh all things clear
and I am waiting
for Ole Man River
to just stop rolling along
past the country club
and I am waiting
for the deepest South
to just stop Reconstructing itself
in its own image
and I am waiting
for a sweet desegregated chariot
to swing low
and carry me back to Ole Virginie
and I am waiting
for Ole Virginie to discover
just why Darkies are born
and I am waiting
for God to lookout
from Lookout Mountain
and see the Ode to the Confederate Dead
as a real farce
and I am awaiting retribution
for what America did
to Tom Sawyer
and I am perpetually awaiting
a rebirth of wonder

I am waiting for Tom Swift to grow up
and I am waiting
for the American Boy
to take off Beauty's clothes
and get on top of her

and I am waiting
for Alice in Wonderland
to retransmit to me
her total dream of innocence
and I am waiting
for Childe Roland to come
to the final darkest tower
and I am waiting
for Aphrodite
to grow live arms
at a final disarmament conference
in a new rebirth of wonder

I am waiting
to get some intimations
of immortality
by recollecting my early childhood
and I am waiting
for the green mornings to come again
youth's dumb green fields come back again
and I am waiting
for some strains of unpremeditated art
to shake my typewriter
and I am waiting to write
the great indelible poem
and I am waiting
for the last long careless rapture
and I am perpetually waiting
for the fleeing lovers on the Grecian Urn
to catch each other up at last
and embrace
and I am awaiting
perpetually and forever
a renaissance of wonder

MONET'S LILIES SHUDDERING

Monet never knew
        he was painting his 'Lilies' for
     a lady from the Chicago Art Institute
      who went to France and filmed
        today's lilies
          by the 'Bridge at Giverny'
            a leaf afloat among them
the film of which now flickers
    at the entrance to his framed visions
      with a Debussy piano soundtrack
flooding with a new fluorescence (fleur-essence?)
   the rooms and rooms
        of waterlilies

Monet caught a Cloud in a Pond
             in 1903
     and got a first glimpse
          of its lilies
   and for twenty years returned
     again and again to paint them
       which now gives us the impression
        that he floated thru life on them
              and their reflections
     which he also didn't know
       we would have occasion
         to reflect upon

Anymore than he could know
      that John Cage would be playing a
        'Cello with Melody-driven Electronics'
          tonight at the University of Chicago
And making those Lilies shudder and shed
             black light

THE PHOTO OF EMILY

She wore a cloche hat
She was Aunt Emily
She spoke French She had a job
as a French governess
She stood on the bridge in Bronxville
over the Bronx River the little river
with its little woods and the little bridge
and the swimming hole and the woods
where we played Robin Hood
I thought I was Robin Hood
or one of his deerskin men
I wanted a deerskin suit
more than anything
I remember that clearly when I was eight
I stayed awake at night
thinking how to make it how to get it
I would have robbed a rich traveller
(That's how rebels are born)
She stood on the bridge in her hat
I came to her from the woods
where I'd been playing
by the little brown river
with its dirty crayfish
I came up to her
in her long lace dress and black pumps
She had elegant feet
long feet
an 'aristocrat's' she would say
She was a bit mad and elegant
Even then I knew it
She was Catholic in a mad way
as if she had some special personal connection
with the Pope
She thought of herself as a writer
as having something special to say
in French

LAWRENCE FERLINGHETTI

I thought of her as my French mother
She was my mother's French sister
the sister who'd been born in France
the family so mixed up
between Portugal and France
and the Virgin Islands
which was the route my mother's family took
to the United States
and Coney Island where the French kept
boardinghouses
and my mother met my father
when he came from Lombardy
speaking only Lombard
and ended up the first night
in that boardinghouse at Coney
My French mother Emily stands on the bridge
in the old photo
the only photo I had of her
A dark bridge and her face in shadow
Or perhaps her face was light once
and the photo darkened
There is a pearly strangeness
in the dark light
It is all I have of her
She must have had a box camera that day
I was wearing short pants
on that little stone bridge
(And who took the picture
of the two of us together
arms around each other?
So silent the old picture—
If it could only speak!)
It is her day off in the Nineteen Twenties
I am nine—
Where now
that elegant cloche hat
that woman lost in time
a shadowy strangeness is all

She had fine skin
gossamer hair
cut like Garbo
or Louise Brooks
but not so beautiful
She had a wen on her breast
Might I not find that hat
and that woman still—
a seamstress in the back
of some small thrift shop—
Come back, come back—
At least the photo
might I not at least
find the photo again
in some lost album
with black cardboard pages
there's the photo
held on the stiff page
by little paper triangles pasted on
the photo of Emily
mad and elegant
thinking herself a great writer
with something to say to the world
in her shadow hat
having her picture taken
with the child she always wanted
She had lovers but no child
She stood by the bedside and took me
Life went on with us
The photo darkened
She was too distracted
too gypsy-like too self-willed
too obsessed too
passionately articulate
burning too bright
too much a lunatic of loving
to keep that child
who ran off finally
into the dark park of those days
by the Bronx River

and sees her now
nowhere else in memory
except by that dark bridge
And saw her never again
And never saw her again
except in the back of old boutiques
peered into now again
with haunting glance
in the Rue de Seine

Isabella Gardner

SUMMERS AGO

For Edith Sitwell

The Ferryman fairied us out to sea
Gold gold gold sang the apple-tree

Children I told you I tell you our sun was a hail of gold!
I say that sun stoned, that sun stormed our tranquil, our blue bay
bellsweet saltfresh water (bluer than tongue-can-tell, daughter)
and dazed us, darlings, and dazzled us, I say that sun crazed
(that sun clove) our serene as ceramic selves and our noon glazed cove,
and children all that grew wild by the wonderful water shot tall
as tomorrow, reeds suddenly shockingly green had sprouted like sorrow
and crimson explosions of roses arose in that flurry of Danaean glory
while at night we did swoon ah we swanned to a silverer moonlight than
    listen or lute,
we trysted in gondolas blown from glass and kissed in fluted Venetian
    bliss.

       Sister and brother I your mother
       Once was a girl in skirling weather
       Though summer and swan must alter, falter,
       I waltzed on the water once, son and daughter.

LINES TO A SEAGREEN LOVER

For Maurice English

My lover never danced with me
Not minuet nor sarabande
We walked (embracing) on the sand

ISABELLA GARDNER

My lover never swam with me
We waded to our ankle bones
And winced and shivered on the stones

My lover never flew with me
We stared at sea birds slicing space
And cried What freedom Look what grace

I wish my love had lain with me
Not on the sand beside the sea
But under my ailanthus tree

IN THE MUSEUM

Small and emptied woman you lie here a thousand years dead
your hands on your diminished loins flat in this final bed
teeth jutting from your unwound head your spiced bones black and
     dried,
who knew you and kissed you and kept you and wept when you died;
died you young had you grace? Risus sardonicus replied.
Then quick I seized my husband's hand while he stared at his bride.

THE WIDOW'S YARD

For Myra

"Snails lead slow idyllic lives . . ."
The rose and the laurel leaves
in the raw young widow's yard
were littered with silver. Hard-
ly a leaf lacked the decimal scale
of the self of a snail. Frail
in friendship I observed with care
these creatures (meaning to spare
the widow's vulnerable eyes
the hurting pity in my gaze).

Snails, I said, are tender skinned.
Excess in nature . . . sun rain wind
are killers. To save themselves

snails shrink to shelter in their shells
where they wait safe and patient
until the elements are gent-
ler. And do they not have other foes?
the widow asked. Turtles crows
foxes rats, I replied, and canned
heat that picnickers aband-
on. Also parasites invade
their flesh and alien eggs are laid
inside their skins. Their mating
too is perilous. The meeting
turns their faces blue with bliss
and consummation of this
absolute embrace is so
extravagantly slow
in coming that love begun
at dawn may end in fatal sun.

The widow told me that her
husband knew snails' ways and his gar-
den had been Eden for them. He
said the timid snail could lift three
times his weight straight up and haul
a wagon toy loaded with a whole
two hundred times his body's burden.
Then as we left the garden
she said that at the first faint chill
the first premonition of fall
the snails go straight to earth . . . excrete
the lime with which they then secrete
the openings in their shells . . . and wait for spring.
It is those little doors which sing,
she said, when they are boiled.
She smiled at me when I recoiled.

THE MILKMAN

The door was bolted and the windows of my porch
were screened to keep invaders out, the mesh of rust-
proof wire sieved the elements. Did my throat parch
then sat I at my table there and ate with lust
most chaste, the raw red apples; juice, flesh, rind and core.

ISABELLA GARDNER

One still and summer noon while dining in the sun
I was poulticing my thirst with apples, slaking care,
when suddenly I felt a whir of dread. Soon, soon,
stiff as bone, I listened for the Milkman's tread.
I heard him softly bang the door of the huge truck
and then his boots besieged my private yard. I tried
to keep my eyes speared to the table, but the suck
of apprehension milked my force. At last he mounted
my backstairs, climbed to the top, and there he stood still
outside the bolted door. The sun's color fainted.
I felt the horror of his quiet melt me, steal
into my sockets, and seduce me to him from
my dinner. His hand clung round the latch like rubber.
I felt him ooze against the screen and shake the frame.
I had to slide the bolt; and thus I was the robber
of my porch. Breathing smiling shape of fright,
the Milkman made his entrance; insistent donor,
he held in soft bleached hands the bottled sterile fruit,
and gave me this fatal, this apostate dinner.
Now in winter I have retreated from the porch
into the house and the once red apples rot where
I left them on the table. Now if my throat parch
for fruit the Milkman brings a quart for my despair.

LETTER FROM SLOUGH POND

Here where you left me alone
the soft wind sighs through my wishbone
the sun is lapping at my flesh
I couple with the ripples of the fresh
pond water I am rolled by the roiling sea.
Love, in our wide bed, do you lie lonely?
The spoon of longing stirs my marrow
and I thank God this bed is narrow.

ISABELLA GARDNER

PART OF THE DARKNESS

I had thought of the bear in his lair as fiercely free, feasting on honey and
   wildwood fruits;

I had imagined a forest lunge, regretting the circus shuffle and the zoo's
   prescribed pursuits.

Last summer I took books and children to Wisconsin's Great North woods.
   We drove

one night through miles of pines and rainy darkness to a garbage grove

that burgeoned broken crates and bulging paper bags and emptied cans of beer,

to watch for native bears, who local guides had told us, scavenged there.

After parking behind three other cars (leaving our headlights on but dim)

We stumbled over soggy moss to join the families blinking on the rim

of mounded refuse bounded east north and west by the forest.

The parents hushed and warned their pushing children each of whom
   struggled to stand nearest

the arena, and presently part of the darkness humped away from the foliage
   and lumbered bear-shaped

toward the heaping spoilage. It trundled into the litter while we gaped,

and for an instant it gaped too, bear-faced, but not a tooth was bared. It
   grovelled

carefully while tin cans clattered and tense tourists tittered. Painstakingly it
   nosed and ravelled

rinds and husks and parings, the used and the refused; bear-skinned and
   doggedly explored

the second-hand remains while headlights glared and flashlights stared and
   shamed bored

children booed, wishing aloud that it would trudge away so they might read
    its tracks.

They hoped to find an as yet unclassified spoor, certain that no authentic
    bear would turn his back

upon the delicacies of his own domain to flounder where mere housewives'
    leavings rot.

I also was reluctant to concede that there is no wild honey in the forest and
    no forest in the bear.

Bereaved, we started home, leaving that animal there.

ON LOOKING IN THE LOOKING GLASS

Your small embattled eyes dispute a face
that middle-aging sags and creases.
Besieged, your eyes protest and plead,
your wild little eyes are bright, and bleed.

And now in an instant's blink my stare
seizes in your beleaguered glare
the pristine gaze the blown-glass stance
of your once
total innocence.
I see and dare the child you were.

And for a wink's lasting, There
Now in your blistered eyes dazzles the flare
of Youth with years and love to swear
the kindling enkindled fire
heedless and sheer . . .
I see and fear the girl you were.

And now for a tic's lending, Now for the stint
of a second's fission I light to the glint
of your Daemon, that familiar whom you stint
so prodigally. Shunting, shan't-
ing, wincing fabricant
I see the maker that you want
and aren't.

And now just now I closed your eyes
your infant ancient naked eyes.
Gaze glare and flare and glint are buried by
my neutral eye-
lids. These island citadels are now surrendered
and with imagination's eye I see you dead.

TO THOREAU ON REREADING WALDEN

I long ago lost a hound, a bay horse, and a turtle-dove.
There too, as everywhere, I sometimes expected the visitor who never comes.

—*Henry Thoreau*

Your passion was ever plural, apart
from that one twig ("the twig") you never found.
Herds of birds and fishes, stars in droves
received your taut and tender gaze
but gills beaks planets can't reciprocate
and gratefully you prayed their praise.
You loved the faces in the fire, Thoreau,
the goldgreen pickerel, the huddling snow.
I too love these, and O love you, fierceheart,
and yet were you, like Lazarus, to rise,
you would look everywhere but in my eyes.
You'd hear the loud spring ice the greening ground,
but not the caller knocking at your gate
nor the nickering in your maple groves
nor the howling for home of the hound.
You did not listen to the turtle-dove
(singular bird) sing on your lintel: LOVE
And now no visitor will come to crowd
Your peace. You have dried safely in your shroud.

THAT WAS THEN

for Riva Blevitsky

Union Pier Michigan. We called it Shapiro
Shangri La. People said I needed a passport.
I was the only Shicksa there Kolya Shura
Manya Tanya and Sonya, Sulya Myra and
Vera they were there. And Riva a young girl then.
Soda pop and ice cream parlors, no bars,
Delicatessens but no liquor stores.
They spoke fractured English fractured Yiddish
and fractured Russian when they did not want
their children to understand. Most husbands
drove down from Chicago fridays but mine
came to me thursdays bringing the squat green
bottles of Chilean white wine I drank
(he was angry if I forgot to buy
cucumbers). My daughter then five, now in
Bedlam, chased butterflies and thirty years
ago my infant son, now for some years
lost, was happy too. I washed his diapers
in a tub and hung them up in the sun.
Instead of a play-pen, my husband, Seymour,
called Simcha which means joy, made a paddock
for him. Dan did not like to be cooped up
(nor did Rose, my daughter Rosy; nor did she)
not then, not later, never. Dan was last
seen in Columbia, South America.
Simcha little Rosy littler Daniel
and the Shicksa we were all of us joy-
full then in Shapiro Shangri La when
we were young and laughing. On the lake beach
the women waded and gossiped. The men,
supine on the hot sand sucked in the sun
through every work and city tired pore
and on the blithe beach played chess needling each
other, "singing" they called it. The Shicksa
swam and her daughter, round pink Rosy made
castles out of sand and when the big rough
boy's unseeing feet crushed her battlements
she cried. (As she would later, as she did
later, as she does now and must again
in inexorable time.) Ah but then
it was different. The first summer at our

Michigan Shangri La we shared one half
a cottage with Seymour's sister Molly
Molly the matriarch and my mother
too Molly ample Yiddish mama
bountiful heart bountiful flesh married
to tender Ben Blevitsky book-binder
and Bolshevik, not Communist though he
thought he was and paid his Party dues.
He pressed on me, a bemused fellow traveller
The Daily Worker which I occasionally
scanned. Aside from Ben's misguided fealty
to a party that betrayed his each, his
every dream, he taught the Shicksa wisdom,
ancient, Hebraic, of the heart and pulse.
This Shicksa loved him all his life. He died
attacking Zionists. In the debate
the heckling hit his heart and aged eighty-two
gentle Ben Blevitsky fell down and died.

That first summer the Shicksa shared the stove
with Molly who wouldn't let her cook
a meal but did teach her to cook kugel
and fix gefilte fish. (It was only
the Shicksa's second marriage and so she
had not yet lost her appetite for cooking,
that came after the fourth marriage when
she recklessly played house with a fifth man.)
Political not pious there was not
kept, a kosher kitchen. Molly and Ben
once took the bus to Chicago saying
they'd be back saturday night for supper
saying Be well Bellotchka but don't cook!
Later Molly's cheeks streaming with laughter
crowed to cronies "The Shicksa cooked a haser
for the Shabbas!" Stuck with cloves it was,
the scored cuts thumbed full of dark brown sugar
hot powdered mustard and the fresh squeezed juice
of sweet oranges and the whole ham smeared
with that luscious mixture and therewith glazed
and all ate that haser with high delight
the Blevitskys, Molly, Ben, and their Bob and Riva
Rose, Simcha and his Bellotchka — the cook
ate and ate while the infant Daniel slept.

That was then. That was then.

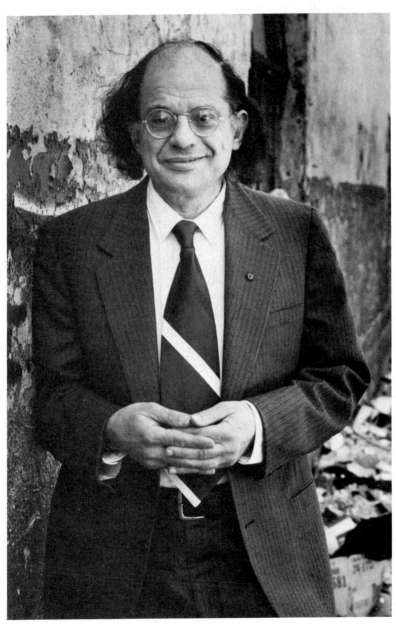

Allen Ginsberg

HOWL

for Carl Solomon

I

I saw the best minds of my generation destroyed by madness, starving
   hysterical naked,
dragging themselves through the negro streets at dawn looking for an
   angry fix,
angelheaded hipsters burning for the ancient heavenly connection to the
   starry dynamo in the machinery of night,
who poverty and tatters and hollow-eyed and high sat up smoking in the
   supernatural darkness of cold-water flats floating across the tops of
   cities contemplating jazz,
who bared their brains to Heaven under the El and saw Mohammedan
   angels staggering on tenement roofs illuminated,
who passed through universities with radiant cool eyes hallucinating
   Arkansas and Blake-light tragedy among the scholars of war,
who were expelled from the academies for crazy & publishing obscene
   odes on the windows of the skull,
who cowered in unshaven rooms in underwear, burning their money in
   wastebaskets and listening to the Terror through the wall,
who got busted in their pubic beards returning through Laredo with a
   belt of marijuana for New York,
who ate fire in paint hotels or drank turpentine in Paradise Alley, death,
   or purgatoried their torsos night after night
with dreams, with drugs, with waking nightmares, alcohol and cock and
   endless balls,
incomparable blind streets of shuddering cloud and lightning in the mind
   leaping toward poles of Canada & Paterson, illuminating all the
   motionless world of Time between,
Peyote solidities of halls, backyard green tree cemetery dawns, wine drunk-
   enness over the rooftops, storefront boroughs of teahead joyride neon
   blinking traffic light, sun and moon and tree vibrations in the roaring
   winter dusks of Brooklyn, ashcan rantings and kind king light of mind,
who chained themselves to subways for the endless ride from Battery to
   holy Bronx on benzedrine until the noise of wheels and children

brought them down shuddering mouth-wracked and battered bleak of brain all drained of brilliance in the drear light of Zoo,

who sank all night in submarine light of Bickford's floated out and sat through the stale beer afternoon in desolate Fugazzi's, listening to the crack of doom on the hydrogen jukebox,

who talked continuously seventy hours from park to pad to bar to Bellevue to museum to the Brooklyn Bridge,

a lost battalion of platonic conversationalists jumping down the stoops off fire escapes off windowsills off Empire State out of the moon,

yacketayakking screaming vomiting whispering facts and memories and anecdotes and eyeball kicks and shocks of hospitals and jails and wars,

whole intellects disgorged in total recall for seven days and nights with brilliant eyes, meat for the Synagogue cast on the pavement,

who vanished into nowhere Zen New Jersey leaving a trail of ambiguous picture postcards of Atlantic City Hall,

suffering Eastern sweats and Tangerian bone-grindings and migraines of China under junk-withdrawal in Newark's bleak furnished room,

who wandered around and around at midnight in the railroad yard wondering where to go, and went, leaving no broken hearts,

who lit cigarettes in boxcars boxcars boxcars racketing through snow toward lonesome farms in grandfather night,

who studied Plotinus Poe St. John of the Cross telepathy and bop kaballa because the cosmos instinctively vibrated at their feet in Kansas,

who loned it through the streets of Idaho seeking visionary indian angels who were visionary indian angels,

who thought they were only mad when Baltimore gleamed in supernatural ecstasy,

who jumped in limousines with the Chinaman of Oklahoma on the impulse of winter midnight streetlight smalltown rain,

who lounged hungry and lonesome through Houston seeking jazz or sex or soup, and followed the brilliant Spaniard to converse about America and Eternity, a hopeless task, and so took ship to Africa,

who disappeared into the volcanoes of Mexico leaving behind nothing but the shadow of dungarees and the lava and ash of poetry scattered in fireplace Chicago,

who reappeared on the West Coast investigating the F.B.I. in beards and shorts with big pacifist eyes sexy in their dark skin passing out incomprehensible leaflets,

who burned cigarette holes in their arms protesting the narcotic tobacco haze of Capitalism,

who distributed Supercommunist pamphlets in Union Square weeping and undressing while the sirens of Los Alamos wailed them down, and wailed down Wall, and the Staten Island ferry also wailed,

who broke down crying in white gymnasiums naked and trembling before the machinery of other skeletons, who bit detectives in the neck and shrieked with delight in policecars for committing no crime but their own wild cooking pederasty and intoxication,

who howled on their knees in the subway and were dragged off the roof waving genitals and manuscripts,

who let themselves be fucked in the ass by saintly motorcyclists, and screamed with joy,

who blew and were blown by those human seraphim, the sailors, caresses of Atlantic and Caribbean love,

who balled in the morning in the evenings in rosegardens and the grass of public parks and cemeteries scattering their semen freely to whomever come who may,

who hiccupped endlessly trying to giggle but wound up with a sob behind a partition in a Turkish Bath when the blonde & naked angel came to pierce them with a sword,

who lost their loveboys to the three old shrews of fate the one eyed shrew of the heterosexual dollar the one eyed shrew that winks out of the womb and the one eyed shrew that does nothing but sit on her ass and snip the intellectual golden threads of the craftsman's loom,

who copulated ecstatic and insatiate with a bottle of beer a sweetheart a package of cigarettes a candle and fell off the bed, and continued along the floor and down the hall and ended fainting on the wall with a vision of ultimate cunt and come eluding the last gyzym of consciousness,

who sweetened the snatches of a million girls trembling in the sunset, and were red eyed in the morning but prepared to sweeten the snatch of the sunrise, flashing buttocks under barns and naked in the lake,

who went out whoring through Colorado in myriad stolen night-cars, N.C., secret hero of these poems, cocksman and Adonis of Denver— joy to the memory of his innumerable lays of girls in empty lots & diner backyards, moviehouses' rickety rows, on mountaintops in caves or with gaunt waitresses in familiar roadside lonely petticoat upliftings & especially secret gas-station solipsisms of johns, & hometown alleys too,

who faded out in vast sordid movies, were shifted in dreams, woke on a sudden Manhattan, and picked themselves up out of basements hungover with heartless Tokay and horrors of Third Avenue iron dreams & stumbled to unemployment offices,

who walked all night with their shoes full of blood on the snowbank docks waiting for a door in the East River to open to a room full of steamheat and opium,

who created great suicidal dramas on the apartment cliff-banks of the Hudson under the wartime blue floodlight of the moon & their heads shall be crowned with laurel in oblivion,

who ate the lamb stew of the imagination or digested the crab at the
    muddy bottom of the rivers of Bowery,

who wept at the romance of the streets with their pushcarts full of
    onions and bad music,

who sat in boxes breathing in the darkness under the bridge, and rose up
    to build harpsichords in their lofts,

who coughed on the sixth floor of Harlem crowned with flame under the
    tubercular sky surrounded by orange crates of theology,

who scribbled all night rocking and rolling over lofty incantations which
    in the yellow morning were stanzas of gibberish,

who cooked rotten animals lung heart feet tail borsht & tortillas dreaming
    of the pure vegetable kingdom,

who plunged themselves under meat trucks looking for an egg,

who threw their watches off the roof to cast their ballot for Eternity
    outside of Time, & alarm clocks fell on their heads every day for the
    next decade,

who cut their wrists three times successively unsuccessfully, gave up and
    were forced to open antique stores where they thought they were
    growing old and cried,

who were burned alive in their innocent flannel suits on Madison Avenue
    amid blasts of leaden verse & the tanked-up clatter of the iron
    regiments of fashion & the nitroglycerine shrieks of the fairies of
    advertising & the mustard gas of sinister intelligent editors, or were
    run down by the drunken taxicabs of Absolute Reality,

who jumped off the Brooklyn Bridge this actually happened and walked
    away unknown and forgotten into the ghostly daze of Chinatown
    soup alleyways & firetrucks, not even one free beer,

who sang out of their windows in despair, fell out of the subway window,
    jumped in the filthy Passaic, leaped on negroes, cried all over the
    street, danced on broken wineglasses barefoot smashed phonograph
    records of nostalgic European 1930's German jazz finished the whiskey
    and threw up groaning into the bloody toilet, moans in their ears and
    the blast of colossal steamwhistles,

who barreled down the highways of the past journeying to each other's
    hotrod-Golgotha jail-solitude watch or Birmingham jazz incarnation,

who drove crosscountry seventytwo hours to find out if I had a vision or
    you had a vision or he had a vision to find out Eternity,

who journeyed to Denver, who died in Denver, who came back to Denver
    & waited in vain, who watched over Denver & brooded & loned in
    Denver and finally went away to find out the Time, & now Denver is
    lonesome for her heroes,

who fell on their knees in hopeless cathedrals praying for each other's
    salvation and light and breasts, until the soul illuminated its hair for
    a second,

who crashed through their minds in jail waiting for impossible criminals
with golden heads and the charm of reality in their hearts who sang
sweet blues to Alcatraz,

who retired to Mexico to cultivate a habit, or Rocky Mount to tender
Buddha or Tangiers to boys or Southern Pacific to the black loco-
motive or Harvard to Narcissus to Woodlawn to the daisychain or
grave,

who demanded sanity trials accusing the radio of hypnotism & were
left with their insanity & their hands & a hung jury,

who threw potato salad at CCNY lecturers on Dadaism and subsequently
presented themselves on the granite steps of the madhouse with
shaven heads and harlequin speech of suicide, demanding instanta-
neous lobotomy,

and who were given instead the concrete void of insulin metrasol elec-
tricity hydrotherapy psychotherapy occupational therapy pingpong &
amnesia,

who in humorless protest overturned only one symbolic pingpong table,
resting briefly in catatonia,

returning years later truly bald except for a wig of blood, and tears and
fingers, to the visible madman doom of the wards of the madtowns
of the East,

Pilgrim State's Rockland's and Greystone's foetid halls, bickering with
the echoes of the soul, rocking and rolling in the midnight solitude-
bench dolmen-realms of love, dream of life a nightmare, bodies turned
to stone as heavy as the moon,

with mother finally ******, and the last fantastic book flung out of the
tenement window, and the last door closed at 4 AM and the last
telephone slammed at the wall in reply and the last furnished room
emptied down to the last piece of mental furniture, a yellow paper
rose twisted on a wire hanger in the closet, and even that imaginary,
nothing but a hopeful little bit of hallucination—

ah, Carl, while you are not safe I am not safe, and now you're really in
the total animal soup of time—

and who therefore ran through the icy streets obsessed with a sudden
flash of the alchemy of the use of the ellipse the catalog the meter &
the vibrating plane,

who dreamt and made incarnate gaps in Time & Space through images
juxtaposed, and trapped the archangel of the soul between 2 visual
images and joined the elemental verbs and set the noun and dash of
consciousness together jumping with sensation of Pater Omnipotens
Aeterna Deus

to recreate the syntax and measure of poor human prose and stand before
you speechless and intelligent and shaking with shame, rejected yet
confessing out the soul to conform to the rhythm of thought in his
naked and endless head,

the madman bum and angel beat in Time, unknown, yet putting down
here what might be left to say in time come after death,
and rose reincarnate in the ghostly clothes of jazz in the goldhorn shadow
of the band and blew the suffering of America's naked mind for love
into an eli eli lamma lamma sabacthani saxophone cry that shivered
the cities down to the last radio
with the absolute heart of the poem of life butchered out of their own
bodies good to eat a thousand years.

II

What sphinx of cement and aluminum bashed open their skulls and ate
up their brains and imagination?
Moloch! Solitude! Filth! Ugliness! Ashcans and unobtainable dollars!
Children screaming under the stairways! Boys sobbing in armies! Old
men weeping in the parks!
Moloch! Moloch! Nightmare of Moloch! Moloch the loveless! Mental
Moloch! Moloch the heavy judger of men!
Moloch the incomprehensible prison! Moloch the crossbone soulless
jailhouse and Congress of sorrows! Moloch whose buildings are
judgement! Moloch the vast stone of war! Moloch the stunned
governments!
Moloch whose mind is pure machinery! Moloch whose blood is running
money! Moloch whose fingers are ten armies! Moloch whose breast is
a cannibal dynamo! Moloch whose ear is a smoking tomb!
Moloch whose eyes are a thousand blind windows! Moloch whose sky-
scrapers stand in the long streets like endless Jehovahs! Moloch whose
factories dream and croak in the fog! Moloch whose smokestacks and
antennae crown the cities!
Moloch whose love is endless oil and stone! Moloch whose soul is elec-
tricity and banks! Moloch whose poverty is the specter of genius!
Moloch whose fate is a cloud of sexless hydrogen! Moloch whose
name is the Mind!
Moloch in whom I sit lonely! Moloch in whom I dream Angels! Crazy
in Moloch! Cocksucker in Moloch! Lacklove and manless in Moloch!
Moloch who entered my soul early! Moloch in whom I am a conscious-
ness without a body! Moloch who frightened me out of my natural
ecstasy! Moloch whom I abandon! Wake up in Moloch! Light
streaming out of the sky!
Moloch! Moloch! Robot apartments! invisible suburbs! skeleton treas-
uries! blind capitals! demonic industries! spectral nations! invincible
madhouses! granite cocks! monstrous bombs!
They broke their backs lifting Moloch to Heaven! Pavements, trees,

radios, tons! lifting the city to Heaven which exists and is everywhere
about us!

Visions! omens! hallucinations! miracles! ecstasies! gone down the Ameri-
can river!

Dreams! adorations! illuminations! religions! the whole boatload of sensi-
tive bullshit!

Breakthroughs! over the river! flips and crucifixions! gone down the flood!
Highs! Epiphanies! Despairs! Ten years' animal screams and suicides!
Minds! New loves! Mad generation! down on the rocks of Time!

Real holy laughter in the river! They saw it all! the wild eyes! the holy
yells! They bade farewell! They jumped off the roof! to solitude!
waving! carrying flowers! Down to the river! into the street!

III

Carl Solomon! I'm with you in Rockland
    where you're madder than I am
I'm with you in Rockland
    where you must feel very strange
I'm with you in Rockland
    where you imitate the shade of my mother
I'm with you in Rockland
    where you've murdered your twelve secretaries
I'm with you in Rockland
    where you laugh at this invisible humor
I'm with you in Rockland
    where we are great writers on the same dreadful typewriter
I'm with you in Rockland
    where your condition has become serious and is reported on the radio
I'm with you Rockland
    where the faculties of the skull no longer admit the worms of the senses
I'm with you in Rockland
    where you drink the tea of the breasts of the spinsters of Utica
I'm with you in Rockland
    where you pun on the bodies of your nurses the harpies of the Bronx
I'm with you in Rockland
    where you scream in a straightjacket that you're losing the game of
    the actual pingpong of the abyss
I'm with you in Rockland
    where you bang on the catatonic piano the soul is innocent and
    immortal it should never die ungodly in an armed madhouse
I'm with you in Rockland
    where fifty more shocks will never return your soul to its body again
    from its pilgrimage to a cross in the void

I'm with you in Rockland
> where you accuse your doctors of insanity and plot the Hebrew
> socialist revolution against the fascist national Golgotha

I'm with you in Rockland
> where you will split the heavens of Long Island and resurrect your
> living human Jesus from the superhuman tomb

I'm with you in Rockland
> where there are twentyfive-thousand mad comrades all together singing
> the final stanzas of the Internationale

I'm with you in Rockland
> where we hug and kiss the United States under our bedsheets the
> United States that coughs all night and won't let us sleep

I'm with you in Rockland
> where we wake up electrified out of the coma by our own souls'
> airplanes roaring over the roof they've come to drop angelic bombs
> the hospital illuminates itself imaginary walls collapse   O skinny
> legions run outside   O starry spangled shock of mercy the eternal war
> is here   O victory forget your underwear we're free

I'm with you in Rockland
> in my dreams you walk dripping from a sea-journey on the highway
> across America in tears to the door of my cottage in the Western
> night

San Francisco 1955–56

AMERICA

America I've given you all and now I'm nothing.
America two dollars and twentyseven cents January 17, 1956.
I can't stand my own mind.
America when will we end the human war?
Go fuck yourself with your atom bomb.
I don't feel good don't bother me.
I won't write my poem till I'm in my right mind.
America when will you be angelic?
When will you take off your clothes?
When will you look at yourself through the grave?
When will you be worthy of your million Trotskyites?
America why are your libraries full of tears?
America when will you send your eggs to India?
I'm sick of your insane demands.
When can I go into the supermarket and buy what I need with my
> good looks?

America after all it is you and I who are perfect not the next world.
Your machinery is too much for me.
You made me want to be a saint.
There must be some other way to settle this argument.
Burroughs is in Tangiers I don't think he'll come back it's sinister.
Are you being sinister or is this some form of practical joke?
I'm trying to come to the point.
I refuse to give up my obsession.
America stop pushing I know what I'm doing.
America the plum blossoms are falling.
I haven't read the newspapers for months, everyday somebody goes on
    trial for murder.
America I feel sentimental about the Wobblies.
America I used to be a communist when I was a kid I'm not sorry.
I smoke marijuana every chance I get.
I sit in my house for days on end and stare at the roses in the closet.
When I go to Chinatown I get drunk and never get laid.
My mind is made up there's going to be trouble.
You should have seen me reading Marx.
My psychoanalyst thinks I'm perfectly right.
I won't say the Lord's Prayer.
I have mystical visions and cosmic vibrations.
America I still haven't told you what you did to Uncle Max after he
    came over from Russia.

I'm addressing you.
Are you going to let your emotional life be run by Time Magazine?
I'm obsessed by Time Magazine.
I read it every week.
Its cover stares at me every time I slink past the corner candystore.
I read it in the basement of the Berkeley Public Library.
It's always telling me about responsibility. Businessmen are serious.
    Movie producers are serious. Everybody's serious but me.
It occurs to me that I am America.
I am talking to myself again.

Asia is rising against me.
I haven't got a chinaman's chance.
I'd better consider my national resources.
My national resources consist of two joints of marijuana millions of geni-
    tals an unpublishable private literature that goes 1400 miles an hour
    and twentyfive-thousand mental institutions.
I say nothing about my prisons nor the millions of underprivileged who
    live in my flowerpots under the light of five hundred suns.

I have abolished the whorehouses of France, Tangiers is the next to go.
My ambition is to be President despite the fact that I'm a Catholic.

America how can I write a holy litany in your silly mood?
I will continue like Henry Ford my strophes are as individual as his auto-
   mobiles more so they're all different sexes.
America I will sell you strophes $2500 apiece $500 down on your old
   strophe
America free Tom Mooney
America save the Spanish Loyalists
America Sacco & Vanzetti must not die
America I am the Scottsboro boys.
America when I was seven momma took me to Communist Cell meetings
   they sold us garbanzos a handful per ticket a ticket costs a nickel and
   the speeches were free everybody was angelic and sentimental about
   the workers it was all so sincere you have no idea what a good thing
   the party was in 1835 Scott Nearing was a grand old man a real
   mensch Mother Bloor made me cry I once saw Israel Amter plain.
   Everybody must have been a spy.
America you don't really want to go to war.
America it's them bad Russians.
Them Russians them Russians and them Chinamen. And them Russians.
The Russia wants to eat us alive. The Russia's power mad. She wants to
   take our cars from out our garages.
Her wants to grab Chicago. Her needs a Red Readers' Digest. Her wants
   our auto plants in Siberia. Him big bureaucracy running our filling-
   stations.
That no good. Ugh. Him make Indians learn read. Him need big black
   niggers. Hah. Her make us all work sixteen hours a day. Help.
America this is quite serious.
America this is the impression I get from looking in the television set.
America is this correct?
I'd better get right down to the job.
It's true I don't want to join the Army or turn lathes in precision parts
   factories, I'm nearsighted and psychopathic anyway.
America I'm putting my queer shoulder to the wheel.

LOVE POEM ON THEME BY WHITMAN

I'll go into the bedroom silently and lie down between the bridegroom
   and the bride,

those bodies fallen from heaven stretched out waiting naked and restless,
arms resting over their eyes in the darkness,
bury my face in their shoulders and breasts, breathing their skin,
and stroke and kiss neck and mouth and make back be open and known,
legs raised up crook'd to receive, cock in the darkness driven tormented
    and attacking
roused up from hole to itching head,
bodies locked shuddering naked, hot lips and buttocks screwed into each
    other
and eyes, eyes glinting and charming, widening into looks and abandon,
and moans of movement, voices, hands in air, hands between thighs,
hands in moisture on softened hips, throbbing contraction of bellies
till the white come flow in the swirling sheets,
and the bride cry for forgiveness, and the groom be covered with tears of
    passion and compassion,
and I rise up from the bed replenished with last intimate gestures and
    kisses of farewell—
all before the mind wakes, behind shades and closed doors in a darkened
    house
where the inhabitants roam unsatisfied in the night,
nude ghosts seeking each other out in the silence.

PSALM III

    To God: to illuminate all men. Beginning with Skid Road.
    Let Occidental and Washington be transformed into a
higher place, the plaza of eternity.
    Illuminate the welders in shipyards with the brilliance of
their torches.
    Let the crane operator lift up his arm for joy.
    Let elevators creak and speak, ascending and descending in
awe.
    Let the mercy of the flower's direction beckon in the eye.
    Let the straight flower bespeak its purpose in straightness—
to seek the light.
    Let the crooked flower bespeak its purpose in crookedness—
to seek the light.
    Let the crookedness and straightness bespeak the light.
    Let Puget Sound be a blast of light.

I feed on your Name like a cockroach on a crumb—this cockroach is holy.

Seattle 1956

WALES VISITATION

White fog lifting & falling on mountain-brow
    Trees moving in rivers of wind
            The clouds arise
  as on a wave, gigantic eddy lifting mist
    above teeming ferns exquisitely swayed
              along a green crag
    glimpsed thru mullioned glass in valley raine—

Bardic, O Self, Visitacione, tell naught
  but what seen by one man in a vale in Albion,
    of the folk, whose physical sciences end in Ecology,
      the wisdom of earthly relations,
    of mouths & eyes interknit ten centuries visible
      orchards of mind language manifest human,
  of the satanic thistle that raises its horned symmetry
    flowering above sister grass-daisies' pink tiny
        bloomlets angelic as lightbulbs—

Remember 160 miles from London's symmetrical thorned tower
    & network of TV pictures flashing bearded your Self
  the lambs on the tree-nooked hillside this day bleating
  heard in Blake's old ear, & the silent thought of Wordsworth in
              eld Stillness
  clouds passing through skeleton arches of Tintern Abbey—
    Bard Nameless as the Vast, babble to Vastness!
All the Valley quivered, one extended motion, wind
      undulating on mossy hills
  a giant wash that sank white fog delicately down red runnels
      on the mountainside
  whose leaf-branch tendrils moved asway
      in granitic undertow down—
and lifted the floating Nebulous upward, and lifted the arms of the
                         trees
    and lifted the grasses an instant in balance
    and lifted the lambs to hold still
  and lifted the green of the hill, in one solemn wave

ALLEN GINSBERG

A solid mass of Heaven, mist-infused, ebbs thru the vale,
    a wavelet of Immensity, lapping gigantic through Llanthony
                        Valley,
    the length of all England, valley upon valley under Heaven's ocean
                  tonned with cloud-hang,
       Heaven balanced on a grassblade—
Roar of the mountain wind slow, sigh of the body,
     One Being on the mountainside stirring gently
       Exquisite scales trembling everywhere in balance,
one motion thru the cloudy sky-floor shifting on the million
               feet of daisies,
one Majesty the motion that stirred wet grass quivering
    to the farthest tendril of white fog poured down
        through shivering flowers on the mountain's
              head—
No imperfection in the budded mountain,
    Valleys breathe, heaven and earth move together,
   daisies push inches of yellow air, vegetables tremble
     green atoms shimmer in grassy mandalas,
sheep speckle the mountainside, revolving their jaws with empty
              eyes,

      horses dance in the warm rain,
   tree-lined canals network through live farmland,
     blueberries fringe stone walls
    on hill breasts nippled with hawthorn,
    pheasants croak up meadow-bellies haired with fern—
Out, out on the hillside, into the ocean sound, into delicate
       gusts of wet air,
Fall on the ground, O great Wetness, O Mother, No harm on
           thy body!
Stare close, no imperfection in the grass,
    each flower Buddha-eye, repeating the story,
    the myriad-formed soul
Kneel before the foxglove raising green buds, mauve bells drooped
   doubled down the stem trembling antennae,
   & look in the eyes of the branded lambs that stare
   breathing stockstill under dripping hawthorn—
I lay down mixing my beard with the wet hair of the mountainside,
   smelling the brown vagina-moist ground, harmless,
    tasting the violet thistle-hair, sweetness—
One being so balanced, so vast, that its softest breath
   moves every floweret in the stillness on the valley floor,
   trembles lamb-hair hung gossamer rain-beaded in the grass,

lifts trees on their roots, birds in the great draught
       hiding their strength in the rain, bearing same weight,

Groan thru breast and neck, a great Oh! to earth heart
       Calling our Presence together
    The great secret is no secret
      Senses fit the winds,
       Visible is visible,
    rain-mist curtains wave through the bearded vale,
      grey atoms wet the wind's Kaballah
Crosslegged on a rock in dusk rain,
    rubber booted in soft grass, mind moveless,
   breath trembles in white daisies by the roadside,
      Heaven breath and my own symmetric
   Airs wavering thru antlered green fern
drawn in my navel, same breath as breathes thru Capel-Y-Ffn,
    Sounds of Aleph and Aum
      through forests of gristle,
  my skull and Lord Hereford's Knob equal,
      All Albion one.
What did I notice? Particulars! The
   vision of the great One is myriad—
smoke curls upward from ash tray,
   house fire burned low,
The night, still wet & moody black heaven
    starless
upward in motion with wet wind.

July 29, 1967 (LSD)—August 3, 1967 (London)

ON NEAL'S ASHES

Delicate eyes that blinked blue Rockies all ash
nipples, Ribs I touched w/ my thumb are ash
mouth my tongue touched once or twice all ash
bony cheeks soft on my belly are cinder, ash
earlobes & eyelids, youthful cock tip, curly pubis
breast warmth, man palm, high school thigh,
baseball bicept arm, asshole anneal'd to silken skin
    all ashes, all ashes again.

August 1968

ALLEN GINSBERG

FOURTH FLOOR, DAWN, UP ALL NIGHT WRITING LETTERS

Pigeons shake their wings on the copper church roof
out my window across the street, a bird perched on the cross
surveys the city's blue-grey clouds. Larry Rivers
'll come at 10 AM and take my picture. I'm taking
your picture, pigeons. I'm writing you down, Dawn.
I'm immortalizing your exhaust, Avenue A bus.
O Thought, now you'll have to think the same thing forever!

6:48 am June 7, 1980

ODE TO FAILURE

Many prophets have failed, their voices silent
ghost-shouts in basements nobody heard dusty laughter in family attics
nor glanced them on park benches weeping with relief under empty sky
Walt Whitman viva'd local losers—courage to Fat Ladies in the Freak Show!
   nervous prisoners whose mustached lips dripped sweat on chow lines—
Mayakovsky cried, Then die! my verse, die like the workers' rank & file
   fusilladed in Petersburg!
Prospero burned his Power books & plummeted his magic wand to the
   bottom of dragon seas
Alexander the Great failed to find more worlds to conquer!
O Failure I chant your terrifying name, accept me your 54 year old Prophet
epicking Eternal Flop! I join your Pantheon of mortal bards, & hasten this
   ode with high blood pressure
rushing to the top of my skull as if I wouldn't last another minute, like the
   Dying Gaul! to
You, Lord of blind Monet, deaf Beethoven, armless Venus de Milo, headless
   Winged Victory!
I failed to sleep with every bearded rosy-cheeked boy I jacked off over
My tirades destroyed no Intellectual Unions of KGB & CIA in turtlenecks
   & underpants, their woolen suits and tweeds
I never dissolved Plutonium or dismantled the nuclear Bomb before my skull
   lost hair
I have not yet stopped the Armies of entire Mankind in their march toward
   World War III
I never got to Heaven, Nirvana, X, Whatchamacallit, I never left Earth,
I never learned to die.

March 7 – October 10, 1980

Donald Hall

MY SON, MY EXECUTIONER

My son, my executioner,
    I take you in my arms,
Quiet and small and just astir,
    And whom my body warms.

Sweet death, small son, our instrument
    Of immortality,
Your cries and hungers document
    Our bodily decay.

We twenty-five and twenty-two,
    Who seemed to live forever,
Observe enduring life in you
    And start to die together.

DIGGING

One midnight, after a day when lilies
lift themselves out of the ground while you watch them,
and you come into the house at dark
your fingers grubby with digging, your eyes
vague with the pleasure of digging,

let a wind raised from the South
climb through your bedroom window, lift you in its arms
—you have become as small as a seed—
and carry you out of the house, over the black garden,
spinning and fluttering,

and drop you in cracked ground.
The dirt will be cool, rough to your clasped skin
like a man you have never known.

177

You will die into the ground
in a dead sleep, surrendered to water.

You will wake suffering
a widening pain in your side, a breach
gapped in your right ribs
where a green shoot struggles to lift itself upwards
through the tomb of your dead flesh

to the sun, to the air of your garden
where you will blossom
in the shape of your own self, thoughtless
with flowers, speaking
to bees, in the language of green and yellow, white and red.

THE MAN IN THE DEAD MACHINE

High on a slope in New Guinea
the Grumman Hellcat
lodges among bright vines
as thick as arms. In nineteen-forty-three,
the clenched hand of a pilot
glided it here
where no one has ever been.

In the cockpit the helmeted
skeleton sits
upright, held
by dry sinews at neck
and shoulder, and by webbing
that straps the pelvic cross
to the cracked
leather of the seat, and the breastbone
to the canvas cover
of the parachute.

Or say that the shrapnel
missed me, I flew
back to the carrier, and every morning
take the train, my pale

hands on a black case, and sit
upright, held
by the firm webbing.

THE TOWN OF HILL

Back of the dam, under
a flat pad

of water, church
bells ring

in the ears of lilies,
a child's swing

curls in the current
of a yard, horned

pout sleep
in a green

mailbox, and
a boy walks

from a screened
porch beneath

the man-shaped
leaves of an oak

down the street looking
at the town

of Hill that water
covered forty

years ago,
and the screen

door shuts
under dream water.

DONALD HALL

MAPLE SYRUP

August, goldenrod blowing. We walk
into the graveyard, to find
my grandfather's grave. Ten years ago
I came here last, bringing
marigolds from the round garden
outside the kitchen.
I didn't know you then.
　　　　　　　We walk
among carved names that go with photographs
on top of the piano at the farm:
Keneston, Wells, Fowler, Batchelder, Buck.
We pause at the new grave
of Grace Fenton, my grandfather's
sister. Last summer
we called on her at the nursing home,
eighty-seven, and nodding
in a blue housedress. We cannot find
my grandfather's grave.
　　　　　　　Back at the house
where no one lives, we potter
and explore the back chamber
where everything comes to rest: spinning wheels,
pretty boxes, quilts,
bottles, books, albums of postcards.
Then with a flashlight we descend
firm steps to the root cellar—black,
cobwebby, huge,
with dirt floors and fieldstone walls,
and above the walls, holding the hewn
sills of the house, enormous
granite foundation stones.
Past the empty bins
for squash, apples, carrots, and potatoes,
we discover the shelves for canning, a few
pale pints
of tomato left, and—what
is this?—syrup, maple syrup
in a quart jar, syrup
my grandfather made twenty-five
years ago
for the last time.

I remember
coming to the farm in March
in sugaring time, as a small boy.
He carried the pails of sap, sixteen-quart
buckets, dangling from each end
of a wooden yoke
that lay across his shoulders, and emptied them
into a vat in the saphouse
where fire burned day and night
for a week.
              Now the saphouse
tilts, nearly to the ground,
like someone exhausted
to the point of death, and next winter
when snow piles three feet thick
on the roofs of the cold farm,
the saphouse will shudder and slide
with the snow to the ground.
                          Today
we take my grandfather's last
quart of syrup
upstairs, holding it gingerly,
and we wash off twenty-five years
of dirt, and we pull
and pry the lid up, cutting the stiff,
dried rubber gasket, and dip our fingers
in, you and I both, and taste
the sweetness, you for the first time,
the sweetness preserved, of a dead man
in the kitchen he left
when his body slid
like anyone's into the ground.

KICKING THE LEAVES

1

Kicking the leaves, October, as we walk home together
from the game, in Ann Arbor,
on a day the color of soot, rain in the air;
I kick at the leaves of maples,

reds of seventy different shades, yellow
like old paper; and poplar leaves, fragile and pale;
and elm leaves, flags of a doomed race.
I kick at the leaves, making a sound I remember
as the leaves swirl upward from my boot,
and flutter; and I remember
Octobers walking to school in Connecticut,
wearing corduroy knickers that swished
with a sound like leaves; and a Sunday buying
a cup of cider at a roadside stand
on a dirt road in New Hampshire; and kicking the leaves,
autumn 1955 in Massachusetts, knowing
my father would die when the leaves were gone.

2

Each fall in New Hampshire, on the farm
where my mother grew up, a girl in the country,
my grandfather and grandmother
finished the autumn work, taking the last vegetables in
from the cold fields, canning, storing roots and apples
in the cellar under the kitchen. Then my grandfather
raked leaves against the house
as the final chore of autumn.
One November I drove up from college to see them.
We pulled big rakes, as we did when we hayed in summer,
pulling the leaves against the granite foundations
around the house, on every side of the house,
and then, to keep them in place, we cut spruce boughs
and laid them across the leaves,
green on red, until the house
was tucked up, ready for snow
that would freeze the leaves in tight, like a stiff skirt.
Then we puffed through the shed door,
taking off boots and overcoats, slapping our hands,
and sat in the kitchen, rocking, and drank
black coffee my grandmother made,
three of us sitting together, silent, in gray November.

3

One Saturday when I was little, before the war,
my father came home at noon from his half day at the office
and wore his Bates sweater, black on red,
with the crossed hockey sticks on it, and raked beside me
in the back yard, and tumbled in the leaves with me,
laughing, and carried me, laughing, my hair full of leaves,
to the kitchen window
where my mother could see us, and smile, and motion
to set me down, afraid I would fall and be hurt.

4

Kicking the leaves today, as we walk home together
from the game, among crowds of people
with their bright pennants, as many and bright as leaves,
my daughter's hair is the red-yellow color
of birch leaves, and she is tall like a birch,
growing up, fifteen, growing older; and my son
flamboyant as maple, twenty,
visits from college, and walks ahead of us, his step
springing, impatient to travel
the woods of the earth. Now I watch them
from a pile of leaves beside this clapboard house
in Ann Arbor, across from the school
where they learned to read,
as their shapes grow small with distance, waving,
and I know that I
diminish, not them, as I go first
into the leaves, taking
the step they will follow, Octobers and years from now.

5

This year the poems came back, when the leaves fell.
Kicking the leaves, I heard the leaves tell stories,
remembering, and therefore looking ahead, and building
the house of dying. I looked up into the maples
and found them, the vowels of bright desire.

I thought they had gone forever
while the bird sang *I love you, I love you*
and shook its black head
from side to side, and its red eye with no lid,
through years of winter, cold
as the taste of chicken wire, the music of cinder block.

6

Kicking the leaves, I uncover the lids of graves.
My grandfather died at seventy-seven, in March
when the sap was running; and I remember my father
twenty years ago,
coughing himself to death at fifty-two in the house
in the suburbs. Oh, how we flung
leaves in the air! How they tumbled and fluttered around us,
like slowly cascading water, when we walked together
in Hamden, before the war, when Johnson's Pond
had not surrendered to houses, the two of us
hand in hand, and in the wet air the smell of leaves
burning;
and in six years I will be fifty-two.

7

Now I fall, now I leap and fall
to feel the leaves crush under my body, to feel my body
buoyant in the ocean of leaves, the night of them,
night heaving with death and leaves, rocking like the ocean.
Oh, this delicious falling into the arms of leaves,
into the soft laps of leaves!
Face down, I swim into the leaves, feathery,
breathing the acrid odor of maple, swooping
in long glides to the bottom of October—
where the farm lies curled against winter, and soup steams
its breath of onion and carrot
onto damp curtains and windows; and past the windows
I see the tall bare maple trunks and branches, the oak
with its few brown weathery remnant leaves,
and the spruce trees, holding their green.

Now I leap and fall, exultant, recovering
from death, on account of death, in accord with the dead,
the smell and taste of leaves again,
and the pleasure, the only long pleasure, of taking a place
in the story of leaves.

THE TOY BONE

Looking through boxes
in the attic at my mother's house in Hamden,
I find a model airplane snapshots
of a dog wearing baby clothes,
a catcher's mitt—the oiled
pocket eaten
by mice—and I discover
the toy bone, the familiar smell of it.
*
I sat alone each day
after school, in the living room
of my parents' house in Hamden, ten
years old, eating
slices of plain white bread.
I listened to the record, Connie
Boswell singing
again and again, her voice
turning like a heel, "The Kerry Dancers",
and I knew she was crippled, and sang
from a wheelchair. I played
with Tommy, my red-and-white
Shetland collie, throwing
his toy bone
into the air and catching it, or letting it fall,
while he watched me
with intent, curious eyes.
I was happy
in the room dark with shades drawn.

DONALD HALL

NAMES OF HORSES

All winter your brute shoulders strained against collars, padding
and steerhide over the ash hames, to haul
sledges of cordwood for drying through spring and summer,
for the Glenwood stove next winter, and for the simmering range.

In April you pulled cartloads of manure to spread on the fields,
dark manure of Holsteins, and knobs of your own clustered with oats.
All summer you mowed the grass in meadow and hayfield, the mowing
   machine
clacketing beside you, while the sun walked high in the morning;

and after noon's heat, you pulled a clawed rake through the same acres,
gathering stacks, and dragged the wagon from stack to stack,
and the built hayrack back, up hill to the chaffy barn,
three loads of hay a day from standing grass in the morning.

Sundays you trotted the two miles to church with the light load
of a leather quartertop buggy, and grazed in the sound of hymns.
Generation on generation, your neck rubbed the windowsill
of the stall, smoothing the wood as the sea smooths glass.

When you were old and lame, when your shoulders hurt bending to
   graze,
one October the man who fed you and kept you, and harnessed you
   every morning,
led you through corn stubble to sandy ground above Eagle Pond,
and dug a hole beside you where you stood shuddering in your skin,

and lay the shotgun's muzzle on the boneless hollow behind your ear,
and fired the slug into your brain, and felled you into your grave,
shoveling sand to cover you, setting goldenrod upright above you,
where by next summer a dent in the ground made your monument.

For a hundred and fifty years, in the pasture of dead horses,
roots of pine trees pushed through the pale curves of your ribs,
yellow blossoms flourished above you in autumn, and in winter
frost heaved your bones in the ground—old toilers, soil makers:

O Roger, Mackerel, Riley, Ned, Nellie, Chester, Lady Ghost.

DONALD HALL

OX CART MAN

In October of the year,
he counts potatoes dug from the brown field,
counting the seed, counting
the cellar's portion out,
and bags the rest on the cart's floor.

He packs wool sheared in April, honey
in combs, linen, leather
tanned from deerhide,
and vinegar in a barrel
hooped by hand at the forge's fire.

He walks by his ox's head, ten days
to Portsmouth Market, and sells potatoes,
and the bag that carried potatoes,
flaxseed, birch brooms, maple sugar, goose
feathers, yarn.

When the cart is empty he sells the cart.
When the cart is sold he sells the ox,
harness and yoke, and walks
home, his pockets heavy
with the year's coin for salt and taxes,

and at home by fire's light in November cold
stitches new harness
for next year's ox in the barn,
and carves the yoke, and saws planks
building the cart again.

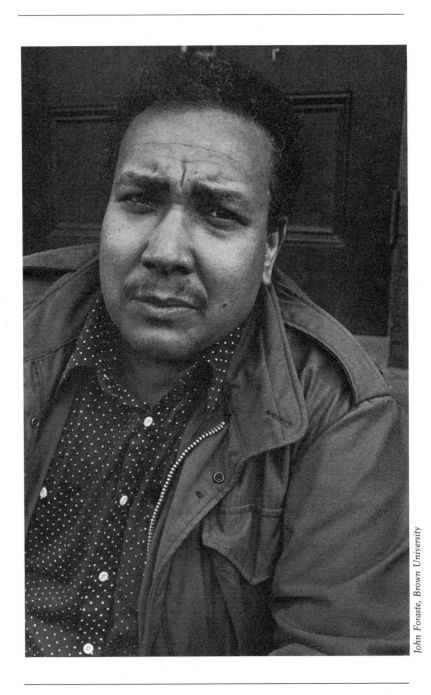

Michael S. Harper

NEW SEASON

My woman has picked
all the leaves,
rolled her hands into locks,
gone into the woods
where I have taught her
the language of these wood leaves,
and the red sand plum trees.
It is a digest
of my taking these leaves with hunger;
it is love she understands.
From my own wooden smell
she has shed her raisin skin
and come back
sweetened into brilliant music:
Her song is our new season.

BLACK STUDY

No one's been told
that black men
went first to the moon
the dark side
for dark brothers
without space ship
gravity complex
in our computer centers
government campuses
instant play and replay
white mice and pig-guineas
in concentric digital rows.

Someone has been
pulling brother's curls

189

into fancy barbed wire,
measuring his forelegs,
caressing his dense innards
into formaldehyde
pruning the jellied marrow:
a certain formula is appearing:
someone has been studying you.

HERE WHERE COLTRANE IS

Soul and race
are private dominions,
memories and modal
songs, a tenor blossoming,
which would paint suffering
a clear color but is not in
this Victorian house
without oil in zero degree
weather and a forty-mile-an-hour wind;
it is all a well-knit family:
a love supreme.
Oak leaves pile up on walkway
and steps, catholic as apples
in a special mist of clear white
children who love my children.
I play "Alabama"
on a warped record player
skipping the scratches
on your faces over the fibrous
conical hairs of plastic
under the wooden floors.

Dreaming on a train from New York
to Philly, you hand out six
notes which become an anthem
to our memories of you:
oak, birch, maple,
apple, cocoa, rubber.
For this reason Martin is dead;
for this reason Malcolm is dead;

for this reason Coltrane is dead;
in the eyes of my first son are the browns
of these men and their music.

THE BORNING ROOM

I stand in moonlight
in our borning room,
now a room of closets
changed by the owners.
Once only the old
and newborn slept
on this first floor,
this boarded door
closed now to the hearth
of our wood burning.

I look over the large bed
at the shape of my woman;
there is no image
for her, no place
for the spring child.
Her cornered shape dreams
a green robed daughter
warmed in a bent room
close to fireplace oven,
warmed by an apple tree:
the old tried to make it new,
the new old; we will not die here.

SONG: *I WANT A WITNESS*

Blacks in frame houses
call to the helicopters,
their antlered arms
spinning; jeeps pad
these glass-studded streets;
on this hill are tanks painted gold.

Our children sing
spirituals of *Motown,*
idioms these streets suckled
on a southern road.
This scene is about power,
terror, producing
love and pain and pathology;
in an army of white dust,
blacks here to *testify*
and *testify,* and *testify,*
and *redeem,* and *redeem,*
in black smoke coming,
as they wave their arms,
as they wave their tongues.

NIGHTMARE BEGINS RESPONSIBILITY

I place these numbed wrists to the pane
watching white uniforms whisk over
him in the tube-kept
prison
fear what they will do in experiment
watch my gloved stickshifting gasolined hands
breathe *boxcar-information-please* infirmary tubes
distrusting white-pink mending paperthin
silkened end hairs, distrusting tubes
shrunk in his *trunk-skincapped*
shaven head, in thighs
distrusting-white-hands-picking-baboon-light
on this son who will not make his second night
of this ward strewn intensive airpocket
where his father's asthmatic
hymns of *night-train,* train done gone
his mother can only know that he has flown
up into essential calm unseen corridor
going boxscarred home, *mamaborn, sweetsonchild*
gonedowntown into *researchtestingwarehousebatteryacid*
mam-son-done-gone/me telling her 'nother
train tonight, no music, no breathstroked
heartbeat in my infinite distrust of them:

and of my distrusting self
white-doctor-who-breathed-for-him-all-night
say it for two sons gone,
say nightmare, say it loud
panebreaking heartmadness:
nightmare begins responsibility.

BUCK

I owe him for pictures
of champions I'd known,
or never seen,
or never known
and seen as men like
him, arched now
on a drunk
to ease arthritis,
his red tie
soaked in vomit,
his blue-ringed eyes
etched in glaucoma,
menace in serge-body
on his day off
near the cubicle
where he polishes
shoes, downtown
handballers at this Y.

Tomorrow
he will kneel
over the soft leather
of his polished nails,
his glasses pouched
as two black circles,
past years at sea,
his prison blindness,
concessions lost
to three promoters
the night Joe Louis
broke in the garden;

that he could box Sugar
in his prime,
hit like Archie,
teach Gavilan to bolo,
all this in signed
photos of his gallery,
is his hangover and cure
of the future of brushes.

Four bits,
he's changed men into boys
when they ask of his photos,
black and greased
in red velvet,
buckdancing in high-topped shoes,
he'll tell a lawyer
his two cushions
are his hero chamber;
'even with glasses off
I can tell you're a boy.'
He'll speak of his father
in Panama, lost and broken
in the canal
where ships cruise
to Frisco
keelhauling his shadow,
how he followed
his known sister
who'd died ironing
his suit cleaned
on her kitchen benches.

When my third son
died in intensive,
after early birth,
he took two photos
of his champions
for two sons I'd lost,
and signed their backs;
patting my shoulder
with mahogany nails
he called them grandsons,

turned toward two men
with black unlaced shoes
patting their sleeping soles.

GRANDFATHER

In 1915 my grandfather's
neighbors surrounded his house
near the dayline he ran
on the Hudson
in Catskill, NY
and thought they'd burn
his family out
in a movie they'd just seen
and be rid of his kind:
the death of a lone black
family is *the Birth
of a Nation,*
or so they thought.
His 5'4" waiter gait
quenched the white jacket smile
he'd brought back from watered
polish of my father
on the turning seats,
and he asked his neighbors
up on his thatched porch
for the first blossom of fire
that would burn him down.

They went away, his nation,
spittooning their torched necks
in the shadows of the riverboat
they'd seen, posse decomposing;
and I see him on Sutter
with white bag from your
restaurant, challenged by his first
grandson to a foot-race
he will win in white clothes.

I see him as he buys galoshes
for his railed yard near Mineo's

metal shop, where roses jump
as the el circles his house
toward Brooklyn, where his rain fell;
and I see cigar smoke in his eyes,
chocolate Madison Square Garden chews
he breaks on his set teeth,
stitched up after cancer,
the great white nation immovable
as his weight wilts
and he is on a porch
that won't hold my arms,
or the legs of the race run
forwards, or the film
played backwards on his grandson's eyes.

HEALING SONG

He stoops down eating sunflowers
snowballed at his prayer-rugged
table, 'message/solution/masses'
his ghetto-blues-plantation,
driven into inner/outer realities
as buffers drawn from his eyes.

Penned in that magnificent voice
where *victorola* mutters 'Koppin' songs,
his sedge burning night-trains,
this serape-man found wanting
only in that 'God Don't Like Ugly'
phrase; he draws his own lightning,
believing differently,
an angel surrendering angles of desire:
his masked heart-centered soul reveals.

Rused in dance steps of jubilo,
atavisms of worship shutting out sound,
his full essential flowering
balances in the 4 a.m. traduction,
his Emancipation Tree.

MICHAEL S. HARPER

Hidden in ancient tetters
of autobiography,
he tropes of 1863 *moverings*,
his Osceolas already sacrificed
as Lincoln's mass production lines
funnel bodies to the Crater;
his Easter families agonize
at blue doors of transformation.

Self-accused in venial sins, his gorgeous
offerings lift blind pigs to Bessie's
witchdoctoring, her blue-black tongue
singing down Jesus,
'watch your goin' be like comin' back,'
he witnesses flesh pull down in anger,
killing calves of hunger to no higher law.

Ragboned Bob Hayden, shingled in slime,
reaches for his cereus ladder of midnight flight,
his seismographic heartbeats
sphinctered in rhiney polygraphs of light;
Dee-troit born and half-blind
in diction of arena and paradise,
his ambient nightmare-dreams streak his tongue;
mementos of his mother, of Erma, he image-makes
peopling the human family of God's mirror,
mingling realities, this creature of transcendence
a love-filled shadow, congealed and clarified.

Robert Hayden

FREDERICK DOUGLASS

When it is finally ours, this freedom, this liberty, this beautiful
and terrible thing, needful to man as air,
usable as earth; when it belongs at last to all,
when it is truly instinct, brain matter, diastole, systole,
reflex action; when it is finally won; when it is more
than the gaudy mumbo jumbo of politicians:
this man, this Douglass, this former slave, this Negro
beaten to his knees, exiled, visioning a world
where none is lonely, none hunted, alien,
this man, superb in love and logic, this man
shall be remembered. Oh, not with statues' rhetoric,
not with legends and poems and wreaths of bronze alone,
but with the lives grown out of his life, the lives
fleshing his dream of the beautiful, needful thing.

"FROM THE CORPSE WOODPILES, FROM THE ASHES"

From the corpse woodpiles, from the ashes
and staring pits of Dachau,
Buchenwald they come—

O David, Hirschel, Eva,
cops and robbers with me once,
their faces are like yours—

From Johannesburg, from Seoul.
Their struggles are all horizons.
Their deaths encircle me.

Through target streets I run,
in light part nightmare
and part vision fleeing

What I cannot flee, and reach
that cold cloacal cell
where He, who is man beatified

And Godly mystery,
lies chained, His pain
our anguish and our anodyne.

THOSE WINTER SUNDAYS

Sundays too my father got up early
and put his clothes on in the blueblack cold,
then with cracked hands that ached
from labor in the weekday weather made
banked fires blaze. No one ever thanked him.

I'd wake and hear the cold splintering, breaking.
When the rooms were warm, he'd call,
and slowly I would rise and dress,
fearing the chronic angers of that house,

Speaking indifferently to him,
who had driven out the cold
and polished my good shoes as well.
What did I know, what did I know
of love's austere and lonely offices?

NIGHT, DEATH, MISSISSIPPI

I

A quavering cry. Screech-owl?
Or one of them?
The old man in his reek
and gauntness laughs—

ROBERT HAYDEN

One of them, I bet—
and turns out the kitchen lamp,
limping to the porch to listen
in the windowless night.

Be there with Boy and the rest
if I was well again.
Time was. Time was.
White robes like moonlight

In the sweetgum dark.
Unbucked that one then
and him squealing bloody Jesus
as we cut it off.

Time was. A cry?
A cry all right.
He hawks and spits,
fevered as by groinfire.

Have us a bottle,
Boy and me—
he's earned him a bottle—
when he gets home.

II

Then we beat them, he said,
beat them till our arms was tired
and the big old chains
messy and red.

O Jesus burning on the lily cross

Christ, it was better
than hunting bear
which don't know why
you want him dead.

O night, rawhead and bloodybones night

You kids fetch Paw
some water now so's he
can wash that blood
off him, she said.

O night betrayed by darkness not its own

MONET'S "WATERLILIES"

(for Bill and Sonja)

Today as the news from Selma and Saigon
poisons the air like fallout,
    I come again to see
the serene great picture that I love.

Here space and time exist in light
the eye like the eye of faith believes.
    The seen, the known
dissolve in iridescence, become
illusive flesh of light
    that was not, was, forever is.

O light beheld as through refracting tears.
Here is the aura of that world
    each of us has lost.
Here is the shadow of its joy.

SOLEDAD

(And I, I am no longer of that world)

Naked, he lies in the blinded room
chainsmoking, cradled by drugs, by jazz
as never by any lover's cradling flesh.

Miles Davis coolly blows for him:
O *pena negra,* sensual Flamenco blues;
the red clay foxfire voice of Lady Day

ROBERT HAYDEN

(lady of the pure black magnolias)
sobsings her sorrow and loss and fare you well,
dryweeps the pain his treacherous jailers

have released him from for awhile.
His fears and his unfinished self
await him down in the anywhere streets.

He hides on the dark side of the moon,
takes refuge in a stained-glass cell,
flies to a clockless country of crystal.

Only the ghost of Lady Day knows where
he is. Only the music. And he swings
oh swings: beyond complete immortal now.

THE NIGHT-BLOOMING CEREUS

And so for nights
we waited, hoping to see
the heavy bud
        break into flower.

On its neck-like tube
hooking down from the edge
of the leaf-branch
        nearly to the floor,

the bud packed
tight with its miracle swayed
stiffly on breaths
        of air, moved

as though impelled
by stirrings within itself.
It repelled as much
        as it fascinated me

sometimes—snake,
eyeless bird head,
beak that would gape
        with grotesque life-squawk.

But you, my dear,
conceded less to the bizarre
than to the imminence
        of bloom. Yet we agreed

we ought
to celebrate the blossom,
paint ourselves, dance
        in honor of

archaic mysteries
when it appeared. Meanwhile
we waited, aware
        of rigorous design.

Backster's
polygraph, I thought,
would have shown
        (as clearly as it had

a philodendron's
fear) tribal sentience
in the cactus, focused
        energy of will.

That belling of
tropic perfume—that
signalling
        not meant for us;

the darkness
cloyed with summoning
fragrance. We dropped
        trivial tasks

and marvelling
beheld at last the achieved
flower. Its moonlight
        petals were

ROBERT HAYDEN

still unfold-
ing, the spike fringe of the outer
perianth recessing
    as we watched.

Lunar presence,
foredoomed, already dying,
it charged the room
    with plangency

older than human
cries, ancient as prayers
invoking Osiris, Krishna,
    Tezcátlipóca.

We spoke
in whispers when
we spoke
    at all . . .

THE PRISONERS

Steel doors — guillotine gates —
of the doorless house closed massively.
We were locked in with loss.

Guards frisked us, marked our wrists,
then let us into the drab Rec Hall —
splotched green walls, high windows barred —

where the dispossessed awaited us.
Hands intimate with knife and pistol,
hands that had cruelly grasped and throttled

clasped ours in welcome. I sensed the plea
of men denied: Believe us human
like yourselves, who but for Grace. . . .

We shared reprieving Hidden Words
revealed by the Godlike imprisoned
One, whose crime was truth.

ROBERT HAYDEN

And I read poems I hoped were true.
It's like you been there, brother, been there,
the scarred young lifer said.

THE TATTOOED MAN

I gaze at you,
longing longing,
as from a gilt
and scarlet cage;
silent, speak
your name, cry—
Love me.
To touch you, once
to hold you close—
My jungle arms,
their prized chimeras,
appall. You fear
the birds-of-paradise
perched on my thighs.
Oh to break through,
to free myself—
lifer in The Hole—
from servitude
I willed. Or was
it evil circumstance
that drove me to seek
in strangeness strange
abiding-place?
Born alien,
homeless everywhere,
did I, then, choose
bizarrity,
having no other choice?

Hundreds have paid
to gawk at me—
grotesque outsider whose
unnaturalness
assures them they

are natural, they indeed
belong.
But you but you,
for whom I would
endure caustic acids,
keenest knives—
you look at me with pain,
avert your face,
love's own,
ineffable and pure
and not for gargoyle
kisses such as mine.
Da Vinci's Last Supper—
a masterpiece
in jewel colors
on my breast
(I clenched my teeth in pain;
all art is pain
suffered and outlived);
gryphons, naked Adam
embracing naked Eve,
a gaiety of imps
in cinnabar;
the Black Widow
peering from the web
she spun, belly to groin—
These that were my pride
repel the union of
your flesh with mine.
I yearn I yearn.
And if I dared
the agonies
of metamorphosis,
would I not find
you altered then?
I do not want
you other than you are.
And I—I cannot
(will not?) change.
It is too late
for any change
but death.
I am I.

Richard Hugo

DEATH OF THE KAPOWSIN TAVERN

I can't ridge it back again from char.
Not one board left. Only ash a cat explores
and shattered glass smoked black and strung
about from the explosion I believe
in the reports. The white school up for sale
for years, most homes abandoned to the rocks
of passing boys—the fire, helped by wind
that blew the neon out six years before,
simply ended lots of ending.

A damn shame. Now, when the night chill
of the lake gets in a troller's bones
where can the troller go for bad wine
washed down frantically with beer?
And when wise men are in style again
will one recount the two-mile glide of cranes
from dead pines or the nameless yellow
flowers thriving in the useless logs,
or dots of light all night about the far end
of the lake, the dawn arrival of the idiot
with catfish—most of all, above the lake
the temple and our sanctuary there?

Nothing dies as slowly as a scene.
The dusty jukebox cracking through
the cackle of a beered-up crone—
wagered wine—sudden need to dance—
these remain in the black debris.
Although I know in time the lake will send
wind black enough to blow it all away.

G.I. GRAVES IN TUSCANY

They still seem G.I., the uniform lines
of white crosses, the gleam that rolls
white drums over the lawn. Machines

209

that cut the grass left their maneuvers plain.
Our flag doesn't seem silly though plainly
it flies only because there is wind.

Let them go by. I don't want to turn in.
After ten minutes I'd be sick of their names
or the names of their towns. Then
some guide would offer a tour
for two thousand lire, smiling the places
of battle, feigning hate for the Krauts.
I guess visitors come. A cross here and there
is rooted in flowers. Maybe in Scranton
a woman is saving. Maybe in books
what happened and why is worked out.

The loss is so damn gross. I remember
a washtub of salad in basic, blacktop acres
of men waiting to march, passing three hours
of bombers, en route to Vienna, and bombing
and passing two hours of planes, coming back.
Numbers are vulgar. If I stayed
I'd count the men in years of probable loss.

I'm a liar. I'm frightened to stop.
Afraid of a speech I might make,
corny over some stone with a name
that indicates Slavic descent—you there,
you must be first generation,
I'm third. The farm, I'm told, was hard
but it all means something. Think
of Jefferson, of the Constitution,
not of these children
beside me, bumming a smoke and laughing.

DEGREES OF GRAY IN PHILIPSBURG

You might come here Sunday on a whim.
Say your life broke down. The last good kiss
you had was years ago. You walk these streets

laid out by the insane, past hotels
that didn't last, bars that did, the tortured try
of local drivers to accelerate their lives.
Only churches are kept up. The jail
turned 70 this year. The only prisoner
is always in, not knowing what he's done.

The principal supporting business now
is rage. Hatred of the various grays
the mountain sends, hatred of the mill,
The Silver Bill repeal, the best liked girls
who leave each year for Butte. One good
restaurant and bars can't wipe the boredom out.
The 1907 boom, eight going silver mines,
a dance floor built on springs—
all memory resolves itself in gaze,
in panoramic green you know the cattle eat
or two stacks high above the town,
two dead kilns, the huge mill in collapse
for fifty years that won't fall finally down.

Isn't this your life? That ancient kiss
still burning out your eyes? Isn't this defeat
so accurate, the church bell simply seems
a pure announcement: ring and no one comes?
Don't empty houses ring? Are magnesium
and scorn sufficient to support a town,
not just Philipsburg, but towns
of towering blondes, good jazz and booze
the world will never let you have
until the town you came from dies inside?

Say no to yourself. The old man, twenty
when the jail was built, still laughs
although his lips collapse. Someday soon,
he says, I'll go to sleep and not wake up.
You tell him no. You're talking to yourself.
The car that brought you here still runs.
The money you buy lunch with,
no matter where it's mined, is silver
and the girl who serves you food
is slender and her red hair lights the wall.

MONTGOMERY HOLLOW

Birds here should have names so hard to say
you name them over. They finally found
the farmer hanging near the stream.
Only insect hum today and the purple odor
of thyme. You'd bet your throat against
the way a mind goes bad. You conquer loss
by going to the place it happened
and replaying it, saying the name
of the face in the open casket right.

People die in cities. Unless it's war
you never see the bodies. They die in print,
over phones in paramouric flats.
Here, you find them staring down the sun,
flies crawling them like bacon. Wives
scream two days running and the pain is gone.
Here, you find them living.

To know a road you own it, every bend
and pebble and the weeds along it,
dust that itches when the August hayrake
rambles home. You own the home.
You own the death of every bird you name.
To live good, keep your life and the scene.
Cow, brook, hay: these are names of coins.

for Stanley Kauffmann

MONTANA RANCH ABANDONED

Cracks in eight log buildings, counting sheds
and outhouse, widen and a ghost peeks out.
Nothing, tree or mountain, weakens wind
coming for the throat. Even wind must work
when land gets old. The rotting wagon tongue
makes fun of girls who begged to go to town.
Broken brakerods dangle in the dirt.

Alternatives were madness or a calloused moon.
Wood they carved the plowblade from
turned stone as nameless gray. Indifferent flies
left dung intact. One boy had to leave
when horses pounded night, and miles away
a neighbor's daughter puked. Mother's cry
to dinner changed to caw in later years.

Maybe raiding bears or eelworms made them quit,
or daddy died, or when they planted wheat
dead Flatheads killed the plant. That stove
without a grate can't warm the ghost.
Tools would still be good if cleaned, but mortar
flakes and log walls sag. Even if you shored,
cars would still boom by beyond the fence, no glance
from drivers as you till the lunar dust.

THE HOUSE ON 15TH S.W.

Cruelty and rain could be expected.
Any season. The talk was often German
and we cried at the death of strangers.
Potatoes mattered and neighbors who came
to marvel at our garden. I never helped
with the planting. I hid in woods these houses
built on either side replaced. Ponds
duplicated sky. I watched my face
play out dreams of going north with clouds.

North surely was soft. North was death
and women and the women soft. The tongue
there was American and kind. Acres of women
would applaud me as I danced, and acres
of graves would dance when sun announced
another cloud was dead. No grating scream
to meals or gratuitous beatings,
no crying, raging fists against closed doors,
twisted years I knew were coming at me,
hours alone in bars with honest mirrors,
being fun with strangers, being liked

so much the chance of jail was weak
from laughter, and my certainty of failure
mined by a tyrant for its pale perverted ore.

My pride in a few poems, my shame
of a wasted life, no wife, no children,
cancel out. I'm left neutral as this house,
not caring to go in. Light would be soft
and full, not harsh and dim remembered.
The children, if there are children inside,
would be normal, clean, not at all
the soiled freaks I had counted on.

FARMER, DYING

Seven thousand acres of grass have faded yellow
from his cough. These limp days, his anger,
legend forty years from moon to Stevensville,
lives on, just barely, in a Great Falls whore.
Cruel times, he cries, cruel winds. His geese roam
unattended in the meadow. The gold last leaves
of cottonwoods ride Burnt Fork creek away.
His geese grow fat without him. Same old insult.
Same indifferent rise of mountains south,
hunters drunk around the fire ten feet from his fence.

What's killing us is something autumn. Call it
war or fever. You know it when you see it: flare.
Vine and fire and the morning deer come half
a century to sip his spring, there, at the far end
of his land, wrapped in cellophane by light.
What lives is what he left in air, definite,
unseen, hanging where he stood the day he roared.
A bear prowls closer to his barn each day.
Farmers come to watch him die. They bring crude offerings
of wine. Burnt Fork creek is caroling. He dies white
in final anger. The bear taps on his pane.

And we die silent, our last day loaded with the scream
of Burnt Fork creek, the last cry of that raging farmer.
We have aged ourselves to stone trying to summon

RICHARD HUGO

mercy for ungrateful daughters. Let's live him
in ourselves, stand deranged on the meadow rim
and curse the Baltic back, moon, bear and blast.
And let him shout from his grave for us.

for Hank and Nancy

THE HILLTOP

I like bars close to home and home run down,
a signal to the world, I'm weak. I like a bar
to be a home. Take this one. Same men every night.
Same jokes. Traffic going by
fifteen feet away and punchboards never paying off.
Churn of memory and ulcer. Most of all
the stale anticipation of the girl
sure to walk in someday fresh from '39,
not one day older, holding out her arms.

Soon, I say to no one late each night,
I'll be all right. I put five dollars
in the jukebox and never hear a tune.
I take pride drinking alone and being kind.
When I walk in, people say my name.
By ten, the loveliest girl in Vegas
swims about the room, curving in and counter
to the flow of smoke. Her evil sister
swings her legs and giggles in my drink.

When I'm at home, the kitchen light stays on.
Help me, friend. By dawn, a hundred dogs
are gnawing at my throat. My gnarled phlegm
chokes up yellow. My empty room
revolves tornado and my relatives
are still unnamed. A dozen practiced gestures
get me through the day. By five, I'm crawling
up the hill, certain I'll live, my Hilltop smile
perfected and my coin naïve.

for Susan Zwinger

RICHARD HUGO

HERE, BUT UNABLE TO ANSWER

in memory, Herbert Hugo

A small dawn, sailor. First light glints
off water and it rays across your face
some ill-defined religion. I see you
always on the bridge alone, vigorous
and handsome. Eight bells. You bellow orders.
Your voice rolls back the wind.
Your eyes light numbers on the compass green.

Had I found you lost, I swear
I would have torn the clouds apart right
beneath the north star long enough
for you to fix position, and we'd have gone
sailing, sailing down our boyhood rivers
out to open sea, you proud of my power
over uncooperative sky. What a team
and never to be. You gone to China. I alone
with two old people and in nightmare earth
becoming drier. No new crop. No growth.

Even in war we lived a war apart.
You who desperately wanted combat
stuck piloting new ships from Pittsburgh
to the gulf. Me and my unwanted self
praying the final bomb run out, praying me alone
home safe, then all the others I forgot.
Forgive the bad nerves I brought home,
these hands still trembling with sky, that deafening
dream exploding me awake. Books will call
that war the last one worth the toll.

Father, now you're buried much too close for me
to a busy highway, I still see you up there
on the bridge, night sky wide open and you naming
wisely every star again, your voice enormous
with the power of moon, of tide. I seldom
sail off course. I swim a silent green.
When I dream, the compass lights stay on.

RICHARD HUGO

DISTANCES

Driving a prairie, we see a mill far off
and though clouds climbing out of the stack
pollute the air we find the sight lovely.
Horses on the rim of a distant rise
move faintly. We barely see them move
though they run wild. Or when a mile offshore
whales romp and spout, we admire
fountains in Rome, and the distant cathedral
that makes all daylit hours dawn. Artillery
lights a glorious horizon too far for us
to hear the thundering guns. We remain
out of earshot of scream.

Clouds bring rivers closer, bring closer
the homesteader's cabin, the antelope herd.
Clouds move on and the day opens to distance.
Animals are dots. They could be cattle or sheep.
Whatever, they no doubt graze safely and sky
drums wide. Whole symphonies live between
here and a distant whatever-we-look-at.
At night, what we can't see advances
fast and armed over the quaking plain.

All things came close and harmless
first thing this morning, a new trick of light.
Let's learn that trick. If we can, it will mean
we live in this world, neighbor to goat,
neighbor to trout, and we can take comfort
in low birds that hang long enough for us
to read markings and look up names
we'll whisper to them from now on.

David Ignatow

COMMUNION

Let us be friends, said Walt,
and buildings sprang up
quick as corn and people
were born into them, stock
brokers, admen, lawyers and doctors
and they contended
                        among themselves
that they might know
                        each other.

Let us be friends, said Walt.
We are one and occasionally two
of which the one is made
and cemeteries were laid out
miles in all directions
to fill the plots with the old
and young, dead of murder, disease,
rape, hatred, heartbreak and insanity
to make way for the new
and the cemeteries spread over the land
their white scab monuments.

Let us be friends, said Walt, and the graves
were opened and coffins laid on top
of one another for lack of space.
It was then the gravediggers slit
their throats, being alone in the world,
not a friend to bury.

SUNDAY AT THE STATE HOSPITAL

I am sitting across the table
eating my visit sandwich.
The one I brought him stays suspended
near his mouth; his eyes focus
on the table and seem to think,
his shoulders hunched forward.
I chew methodically,
pretending to take him
as a matter of course.
The sandwich tastes mad
and I keep chewing.
My past is sitting in front of me
filled with itself
and trying with almost no success
to bring the present to its mouth.

MY PLACE

I have a place to come to.
It's my place. I come to it
morning, noon and night
and it is there. I expect it
to be there whether or not
it expects me—my place
where I start from and go
towards so that I know
where I am going and what
I am going from, making me
firm in my direction.

I am good to talk to,
you feel in my speech
a location, an expectation
and all said to me in reply
is to reinforce this feeling
because all said is towards

my place and the speaker
too grows his
from which he speaks to mine
having located himself
through my place.

EPITAPH

There were no hidden motives to his life,
he is remembered for his meanness.
Beyond that we may look into the sky
and lose ourselves in the blue air.

Reason with me,
I'll believe in reason
though my father is dead,
and when I die
remember of me
I sought for a reason.

In the mirror the face I see
before me is my father's face,
as if I were thinking his thoughts
about me, in love
and disapproval.
I turn my face away.

Forgive me, father,
as I have forgiven you
my sins.

THE BAGEL

I stopped to pick up the bagel
rolling away in the wind,
annoyed with myself

for having dropped it
as it were a portent.
Faster and faster it rolled,
with me running after it
bent low, gritting my teeth,
and I found myself doubled over
and rolling down the street
head over heels, one complete somersault
after another like a bagel
and strangely happy with myself.

RESCUE THE DEAD

Finally, to forgo love is to kiss a leaf,
is to let rain fall nakedly upon your head,
is to respect fire,
is to study man's eyes and his gestures
as he talks,
is to set bread upon the table
and a knife discreetly by,
is to pass through crowds
like a crowd of oneself.
Not to love is to live.

To love is to be led away
into a forest where the secret grave
is dug, singing, praising darkness
under the trees.

To live is to sign your name,
is to ignore the dead,
is to carry a wallet
and shake hands.

To love is to be a fish.
My boat wallows in the sea.
You who are free,
rescue the dead.

DAVID IGNATOW

AGAINST THE EVIDENCE

As I reach to close each book
lying open on my desk, it leaps up
to snap at my fingers. My legs
won't hold me, I must sit down.
My fingers pain me
where the thick leaves snapped together
at my touch.

        All my life
I've held books in my hands
like children, carefully turning
their pages and straightening out
their creases. I use books
almost apologetically. I believe
I often think their thoughts for them.
Reading, I never know where theirs leave off
and mine begin. I am so much alone
in the world, I can observe the stars
or study the breeze, I can count the steps
on a stair on the way up or down,
and I can look at another human being
and get a smile, knowing
it is for the sake of politeness.
Nothing must be said of estrangement
among the human race and yet
nothing is said at all
because of that.
But no book will help either.
I stroke my desk,
its wood so smooth, so patient and still.
I set a typewriter on its surface
and begin to type
to tell myself my troubles.
Against the evidence, I live by choice.

DAVID IGNATOW

FIRST COFFIN POEM

I love you, my plain pine box,
because you also are a bench,
with the lid down. Can you see
my friends in a row seated
at ease with themselves?
I am in a coffin
and it has been set against the wall
of a living room. It is just before
dinner and several friends are standing
about with glasses in their hands,
drinking to the possibilities
that life offers.
    The coffin also
could be placed as a table
in front of a grand sofa, with food
and drinks served on it, and an ashtray.

It would be so much simpler, less gruesome
to use an actual coffee table, you say,
or a real bench, but ah, that would prove
how rigid we must be about ourselves
and cause us to languish, caught
in a limitation. We must make one thing
do for another.
    I am hope, in urging you
to use my pine box. Take me to your home
when I die imperceptibly. Without fuss
place me against the wall in my coffin,
a conversation piece, an affirmation of change.
I am, sincerely, yours.

WAITING INSIDE

I protest my isolation
but protest is a mark of my defeat,
even as I write.
    Being a victim,

I am an accuser. Being human,
others feel my fallen weight
upon their thoughts and are oppressed—
as I am, their guilt unlike mine
and unrelated and without hope in it
of change for me.
              Guilty, my oppressor
and I go separate ways
though we could relieve each other
by going together, as Whitman wrote,
with our arms around each other's waists,
in support.

THE QUESTION

I dream I am flying above the city
on the strength of my two outflung arms
and looking down upon the streets
where people are like so many
bacteria moving about upon a slide.
I am alone up here, with no one
to contradict me, free of the noise,
tumult and violence of the living.
Here is my true residence,
and if I say the people are bacteria
who will deny it? I declare
in my circumstances that the people
are what I say they are. The only
question now is whether I can
keep flying.

from SUNLIGHT: A SEQUENCE FOR MY DAUGHTER

[I am proud of your soft, brown eyes]

I am proud of your soft, brown eyes
looking at me to understand my presence.
You have smiled and you have thrown your hands

and legs into the air in a rhapsody
of well being and I have followed
with laughter, awed to think it is possible
to be as small as you and yet human,
for I have confused love with size,
and you look at me steadily
when I cluck and coo.

I am proud of your brown eyes
I have not known could be so soft
and questioning, and I lift you
from the crib to carry you cheek to cheek
to see if I can rub your gentleness on me.

[My infinite child, hold me to sleep]

My infinite child, hold me to sleep
in your certitude where we play house
holding the doll for a baby being fed
the bottle. I am not the happiness
you find in me, nor is it in my love.
My sadness buoys you up,
as watching you asleep your childhood
slays my old age back into beginnings,
your lips parted in dream,
face softly strange
as with difficulty delighted in.

from LEAVING THE DOOR OPEN

[He got his friends to agree to shoot him]

He got his friends to agree to shoot him standing against a stone wall, somewhere in the country on a deserted farm. It was to resemble an execution, the plan cleared with the police, at whose headquarters he had signed attesting to his desire to be shot and, in clearing his friends, declaring his death a suicide that they were to help him to—at the peak of his strength.

Never to return to life in any form but that of earth itself, since earth was not fearful or joyous. And then he was followed, on inspiration, by his friends, one by one, each fired on by a diminishing squad until the last left was shot, as a courtesy by the police. Afterwards, the police shook their heads, puzzled, grieved and somehow angry at those bodies lying sprawled with outstretched arms and legs against the ground, as if pleading with the earth to let them in.

[Lying quietly on the bed]

Lying quietly on the bed
I've become an object of the room
the way my book in hand exists
from moment to moment, its contents fixed.

How lovely it is to exist as an object.
How sweet and tranquil are the filing cabinets
and ceiling. I have found in myself
their separation from thought: never confused
in themselves or seen by others as anything
but what they are
to the touch and to the eye.

[In the spaces between the stars]

In the spaces between the stars still water dances.
In the clouds of morning the evening is flowing
backwards to its evanescence—also meaningless to you.

I had not expected to convey to you my self
in transport in a vision, and now I must start again
to express it in yet another way, as the silent flower
in the silent desert that instantly begins to bloom
more silent flowers, as I am writing this.

Now you are surely in the desert there with me
because no such desert exists, we are
both at a loss. "This is my brother." I am
introducing you to the silent flowers,
and they understand.

Randall Jarrell

THE BLACK SWAN

When the swans turned my sister into a swan
    I would go to the lake, at night, from milking:
The sun would look out through the reeds like a swan,
    A swan's red beak; and the beak would open
And inside there was darkness, the stars and the moon.

Out on the lake a girl would laugh.
    "Sister, here is your porridge, sister,"
I would call; and the reeds would whisper,
    "Go to sleep, go to sleep, little swan."
My legs were all hard and webbed, and the silky

Hairs of my wings sank away like stars
    In the ripples that ran in and out of the reeds:
I heard through the lap and hiss of water
    Someone's "Sister . . . sister," far away on the shore,
And then as I opened my beak to answer

I heard my harsh laugh go out to the shore
    And saw—saw at last, swimming up from the green
Low mounds of the lake, the white stone swans:
    The white, named swans . . . "It is all a dream,"
I whispered, and reached from the down of the pallet

To the lap and hiss of the floor.
    And "Sleep, little sister," the swans all sang
From the moon and stars and frogs of the floor.
    But the swan my sister called, "Sleep at last, little sister,"
And stroked all night, with a black wing, my wings.

TO THE NEW WORLD

(For an emigrant of 1939)

In that bad year and city of your birth
They traded bread for bank-notes weight for weight,
And nothing but the statues kept the smile
The waltzers wore once: excluding, innocent,
The face of old and comfortable injustice.
And if you wept,
Dropped red into a city where the husbandless
And fatherless were weeping too, who cared
For one more cry or one more child? You grew,

Time put words into your mouth, and you put sugar
Upon your windowsill and waited for a brother—
The stork was greedy, ate, brought nothing in return.
But your life was thinking of you, took you back to Prague,
At school there, timid, boisterous, you spoke
The unaccustomed Czech—
The children laughed at you. For you were learning
New words and a new life, the old
City and its new country too were learning
An old wish: to be just; yes, to be free.

"I saw summer in my time." Summer is ending.
The storms plunge from the tree of winter, death
Moves like an impulse over Europe. Child,
What man is just or free?—but fortunate,
Warm in time's hand, turning and trusting to his face;
And that face changes.
Time is a man for men, and He is willing
For many a new life, for others death. Already
He buys His trench-coat, falls, writes His big book;

Points here, points here: to Jews, to wicked friends—
His words are the moments of a man's life . . .
And now the men march. One morning you awoke
And found Vienna gone, your father said:
"Us next!" And you were next.

Us next!
Cried map and mouth, oppressors and oppressed,
The appeasers as they gave you—but you were gone.
"I had a speech, a city." *What is your name?*
"My name is what my name was." *You have no name.*

So the dream spoke to you: in Zurich, Paris,
In London on a lawn. The unbefriending sea
Cried to you, "Stranger!" Superb, inhospitable,
The towers of the island turned their gaze
Past the girl who looked to the great statue:
So green, so gay . . .
That is how you came. Your face shows white
Against the dark time, your words are indistinct,
One cry among so many, lost in the sound

Of degradation and of agony, the peoples dying.
The net was laid for you, and you are free.
Past the statue there is summer, and the summer smiles
The smile of justice or injustice: blind,
Comfortable, including. Here are the lives
And their old world;
Far off, inside you, a conclusive face
Watches in accusation, in acceptance. It is He.
You escaped from nothing: the westering soul
Finds Europe waiting for it over every sea.

90 NORTH

At home, in my flannel gown, like a bear to its floe,
I clambered to bed; up the globe's impossible sides
I sailed all night—till at last, with my black beard,
My furs and my dogs, I stood at the northern pole.

There in the childish night my companions lay frozen,
The stiff furs knocked at my starveling throat,
And I gave my great sigh: the flakes came huddling,
Were they really my end? In the darkness I turned to my rest.

RANDALL JARRELL

—Here, the flag snaps in the glare and silence
Of the unbroken ice. I stand here,
The dogs bark, my beard is black, and I stare
At the North Pole . . .
                    And now what? Why, go back.

Turn as I please, my step is to the south.
The world—my world spins on this final point
Of cold and wretchedness: all lines, all winds
End in this whirlpool I at last discover.

And it is meaningless. In the child's bed
After the night's voyage, in that warm world
Where people work and suffer for the end
That crowns the pain—in that Cloud-Cuckoo-Land

I reached my North and it had meaning.
Here at the actual pole of my existence,
Where all that I have done is meaningless,
Where I die or live by accident alone—

Where, living or dying, I am still alone;
Here where North, the night, the berg of death
Crowd me out of the ignorant darkness,
I see at last that all the knowledge

I wrung from the darkness—that the darkness flung me—
Is worthless as ignorance: nothing comes from nothing,
The darkness from the darkness. Pain comes from the darkness
And we call it wisdom. It is pain.

THE SNOW-LEOPARD

His pads furring the scarp's rime,
Weightless in greys and ecru, gliding
Invisibly, incuriously
As the crystals of the cirri wandering
A mile below his absent eyes,
The leopard gazes at the caravan.

The yaks groaning with tea, the burlaps
Lapping and lapping each stunned universe
That gasps like a kettle for its thinning life
Are pools in the interminable abyss
That ranges up through ice, through air, to night.
Raiders of the unminding element,
The last cold capillaries of their kind,
They move so slowly they are motionless
To any eye less stubborn than a man's. . . .
From the implacable jumble of the blocks
The grains dance icily, a scouring plume,
Into the breath, sustaining, unsustainable,
They trade to that last stillness for their death.
They sense with misunderstanding horror, with desire,
Behind the world their blood sets up in mist
The brute and geometrical necessity:
The leopard waving with a grating purr
His six-foot tail; the leopard, who looks sleepily—
Cold, fugitive, secure—at all that he knows,
At all that he is: the heart of heartlessness.

THE DEATH OF THE BALL TURRET GUNNER

From my mother's sleep I fell into the State,
And I hunched in its belly till my wet fur froze.
Six miles from earth, loosed from its dream of life,
I woke to black flak and the nightmare fighters.
When I died they washed me out of the turret with a hose.

EIGHTH AIR FORCE

If, in an odd angle of the hutment,
A puppy laps the water from a can
Of flowers, and the drunk sergeant shaving
Whistles O Paradiso!—shall I say that man
Is not as men have said: a wolf to man?

The other murderers troop in yawning;
Three of them play Pitch, one sleeps, and one
Lies counting missions, lies there sweating
Till even his heart beats: One; One; One.
O *murderers!* . . . Still, this is how it's done:

This is a war. . . . But since these play, before they die,
Like puppies with their puppy; since, a man,
I did as these have done, but did not die—
I will content the people as I can
And give up these to them: Behold the man!

I have suffered, in a dream, because of him,
Many things; for this last saviour, man,
I have lied as I lie now. But what is lying?
Men wash their hands, in blood, as best they can:
I find no fault in this just man.

A CAMP IN THE PRUSSIAN FOREST

I walk beside the prisoners to the road.
Load on puffed load,
Their corpses, stacked like sodden wood,
Lie barred or galled with blood

By the charred warehouse. No one comes today
In the old way
To knock the fillings from their teeth;
The dark, coned, common wreath

Is plaited for their grave—a kind of grief.
The living leaf
Clings to the planted profitable
Pine if it is able;

The boughs sigh, mile on green, calm, breathing mile,
From this dead file
The planners ruled for them. . . . One year
They sent a million here:

Here men were drunk like water, burnt like wood.
The fat of good
And evil, the breast's star of hope
Were rendered into soap.

I paint the star I sawed from yellow pine—
And plant the sign
In soil that does not yet refuse
Its usual Jews

Their first asylum. But the white, dwarfed star—
This dead white star—
Hides nothing, pays for nothing; smoke
Fouls it, a yellow joke,

The needles of the wreath are chalked with ash,
A filmy trash
Litters the black woods with the death
Of men; and one last breath

Curls from the monstrous chimney. . . . I laugh aloud
Again and again;
The star laughs from its rotting shroud
Of flesh. O star of men!

THE WOMAN AT THE WASHINGTON ZOO

The saris go by me from the embassies.

Cloth from the moon. Cloth from another planet.
They look back at the leopard like the leopard.

And I. . . .
                this print of mine, that has kept its color
Alive through so many cleanings; this dull null
Navy I wear to work, and wear from work, and so
To my bed, so to my grave, with no
Complaints, no comment: neither from my chief,
The Deputy Chief Assistant, nor his chief—

Only I complain. . . . this serviceable
Body that no sunlight dyes, no hand suffuses
But, dome-shadowed, withering among columns,
Wavy beneath fountains—small, far-off, shining
In the eyes of animals, these beings trapped
As I am trapped but not, themselves, the trap,
Aging, but without knowledge of their age,
Kept safe here, knowing not of death, for death—
Oh, bars of my own body, open, open!

The world goes by my cage and never sees me.
And there come not to me, as come to these,
The wild beasts, sparrows pecking the llamas' grain,
Pigeons settling on the bears' bread, buzzards
Tearing the meat the flies have clouded. . . .
        Vulture,
When you come for the white rat that the foxes left,
Take off the red helmet of your head, the black
Wings that have shadowed me, and step to me as man:
The wild brother at whose feet the white wolves fawn,
To whose hand of power the great lioness
Stalks, purring. . . .
     You know what I was,
You see what I am: change me, change me!

KIRILOV ON A SKYSCRAPER

Something gnaws inside my head
That changes everything I see:
An indolent and cloudy time,
The treasures of a barbarous scene,—

What use the crow's malignant look
Or joints as aching as a song
To show that aimless dignity
And ease that even an eye can own?—

The faces by the parapet,
Infected with their gazing, glare
As savagely as though they'd build
Another Eden, and a fruit

To reave from us the knowledge that we got.
What's good or evil to the man
So soon diminished to a doll,
Too rapid to catch a window's stare?—

His love, his mother, ranged at them—
Too fast! too fast! They gaze at, in their hour,
One instant in one instant's world—
Mortality distending like a flower.

© Joseph Levy

Donald Justice

LANDSCAPE WITH LITTLE FIGURES

There were some pines, a canal, a piece of sky.
The pines are the houses now of the very poor,
Huddled together, in a blue, ragged wind.
Children go whistling their dogs, down by the mudflats,
Once the canal. There's a red ball lost in the weeds.
It's winter, it's after supper, it's goodbye.
O goodbye to the houses, the children, the little red ball,
And the pieces of sky that will go on falling for days.

COUNTING THE MAD

This one was put in a jacket,
This one was sent home,
This one was given bread and meat
But would eat none,
And this one cried No No No No
All day long.

This one looked at the window
As though it were a wall,
This one saw things that were not there,
This one things that were,
And this one cried No No No No
All day long.

This one thought himself a bird,
This one a dog,
And this one thought himself a man,
An ordinary man,
And cried and cried No No No No
All day long.

BUS STOP

Lights are burning
In quiet rooms
Where lives go on
Resembling ours.

The quiet lives
That follow us—
These lives we lead
But do not own—

Stand in the rain
So quietly
When we are gone,
So quietly . . .

And the last bus
Comes letting dark
Umbrellas out—
Black flowers, black flowers.

And lives go on.
And lives go on
Like sudden lights
At street corners

Or like the lights
In quiet rooms
Left on for hours,
Burning, burning.

DONALD JUSTICE

THE TOURIST FROM SYRACUSE

*One of those men who can be a car salesman or a tourist from Syracuse
or a hired assassin.*

John D. MacDonald

You would not recognize me.
Mine is the face which blooms in
The dank mirrors of washrooms
As you grope for the light switch.

My eyes have the expression
Of the cold eyes of statues
Watching their pigeons return
From the feed you have scattered,

And I stand on my corner
With the same marble patience.
If I move at all, it is
At the same pace precisely

As the shade of the awning
Under which I stand waiting
And with whose blackness it seems
I am already blended.

I speak seldom, and always
In a murmur as quiet
As that of crowds which surround
The victims of accidents.

Shall I confess who I am?
My name is all names, or none.
I am the used-car salesman,
The tourist from Syracuse,

The hired assassin, waiting.
I will stand here forever
Like one who has missed his bus—
Familiar, anonymous—

On my usual corner,
The corner at which you turn
To approach that place where now
You must not hope to arrive.

MEN AT FORTY

Men at forty
Learn to close softly
The doors to rooms they will not be
Coming back to.

At rest on a stair landing,
They feel it
Moving beneath them now like the deck of a ship,
Though the swell is gentle.

And deep in mirrors
They rediscover
The face of the boy as he practices tying
His father's tie there in secret

And the face of that father,
Still warm with the mystery of lather.
They are more fathers than sons themselves now.
Something is filling them, something

That is like the twilight sound
Of the crickets, immense,
Filling the woods at the foot of the slope
Behind their mortgaged houses.

DONALD JUSTICE

THE MISSING PERSON

He has come to report himself
A missing person.

The authorities
Hand him the forms.

He knows how they have waited
With the learned patience of barbers

In small shops, idle,
Stropping their razors.

But now that these spaces in his life
Stare up at him blankly,

Waiting to be filled in,
He does not know how to begin.

Afraid that he may not answer
To his description of himself,

He asks for a mirror.
They reassure him

That he can be nowhere
But wherever he finds himself

From moment to moment
Which, for the moment, is here.

And he might like to believe them.
But in the mirror

He sees what is missing.
It is himself

He sees there emerging
Slowly, as from the dark

DONALD JUSTICE

Of a furnished room
Only by darkness,

One who receives no mail
And is known to the landlady only

For keeping himself to himself,
And for whom it will be years yet

Before he can trust to the light
This last disguise, himself.

THE ASSASSINATION

It begins again, the nocturnal pulse.
It courses through the cables laid for it.
It mounts to the chandeliers and beats there, hotly.
We are too close. Too late, we would move back.
We are involved with the surge.

Now it bursts. Now it has been announced.
Now it is being soaked up by newspapers.
Now it is running through the streets.
The crowd has it. The woman selling carnations
And the man in the straw hat stand with it in their shoes.

Here is the red marquee it sheltered under,
Here is the ballroom, here
The sadly various orchestra led
By a single gesture. My arms open.
It enters. Look, we are dancing.

June 5, 1968

DONALD JUSTICE

POEM

This poem is not addressed to you.
You may come into it briefly,
But no one will find you here, no one.
You will have changed before the poem will.

Even while you sit there, unmovable,
You have begun to vanish. And it does not matter.
The poem will go on without you.
It has the spurious glamor of certain voids.

It is not sad, really, only empty.
Once perhaps it was sad, no one knows why.
It prefers to remember nothing.
Nostalgias were peeled from it long ago.

Your type of beauty has no place here.
Night is the sky over this poem.
It is too black for stars.
And do not look for any illumination.

You neither can nor should understand what it means.
Listen, it comes without guitar,
Neither in rags nor any purple fashion.
And there is nothing in it to comfort you.

Close your eyes, yawn. It will be over soon.
You will forget the poem, but not before
It has forgotten you. And it does not matter.
It has been most beautiful in its erasures.

O bleached mirrors! Oceans of the drowned!
Nor is one silence equal to another.
And it does not matter what you think.
This poem is not addressed to you.

VARIATIONS ON A TEXT BY VALLEJO

Me moriré en París con aguacero . . .

I will die in Miami in the sun,
On a day when the sun is very bright,
A day like the days I remember, a day like other days,
A day that nobody knows or remembers yet,
And the sun will be bright then on the dark glasses of strangers
And in the eyes of a few friends from my childhood
And of the surviving cousins by the graveside,
While the diggers, standing apart, in the still shade of the palms,
Rest on their shovels, and smoke,
Speaking in Spanish softly, out of respect.

I think it will be on a Sunday like today,
Except that the sun will be out, the rain will have stopped,
And the wind that today made all the little shrubs kneel down;
And I think it will be a Sunday because today,
When I took out this paper and began to write,
Never before had anything looked so blank,
My life, these words, the paper, the gray Sunday;
And my dog, quivering under a table because of the storm,
Looked up at me, not understanding,
And my son read on without speaking, and my wife slept.

Donald Justice is dead. One Sunday the sun came out,
It shone on the bay, it shone on the white buildings,
The cars moved down the street slowly as always, so many,
Some with their headlights on in spite of the sun,
And after a while the diggers with their shovels
Walked back to the graveside through the sunlight,
And one of them put his blade into the earth
To lift a few clods of dirt, the black marl of Miami,
And scattered the dirt, and spat,
Turning away abruptly, out of respect.

DONALD JUSTICE

SONATINA IN YELLOW

Du schnell vergehendes Daguerrotyp
In meinen langsamer vergehenden Händen.

Rilke

The pages of the album,
As they are turned, turn yellow; a word,
Once spoken, obsolete,
No longer what was meant. Say it.
The meanings come, or come back later,
Unobtrusive, taking their places.

Think of the past. Think of forgetting the past.
It was an exercise requiring further practice;
A difficult exercise, played through by someone else.
Overheard from another room, now,
It seems full of mistakes.
                                    So the voice of your father,
Rising as from the next room still
With all the remote but true affection of the dead,
Repeats itself, insists,
Insisting you must listen, rises
In the familiar pattern of reproof
For some childish error, a nap disturbed,
Or vase, broken or overturned;
Rises and subsides. And you do listen.
Listen and forget. Practice forgetting.

Forgotten sunlight still
Blinds the eyes of faces in the album.
The faces fade, and there is only
A sort of meaning that comes back,
Or for the first time comes, but comes too late
To take the places of the faces.

                                                Remember
The dead air of summer. Remember
The trees drawn up to their full height like fathers,
The underworld of shade you entered at their feet.
Enter the next room. Enter it quietly now,
Not to disturb your father sleeping there. *He stirs.*

Notice his clothes, how scrupulously clean,
Unwrinkled from the nap; his face, freckled with work,
Smoothed by a passing dream. The vase
Is not yet broken, still young roses
Drink there from perpetual waters. *He rises,
speaks* . . .

Repeat it now, no one was listening.
So your hand moves, moving across the keys,
And slowly the keys grow darker to the touch.

PRESENCES

Everyone, everyone went away today.
They left without a word, and I think
I did not hear a single goodbye today.

And all that I saw was someone's hand, I think,
Thrown up out there like the hand of someone drowning,
But far away, too far to be sure what it was or meant.

No, but I saw how everything had changed
Later, just as the light had; and at night
I saw that from dream to dream everything changed.

And those who might have come to me in the night,
The ones who did come back but without a word,
All those I remembered passed through my hands like clouds—

Clouds out of the south, familiar clouds—
But I could not hold onto them, they were drifting away,
Everything going away in the night again and again.

DONALD JUSTICE

COMPLAINT OF THE GRANDPARENTS

Les morts
C'est sous terre;
Ça n'en sort
  Guère.

    — *Laforgue*

    Our diaries squatted, toad-like,
    On dark closet ledges.
    Forget-me-not and thistle
    Decalcomaned the pages.
    Where, where are they now,
      The sad squalors
    Of those between-wars parlors? —
Cut flowers; and the sunlight spilt like soda
    On torporous rugs; the photo
    Albums all outspread . . .
      The dead
Don't get around much anymore.

    There was an hour when daughters
    Practiced arpeggios;
    And their mothers, awkward and proud,
    Would listen, smoothing their hose —
    Sundays, half-past five!
      Do you recall
    How the sun used to loll,
Lazily, just beyond the roof,
    Bloodshot and aloof?
    We thought it would never set.
      The dead don't get
    Around much anymore.

    Eternity resembles
    One long Sunday afternoon.
    No traffic passes; the cigar-smoke
    Coils in a blue cocoon.
    Children, have you nothing
      For our cold sakes?

DONALD JUSTICE

No tea? No little tea-cakes?
Sometimes now the rains disturb
Even our remote suburb.
There's a dampness underground . . .
The dead don't get around
Much anymore.

IN MEMORY OF THE UNKNOWN POET
ROBERT BOARDMAN VAUGHN

But the essential advantage for a poet is not, to have a beautiful world with which to deal: it is to be able to see beneath both beauty and ugliness; to see the boredom, and the horror, and the glory.

— T. S. Eliot

It was his story. It would always be his story.
It followed him; it overtook him finally—
The boredom, and the horror, and the glory.

Probably at the end he was not yet sorry,
Even as the boots were brutalizing him in the alley.
It was his story. It would always be his story,

Blown on a blue horn, full of sound and fury,
But signifying, O signifying magnificently
The boredom, and the horror, and the glory.

I picture the snow as falling without hurry
To cover the cobbles and the toppled ashcans completely.
It was his story. It would always be his story.

Lately he had wandered between St. Mark's Place and the Bowery,
Already half a spirit, mumbling and muttering sadly.
O the boredom, and the horror, and the glory!

DONALD JUSTICE

All done now. But I remember the fiery,
Hypnotic eye and the raised voice blazing with poetry.
It was his story and would always be his story—
The boredom, and the horror, and the glory.

Galway Kinnell

FIRST SONG

Then it was dusk in Illinois, the small boy
After an afternoon of carting dung
Hung on the rail fence, a sapped thing
Weary to crying. Dark was growing tall
And he began to hear the pond frogs all
Calling on his ear with what seemed their joy.

Soon their sound was pleasant for a boy
Listening in the smoky dusk and the nightfall
Of Illinois, and from the fields two small
Boys came bearing cornstalk violins
And they rubbed the cornstalk bows with resins
And the three sat there scraping of their joy.

It was now fine music the frogs and the boys
Did in the towering Illinois twilight make
And into dark in spite of a shoulder's ache
A boy's hunched body loved out of a stalk
The first song of his happiness, and the song woke
His heart to the darkness and into the sadness of joy.

ON FROZEN FIELDS

1

We walk across the snow,
The stars can be faint,
The moon can be eating itself out,
There can be meteors flaring to death on earth,
The Northern Lights can be blooming and seething
And tearing themselves apart all night,
We walk arm in arm, and we are happy.

253

2

You in whose ultimate madness we live,
You flinging yourself out into the emptiness,
You—like us—great an instant,

O only universe we know, forgive us.

HOW MANY NIGHTS

How many nights
have I lain in terror,
O Creator Spirit, Maker of night and day,

only to walk out
the next morning over the frozen world
hearing under the creaking of snow
faint, peaceful breaths . . .
snake,
bear, earthworm, ant . . .

and above me
a wild crow crying 'yaw yaw yaw'
from a branch nothing cried from ever in my life.

VAPOR TRAIL REFLECTED IN THE FROG POND

1

The old watch: their
thick eyes
puff and foreclose by the moon. The young, heads
trailed by the beginnings of necks,
shiver,
in the guarantee they shall be bodies.

In the frog pond
the vapor trail of a SAC bomber creeps,

I hear its drone, drifting, high up
in immaculate ozone.

2

And I hear,
coming over the hills, America singing,
her varied carols I hear:
crack of deputies' rifles practicing their aim on stray dogs
      at night,
sput of cattleprod,
TV groaning at the smells of the human body,
curses of the soldier as he poisons, burns, grinds, and stabs
the rice of the world,
with open mouth, crying strong, hysterical curses.

3

And by rice paddies in Asia
bones
wearing a few shadows
walk down a dirt road, smashed
bloodsuckers on their heel, knowing
the flesh a man throws down in the sunshine
dogs shall eat
and the flesh that is upthrown in the air
shall be seized by birds,
shoulder blades smooth, unmarked by old feather-holes,
hands rivered
by blue, erratic wanderings of the blood,
eyes crinkled up
as they gaze up at the drifting sun that gives us our lives,
seed dazzled over the footbattered blaze of the earth.

GALWAY KINNELL

THE BEAR

1

In late winter
I sometimes glimpse bits of steam
coming up from
some fault in the old snow
and bend close and see it is lung-colored
and put down my nose
and know
the chilly, enduring odor of bear.

2

I take a wolf's rib and whittle
it sharp at both ends
and coil it up
and freeze it in blubber and place it out
on the fairway of the bears.

And when it has vanished
I move out on the bear tracks,
roaming in circles
until I come to the first, tentative, dark
splash on the earth.

And I set out
running, following the splashes
of blood wandering over the world.
At the cut, gashed resting places
I stop and rest,
at the crawl-marks
where he lay out on his belly
to overpass some stretch of bauchy ice
I lie out
dragging myself forward with bear-knives in my fists.

3

On the third day I begin to starve,
at nightfall I bend down as I knew I would
at a turd sopped in blood,
and hesitate, and pick it up,
and thrust it in my mouth, and gnash it down,
and rise
and go on running.

4

On the seventh day,
living by now on bear blood alone,
I can see his upturned carcass far out ahead, a scraggled,
steamy hulk,
the heavy fur riffling in the wind.

I come up to him
and stare at the narrow-spaced, petty eyes,
the dismayed
face laid back on the shoulder, the nostrils
flared, catching
perhaps the first taint of me as he
died.

I hack
a ravine in his thigh, and eat and drink,
and tear him down his whole length
and open him and climb in
and close him up after me, against the wind,
and sleep.

5

And dream
of lumbering flatfooted
over the tundra,

stabbed twice from within,
splattering a trail behind me,
splattering it out no matter which way I lurch,
no matter which parabola of bear-transcendence,
which dance of solitude I attempt,
which gravity-clutched leap,
which trudge, which groan.

6

Until one day I totter and fall—
fall on this
stomach that has tried so hard to keep up,
to digest the blood as it leaked in,
to break up
and digest the bone itself: and now the breeze
blows over me, blows off
the hideous belches of ill-digested bear blood
and rotted stomach
and the ordinary, wretched odor of bear,

blows across
my sore, lolled tongue a song
or screech, until I think I must rise up
and dance. And I lie still.

7

I awaken I think. Marshlights
reappear, geese
come trailing again up the flyway.
In her ravine under old snow the dam-bear
lies, licking
lumps of smeared fur
and drizzly eyes into shapes
with her tongue. And one
hairy-soled trudge stuck out before me,
the next groaned out,
the next,

the next,
the rest of my days I spend
wandering: wondering
what, anyway,
was that sticky infusion, that rank flavor of blood, that
    poetry, by which I lived?

UNDER THE MAUD MOON

1

On the path,
by this wet site
of old fires—
black ashes, black stones, where tramps
must have squatted down,
gnawing on stream water,
unhouseling themselves on cursed bread,
failing to get warm at a twigfire—

I stop,
gather wet wood,
cut dry shavings, and for her,
whose face
I held in my hands
a few hours, whom I gave back
only to keep holding the space where she was,

I light
a small fire in the rain.

The black
wood reddens, the deathwatches inside
begin running out of time, I can see
the dead, crossed limbs
longing again for the universe, I can hear
in the wet wood the snap
and re-snap of the same embrace being torn.

The raindrops trying
to put the fire out
fall into it and are
changed: the oath broken,
the oath sworn between earth and water, flesh and spirit, broken,
to be sworn again,
over and over, in the clouds, and to be broken again,
over and over, on earth.

2

I sit a moment
by the fire, in the rain, speak
a few words into its warmth—
stone saint smooth stone—and sing
one of the songs I used to croak
for my daughter, in her nightmares.

Somewhere out ahead of me
a black bear sits alone
on his hillside, nodding from side
to side. He sniffs
the blossom-smells, the rained earth,
finally he gets up,
eats a few flowers, trudges away,
his fur glistening
in the rain.

The singed grease streams
out of the words, the one
held note
remains—a love-note
twisting under my tongue, like the coyote's bark,
curving off, into a
howl.

3

A round-
cheeked girlchild comes awake
in her crib. The green

swaddlings tear open,
a filament or vestment
tears, the blue
flower opens.

And she who is born,
she who sings and cries,
she who begins the passage, her hair
sprouting out,
her gums budding for her first spring on earth,
the mist still clinging about
her face, puts
her hand
into her father's mouth, to take hold of
his song.

4

It is all over,
little one, the flipping
and overleaping, the watery
somersaulting alone in the oneness
under the hill, under
the old, lonely bellybutton
pushing forth again
in remembrance,
the drifting there furled in the dark,
pressing a knee or elbow
along a slippery wall, sculpting
the world with each thrash—the stream
of omphalos blood humming all about you.

5

Her head
enters the headhold
which starts sucking her forth: being itself
closes down all over her, gives her
into the shuddering
grip of departure, the slow,
agonized clenches making
the last molds of her life in the dark.

6

The black eye
opens, the pupil
droozed with black hairs
stops, the chakra
on top of the brain throbs a long moment in world light,

and she skids out on her face into light,
this peck
of stunned flesh
clotted with celestial cheesiness, glowing
with the astral violet
of the underlife. And as they cut

her tie to the darkness
she dies
a moment, turns blue as a coal,
the limbs shaking
as the memories rush out of them. When

they hang her up
by the feet, she sucks
air, screams
her first song—and turns rose,
the slow,
beating, featherless arms
already clutching at the emptiness.

7

When it was cold
on our hillside, and you cried
in the crib rocking
through the darkness, on wood
knifed down to the curve of the smile, a sadness
stranger than ours, all of it
flowing from the other world,

GALWAY KINNELL

I used to come to you
and sit by you
and sing to you. You did not know,
and yet you will remember,
in the silent zones
of the brain, a specter, descendant
of the ghostly forefathers, singing
to you in the nighttime—
not the songs
of light said to wave
through the bright hair of angels,
but a blacker
rasping flowering on that tongue.

For when the Maud moon
glimmered in those first nights,
and the Archer lay
sucking the icy biestings of the cosmos,
in his crib of stars,

I had crept down
to riverbanks, their long rustle
of being and perishing, down to marshes
where the earth oozes up
in cold streaks, touching the world
with the underglimmer
of the beginning,
and there learned my only song.

And in the days
when you find yourself orphaned,
emptied
of all wind-singing, of light,
the pieces of cursed bread on your tongue,

may there come back to you
a voice,
spectral, calling you
sister!
from everything that dies.

And then
you shall open
this book, even if it is the book of nightmares.

LAST SONGS

1

What do they sing, the last birds
coasting down the twilight,
banking
across woods filled with darkness, their
frayed wings
curved on the world like a lover's arms
which form, night after night, in sleep,
an irremediable absence?

2

Silence. Ashes
in the grate. Whatever it is
that keeps us from heaven,
sloth, wrath, greed, fear, could we only
reinvent it on earth
as song.

SAINT FRANCIS AND THE SOW

The bud
stands for all things,
even for those things that don't flower,

because everything flowers from within, of self-blessing.
Though sometimes it's necessary
to reteach a thing its loveliness,
to put a hand on its brow
of the flower
and retell it in words and in touch
it is lovely
until it flowers again from within, of self-blessing.
As Saint Francis
put his hand on the creased forehead
of the sow, and told her in words and in touch
blessings of earth on the sow, and the sow
began remembering all down her thick length,
from the earthen snout all the way through the fodder and slops
to the spiritual curl of the tail,
from the hard spininess spiked out from the spine
down through the great, unbreakable heart
to the sheer blue milken dreaminess shuddering and squirting
from the fourteen teats into the fourteen mouths sucking and blowing
    beneath them:
the long, perfect loveliness of sow.

THE FUNDAMENTAL PROJECT
OF TECHNOLOGY

"A flash! A white flash sparkled!"

                Tatsuichiro Akizuki, Concentric Circles of Death

    Under glass, glass dishes which changed
    in color; pieces of transformed beer bottles;
    a household iron; bundles of wire become solid
    lumps of iron; a pair of pliers; a ring of skull-
    bone fused to the inside of a helmet; a pair of eyeglasses
    taken off the eyes of an eyewitness, without glass,
    which vanished, when a white flash sparkled.

An old man, possibly a soldier back then,
now reduced down to one who soon will die,
sucks at the cigarette dangling from his lip, peers
at the uniform, scorched, of some tiniest schoolboy,
sighs out bluish mists of his own ashes over
a pressed tin lunch box well crushed back then when
the word *future* first learned, in a white flash, to jerk tears.

On the bridge outside, in navy black, a group
of schoolchildren line up, hold it, grin at a flash-pop,
scatter across grass, see a stranger, cry,
hello! hello! hello! and soon, *goodbye! goodbye! goodbye!*
having pecked up the greetings that fell half unspoken
and the going-sayings that those who went the day
it happened a white flash sparkled did not get to say.

If all a city's faces were to shrink back all at once
from their skulls, would a new sound come into existence,
audible above moans eaves extract from wind that smoothes
the grass on graves; or raspings heart's-blood greases still;
or wails babies trill born already skillful at the grandpa's rattle;
or infra-screams bitter-knowledge's speechlessness
memorized, at that white flash, inside closed-forever mouths?

To de-animalize human mentality, to purge it of obsolete
evolutionary characteristics, in particular of death,
which foreknowledge terrorizes the contents of skulls with,
is the fundamental project of technology; however,
the mechanisms of *pseudologica fantastica* require:
to establish deathlessness it is necessary first to eliminate
those who die; a task attempted, when a white flash sparkled.

Unlike the trees of home, which continually evaporate
along the skyline, the trees here have been enticed down
toward world-eternity. No one knows which gods they enshrine.
Does it matter? Awareness of ignorance is as devout
as knowledge of knowledge. Or more so. Even though not knowing,
sometimes we weep, from surplus of gratitude, even though knowing,
twice already on earth sparkled a flash, a white flash.

The children go away. By nature they do. And by memory:
in scorched uniforms, holding tiny crushed-metal lunch tins.
All the ecstasy-groans of each night call them back, satori
their ghostliness back into the ashes, in the momentary shrines,
the thankfulness of arms, from which they will go
again and again, until the day flashes and no one lives
to look back and say, a flash, a white flash sparkled.

Carolyn Kizer

from PRO FEMINA

I will speak about women of letters, for I'm in the racket.
Our biggest successes to date? Old maids to a woman.
And our saddest conspicuous failures? The married spinsters
On loan to the husbands they treated like surrogate fathers.
Think of that crew of self-pitiers, not-very-distant,
Who carried the torch for themselves and got first-degree burns.
Or the sad sonneteers, toast-and-teasdales we loved at thirteen;
Middle-aged virgins seducing the puerile anthologists
Through lust-of-the-mind; barbiturate-drenched Camilles
With continuous periods, murmuring softly on sofas
When poetry wasn't a craft but a sickly effluvium,
The air thick with incense, musk, and emotional blackmail.

I suppose they reacted from an earlier womanly modesty
When too many girls were scabs to their stricken sisterhood,
Impugning our sex to stay in good with the men,
Commencing their insecure bluster. How they must have swaggered
When women themselves indorsed their own inferiority!
Vestals, vassals and vessels, rolled into several,
They took notes in rolling syllabics, in careful journals,
Aiming to please a posterity that despises them.
But we'll always have traitors who swear that a woman surrenders
Her Supreme Function, by equating Art with aggression
And failure with Femininity. Still it's just as unfair
To equate Art with Femininity, like a prettily-packaged commodity
When we are the custodians of the world's best-kept secret:
Merely the private lives of one-half of humanity.

But even with masculine dominance, we mares and mistresses
Produced some sleek saboteuses, making their cracks
Which the porridge-brained males of the day were too thick to perceive,
Mistaking young hornets for perfectly harmless bumblebees.
Being thought innocuous rouses some women to frenzy;

They try to be ugly by aping the ways of the men
And succeed. Swearing, sucking cigars and scorching the bedspread,
Slopping straight shots, eyes blotted, vanity-blown
In the expectation of glory: *she writes like a man!*
This drives other women mad in a mist of chiffon
(one poetess draped her gauze over red flannels, a practical feminist).

But we're emerging from all that, more or less,
Except for some lady-like laggards and Quarterly priestesses
Who flog men for fun, and kick women to maim competition.
Now, if we struggle abnormally, we may almost seem normal;
If we submerge our self-pity in disciplined industry;
If we stand up and be hated, and swear not to sleep with editors;
If we regard ourselves formally, respecting our true limitations
Without making an unseemly show of trying to unfreeze our assets;
Keeping our heads and our pride while remaining unmarried;
And if wedded, kill guilt in its tracks when we stack up the dishes
And defect to the typewriter. And if mothers, believe in the luck of our
    children,
Whom we forbid to devour us, whom we shall not devour,
And the luck of our husbands and lovers, who keep free women.

THE UNGRATEFUL GARDEN

Midas watched the golden crust
That formed over his streaming sores,
Hugged his agues, loved his lust,
But damned to hell the out-of-doors

Where blazing motes of sun impaled
The serried roses, metal-bright.
"Those famous flowers," Midas wailed,
"Have scorched my retina with light."

This gift, he'd thought, would gild his joys,
Silt up the waters of his grief;
His lawns a wilderness of noise,
The heavy clang of leaf on leaf.

Within, the golden cup is good
To heft, to sip the yellow mead.
Outside, in summer's rage, the rude
Gold thorn has made his fingers bleed.

"I strolled my halls in golden shift,
As ruddy as a lion's meat.
Then I rushed out to share my gift,
And golden stubble cut my feet."

Dazzled with wounds, he limped away
To climb into his golden bed.
Roses, roses can betray.
"Nature is evil," Midas said.

A WIDOW IN WINTERTIME

Last night a baby gargled in the throes
Of a fatal spasm. My children are all grown
Past infant strangles; so, reassured, I knew
Some other baby perished in the snow.
But no. The cat was making love again.

Later, I went down and let her in.
She hung her tail, flagging from her sins.
Though she'd eaten, I forked out another dinner,
Being myself hungry all ways, and thin
From metaphysic famines she knows nothing of,

The feckless beast! Even so, resemblances
Were on my mind: female and feline, though
She preens herself from satisfaction, and does
Not mind lying even in snow. She is
Lofty and bedraggled, without need to choose.

As an ex-animal, I look fondly on
Her excesses and simplicities, and would not return
To them; taking no marks for what I have become,

Merely that my nine lives peal in my ears again
And again, ring in these austerities,

These arbitrary disciplines of mine,
Most of them trivial: like covering
The children on my way to bed, and trying
To live well enough alone, and not to dream
Of grappling in the snow, claws plunged in fur,

Or waken in a caterwaul of dying.

THE COPULATING GODS

Brushing back the curls from your famous brow,
Lingering over the prominent temple vein
Purple as Aegean columns in the dawn,
Calm now, I ponder how self-consciously
The gods must fornicate.
It is that sense of unseen witness:
Those mortals with whom we couple or have coupled,
Clinging to our swan-suits, our bull-skins,
Our masquerades in coin and shrubbery.

We were their religion before they were born.
The spectacle of our carnality
Confused them into spiritual lust.
The headboard of our bed became their altar;
Rare nectar, shared, a common sacrament.
The wet drapery of our sheets, molded
To noble thighs, is made the basis
For a whole new aesthetic:
God is revealed as the first genius.

Men continue to invent our histories,
Deny our equal pleasure in each other.
Club-foot, nymphomaniac, they dub us,
Then fabricate the net that God will cast
Over our raptures: we, trussed up like goats,

CAROLYN KIZER

Paraded past the searchlights of the sky
By God himself, the ringmaster and cuckold,
Amidst a thunderous laughter and applause.

Tracing again the bones of your famous face,
I know we are not their history but our myth.
Heaven prevents time; and our astral raptures
Float buoyant in the universe. Come, kiss!
Come, swoon again, we who invented dying
And the whole alchemy of resurrection.
They will concoct a scripture explaining this.

SEMELE RECYCLED

After you left me forever,
I was broken into pieces,
and all the pieces flung into the river.
Then the legs crawled ashore
and aimlessly wandered the dusty cow-track.
They became, for a while, a simple roadside shrine:
A tiny table set up between the thighs
held a dusty candle, weed, and fieldflower chains
placed reverently there by children and old women.
My knees were hung with tin triangular medals
to cure all forms of hysterical disease.

After I died forever in the river,
my torso floated, bloated in the stream,
catching on logs or stones among the eddies.
White water foamed around it, then dislodged it;
after a whirlwind trip, it bumped ashore.
A grizzled old man who scavenged along the banks
had already rescued my arms and put them by,
knowing everything has its uses, sooner or later.

When he found my torso, he called it his canoe,
and, using my arms as paddles,
he rowed me up and down the scummy river.

When catfish nibbled my fingers, he scooped them up
and blessed his re-usable bait.
Clumsy but serviceable, that canoe!
The trail of blood that was its wake
attracted the carp and eels, and the river turtle,
easily landed, dazed by my tasty red.

A young lad found my head among the rushes
and placed it on a dry stone.
He carefully combed my hair with a bit of shell
and set small offerings before it
which the birds and rats obligingly stole at night,
so it seemed I ate.
And the breeze wound through my mouth and empty sockets
so my lungs would sigh and my dead tongue mutter.
Attached to my throat like a sacred necklace
was a circlet of small snails.
Soon the villagers came to consult my oracular head
with its waterweed crown.
Seers found occupation, interpreting sighs,
and their papyrus rolls accumulated.

Meanwhile, young boys retrieved my eyes
they used for marbles in a simple game
—till somebody's pretty sister snatched at them
and set them, for luck, in her bridal diadem.
Poor girl! When her future groom caught sight of her,
all eyes, he crossed himself in horror,
and stumbled away in haste
through her dowered meadows.

What then of my heart and organs,
my sacred slit
which loved you best of all?
They were caught in a fisherman's net
and tossed at night into a pen for swine.
But they shone so by moonlight that the sows stampeded,
trampled each other in fear, to get away.
And the fisherman's wife, who had 13 living children
and was contemptuous of holy love,
raked the rest of me onto the compost heap.

CAROLYN KIZER

Then in their various places and helpful functions,
the altar, oracle, offal, canoe, and oars
learned the wild rumor of your return.
The altar leapt up and ran to the canoe,
scattering candle grease and wilted grasses.
Arms sprang to their sockets, blind hands with nibbled nails
groped their way, aided by loud lamentation,
to the bed of the bride, snatched up those unlucky eyes
from her discarded veil and diadem,
and rammed them home. O what a bright day it was!
This empty body danced on the river bank.
Hollow, it called and searched among the fields
for those parts that steamed and simmered in the sun,
and never would have found them.

But then your great voice rang out under the skies
my name!—and all those private names
for the parts and places that had loved you best.
And they stirred in their nest of hay and dung.
The distraught old ladies chasing their lost altar,
and the seers pursuing my skull, their lost employment,
and the tumbling boys, who wanted the magic marbles,
and the runaway groom, and the fisherman's 13 children
set up such a clamor, with their cries of "Miracle!"
that our two bodies met like a thunderclap
in mid-day—right at the corner of that wretched field
with its broken fenceposts and startled, skinny cattle.
We fell in a heap on the compost heap
and all our loving parts made love at once,
while the bystanders cheered and prayed and hid their eyes
and then went decently about their business.

And here it is, moonlight again; we've bathed in the river
and are sweet and wholesome once more.
We kneel side by side in the sand;
we worship each other in whispers.
But the inner parts remember fermenting hay,
the comfortable odor of dung, the animal incense,
and passion, its bloody labor,
its birth and rebirth and decay.

CAROLYN KIZER

THE BLESSING

I

Daughter-my-mother,
you have observed my worst.
Holding me together at your expense
has made you burn cool.

So did I in childhood:
nursed her old hurts and doubts,
myself made cool to shallowness.
She grew out as I grew in.
At mid-point our furies met.

My mother's dust has rested
for fifteen years
in the front hall closet
because we couldn't bear to bury it.
Her dust-lined, dust-coated urn
squats among the size-eleven overshoes.
My father, who never forgets
his overshoes,
has forgotten that.

Hysterical-tongued daughter
of a dead marriage,
you shed hot tears in the bed
of that benign old woman
whose fierce joy you were:
tantrums in the closet
taking upon yourself the guilt
the split parents never felt.

Child and old woman
soothing each other,
sharing the same face

in a span of seventy years
the same mother wit.

II

I must go home, says my father,
his mind straying:
this is a hard time
for your mother. But she's been dead
these fifteen years.
Daughter and daughter, we sit
on either side.
Whose? Which? He's not sure.
After long silence,
don't press me, he says.

Mother, hysterical-tongued,
age and grace burned away
your excesses, left
that lavender-sweet child
who turned up the thermostat
on her electric blanket, folded
her hands on her breast.
You had dreamed death
as a silver prince:
Like marrying Nehru, you said.

Dearest, does your dust hum
in the front hall closet—
this is a hard time for me—
among the umbrella points,
the canes, and overshoes
of that cold climate?

Each week she denies it,
my blithe mother

in that green, cloud-free landscape
where we whisper our dream-secrets
to each other.

III

Daughter, you lived through
my difficult affairs
as I tried to console
your burnt-out childhood.
We coped with our fathers,
compared notes
on the old one and the cold one,
learned to moderate our hates.
Risible in suffering,
we grew up together.

Mother-my-daughter,
I have been blessed
on both sides of my life.
Forgive me if sometimes
like my fading father
I see you as one.

Not that I confuse
your two identities
as he does, taking off
or putting on his overshoes
but my own role:

I lean on the bosom
of that double mother,
the ghost by night, the girl by day;
I between my
two mild furies,
alone but comforted.

And I will whisper blithely
in your dreams
when you are as old as I,
my hard time over.

Meanwhile, keep warm
your love, your bed,
and your wise heart and head,
my good daughter.

for Ashley

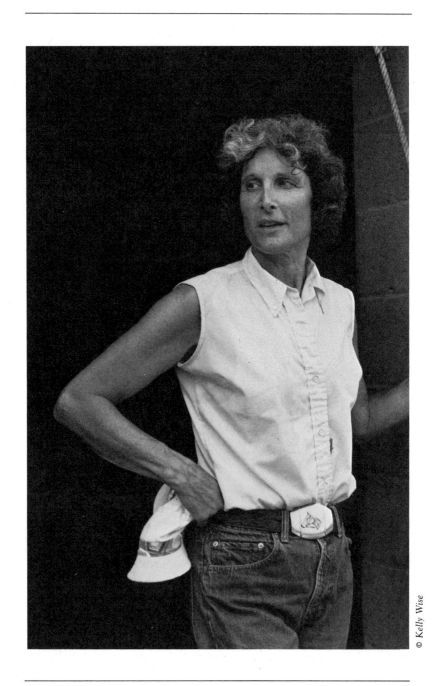

Maxine Kumin

MORNING SWIM

Into my empty head there come
a cotton beach, a dock wherefrom

I set out, oily and nude
through mist, in chilly solitude.

There was no line, no roof or floor
to tell the water from the air.

Night fog thick as terry cloth
closed me in its fuzzy growth.

I hung my bathrobe on two pegs.
I took the lake between my legs.

Invaded and invader, I
went overhand on that flat sky.

Fish twitched beneath me, quick and tame.
In their green zone they sang my name

and in the rhythm of the swim
I hummed a two-four-time slow hymn.

I hummed *Abide with Me*. The beat
rose in the fine thrash of my feet,

rose in the bubbles I put out
slantwise, trailing through my mouth.

My bones drank water; water fell
through all my doors. I was the well

that fed the lake that met my sea
in which I sang *Abide with Me*.

MAXINE KUMIN

STONES

The moving of stones, that sly jockeying thrust
takes place at night underground, shoulders first.

They bud in their bunkers like hydras. They puff
up head after head and allow them to drop off

on their own making quahogs, cow flops, eggs and knee
caps. In this way one stone can infuse a colony.

Eyeless and unsurprised they behave
in the manner of stones: swallow turnips, heave graves

rise up openmouthed into walls and from time
to time imitate oysters or mushrooms.

The doors of my house are held open by stones
and to see the tame herd of them hump their backbones

as cumbrous as bears across the pasture in
an allday rain is to believe for an afternoon

of objects that waver and blur
in some dark obedient order.

WOODCHUCKS

Gassing the woodchucks didn't turn out right.
The knockout bomb from the Feed and Grain Exchange
was featured as merciful, quick at the bone
and the case we had against them was airtight,
both exits shoehorned shut with puddingstone,
but they had a sub-sub-basement out of range.

Next morning they turned up again, no worse
for the cyanide than we for our cigarettes
and state-store Scotch, all of us up to scratch.
They brought down the marigolds as a matter of course
and then took over the vegetable patch
nipping the broccoli shoots, beheading the carrots.

The food from our mouths, I said, righteously thrilling
to the feel of the .22, the bullets' neat noses.
I, a lapsed pacifist fallen from grace
puffed with Darwinian pieties for killing,
now drew a bead on the littlest woodchuck's face.
He died down in the everbearing roses.

Ten minutes later I dropped the mother. She
flipflopped in the air and fell, her needle teeth
still hooked in a leaf of early Swiss chard.
Another baby next. O one-two-three
the murderer inside me rose up hard,
the hawkeye killer came on stage forthwith.

There's one chuck left. Old wily fellow, he keeps
me cocked and ready day after day after day.
All night I hunt his humped-up form. I dream
I sight along the barrel in my sleep.
If only they'd all consented to die unseen
gassed underground the quiet Nazi way.

HOW IT IS

Shall I say how it is in your clothes?
A month after your death I wear your blue jacket.
The dog at the center of my life recognizes
you've come to visit, he's ecstatic.
In the left pocket, a hole.
In the right, a parking ticket
delivered up last August on Bay State Road.
In my heart, a scatter like milkweed,
a flinging from the pods of the soul.
My skin presses your old outline.
It is hot and dry inside.

I think of the last day of your life,
old friend, how I would unwind it, paste
it together in a different collage,
back from the death car idling in the garage,
back up the stairs, your praying hands unlaced,

reassembling the bites of bread and tuna fish
into a ceremony of sandwich,
running the home movie backward to a space
we could be easy in, a kitchen place
with vodka and ice, our words like living meat.

Dear friend, you have excited crowds
with your example. They swell
like wine bags, straining at your seams.
I will be years gathering up our words,
fishing out letters, snapshots, stains,
leaning my ribs against this durable cloth
to put on the dumb blue blazer of your death.

THE LONGING TO BE SAVED

When the barn catches fire
I am wearing the wrong negligee.
It hangs on me like a gunny sack.
I get the horses out, but they
wrench free, wheel, dash back
and three or four trips are required.
Much whinnying and rearing as well.
This happens whenever I travel.

At the next stopover, the children take off
their doctor and lawyer disguises
and turn back into little lambs.
They cower at windows from which flames
shoot like the tattered red cloth
of dimestore devil suits. They refuse
to jump into my waiting arms, although
I drilled them in this technique, years ago.

Finally they come to their senses and leap
but each time, the hoop holds my mother.
Her skin is as dry and papery
as a late onion. I take her
into my bed, an enormous baby
I do not especially want to keep.

Three nights of such disquiet
in and out of dreams as thin as acetate

until, last of all, it's you
trapped in the blazing fortress.
I hold the rope as you slide from danger.
It's tricky in high winds and drifting snow.
Your body swaying in space
grows heavier, older, stranger

and me in the same gunny sack
and the slamming sounds as the gutted building burns.
Now the family's out, there's no holding back.
I go in to get my turn.

THE EXCREMENT POEM

It is done by us all, as God disposes, from
the least cast of worm to what must have been
in the case of the brontosaur, say, spoor
of considerable heft, something awesome.

We eat, we evacuate, survivors that we are.
I think these things each morning with shovel
and rake, drawing the risen brown buns
toward me, fresh from the horse oven, as it were,

or culling the alfalfa-green ones, expelled
in a state of ooze, through the sawdust bed
to take a serviceable form, as putty does,
so as to lift out entire from the stall.

And wheeling to it, storming up the slope,
I think of the angle of repose the manure
pile assumes, how sparrows come to pick
the redelivered grain, how inky-cap

coprinus mushrooms spring up in a downpour.
I think of what drops from us and must then
be moved to make way for the next and next.
However much we stain the world, spatter

it with our leavings, make stenches, defile
the great formal oceans with what leaks down,
trundling off today's last barrowful,
I honor shit for saying: We go on.

THE GRACE OF GELDINGS IN RIPE PASTURES

Glutted, half asleep, browsing in
timothy grown so tall I see them
as through a pale-green stage scrim

they circle, nose to rump,
a trio of trained elephants.
It begins to rain, as promised.

Bit by bit they soak up drops
like laundry dampened to be ironed.
Runnels bedeck them. Their sides

drip like the ribs of very broad
umbrellas. And still they graze
and grazing, one by one let down

their immense, indolent penises
to drench the everlasting grass
with the rich nitrogen

that repeats them.

IN THE PEA PATCH

These as they clack in the wind
saying castanets, saying dance with me,
saying do me, dangle their intricate
nuggety scrota

and these with the light shining through
call up a woman in a gauzy dress

young, with tendrils of hair at her neck,
leaning in a summer doorway

and as the bloom of the lime-green pod
rubs away under the polishing thumb
in the interior
sweet for the taking, nine little fetuses
nod their cloned heads.

SPENDING THE NIGHT

As bubbles are baked
into the risen loaf
so the small hot apprehension
of my death is folded in me
each time you enter my body.

Even while we hold each other
rising more surely than hornflies
to beat against the ceiling
Death tags along like a Saint Bernard
padding across his own night-alp.

Afterward I dial the grave.
My father speaks, his voice
is thin yet clear as lightning forks.
Stay home! No visitors! he calls.

While you sprawl in sleep
arms outflung like a child's
my tongue tries the salt
of this dream.
        In the cup
of your armpit the Spoiler lurks.
Snatched out, held down, this one
time more I pass him in the dark.

APOSTROPHE TO A DEAD FRIEND

(on being interviewed by her biographer)

Little by little my gender drifts away
leaving the bones of this person
whose shoe size was your size
who traded dresses in our pool
of public-occasion costumes:
yours the formal-length jersey
mine the cocktail wool
and your dead mother's mink coat that
I always said looked like muskrat.

It fades, the glint of those afternoons
we lay in the sun by the pond.
Paler, the intimate confidences.
Even the distances we leapt in poems
have shrunk. No more parapets.
The men have grown smaller, drier,
easier to refuse.
Passion subsides like a sunset.
Urgency has been wrung from the rendezvous.

Now that the children have changed
into exacting adults, the warmth
we felt for each other's young
takes on the skin tone of plain daylight.
However well-fed and rosy
they are no kinder or wiser than we.

Soon I will be sixty.
How it was with you now
hardly more vivid than how
it is without you, I carry
the sheer weight of the telling
like a large infant, on one hip.
I who am remaindered in the conspiracy
doom, doom on my lips.

MAXINE KUMIN

FAMILY REUNION

The week in August you come home,
adult, professional, aloof,
we roast and carve the fatted calf
—in our case home-grown pig, the chine
garlicked and crisped, the applesauce
hand-pressed. Hand-pressed the greengage wine.

Nothing is cost-effective here.
The peas, the beets, the lettuces
hand sown, are raised to stand apart.
The electric fence ticks like the slow heart
of something we fed and bedded for a year,
then killed with kindness's one bullet
and paid Jake Mott to do the butchering.

In winter we lure the birds with suet,
thaw lungs and kidneys for the cat.
Darlings, it's all a circle from the ring
of wire that keeps the raccoons from the corn
to the gouged pine table that we lounge around,
distressed before any of you was born.

Benign and dozy from our gluttonies,
the candles down to stubs, defenses down,
love leaking out unguarded the way
juice dribbles from the fence when grounded
by grass stalks or a forgotten hoe,
how eloquent, how beautiful you seem!

Wearing our gestures, how wise you grow,
ballooning to overfill our space,
the almost-parents of your parents now.
So briefly having you back to measure us
is harder than having let you go.

Stanley Kunitz

SINGLE VISION

Before I am completely shriven
I shall reject my inch of heaven.

Cancel my eyes, and, standing, sink
Into my deepest self; there drink

Memory down. The banner of
My blood, unfurled, will not be love,

Only the pity and the pride
Of it, pinned to my open side.

When I have utterly refined
The composition of my mind,

Shaped language of my marrow till
Its forms are instant to my will,

Suffered the leaf of my heart to fall
Under the wind, and, stripping all

The tender blanket from my bone,
Rise like a skeleton in the sun,

I shall have risen to disown
The good mortality I won.

Directly risen with the stain
Of life upon my crested brain,

Which I shall shake against my ghost
To frighten him, when I am lost.

Gladly, as any poison, yield
My halved conscience, brightly peeled;

Infect him, since we live but once,
With the unused evil in my bones.

I'll shed the tear of souls, the true
Sweat, Blake's intellectual dew,

Before I am resigned to slip
A dusty finger on my lip.

FATHER AND SON

Now in the suburbs and the falling light
I followed him, and now down sandy road
Whiter than bone-dust, through the sweet
Curdle of fields, where the plums
Dropped with their load of ripeness, one by one.
Mile after mile I followed, with skimming feet,
After the secret master of my blood,
Him, steeped in the odor of ponds, whose indomitable love
Kept me in chains. Strode years; stretched into bird;
Raced through the sleeping country where I was young,
The silence unrolling before me as I came,
The night nailed like an orange to my brow.

How should I tell him my fable and the fears,
How bridge the chasm in a casual tone,
Saying, "The house, the stucco one you built,
We lost. Sister married and went from home,
And nothing comes back, it's strange, from where she goes.
I lived on a hill that had too many rooms:
Light we could make, but not enough of warmth,
And when the light failed, I climbed under the hill.
The papers are delivered every day;
I am alone and never shed a tear."

At the water's edge, where the smothering ferns lifted
Their arms, "Father!" I cried, "Return! You know
The way. I'll wipe the mudstains from your clothes;

No trace, I promise, will remain. Instruct
Your son, whirling between two wars,
In the Gemara of your gentleness,
For I would be a child to those who mourn
And brother to the foundlings of the field
And friend of innocence and all bright eyes.
O teach me how to work and keep me kind."

Among the turtles and the lilies he turned to me
The white ignorant hollow of his face.

END OF SUMMER

An agitation of the air,
A perturbation of the light
Admonished me the unloved year
Would turn on its hinge that night.

I stood in the disenchanted field
Amid the stubble and the stones,
Amazed, while a small worm lisped to me
The song of my marrow-bones.

Blue poured into summer blue,
A hawk broke from his cloudless tower,
The roof of the silo blazed, and I knew
That part of my life was over.

Already the iron door of the north
Clangs open: birds, leaves, snows
Order their populations forth,
And a cruel wind blows.

THE WAR AGAINST THE TREES

The man who sold his lawn to standard oil
Joked with his neighbors come to watch the show
While the bulldozers, drunk with gasoline,

Tested the virtue of the soil
Under the branchy sky
By overthrowing first the privet-row.

Forsythia-forays and hydrangea-raids
Were but preliminaries to a war
Against the great-grandfathers of the town,
So freshly lopped and maimed.
They struck and struck again,
And with each elm a century went down.

All day the hireling engines charged the trees,
Subverting them by hacking underground
In grub-dominions, where dark summer's mole
Rampages through his halls,
Till a northern seizure shook
Those crowns, forcing the giants to their knees.

I saw the ghosts of children at their games
Racing beyond their childhood in the shade,
And while the green world turned its death-foxed page
And a red wagon wheeled,
I watched them disappear
Into the suburbs of their grievous age.

Ripped from the craters much too big for hearts
The club-roots bared their amputated coils,
Raw gorgons matted blind, whose pocks and scars
Cried Moon! on a corner lot
One witness-moment, caught
In the rear-view mirrors of the passing cars.

INDIAN SUMMER AT LAND'S END

The season stalls, unseasonably fair,
blue-fair, serene, a stack of golden discs,
each disc a day, and the addition slow.
I wish you were here with me to walk the flats,

STANLEY KUNITZ

towards dusk especially when the tide is out
and the bay turns opal, filled with rolling fire
that washes on the mouldering wreck offshore,
our mussel-vineyard, strung with bearded grapes.
Last night I reached for you and shaped you there
lying beside me as we drifted past
the farthest seamarks and the watchdog bells,
and round Long Point throbbing its frosty light,
until we streamed into the open sea.
What did I know of voyaging till now?
Meanwhile I tend my flock, strange golden puffs
diminutive as wrens, with snipped-off tails,
who bounce down from the trees. High overhead,
on the trackless roads, skywriting V and yet
another V, the southbound Canada express
hoots of horizons and distances. . . .

THE ARTIST

His paintings grew darker every year.
They filled the walls, they filled the room;
eventually they filled his world—
all but the ravishment.
When voices faded, he would rush to hear
the scratched soul of Mozart
endlessly in gyre.
Back and forth, back and forth,
he paced the paint-smeared floor,
diminishing in size each time he turned,
trapped in his monumental void,
raving against his adversaries.
At last he took a knife in his hand
and slashed an exit for himself
between the frames of his tall scenery.
Through the holes of his tattered universe
the first innocence and the light
came pouring in.

THE PORTRAIT

My mother never forgave my father
for killing himself,
especially at such an awkward time
and in a public park,
that spring
when I was waiting to be born.
She locked his name
in her deepest cabinet
and would not let him out,
though I could hear him thumping.
When I came down from the attic
with the pastel portrait in my hand
of a long-lipped stranger
with a brave moustache
and deep brown level eyes,
she ripped it into shreds
without a single word
and slapped me hard.
In my sixty-fourth year
I can feel my cheek
still burning.

THE UNQUIET ONES

Years ago I lost
both my parents' addresses.
Father and mother lie
in their neglected cribs,
obscure as moles,
unvisited.
I do not need to summon them.
When I put out the light
I hear them stir, dissatisfied,

in their separate places,
in death as in life
remote from each other,
having no conversation
except in the common ground
of their son's mind.
They slip through narrow crevices
and, suddenly blown tall,
glide into my cave of phantoms,
unwelcome guests, but not
unloved, dark emissaries
of the two-faced god.

THE KNOT

I've tried to seal it in,
that cross-grained knot
on the opposite wall,
scored in the lintel of my door,
but it keeps bleeding through
into the world we share.
Mornings when I wake,
curled in my web,
I hear it come
with a rush of resin
out of the trauma
of its lopping-off.
Obstinate bud,
sticky with life,
mad for the rain again,
it racks itself with shoots
that crackle overhead,
dividing as they grow.
Let be! Let be!
I shake my wings
and fly into its boughs.

THE WELLFLEET WHALE

1

You have your language too,
    an eerie medley of clicks
        and hoots and trills,
location-notes and love calls,
    whistles and grunts. Occasionally,
        it's like furniture being smashed,
or the creaking of a mossy door,
    sounds that all melt into a liquid
        song with endless variations,
as if to compensate
    for the vast loneliness of the sea.
        Sometimes a disembodied voice
breaks in, as if from distant reefs,
    and it's as much as one can bear
        to listen to its long mournful cry,
a sorrow without name, both more
    and less than human. It drags
        across the ear like a record
running down.

2

No wind. No waves. No clouds.
    Only the whisper of the tide,
        as it withdrew, stroking the shore,
a lazy drift of gulls overhead,
    and tiny points of light
        bubbling in the channel.
It was the tag-end of summer.
    From the harbor's mouth
        you coasted into sight,
flashing news of your advent,
    the crescent of your dorsal fin
        clipping the diamonded surface.
We cheered at the sign of your greatness
    when the black barrel of your head

erupted, ramming the water,
and you flowered for us
in the jet of your spouting.

3

All afternoon you swam
tirelessly round the bay,
with such an easy motion,
the slightest downbeat of your tail,
an almost imperceptible
undulation of your flippers,
you seemed like something poured,
not driven; you seemed
to marry grace with power.
And when you bounded into air,
slapping your flukes,
we thrilled to look upon
pure energy incarnate
as nobility of form.
You seemed to ask of us
not sympathy, or love,
or understanding,
but awe and wonder.

That night we watched you
swimming in the moon.
Your back was molten silver.
We guessed your silent passage
by the phosphorescence in your wake.
At dawn we found you stranded on the rocks.

4

There came a boy and a man
and yet other men running, and two
schoolgirls in yellow halters
and a housewife bedecked
with curlers, and whole families in beach
buggies with assorted yelping dogs.

The tide was almost out.
    We could walk around you,
        as you heaved deeper into the shoal,
crushed by your own weight,
    collapsing into yourself,
        your flippers and your flukes
quivering, your blowhole
    spasmodically bubbling, roaring.
        In the pit of your gaping mouth
you bared your fringework of baleen,
    a thicket of horned bristles.
        When the Curator of Mammals
arrived from Boston
    to take samples of your blood
        you were already oozing from below.
Somebody had carved his initials
    in your flank. Hunters of souvenirs
        had peeled off strips of your skin,
a membrane thin as paper.
    You were blistered and cracked by the sun.
        The gulls had been pecking at you.
The sound you made was a hoarse and fitful bleating.

What drew us to the magnet of your dying?
    You made a bond between us,
        the keepers of the nightfall watch,
who gathered in a ring around you,
    boozing in the bonfire light.
        Toward dawn we shared with you
your hour of desolation,
    the huge lingering passion
        of your unearthly outcry,
as you swung your blind head
    toward us and laboriously opened
        a bloodshot, glistening eye,
in which we swam with terror and recognition.

5

Voyager, chief of the pelagic world,
    you brought with you the myth
        of another country, dimly remembered,

STANLEY KUNITZ

where flying reptiles
  lumbered over the steaming marshes
    and trumpeting thunder lizards
wallowed in the reeds.
  While empires rose and fell on land,
    your nation breasted the open main,
rocked in the consoling rhythm
  of the tides. Which ancestor first plunged
    head-down through zones of colored twilight
to scour the bottom of the dark?
  You ranged the North Atlantic track
    from Port-of-Spain to Baffin Bay,
edging between the ice-floes
  through the fat of summer,
    lob-tailing, breaching, sounding,
grazing in the pastures of the sea
  on krill-rich orange plankton
    crackling with life.
You prowled down the continental shelf,
  guided by the sun and stars
    and the taste of alluvial silt
on your way southward
  to the warm lagoons,
    the tropic of desire,
where the lovers lie belly to belly
  in the rub and nuzzle of their sporting;
    and you turned, like a god in exile,
out of your wide primeval element,
  delivered to the mercy of time.
    Master of the whale-roads,
let the white wings of the gulls
  spread out their cover.
    You have become like us,
disgraced and mortal.

THE ABDUCTION

  Some things I do not profess
  to understand, perhaps
  not wanting to, including

STANLEY KUNITZ

whatever it was they did
with you or you with them
that timeless summer day
when you stumbled out of the wood,
distracted, with your white blouse torn
and a bloodstain on your skirt.
"Do you believe?" you asked.
Between us, through the years,
from bits, from broken clues,
we pieced enough together
to make the story real:
how you encountered on the path
a pack of sleek, grey hounds,
trailed by a dumbshow retinue
in leather shrouds; and how
you were led, through leafy ways,
into the presence of a royal stag,
flaming in his chestnut coat,
who kneeled on a swale of moss
before you; and how you were borne
aloft in triumph through the green,
stretched on his rack of budding horn,
till suddenly you found yourself alone
in a trampled clearing.

That was a long time ago,
almost another age, but even now,
when I hold you in my arms,
I wonder where you are.
Sometimes I wake to hear
the engines of the night thrumming
outside the east bay window
on the lawn spreading to the rose garden.
You lie beside me in elegant repose,
a hint of transport hovering on your lips,
indifferent to the harsh green flares
that swivel through the room,
searchlights controlled by unseen hands.
Out there is childhood country,
bleached faces peering in
with coals for eyes.
Our lives are spinning out
from world to world;

STANLEY KUNITZ

the shapes of things
are shifting in the wind.
What do we know
beyond the rapture and the dread?

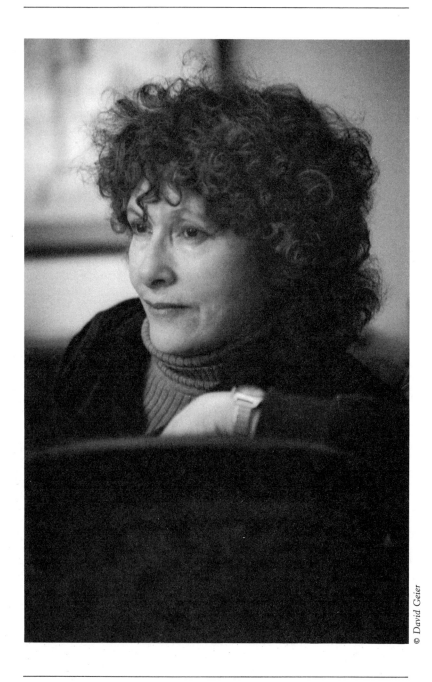

Denise Levertov

THE JACOB'S LADDER

The stairway is not
a thing of gleaming strands
a radiant evanescence
for angels' feet that only glance in their tread, and need not
touch the stone.

It is of stone.
A rosy stone that takes
a glowing tone of softness
only because behind it the sky is a doubtful, a doubting
night gray.

A stairway of sharp
angles, solidly built.
One sees that the angels must spring
down from one step to the next, giving a little
lift of the wings:

and a man climbing
must scrape his knees, and bring
the grip of his hands into play. The cut stone
consoles his groping feet. Wings brush past him.
The poem ascends.

HYPOCRITE WOMEN

Hypocrite women, how seldom we speak
of our own doubts, while dubiously
we mother man in his doubt!

And if at Mill Valley perched in the trees
the sweet rain drifting through western air
a white sweating bull of a poet told us

our cunts are ugly—why didn't we
admit we have thought so too? (And
what shame? They are not for the eye!)

No, they are dark and wrinkled and hairy,
caves of the Moon . . .   And when a
dark humming fills us, a

coldness towards life,
we are too much women to
own to such unwomanliness.

Whorishly with the psychopomp
we play and plead—and say
nothing of this later.   And our dreams,

with what frivolity we have pared them
like toenails, clipped them like ends of
split hair.

A PSALM PRAISING THE HAIR OF MAN'S BODY

My great brother
            Lord of the Song
wears the ruff of
            forest bear.

Husband, thy fleece of silk is black,
            a black adornment;
lies so close to the turns of the flesh,
burns my palm-stroke.

My great brother
            Lord of the Song
wears the ruff of
            forest bear.

Strong legs of our son are dusted
                    dark with hair.
Told of long roads,
we know his stride.

My great brother
                    Lord of the Song
wears the ruff of
                    forest bear.

Hair of man, man-hair, hair of
breast and groin, marking contour as
            silverpoint marks in cross-
            hatching, as river-
            grass on the woven current
            indicates ripple,
praise.

THE WINGS

Something hangs in back of me,
I can't see it, can't move it.

I know it's black,
a hump on my back.

It's heavy. You
can't see it.

What's in it? Don't tell me
you don't know. It's

what you told me about—
black

inimical power, cold
whirling out of it and

around me and
sweeping you flat.

But what if,
like a camel, it's

pure energy I store,
and carry humped and heavy?

Not black, not
that terror, stupidity

of cold rage; or black
only for being pent there?

What if released in air
it became a white

source of light, a fountain
of light? Could all that weight

be the power of flight?
Look inward: see me

with embryo wings, one
feathered in soot, the other

blazing ciliations of ember, pale
flare-pinions. Well—

could I go
on one wing,

the white one?

STEPPING WESTWARD

What is green in me
darkens, muscadine.

If woman is inconstant,
good, I am faithful to

ebb and flow, I fall
in season and now

is a time of ripening.
If her part

is to be true,
a north star,

good, I hold steady
in the black sky

and vanish by day,
yet burn there

in blue or above
quilts of cloud.

There is no savor
more sweet, more salt

than to be glad to be
what, woman,

and who, myself,
I am, a shadow

that grows longer as the sun
moves, drawn out

on a thread of wonder.
If I bear burdens

they begin to be remembered
as gifts, goods, a basket

of bread that hurts
my shoulders but closes me

in fragrance. I can
eat as I go.

THE ALTARS IN THE STREET

On June 17th, 1966, The New York Times reported that, as part of the Buddhist campaign of non-violent resistance, Viet-Namese children were building altars in the streets of Saigon and Hue, effectively jamming traffic.

Children begin at green dawn nimbly to build
topheavy altars, overweighted with prayers,
thronged each instant more densely

with almost-visible ancestors.
Where tanks have cracked the roadway
the frail altars shake; here a boy

with red stumps for hands steadies a corner,
here one adjusts with his crutch the holy base.
The vast silence of Buddha overtakes

and overrules the oncoming roar
of tragic life that fills alleys and avenues;
it blocks the way of pedicabs, police, convoys.

The hale and maimed together
hurry to construct for the Buddha
a dwelling at each intersection. Each altar

made from whatever stones, sticks, dreams, are at hand,
is a facet of one altar; by noon
the whole city in all its corruption,

all its shed blood the monsoon cannot wash away,
has become a temple,
fragile, insolent, absolute.

INTRUSION

After I had cut off my hands
and grown new ones

something my former hands had longed for
came and asked to be rocked.

After my plucked out eyes
had withered, and new ones grown

something my former eyes had wept for
came asking to be pitied.

August, 1969

THE POEM UNWRITTEN

For weeks the poem of your body,
of my hands upon your body
    stroking, sweeping, in the rite of
    worship, going
    their way of wonder down
    from neck-pulse to breast-hair to level
    belly to cock—
for weeks that poem, that prayer,
unwritten.

The poem unwritten, the act
left in the mind, undone. The years
a forest of giant stones, of fossil stumps,
blocking the altar.

1970

MAN ALONE

When the sun goes down, it writes
a secret name in its own blood for remembrance,
the excess of light
an ardor slow to cool:
and man has time to seek shelter.

But when the moon
gains the horizon, though it tarries
a moment, it vanishes
without trace of silver

and he is left with the stars only,
fierce and remote, and not revealing
the stones of the dark roads.

So it is with the gods,
and with the halfgods,
and with the heroes.

WAYS OF CONQUEST

You invaded my country by accident,
not knowing you had crossed the border.
Vines that grew there touched you.

You ran past them,
shaking raindrops off the leaves—you or the wind.
It was toward the hills you ran,
inland—

I invaded your country with all my
'passionate intensity,'
pontoons and parachutes of my blindness.
But living now in the suburbs of the capital
incognito,
          my will to take the heart of the city
          has dwindled. I love
its unsuspecting life,
its adolescents who come to tell me their dreams in the dusty park
among the rocks and benches,
I the stranger who will listen.
I love
the wild herons who return each year to the marshy outskirts.
What I invaded has
invaded me.

WEDDING-RING

My wedding-ring lies in a basket
as if at the bottom of a well.
Nothing will come to fish it back up
and onto my finger again.
              It lies
among keys to abandoned houses,
nails waiting to be needed and hammered
into some wall,
telephone numbers with no names attached,
idle paperclips.
              It can't be given away
for fear of bringing ill-luck.

> It can't be sold
> for the marriage was good in its own
> time, though that time is gone.
> Could some artificer
> beat into it bright stones, transform it
> into a dazzling circlet no one could take
> for solemn betrothal or to make promises
> living will not let them keep? Change it
> into a simple gift I could give in friendship?

PASSAGE

The spirit that walked upon the face of the waters
walks the meadow of long grass;
green shines to silver where the spirit passes.

Wind from the compass points, sun at meridian,
these are forms the spirit enters,
breath, *ruach*, light that is witness and by which we witness.

The grasses numberless, bowing and rising, silently
cry hosanna as the spirit
moves them and moves burnishing

over and again upon mountain pastures
a day of spring, a needle's eye
space and time are passing through like a swathe of silk.

SEEING FOR A MOMENT

I thought I was growing wings—
it was a cocoon.

I thought, now is the time to step
into the fire—
it was deep water.

Eschatology is a word I learned
as a child: the study of Last Things;

facing my mirror—no longer young,
    the news—always of death,
        the dogs—rising from sleep and clamoring
           and howling, howling,

nevertheless
I see for a moment
that's not it: it is
the First Things.

Word after word
floats through the glass.
Towards me.

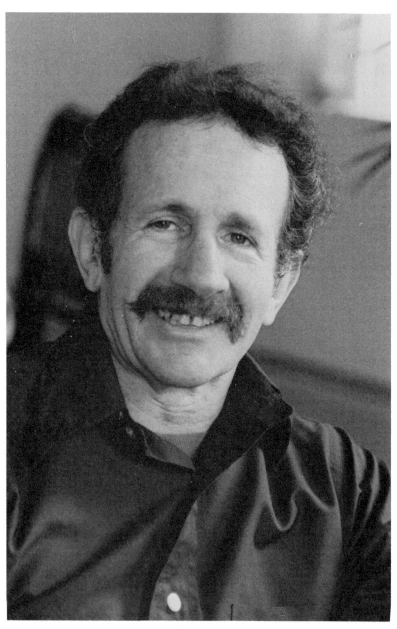

Philip Levine

ANIMALS ARE PASSING FROM OUR LIVES

It's wonderful how I jog
on four honed-down ivory toes
my massive buttocks slipping
like oiled parts with each light step.

I'm to market. I can smell
the sour, grooved block, I can smell
the blade that opens the hole
and the pudgy white fingers

that shake out the intestines
like a hankie. In my dreams
the snouts drool on the marble,
suffering children, suffering flies,

suffering the consumers
who won't meet their steady eyes
for fear they could see. The boy
who drives me along believes

that any moment I'll fall
on my side and drum my toes
like a typewriter or squeal
and shit like a new housewife

discovering television,
or that I'll turn like a beast
cleverly to hook his teeth
with my teeth. No. Not this pig.

PHILIP LEVINE

TO A CHILD TRAPPED IN A BARBER SHOP

You've gotten in through the transom
and you can't get out
till Monday morning or, worse,
till the cops come.

That six-year-old red face
calling for mama
is yours; it won't help you
because your case

is closed forever, hopeless.
So don't drink
the Lucky Tiger, don't
fill up on grease

because that makes it a lot worse,
that makes it a crime
against property and the state
and that costs time.

We've all been here before,
we took our turn
under the electric storm
of the vibrator

and stiffened our wills to meet
the close clippers
and heard the true blade mowing
back and forth

on a strip of dead skin,
and we stopped crying.
You think your life is over?
It's just begun.

COMING HOME

Detroit, 1968

A winter Tuesday, the city pouring fire,
Ford Rouge sulfurs the sun, Cadillac, Lincoln,
Chevy gray. The fat stacks
of breweries hold their tongues. Rags,
papers, hands, the stems of birches
dirtied with words.
                          Near the freeway
you stop and wonder what came off,
recall the snowstorm where you lost it all,
the wolverine, the northern bear, the wolf
caught out, ice and steel raining
from the foundries in a shower
of human breath. On sleds in the false sun
the new material rests. One brown child
stares and stares into your frozen eyes
until the lights change and you go
forward to work. The charred faces, the eyes
boarded up, the rubble of innards, the cry
of wet smoke hanging in your throat,
the twisted river stopped at the color of iron.
We burn this city every day.

THEY FEED THEY LION

Out of burlap sacks, out of bearing butter,
Out of black bean and wet slate bread,
Out of the acids of rage, the candor of tar,
Out of creosote, gasoline, drive shafts, wooden dollies,
They Lion grow.

PHILIP LEVINE

Out of the gray hills
Of industrial barns, out of rain, out of bus ride,
West Virginia to Kiss My Ass, out of buried aunties,
Mothers hardening like pounded stumps, out of stumps,
Out of the bones' need to sharpen and the muscles' to stretch,
They Lion grow.
                    Earth is eating trees, fence posts,
Gutted cars, earth is calling in her little ones,
"Come home, Come home!" From pig balls,
From the ferocity of pig driven to holiness,
From the furred ear and the full jowl come
The repose of the hung belly, from the purpose
They Lion grow.
                    From the sweet glues of the trotters
Come the sweet kinks of the fist, from the full flower
Of the hams the thorax of caves,
From "Bow Down" come "Rise Up,"
Come they Lion from the reeds of shovels,
The grained arm that pulls the hands,
They Lion grow.
                    From my five arms and all my hands,
From all my white sins forgiven, they feed,
From my car passing under the stars,
They Lion, from my children inherit,
From the oak turned to a wall, they Lion,
From they sack and they belly opened
And all that was hidden burning on the oil-stained earth
They feed they Lion and he comes.

ZAYDEE

Why does the sea burn? Why do the hills cry?
My grandfather opens a fresh box
of English Ovals, lights up, and lets the smoke
drift like clouds from his lips.

Where did my father go in my fifth autumn?
In the blind night of Detroit
on the front porch, Grandfather points up
at a constellation shaped like a cock and balls.

A tiny man, at 13 I outgrew his shirts.
I then beheld a closet of stolen suits,
a hive of elevator shoes, crisp hankies,
new bills in the cupboard, old in the wash.

I held the spotted hands that passed over
the breasts of airlines stewardesses,
that moved in the fields like a wind
stirring the long hairs of grain.

Where is the ocean? the flying fish?
the God who speaks from a cloud?
He carries a card table out under the moon
and plays gin rummy and cheats.

He took me up in his arms
when I couldn't walk and carried me
into the grove where the bees sang
and the stream paused forever.

He laughs in the movies, cries in the streets,
the judges in their gowns are monkeys,
the lawyers mice, a cop is a fat hand.
He holds up a strawberry and bites it.

He sings a song of freestone peaches
all in a box,
in the street he sings out Idaho potatoes
California, California oranges.

He sings the months in prison,
sings salt pouring down the sunlight,
shovelling all night in the stove factory
he sings the oven breathing fire.

Where did he go when his autumn came?
He sat before the steering wheel
of the black Packard, he turned the key,
pressed the starter, and he went.

The maples blazed golden and red
a moment and then were still,
the long streets were still and the snow
swirled where I lay down to rest.

PHILIP LEVINE

STARLIGHT

My father stands in the warm evening
on the porch of my first house.
I am four years old and growing tired.
I see his head among the stars,
the glow of his cigarette, redder
than the summer moon riding
low over the old neighborhood. We
are alone, and he asks me if I am happy.
"Are you happy?" I cannot answer.
I do not really understand the word,
and the voice, my father's voice, is not
his voice, but somehow thick and choked,
a voice I have not heard before, but
heard often since. He bends and passes
a thumb beneath each of my eyes.
The cigarette is gone, but I can smell
the tiredness that hangs on his breath.
He has found nothing, and he smiles
and holds my head with both his hands.
Then he lifts me to his shoulder,
and now I too am there among the stars,
as tall as he. Are you happy? I say.
He nods in answer, Yes! oh yes! oh yes!
And in that new voice he says nothing,
holding my head tight against his head,
his eyes closed up against the starlight,
as though those tiny blinking eyes
of light might find a tall, gaunt child
holding his child against the promises
of autumn, until the boy slept
never to waken in that world again.

YOU CAN HAVE IT

My brother comes home from work
and climbs the stairs to our room.
I can hear the bed groan and his shoes drop
one by one. You can have it, he says.

PHILIP LEVINE

The moonlight streams in the window
and his unshaven face is whitened
like the face of the moon. He will sleep
long after noon and waken to find me gone.

Thirty years will pass before I remember
that moment when suddenly I knew each man
has one brother who dies when he sleeps
and sleeps when he rises to face this life,

and that together they are only one man
sharing a heart that always labors, hands
yellowed and cracked, a mouth that gasps
for breath and asks, Am I gonna make it?

All night at the ice plant he had fed
the chute its silvery blocks, and then I
stacked cases of orange soda for the children
of Kentucky, one gray box-car at a time

with always two more waiting. We were twenty
for such a short time and always in
the wrong clothes, crusted with dirt
and sweat. I think now we were never twenty.

In 1948 in the city of Detroit, founded
by de la Mothe Cadillac for the distant purposes
of Henry Ford, no one wakened or died,
no one walked the streets or stoked a furnace,

for there was no such year, and now
that year has fallen off all the old newspapers,
calendars, doctors' appointments, bonds,
wedding certificates, drivers licenses.

The city slept. The snow turned to ice.
The ice to standing pools or rivers
racing in the gutters. Then bright grass rose
between the thousands of cracked squares,

and that grass died. I give you back 1948.
I give you all the years from then
to the coming one. Give me back the moon
with its frail light falling across a face.

Give me back my young brother, hard
and furious, with wide shoulders and a curse
for God and burning eyes that look upon
all creation and say, You can have it.

LET ME BEGIN AGAIN

Let me begin again as a speck
of dust caught in the night winds
sweeping out to sea. Let me begin
this time knowing the world is
salt water and dark clouds, the world
is grinding and sighing all night, and dawn
comes slowly and changes nothing. Let
me go back to land after a lifetime
of going nowhere. This time lodged
in the feathers of some scavenging gull
white above the black ship that docks
and broods upon the oily waters of
your harbor. This leaking freighter
has brought a hold full of hayforks
from Spain, great jeroboams of dark
Algerian wine and quill pens that can't
write English. The sailors have stumbled
off toward the bars or the bright houses.
The captain closes his log and falls asleep.
1/10'28. Tonight I shall enter my life
after being at sea for ages, quietly,
in a hospital named for an automobile.
The one child of millions of children
who has flown alone by the stars
above the black wastes of moonless waters
that stretched forever, who has turned
golden in the full sun of a new day.
A tiny wise child who this time will love
his life because it is like no other.

PHILIP LEVINE

THE HOUSE

This poem has a door, a locked door,
and windows drawn against the day,
but at night the lights come on, one
in each room, and the neighbors swear
they hear music and the sound of dancing.
These days the neighbors will swear
to anything. That is not why
the house is locked and no one goes
in or out all day long. That is because
this is a poem first and a house only
at night when everyone should be asleep.
The milkman tries to stop at dawn,
for he has three frosty white bottles
to place by the back door, but his horse
shakes his head back and forth, and so
he passes on his way. The papers pile
up on the front porch until the rain
turns them into gray earth, and they run
down the stairs and say nothing
to anyone. Who ever made this house
had no idea of beauty — it's all gray —
and no idea of what a happy family
needs on a day in spring when tulips
shout from their brown beds in the yard.
Back there the rows are thick with weeds,
stickers, choke grass, the place has gone
to soggy mulch, and the tools are hanging
unused from their hooks in the tool room.
Think of a marriage taking place at one
in the afternoon on a Sunday in June
in the stuffy front room. The dining table
is set for twenty, and the tall glasses
filled with red wine, the silver sparkling.
But no one is going in or out, not even
a priest in his long white skirt, or a boy
in pressed shorts, or a plumber with a fat bag.

John Logan

THREE MOVES

Three moves in six months and I remain
the same.
Two homes made two friends.
The third leaves me with myself again.
(We hardly speak.)
Here I am with tame ducks
and my neighbors' boats,
only this electric heat
against the April damp.
I have a friend named Frank—
The only one who ever dares to call
and ask me, "How's your soul?"
I hadn't thought about it for a while,
and was ashamed to say I didn't know.
I have no priest for now.
Who
will forgive me then. Will you?
Tame birds and my neighbors' boats.
The ducks honk about the floats . . .
They walk dead drunk onto the land and grounds,
iridescent blue and black and green and brown.
They live on swill
our aged houseboats spill.
But still they are beautiful.
Look! The duck with its unlikely beak
has stopped to pick
and pull
at the potted daffodil.
Then again they sway home
to dream
bright gardens of fish in the early night.
Oh these ducks are all right.
They will survive.
But I am sorry I do not often see them climb.
Poor sons-a-bitching ducks.

JOHN LOGAN

You're all fucked up.
What do you do that for?
Why don't you hover near the sun anymore?
Afraid you'll melt?
These foolish ducks lack a sense of guilt,
and so all their multi-thousand-mile range
is too short for the hope of change.

Seattle, April 1965

TO A YOUNG POET WHO FLED

Your cries make us afraid, but we love your delicious music!

Kierkegaard

So you said you'd go home to work on your father's farm.
We've talked of how it is the poet alone can touch
with words, but I would touch you with my hand, my lost son,
to say good-bye again. You left some work, and have gone.
You don't know what you mean. Oh, not to me as a son,
for I have others. Perhaps too many. I cannot
answer all the letters. If I seem to brag, I add
I know how to shatter an image of the father
(twice have tried to end the yearning of an orphan son,
but opened up in him, and in me, another wound).
No—I say this: you don't know the reason of your gift.
It's not the suffering. Others have that. The gift of tears
is the hope of saints, Monica again and Austin.
I mean the gift of the structure of a poet's jaw,
which makes the mask that's cut out of the flesh of his face
a megaphone—as with the goat clad Greeks—to ampli-
fy the light gestures of his soul toward the high stone seats.
The magic of the mouth that can melt to tears the rock
of hearts. I mean the wand of tongues that charms the exile
of listeners into a bond of brothers, breaking
down the lines of lead that separate a man from a
man, and the husbands from their wives, in these old, burned glass
panels of our lives. The poet's jaw has its tongue ripped

as Philomel, its lips split (and kissed beside the grave),
the jawbone patched and cracked with fists and then with the salve
of his fellows. If they make him bellow, like a slave
cooked inside the ancient, brass bull, still that small machine
inside its throat makes music for an emperor's guest
out of his cries. Thus his curse: the poet cannot weep
but with a public and musical grief, and he laughs
with the joys of others. Yet, when the lean blessings come,
they are sweet, and great. My son, I could not make your choice.
Let me take your hand. I am too old or young to say,
"I'd rather be a swineherd in the hut, understood
by swine, than be a poet misunderstood by men."

SPRING OF THE THIEF

But if I look the ice is gone from the lake
and the altered air
no longer fills with the small
terrible bodies of the snow.
Only once these late winter weeks
the dying flakes
fell instead as manna or as wedding rice
blooming in the light
about the bronze Christ
and the thieves. There these three
still hang, more than man-
sized and heavier than life
on a hill over the lake
where I walk
this Third Sunday of Lent.
I come from Mass
melancholy at its ancient story
of the unclean ghost
a man thought he'd lost.
It came back into his well-swept house
and at the final state that man
was worse than he began.
Yet again today

there is the faintest edge of green
to trees about St. Joseph's Lake.
Ah God if our confessions show contempt
because we let them free us of our guilt
to sin again
forgive us still . . . before the leaves . . .
before the leaves have formed
you can glimpse the Christ and Thieves
on top of the hill. One of them was saved.
That day the snow had seemed to drop like grace
upon the four of us,
or like the peace of intercourse,
suddenly I wanted to confess—
or simply talk.
I paid a visit to the mammoth Sacred Heart
Church, and found it shut.
Who locked him out or in?
The name of God is changing in our time.
What is his winter name?
Where was his winter home.
Oh I've kept my love to myself before.
Even those ducks weave down the shore
together, drunk with hope
for the April water. One spring festival
near here I stripped and strolled
through a rain filled field.
Spread eagled on the soaking earth
I let the rain
move its audible little hands
gently on my skin . . . let the dark rain
raise up my love.
But why? I was alone
and no one saw how ardent I grew.
And when I rolled naked in the snow one night
as St. Francis with his Brother Ass
or a hard bodied Finn
I was alone. Underneath
the howling January moon
I knelt and dug my fist
full of the cold winter sand

JOHN LOGAN

and rubbed and
hid my manhood under it.
Washed up at some ancient or half-heroic shore
I was ashamed that I was naked there.
Before Nausicaä and the saints. Before myself.
But who took off my coat? Who put it on?
Who drove me home?
Blessed be sin if it teaches men shame.
Yet because of it we cannot talk
and I am separated from myself.
So what is all this reveling in snow and rain?
Or in the summer sun when the heavy gold
body weeps with joy or grief or love?
When we speak of God, is it God we speak of?
Perhaps his winter home
is in that field where I rolled or ran . . .
this hill where once the snow
fell serene as rain.
Oh I have walked around the lake
when I was not alone—
sometimes with my wife have seen these swans
dip down their necks
graceful as a girl, showering white and wet!
I've seen their heads delicately turn.
Have gone sailing with my quiet, older son.
And once on a morning walk
a student who had just come back
in fall found a perfect hickory shell
among the bronze and red
leaves and purple flowers of the time
and put its white bread into my hand.
Ekelöf said there is a freshness
nothing can destroy in us—
not even we ourselves.
Perhaps that
Freshness is the changed name of God.
Where all the monsters also hide
I bear him in the ocean of my blood
and in the pulp of my enormous head.
He lives beneath the unkempt potter's grass

of my belly and chest.
I feel his terrible, aged heart
moving under mine . . . can see the shadows
of the gorgeous light
that plays at the edges of his giant eye . . .
or tell the faint press and hum
of his eternal pool of sperm.
Like sandalwood! *Like sandalwood*
the righteous man
perfumes the axe that falls on him.
The cords of elm, of cedar oak and pine
will pile again in fall.
The ribs and pockets of the barns will swell.
Winds and fires in the field rage
and again burn out each
of the ancient roots.
Again at last the late November snow
will fill those fields, change this hill,
throw these figures in relief
and raining on them
will transform
the bronze Christ's brow and cheek,
the white face and thigh of the thief.

March–April, 1962

SUZANNE

You make us want to stay alive, Suzanne,
the way you turn

your blonde head.
The way you curve your slim hand

toward your breast.
When you drew your legs

up, sitting by the fire,
and let your bronze hair

stream about your knees
I could see the grief

of the girl in your eyes.
It touched the high,

formal bones of your face.
Once I heard it in your lovely voice

when you sang—
the terrible time of being young.

Yet you bring us joy with your
self, Suzanne, wherever you are.

And once, although I wasn't here,
you left three roses on my stair.

One party night when you were high
you fled barefoot down the hall,

the fountain of your laughter
showering through the air.

"Chartreuse," you chanted
(the liqueur you always wanted),

"I have yellow chartreuse hair!"
Oh it was a great affair.

You were the most exciting person there.
Yesterday when I wasn't here

again,
you brought a blue, porcelain

egg to me—
colored beautifully

for the Russian Easter.
Since then, I have wanted to be your lover,

but I have only touched your shoulder
and let my fingers brush your hair,

because you left three roses on my stair.

LOVE POEM

Last night you would not come,
and you have been gone so long.
I yearn to find you in my aging, earthen arms
again (your alchemy can change my clay to skin).
I long to turn and watch again
from my half-hidden place
the lost, beautiful slopes and fallings of your face,
the black, rich leaf of each eyelash,
fresh, beach-brightened stones of your teeth.
I want to listen as you breathe yourself to sleep
(for by our human art we mime
the sleeper till we dream).
I want to smell the dark
herb gardens of your hair—touch the thin shock
that drifts over your high brow when
you rinse it clean,
for it is so fine.
I want to hear the light,
long wind of your sigh.
But again tonight I know you will not come.
I will never feel again
your gentle, sleeping calm
from which I took
so much strength, so much of my human heart.
Because the last time
I reached to you
as you sat upon the bed
and talked, you caught both my hands
in yours and crossed them gently on my breast.
I died mimicking the dead.

from POEM IN PROGRESS

Second Prelude. Reality in Albuquerque: The Son

Passing through Albuquerque where I'd read poetry,
I find myself beside a quite young drinking buddy.
Black-haired and bright-eyed Chicano kid, he wants a coke
with three cherries in it. He gets that and then asks me,
as folks next to each other in bars are apt to talk,
why there are no cherries in *my* glass.
"Because," I say, knowing I sound absolutely
absurd, "Screwdrivers just never *have* cherries in them."
Surreal, I think. What's this kid doing in here at ten
o'clock A.M. anyway. "No school today," he says.
"Teacher's convention." He is
only seven and his father is tending the bar.
He asks me where all my kids are.
"In New York where I live," I lie.
Then tell the truth, that I am flying back there tonight.
"And your wife?" Third degree, I think. Well, part of bar talk.
"Why, New York too," I lie again.
How the hell can I tell this kid
I hardly ever see my sons
because they are three thousand miles
away from me (and then some). Perhaps *you* understand
what I mean—but him? Both of us
in the bar at ten A.M. He walks to the juke box
with a quarter given by his father, then looks back,
admits he cannot read well. So
we select together, and agree on two pieces,
playing first that morning song, "Bridge Over Troubled Water."

POEM FOR MY BROTHER

Blue's my older brother's color. Mine is brown, you see.
So today I bought this ring
of gold and lapis lazuli flecked with a bright bronze.

His blue is the light hue of his eyes. Brown's the color
of our dead mother's long hair,
which fell so beautifully about her young shoulders
in the picture, and of my own eyes (I can't tell hers).
I loved my brother, but never quite knew what to think.
For example, he would beat
me up as soon as the folks
left the house, and I would cry big, loud feminine tears.
He was good at sports and played football, and so instead
I was in the marching band.
My brother stole rubbers from the store and smoked cigars
and pipes, which made me sick. But
once we swam together in
the Nishnabotna river
near home, naked, our blue overalls piled together
by the water, their copper
buttons like the bronze glints in my ring. I remember
once when I was very young
I looked deep into a pool
of blue water—we had no mirror—and I was so
amazed I looked over my shoulder, for I did not
imagine it was me, caught
in that cerulean sky.
Thinking it was someone other, I tell you I con-
fused myself with my brother!
Nothing goes with gold, but I can see in this rich blue
stone the meeting of our clothes like the touching of hands
when he taught me to hold my fishing pole well and wound
up the reel for me. You know
blue's the last of the primary colors to be named.
Why, some primitive societies still have no word
for it except "dark." It's associated with black:
in the night brother and I
would play at games that neither of us could understand.
But this is not a confession; it is a question.
We've moved apart and don't write,
and our children don't even know their own cousin!
So, I would have you know I
want this ring to *engage* us
in reconciliation.
Blue's the color of the heart.
I won't live forever. Is it too late now to be

a brother to my brother?
Let the golden snake bend round
again to touch itself and
all at once burst into azure!

AVOCADO

for Robert Bly

It is a green globe like a vegetable light bulb
with a stem to meet either soil or small living tree;
it is mottled like an old man's face or is wizened
like the enormous head of a fetus. Now the stem
has come away from a navel.
It has the stolid heft of a stone. The smell seeps up
and leads the mind far away to the earth's ancient cave.
Its taste is also pungent dirt with a kind of bark
that is quite difficult to chew:
here is the small tomb of woman.
Mother smells its fresh soil even with her dead sense. She feels
its husk. Her body inside is the soft flesh of fruit,
and her heart this oval green core.
Her grief, her anger is that she
no longer has life, but the stuff of her breathes a res-
idue that has remained in earth
and in the minds of the children.
Oh, now I know her skin sighs green
as this fluted fruit: her spirit
is the taste of it, transmuted.

Honolulu
January 30, 1981

HAPPENING ON AEGINA

The beach on Aegina is a bit tawdry, although
the island lies gorgeous beyond.
Rusted cans, a blue abandoned bic and overturned

boats, paint peeling, lying dead on the beach in the sun.
My small friend Al wades gingerly
among the rocks, legs half cut off
by water. His black socks look despairing in their shoes
left behind. What brings this scene alive is a sailboat
quite far out and glowing with a strange brightness in the light
and the goddess on the beach—Daphne, Al's fifteen year old
daughter lying in the sun
in a blue bikini, her luminescent body
oiled, narrow hips, narrow bosom.
Her slim body brings to mind the one pillar still standing
in the temple to Apollo
on this ancient isle of Aegina.
Except for long black hair and eyebrows, unmistakably
a girl's, she's androgynous. Suddenly I feel she has been left behind
by that mysterious boat, its diaphanous sail
like wings just disappearing in the long twilight sun.

June 22 – 23 1982
Aegina, Greece

BELIEVE IT

There is a two-headed goat, a four-winged chicken
and a sad lamb with seven legs
whose complicated little life was spent in Hopland,
California. I saw the man with doubled eyes
who seemed to watch in me my doubts about my spirit.
Will it snag upon this aging flesh?

There is a strawberry that grew
out of a carrot plant, a blade
of grass that lanced through a thick rock,
a cornstalk nineteen-feet-two-inches tall grown by George
Osborne of Silome, Arkansas.
There is something grotesque growing in me I cannot tell.

It has been waxing, burgeoning, for a long time.
It weighs me down like the chains of the man of Lahore
who began collecting links on his naked body

until he crawled around the town carrying the last
thirteen years of his life six-hundred-seventy pounds.
Each link or each lump in me is an offense against love.

I want my own lit candle lamp buried in my skull
like the Lighthouse Man of Chungking,
who could lead the travelers home.
Well, I am still a traveler and I don't know where
I live. If my home is here, inside my breast,
light it up! And I will invite you in as my first guest.

for Tina Logan
After visiting the Believe It or Not Museum
with her in San Francisco
—1980

Robert Lowell

COLLOQUY IN BLACK ROCK

Here the jack-hammer jabs into the ocean;
My heart, you race and stagger and demand
More blood-gangs for your nigger-brass percussions,
Till I, the stunned machine of your devotion,
Clanging upon this cymbal of a hand,
Am rattled screw and footloose. All discussions

End in the mud-flat detritus of death.
My heart, beat faster, faster. In Black Mud
Hungarian workmen give their blood
For the martyre Stephen, who was stoned to death.

Black Mud, a name to conjure with: O mud
For watermelons gutted to the crust,
Mud for the mole-tide harbor, mud for mouse,
Mud for the armored Diesel fishing tubs that thud
A year and a day to wind and tide; the dust
Is on this skipping heart that shakes my house,

House of our Savior who was hanged till death.
My heart, beat faster, faster. In Black Mud
Stephen the martyre was broken down to blood:
Our ransom is the rubble of his death.

Christ walks on the black water. In Black Mud
Darts the kingfisher. On Corpus Christi, heart,
Over the drum-beat of St. Stephen's choir
I hear him, *Stupor Mundi,* and the mud
Flies from his hunching wings and beak—my heart,
The blue kingfisher dives on you in fire.

ROBERT LOWELL

CHRISTMAS EVE UNDER HOOKER'S STATUE

Tonight a blackout. Twenty years ago
I hung my stocking on the tree, and hell's
Serpent entwined the apple in the toe
To sting the child with knowledge. Hooker's heels
Kicking at nothing in the shifting snow,
A cannon and a cairn of cannon balls
Rusting before the blackened Statehouse, know
How the long horn of plenty broke like glass
In Hooker's gauntlets. Once I came from Mass;

Now storm-clouds shelter Christmas, once again
Mars meets his fruitless star with open arms,
His heavy saber flashes with the rime,
The war-god's bronzed and empty forehead forms
Anonymous machinery from raw men;
The cannon on the Common cannot stun
The blundering butcher as he rides on Time—
The barrel clinks with holly. I am cold:
I ask for bread, my father gives me mould;

His stocking is full of stones. Santa in red
Is crowned with wizened berries. Man of war,
Where is the summer's garden? In its bed
The ancient speckled serpent will appear,
And black-eyed susan with her frizzled head.
When Chancellorsville mowed down the volunteer,
"All wars are boyish," Herman Melville said;
But we are old, our fields are running wild:
Till Christ again turn wanderer and child.

MEMORIES OF WEST STREET AND LEPKE

Only teaching on Tuesdays, book-worming
in pajamas fresh from the washer each morning,
I hog a whole house on Boston's
"hardly passionate Marlborough Street,"
where even the man
scavenging filth in the back alley trash cans,
has two children, a beach wagon, a helpmate,

and is a "young Republican."
I have a nine months' daughter,
young enough to be my granddaughter.
Like the sun she rises in her flame-flamingo infants' wear.

These are the tranquillized *Fifties*,
and I am forty. Ought I to regret my seedtime?
I was a fire-breathing Catholic C.O.,
and made my manic statement,
telling off the state and president, and then
sat waiting sentence in the bull pen
beside a Negro boy with curlicues
of marijuana in his hair.

Given a year,
I walked on the roof of the West Street Jail, a short
enclosure like my school soccer court,
and saw the Hudson River once a day
through sooty clothesline entanglements
and bleaching khaki tenements.
Strolling, I yammered metaphysics with Abramowitz,
a jaundice-yellow ("it's really tan")
and fly-weight pacifist,
so vegetarian,
he wore rope shoes and preferred fallen fruit.
He tried to convert Bioff and Brown,
the Hollywood pimps, to his diet.
Hairy, muscular, suburban,
wearing chocolate double-breasted suits,
they blew their tops and beat him black and blue.

I was so out of things, I'd never heard
of the Jehovah's Witnesses.
"Are you a C.O.?" I asked a fellow jailbird.
"No," he answered, "I'm a J.W."
He taught me the "hospital tuck,"
and pointed out the T-shirted back
of *Murder Incorporated's* Czar Lepke,
there piling towels on a rack,
or dawdling off to his little segregated cell full
of things forbidden the common man:
a portable radio, a dresser, two toy American
flags tied together with a ribbon of Easter palm.
Flabby, bald, lobotomized,

he drifted in a sheepish calm,
where no agonizing reappraisal
jarred his concentration on the electric chair—
hanging like an oasis in his air
of lost connections. . . .

MAN AND WIFE

Tamed by *Miltown*, we lie on Mother's bed;
the rising sun in war paint dyes us red;
in broad daylight her gilded bed-posts shine,
abandoned, almost Dionysian.
At last the trees are green on Marlborough Street,
blossoms on our magnolia ignite
the morning with their murderous five days' white.
All night I've held your hand,
as if you had
a fourth time faced the kingdom of the mad—
its hackneyed speech, its homicidal eye—
and dragged me home alive. . . . Oh my *Petite,*
clearest of all God's creatures, still all air and nerve:
you were in your twenties, and I,
once hand on glass
and heart in mouth,
outdrank the Rahvs in the heat
of Greenwich Village, fainting at your feet—
too boiled and shy
and poker-faced to make a pass,
while the shrill verve
of your invective scorched the traditional South.

Now twelve years later, you turn your back.
Sleepless, you hold
your pillow to your hollows like a child;
your old-fashioned tirade—
loving, rapid, merciless—
breaks like the Atlantic Ocean on my head.

ROBERT LOWELL

"TO SPEAK OF WOE THAT IS IN MARRIAGE"

"It is the future generation that presses into being by means of these exuberant feelings and supersensible soap bubbles of ours."

Schopenhauer

"The hot night makes us keep our bedroom windows open.
Our magnolia blossoms. Life begins to happen.
My hopped up husband drops his home disputes,
and hits the streets to cruise for prostitutes,
free-lancing out along the razor's edge.
This screwball might kill his wife, then take the pledge.
Oh the monotonous meanness of his lust. . . .
It's the injustice . . . he is so unjust—
whiskey-blind, swaggering home at five.
My only thought is how to keep alive.
What makes him tick? Each night now I tie
ten dollars and his car key to my thigh. . . .
Gored by the climacteric of his want,
he stalls above me like an elephant."

SKUNK HOUR

(for Elizabeth Bishop)

Nautilus Island's hermit
heiress still lives through winter in her Spartan cottage;
her sheep still graze above the sea.
Her son's a bishop. Her farmer
is first selectman in our village;
she's in her dotage.

Thirsting for
the hierarchic privacy
of Queen Victoria's century,
she buys up all
the eyesores facing her shore,
and lets them fall.

ROBERT LOWELL

The season's ill—
we've lost our summer millionaire,
who seemed to leap from an L. L. Bean
catalogue. His nine-knot yawl
was auctioned off to lobstermen.
A red fox stain covers Blue Hill.

And now our fairy
decorator brightens his shop for fall;
his fishnet's filled with orange cork,
orange, his cobbler's bench and awl;
there is no money in his work,
he'd rather marry.

One dark night,
my Tudor Ford climbed the hill's skull;
I watched for love-cars. Lights turned down,
they lay together, hull to hull,
where the graveyard shelves on the town. . . .
My mind's not right.

A car radio bleats,
"Love, O careless Love. . . ." I hear
my ill-spirit sob in each blood cell,
as if my hand were at its throat. . . .
I myself am hell;
nobody's here—

only skunks, that search
in the moonlight for a bite to eat.
They march on their soles up Main Street:
white stripes, moonstruck eyes' red fire
under the chalk-dry and spar spire
of the Trinitarian Church.

I stand on top
of our back steps and breathe the rich air—
a mother skunk with her column of kittens swills the garbage pail.
She jabs her wedge-head in a cup
of sour cream, drops her ostrich tail,
and will not scare.

ROBERT LOWELL

EYE AND TOOTH

My whole eye was sunset red,
the old cut cornea throbbed,
I saw things darkly,
as through an unwashed goldfish globe.

I lay all day on my bed.
I chain-smoked through the night,
learning to flinch
at the flash of the matchlight.

Outside, the summer rain,
a simmer of rot and renewal,
fell in pinpricks.
Even new life is fuel.

My eyes throb.
Nothing can dislodge
the house with my first tooth
noosed in a knot to the doorknob.

Nothing can dislodge
the triangular blotch
of rot on the red roof,
a cedar hedge, or the shade of a hedge.

No ease from the eye
of the sharp-skinned hawk in the birdbook there,
with reddish-brown buffalo hair
on its shanks, one ascetic talon

clasping the abstract imperial sky.
It says:
an eye for an eye,
a tooth for a tooth.

No ease for the boy at the keyhole,
his telescope,
when the women's white bodies flashed
in the bathroom. Young, my eyes began to fail.

ROBERT LOWELL

Nothing! No oil
for the eye, nothing to pour
on those waters or flames.
I am tired. Everyone's tired of my turmoil.

HISTORY

History has to live with what was here,
clutching and close to fumbling all we had—
it is so dull and gruesome how we die,
unlike writing, life never finishes.
Abel was finished; death is not remote,
a flash-in-the-pan electrifies the skeptic,
his cows crowding like skulls against high-voltage wire,
his baby crying all night like a new machine.
As in our Bibles, white-faced, predatory,
the beautiful, mist-drunken hunter's moon ascends—
a child could give it a face: two holes, two holes,
my eyes, my mouth, between them a skull's no-nose—
O there's a terrifying innocence in my face
drenched with the silver salvage of the mornfrost.

HOMECOMING

What was is . . . since 1930;
the boys in my old gang
are senior partners. They start up
bald like baby birds
to embrace retirement.

At the altar of surrender,
I met you
in the hour of credulity.
How your misfortune came out clearly
to us at twenty.

At the gingerbread casino,
how innocent the nights we made it
on our *Vesuvio* martinis
with no vermouth but vodka
to sweeten the dry gin—

the lash across my face
that night we adored . . .
soon every night and all,
when your sweet, amorous
repetition changed.

EPILOGUE

Those blessèd structures, plot and rhyme—
why are they no help to me now
I want to make
something imagined, not recalled?
I hear the noise of my own voice:
*The painter's vision is not a lens,
it trembles to caress the light.*
But sometimes everything I write
with the threadbare art of my eye
seems a snapshot,
lurid, rapid, garish, grouped,
heightened from life,
yet paralyzed by fact.
All's misalliance.
Yet why not say what happened?
Pray for the grace of accuracy
Vermeer gave to the sun's illumination
stealing like the tide across a map
to his girl solid with yearning.
We are poor passing facts,
warned by that to give
each figure in the photograph
his living name.

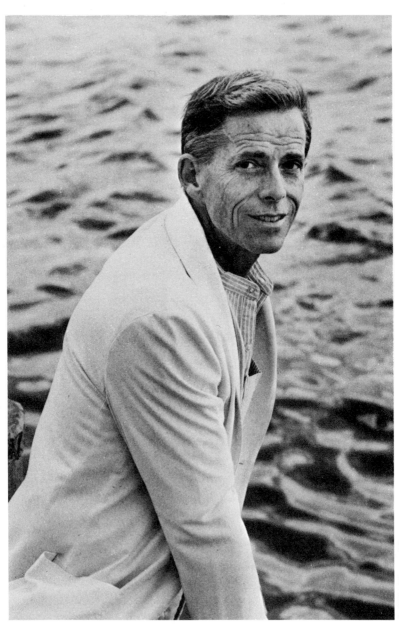

James Merrill

ANGEL

Above my desk, whirring and self-important
(Though not much larger than a hummingbird)
In finely woven robes, school of Van Eyck,
Hovers an evidently angelic visitor.
He points one index finger out the window
At winter snatching to its heart,
To crystal vacancy, the misty
Exhalations of houses and of people running home
From the cold sun pounding on the sea;
While with the other hand
He indicates the piano
Where the Sarabande No. 1 lies open
At a passage I shall never master
But which has already, and effortlessly mastered me.
He drops his jaw as if to say, or sing,
'Between the world God made
And this music of Satie,
Each glimpsed through veils, but whole,
Radiant and willed,
Demanding praise, demanding surrender,
How can you sit there with your notebook?
What do you think you are doing?'
However he says nothing—wisely: I could mention
Flaws in God's world, or Satie's; and for that matter
How did he come by *his* taste for Satie?
Half to tease him, I turn back to my page,
Its phrases thus far clotted, unconnected.
The tiny angel shakes his head.
There is no smile on his round, hairless face.
He does not want even these few lines written.

JAMES MERRILL

AFTER GREECE

Light into the olive entered
And was oil. Rain made the huge pale stones
Shine from within. The moon turned his hair white
Who next stepped from between the columns,
Shielding his eyes. All through
The countryside were old ideas
Found lying open to the elements.
Of the gods' houses only
A minor premise here and there
Would be balancing the heaven of fixed stars
Upon a Doric capital. The rest
Lay spilled, their fluted drums half sunk in cyclamen
Or deep in water's biting clarity
Which just barely upheld me
The next week, when I sailed for home.
But where is home—these walls?
These limbs? The very spaniel underfoot
Races in sleep, toward what?
It is autumn. I did not invite
Those guests, windy and brittle, who drink my liquor.
Returning from a walk I find
The bottles filled with spleen, my room itself
Smeared by reflection on to the far hemlocks.
I some days flee in dream
Back to the exposed porch of the maidens
Only to find my great-great-grandmothers
Erect there, peering
Into a globe of red Bohemian glass.
As it swells and sinks, I call up
Graces, Furies, Fates, removed
To my country's warm, lit halls, with rivets forced
Through draper, and nothing left to bear.
They seem anxious to know
What holds up heaven nowadays.
I start explaining how in that vast fire
Were other irons—well, Art, Public Spirit,
Ignorance, Economics, Love of Self,
Hatred of Self, a hundred more,
Each burning to be felt, each dedicated
To sparing us the worst; how I distrust them
As I should have done those ladies; how I want

JAMES MERRILL

Essentials: salt, wine, olive, the light, the scream—
No! I have scarcely named you,
And look, in a flash you stand full-grown before me,
Row upon row, Essentials,
Dressed like your sister caryatids
Or tombstone angels jealous of their dead,
With undulant coiffures, lips weathered, cracked by grime,
And faultless eyes gone blank beneath the immense
Zinc and gunmetal northern sky. . . .
Stay then. Perhaps the system
Calls for spirits. This first glass I down
To the last time
I ate and drank in that old world. May I
Also survive its meanings, and my own.

A DEDICATION

Hans, there are moments when the whole mind
Resolves into a pair of brimming eyes, or lips
Parting to drink from the deep spring of a death
That freshness they do not yet need to understand.
These are the moments, if ever, an angel steps
Into the mind, as kings into the dress
Of a poor goatherd, for their acts of charity.
There are moments when speech is but a mouth pressed
Lightly and humbly against the angel's hand.

THE OCTOPUS

There are many monsters that a glassen surface
Restrains. And none more sinister
Than vision asleep in the eye's tight translucence.
Rarely it seeks now to unloose
Its diamonds. Having divined how drab a prison
The purest mortal tissue is,
Rarely it wakes. Unless, coaxed out by lusters
Extraordinary, like the octopus
From the gloom of its tank half-swimming half-drifting

Toward anything fair, a handkerchief
Or child's face dreaming near the glass, the writher
Advances in a godlike wreath
Of its own wrath. Chilled by such fragile reeling
A hundred blows of a boot-heel
Shall not quell, the dreamer wakes and hungers.
Percussive pulses, drum or gong,
Build in his skull their loud entrancement,
Volutions of a Hindu dance.
His hands move clumsily in the first conventional
Gestures of assent.
He is willing to undergo the volition and fervor
Of many fleshlike arms, observe
These in their holiness of indirection
Destroy, adore, evolve, reject—
Till on glass rigid with his own seizure
At length the sucking jewels freeze.

LABORATORY POEM

Charles used to watch Naomi, taking heart
And a steel saw, open up turtles, live.
While she swore they felt nothing, he would gag
At blood, at the blind twitching, even after
The murky dawn of entrails cleared, revealing
Contours he knew, egg-yellows like lamps paling.

Well then. She carried off the beating heart
To the kymograph and rigged it there, a rag
In fitful wind, now made to strain, now stopped
By her solutions tonic or malign
Alternately in which it would be steeped.
What the heart bore, she noted on a chart,

For work did not stop only with the heart.
He thought of certain human hearts, their climb
Through violence into exquisite disciplines
Of which, as it now appeared, they all expired.
Soon she would fetch another and start over,
Easy in the presence of her lover.

JAMES MERRILL

CHARLES ON FIRE

Another evening we sprawled about discussing
Appearances. And it was the consensus
That while uncommon physical good looks
Continued to launch one, as before, in life
(Among its vaporous eddies and false calms),
Still, as one of us said into his beard,
"Without your intellectual and spiritual
Values, man, you are sunk." No one but squared
The shoulders of his own unloveliness.
Long-suffering Charles, having cooked and served the meal,
Now brought out little tumblers finely etched
He filled with amber liquor and then passed.
"Say," said the same young man, "in Paris, France,
They do it this way"—bounding to his feet
And touching a lit match to our host's full glass.
A blue flame, gentle, beautiful, came, went
Above the surface. In a hush that fell
We heard the vessel crack. The contents drained
As who should step down from a crystal coach.
Steward of spirits, Charles's glistening hand
All at once gloved itself in eeriness.
The moment passed. He made two quick sweeps and
Was flesh again. "It couldn't matter less,"
He said, but with a shocked, unconscious glance
Into the mirror. Finding nothing changed,
He filled a fresh glass and sank down among us.

from UP AND DOWN

The Emerald

Hearing that on Sunday I would leave,
My mother asked if we might drive downtown.
Why certainly—off with my dressing gown!
The weather had turned fair. We were alive.

Only the gentle General she married
Late, for both an old way out of harm's,

Fought for breath, surrendered in her arms,
With military honors now lay buried.

That week the arcana of his medicine chest
Had been disposed of, and his clothes. Gold belt
Buckle and the letter from President Roosevelt
Went to an unknown grandchild in the West.

Downtown, his widow raised her parasol
Against the Lenten sun's not yet detectable
Malignant atomies which an electric needle
Unfreckles from her soft white skin each fall.

Hence too her chiffon scarf, pale violet,
And spangle-paste dark glasses. Each spring we number
The new dead. Above ground, who can remember
Her as she once was? Even I forget,

Fail to attend her, seem impervious . . .
Meanwhile we have made through a dense shimmy
Of parked cars burnished by the midday chamois
For Mutual Trust. Here cool gloom welcomes us,

And all, director, guard, quite palpably
Adore her. Spinster tellers one by one
Darting from cages, sniffling to meet her son,
Think of her having a son—! She holds the key

Whereby palatial bronze gates shut like jaws
On our descent into this inmost vault.
The keeper bends his baldness to consult,
Brings a tin box painted mud-brown, withdraws.

She opens it. Security. Will. Deed.
Rummages further. Rustle of tissue, a sprung
Lid. Her face gone queerly lit, fair, young,
Like faces of our dear ones who have died.

No rhinestone now, no dilute amethyst,
But of the first water, linking star to pang,
Teardrop to fire, my father's kisses hang
In lipless concentration round her wrist.

JAMES MERRILL

Gray are these temple-drummers who once more
Would rouse her, girl-bride jeweled in his grave.
Instead, she next picks out a ring. "He gave
Me this when you were born. Here, take it for—

For when you marry. For your bride. It's yours."
A den of greenest light, it grows, shrinks, glows,
Hermetic stanza bedded in the prose
Of the last thirty semiprecious years.

I do not tell her, it would sound theatrical,
Indeed this green room's mine, my very life.
We are each other's; there will be no wife;
The little feet that patter here are metrical.

But onto her worn knuckle slip the ring.
Wear it for me, I silently entreat,
Until—until the time comes. Our eyes meet.
The world beneath the world is brightening.

THE VICTOR DOG

for Elizabeth Bishop

Bix to Buxtehude to Boulez,
The little white dog on the Victor label
Listens long and hard as he is able.
It's all in a day's work, whatever plays.

From judgment, it would seem, he has refrained.
He even listens earnestly to Bloch,
Then builds a church upon our acid rock.
He's man's—no—he's the Leiermann's best friend,

Or would be if hearing and listening were the same.
Does he hear? I fancy he rather smells
Those lemon-gold arpeggios in Ravel's
'Les jets d'eau du palais de ceux qui s'aiment.'

He ponders the Schumann Concerto's tall willow hit
By lightning, and stays put. When he surmises
Through one of Bach's eternal boxwood mazes
The oboe pungent as a bitch in heat,

Or when the calypso decants its raw bay rum
Or the moon in *Wozzeck* reddens ripe for murder,
He doesn't sneeze or howl; just listens harder.
Adamant needles bear down on him from

Whirling of outer space, too black, too near—
But he was taught as a puppy not to flinch,
Much less to imitate his bête noire Blanche
Who barked, fat foolish creature, at King Lear.

Still others fought in the road's filth over Jezebel,
Slavered on hearths of horned and pelted barons.
His forebears lacked, to say the least, forbearance.
Can nature change in him? Nothing's impossible.

The last chord fades. The night is cold and fine.
His master's voice rasps through the grooves' bare groves.
Obediently, in silence like the grave's
He sleeps there on the still-warm gramophone

Only to dream he is at the première of a Handel
Opera long thought lost—*Il Cane Minore*.
Its allegorical subject is his story!
A little dog revolving round a spindle

Gives rise to harmonies beyond belief,
A cast of stars. . . . Is there in Victor's heart
No honey for the vanquished? Art is art.
The life it asks of us is a dog's life.

JAMES MERRILL

WATERSPOUT

Where foam-white openwork
Rumples over slate,
Flash of a fork, the first
Wild syllables in flight,
The massive misty forces
Here to be faced are not
Of wind or water quite
So much as thought uptwisted
Helplessly by thought,
A fullblown argument
Sucked racing through whose veins
Whitebait and jellyfish
Repeat the lacy helices
Threaded into the stem
Of a Murano—wait:
Spirits intoxicate
The drinker, not the glass;
Yet *goblets*—three of them—
Weave up to be counted
Like drunks in the stormlight.
Poor crazy scene, poor brain
That cries and reels and clouds . . .
From somewhere above clouds,
Above thunder and levin
And the herring gull's high scream
(At which one glass may seem
To shatter), from this heaven
Slaked by the spinal fluid,
A bright-eyed reveller
Looks down on cloth outspread,
Strewn silver, fruits de mer,
The lighthouse salt-cellar—
A world exhausted, drained
But, like his word, unbroken;
Looks down and keeps his head.

W. S. Merwin

THE DRUNK IN THE FURNACE

For a good decade
The furnace stood in the naked gully, fireless
And vacant as any hat. Then when it was
No more to them than a hulking black fossil
To erode unnoticed with the rest of the junk-hill
By the poisonous creek, and rapidly to be added
     To their ignorance,

     They were afterwards astonished
To confirm, one morning, a twist of smoke like a pale
Resurrection, staggering out of its chewed hole,
And to remark then other tokens that someone,
Cosily bolted behind the eye-holed iron
Door of the drafty burner, had there established
     His bad castle.

     Where he gets his spirits
It's a mystery. But the stuff keeps him musical:
Hammer-and-anvilling with poker and bottle
To his jugged bellowings, till the last groaning clang
As he collapses onto the rioting
Springs of a litter of car-seats ranged on the grates,
     To sleep like an iron pig.

     In their tar-paper church
On a text about stoke-holes that are sated never
Their Reverend lingers. They nod and hate trespassers.
When the furnace wakes, though, all afternoon
Their witless offspring flock like piped rats to its siren
Crescendo, and agape on the crumbling ridge
     Stand in a row and learn.

DEAD HAND

Temptations still nest in it like basilisks.
Hang it up till the rings fall.

AIR

Naturally it is night.
Under the overturned lute with its
One string I am going my way
Which has a strange sound.

This way the dust, that way the dust.
I listen to both sides
But I keep right on.
I remember the leaves sitting in judgment
And then winter.

I remember the rain with its bundle of roads.
The rain taking all its roads.
Nowhere.

Young as I am, old as I am,

I forget tomorrow, the blind man.
I forget the life among the buried windows.
The eyes in the curtains.
The wall
Growing through the immortelles.
I forget silence
The owner of the smile.

This must be what I wanted to be doing,
Walking at night between the two deserts,
Singing.

W. S. MERWIN

WE CONTINUE

for Galway Kinnell

The rust, a little pile of western color, lies
At the end of its travels,
Our instrument no longer.

Those who believe
In death have their worship cut out for them.
As for myself, we
Continue,

An old
Scar of light our trumpet,

Pilgrims with thorns
To the eye of the cold
Under flags made by the blind,
In one fist

This letter that vanishes
If the hand opens:

Charity, come home,
Begin.

SOME LAST QUESTIONS

What is the head
     A. Ash
What are the eyes
     A. The wells have fallen in and have
        Inhabitants
What are the feet
     A. Thumbs left after the auction

No what are the feet
      A. Under them the impossible road is moving
         Down which the broken necked mice push
         Balls of blood with their noses
What is the tongue
      A. The black coat that fell off the wall
         With sleeves trying to say something
What are the hands
      A. Paid
No what are the hands
      A. Climbing back down the museum wall
         To their ancestors the extinct shrews that will
         Have left a message
What is the silence
      A. As though it had a right to more
Who are the compatriots
      A. They make the stars of bone

DECEMBER NIGHT

The cold slope is standing in darkness
But the south of the trees is dry to the touch

The heavy limbs climb into the moonlight bearing feathers
I came to watch these
White plants older at night
The oldest
Come first to the ruins

And I hear magpies kept awake by the moon
The water flows through its
Own fingers without end

Tonight once more
I find a single prayer and it is not for men

FOR THE ANNIVERSARY OF MY DEATH

Every year without knowing it I have passed the day
When the last fires will wave to me
And the silence will set out
Tireless traveller
Like the beam of a lightless star
Then I will no longer
Find myself in life as in a strange garment
Surprised at the earth
And the love of one woman
And then shamelessness of men
As today writing after three days of rain
Hearing the wren sing and the falling cease
And bowing not knowing to what

TERGVINDER'S STONE

One time my friend Tergvinder brought a large round boulder into his living room. He rolled it up the steps with the help of some two-by-fours, and when he got it out into the middle of the room, where some people have coffee tables (though he had never had one there himself) he left it. He said that was where it belonged.

It is really a plain-looking stone. Not as large as Plymouth Rock by a great deal, but then it does not have all the claims of a big shaky promotion campaign to support. That was one of the things Tergvinder said about it. He made no claims at all for it, he said. It was other people who called it Tergvinder's Stone. All he said was that according to him it belonged there.

His dog took to peeing on it, which created a problem (Tergvinder had not moved the carpet before he got the stone to where he said it belonged). Their tomcat took to squirting it, too. His wife fell over it quite often at first and it did not help their already strained marriage. Tergvinder said there was nothing to be done about it. It was in the order of things. That was a phrase he seldom employed, and never when he conceived that there was any room left for doubt.

W. S. MERWIN

He confided in me that he often woke in the middle of the night, troubled by the ancient, nameless ills of the planet, and got up quietly not to wake his wife, and walked through the house naked, without turning on any lights. He said that at such times he found himself listening, listening, aware of how some shapes in the darkness emitted low sounds like breathing, as they never did by day. He said he had become aware of a hole in the darkness in the middle of the living room, and out of that hole a breathing, a mournful dissatisfied sound of an absence waiting for what belonged to it, for something it had never seen and could not conceive of, but without which it could not rest. It was a sound, Tergvinder said, that touched him with fellow-feeling, and he had undertaken—oh, without saying anything to anybody—to assuage, if he could, that wordless longing that seemed always on the verge of despair. How to do it was another matter, and for months he had circled the problem, night and day, without apparently coming any closer to a solution. Then one day he had seen the stone. It had been there all the time at the bottom of his drive, he said, and he had never really seen it. Never recognized it for what it was. The nearer to the house he had got it, the more certain he had become. The stone had rolled into its present place like a lost loved one falling into arms that had long ached for it.

Tergvinder says that now on nights when he walks through the dark house he comes and stands in the living room doorway and listens to the peace in the middle of the floor. He knows its size, its weight, the touch of it, something of what is thought of it. He knows that it is peace. As he listens, some hint of that peace touches him too. Often, after a while, he steps down into the living room and goes and kneels beside the stone and they converse for hours in silence—a silence broken only by the sound of his own breathing.

DO NOT DIE

In each world they may put us
farther apart
do not die
as this world is made I might
live forever

W. S. MERWIN

ANIMULA

Look soul
soul
barefoot presence
through whom blood falls as through
a water clock
and tears rise before they wake
I will take you

at last to
where the wind stops
by the river we
know
by that same water
and the nights are not separate
remember

A DOOR

This is a place where a door might be
here where I am standing
in the light outside all the walls

there would be a shadow here
all day long
and a door into it
where now there is me

and somebody would come and knock
on this air
long after I have gone
and there in front of me a life
would open

THE FALCONS

There were years when I knew
the flowers in the red stone walls

now in the courtyard where I have returned with you
we drink the wine of visitors
the temperature of the cellars

dusk is welling
out of the dried blood of the masonry
no hour remains on the sundial
by now the owls of the tower corners
are waking on their keepers' fists
but it is still day
out in the air
and three falcons appear there
over the courtyard

no feathers on heads or breasts
and they fly down to us
to our wrists and between them
then hover and perch just above us
keeping us in sight
waiting
they are waiting for us

this time they will come with us
when we leave the island
tonight for the rest of our lives

THE BLACK JEWEL

In the dark
there is only the sound of the cricket

W. S. MERWIN

south wind in the leaves
is the cricket
so is the surf on the shore
and the barking across the valley

the cricket never sleeps
the whole cricket is the pupil of one eye
it can run it can leap it can fly
in its back the moon
crosses the night

there is only one cricket
when I listen

the cricket lives in the unlit ground
in the roots
out of the wind
it has only the one sound

before I could talk
I heard the cricket
under the house
then I remembered summer

mice too and the blind lightning
are born hearing the cricket
dying they hear it
bodies of light turn listening to the cricket
the cricket is neither alive nor dead
the death of the cricket
is still the cricket
in the bare room the luck of the cricket
echoes

THE FIELDS

Saturday on Seventh Street
full-waisted gray-haired women in Sunday sweaters

moving through the tan shades of their booths
bend over cakes they baked at home
they gaze down onto the sleep of stuffed cabbages
they stir with huge spoons sauerkraut and potato dumplings
cooked as those dishes were cooked on deep
misty plains among the sounds of horses
beside fields of black earth on the other side of the globe
that only the oldest think they remember
looking down from their windows into the world
where everybody is now

none of the young has yet wept at the smell
of cabbages
those leaves all face
none of the young after long journeys
weeks in vessels
and staring at strange coasts through fog in first light
has been recognized by the steam of sauerkraut
that is older than anyone living
so on the street they play the music
of what they do not remember
they sing of places they have not known
they dance in new costumes under the windows
in the smell of cabbages from fields
nobody has seen

A FAMILY

Would you believe me
if I told you the name of the farmers
at the end of the lake
where it grew shallow over the mossy rocks

W. S. MERWIN

and if you came in the morning the grass was blue
the fur of the rocks was wet the small frogs jumped
and the lake was silent behind you
except for echoes

you tied your boat carefully to a tree
before setting out across the cool pasture
watching for the bull
all the way to the barn

or if you came in the afternoon
the pasture glared and hummed the dark leaves smelled
from beside the water and the barn was drunk
by the time you got to it

to climb on the beams
to dive into the distant hay
will you believe
the names of the farmer's children

THE WAVING OF A HAND

First rose a low shore   pastures green to the water
that my father must have seen   but did he know it at the time
and maybe it seemed to him then   that he was arriving
    a few white facades   far off on the land's edge
lighthouse not yet flashing   small coast guard station
all faintly gleaming   under low sky
by the wide river mouth   late in the day
cold wind sweeping   green estuary
but everything still   calm and as it should be

W. S. MERWIN

water sound sliding   close by under wood
everyone lying down   in the thin vessel
except the one sailor   leaning against the mast
face never seen   turned away forward
catching last sunlight   eyes toward the sea
waves out there suddenly blue   and sky darkening
    yet I was standing   in an old wooden house
where surely my father had stood   but had he known it then
I was among friends   he had never met
    out in back through the window   the same quiet yard
and small wooden study   beyond it under trees
it was growing dark in the room   but no one turned a light on
and the next time   I looked through that window
there was nothing to see in the yard   but a cloud
a white cloud   full of moonlight
and I tapped someone's shoulder   and we both stared
    then we talked of other things   I did not stay
soon it was really night   I ate with friends it rained
three times I climbed   a long staircase
the first time and the second   someone was at the top
    hundreds of miles   to the west
my father died   just before one in the morning

SON

As the shadow closed   on the face once my father's
three times leaning forward   far off she called
Good night in a whisper   from before I was born
later through the burial   a wren went on singing

then it was that I left   for the coast to live
a single long mountain   close to the shore
from it the sun rose   and everyone there asked me
who I was   I asked them who they were

at that time I found the cave   under the mountain
drawings still on the walls   carved fragments in the dirt
all my days I spent there   groping in the floor

but some who came from nearby   were wrecking the place for a game
garbage through holes overhead   broken cars dead animals
in the evenings they rolled huge rocks   down to smash the roof
nothing that I could do   kept them from it for long

the old story   the old story

and in the mornings the cave   full of new daylight

Frank O'Hara

AUTOBIOGRAPHIA LITERARIA

When I was a child
I played by myself in a
corner of the schoolyard
all alone.

I hated dolls and I
hated games, animals were
not friendly and birds
flew away.

If anyone was looking
for me I hid behind a
tree and cried out "I am
an orphan."

And here I am, the
center of all beauty!
writing these poems!
Imagine!

POEM

The eager note on my door said "Call me,
call when you get in!" so I quickly threw
a few tangerines into my overnight bag,
straightened my eyelids and shoulders, and

headed straight for the door. It was autumn
by the time I got around the corner, oh all
unwilling to be either pertinent or bemused, but
the leaves were brighter than grass on the sidewalk!

Funny, I thought, that the lights are on this late
and the hall door open; still up at this hour, a
champion jai-alai player like himself? Oh fie!
for shame! What a host, so zealous! And he was

there in the hall, flat on a sheet of blood that
ran down the stairs. I did appreciate it. There are few
hosts who so thoroughly prepare to greet a guest
only casually invited, and that several months ago.

POEM

All the mirrors in the world
don't help, nor am I moved

by the calm emergence of my
image in the rain, it is not

I who appears or imagines. See,
if you can, if you can make

the unpleasant trip, the
house where shadows of my own

childhood are watered and forced
like overgrown bludgeons, you

must look, for I cannot. I
cannot face that fearful usage,

and my eyes in, say, the glass
of a public bar, become a

depraved hunt for other re-
flections. And what a blessed

relief! when it is some
disgusting sight, anything

but the old shadowy bruising,
anything but my private haunts.

When I am fifty shall my
face drift into those elongations

of innocence and confront me?
Oh rain, melt me! mirror, kill!

TO MY DEAD FATHER

Don't call to me father
wherever you are I'm
still your little son
running through the dark

I couldn't do what you
say even if I could hear
your roses no longer grow
my heart's black as their

bed their dainty thorns
have become my face's
troublesome stubble you
must not think of flowers

And do not frighten my
blue eyes with hazel flecks
or thicken my lips when
I face my mirror don't ask

that I be other than your
strange son understanding
minor miracles not death
father I am alive! father

forgive the roses and me

FRANK O'HARA

MEDITATIONS IN AN EMERGENCY

Am I to become profligate as if I were a blonde? Or religious as if I were French?

Each time my heart is broken it makes me feel more adventurous (and how the same names keep recurring on that interminable list!), but one of these days there'll be nothing left with which to venture forth.

Why should I share you? Why don't you get rid of someone else for a change?

I am the least difficult of men. All I want is boundless love.

Even trees understand me! Good heavens, I lie under them, too, don't I? I'm just like a pile of leaves.

However, I have never clogged myself with the praises of pastoral life, nor with nostalgia for an innocent past of perverted acts in pastures. No. One need never leave the confines of New York to get all the greenery one wishes—I can't even enjoy a blade of grass unless I know there's a subway handy, or a record store or some other sign that people do not totally *regret* life. It is more important to affirm the least sincere; the clouds get enough attention as it is and even they continue to pass. Do they know what they're missing? Uh huh.

My eyes are vague blue, like the sky, and change all the time; they are indiscriminate but fleeting, entirely specific and disloyal, so that no one trusts me. I am always looking away. Or again at something after it has given me up. It makes me restless and that makes me unhappy, but I cannot keep them still. If only I had grey, green, black, brown, yellow eyes; I would stay at home and do something. It's not that I'm curious. On the contrary, I am bored but it's my duty to be attentive, I am needed by things as the sky must be above the earth. And lately, so great has *their* anxiety become, I can spare myself little sleep.

Now there is only one man I love to kiss when he is unshaven. Heterosexuality! you are inexorably approaching. (How discourage her?)

St. Serapion, I wrap myself in the robes of your whiteness which is like midnight in Dostoevsky. How am I to become a legend, my dear? I've tried love, but that hides you in the bosom of another and I am always springing forth from it like the lotus—the ecstasy of always bursting forth! (but one must not be distracted by it!) or like a hyacinth, "to keep the filth of life away," yes, there, even in the heart, where the filth is pumped in and slanders and pollutes and determines. I will my will, though I may become famous for a mysterious vacancy in that department, that greenhouse.

Destroy yourself, if you don't know!

It is easy to be beautiful; it is difficult to appear so. I admire you, beloved, for the trap you've set. It's like a final chapter no one reads because the plot is over.

"Fanny Brown is run away—scampered off with a Cornet of Horse; I do love that little Minx, & hope She may be happy, tho' She has vexed me by this Exploit a little too. —Poor silly Cecchina! or F: B: as we used to call her. —I wish She had a good Whipping and 10,000 pounds." —Mrs. Thrale.

I've got to get out of here. I choose a piece of shawl and my dirtiest suntans. I'll be back, I'll re-emerge, defeated, from the valley; you don't want me to go where you go, so I go where you don't want me to. It's only afternoon, there's a lot ahead. There won't be any mail downstairs. Turning, I spit in the lock and the knob turns.

TO JOHN ASHBERY

I can't believe there's not
another world where we will sit
and read new poems to each other
high on a mountain in the wind.
You can be Tu Fu, I'll be Po Chü-i
and the Monkey Lady'll be in the moon,
smiling at our ill-fitting heads
as we watch snow settle on a twig.
Or shall we be really gone? this
is not the grass I saw in my youth!
and if the moon, when it rises
tonight, is empty—a bad sign,
meaning "You go, like the blossoms."

WHY I AM NOT A PAINTER

I am not a painter, I am a poet.
Why? I think I would rather be
a painter, but I am not. Well,

for instance, Mike Goldberg
is starting a painting. I drop in.
"Sit down and have a drink" he
says. I drink; we drink. I look
up. "You have SARDINES in it."
"Yes, it needed something there."

"Oh." I go and the days go by
and I drop in again. The painting
is going on, and I go, and the days
go by. I drop in. The painting is
finished. "Where's SARDINES?"
All that's left is just
letters, "It was too much," Mike says.

But me? One day I am thinking of
a color: orange. I write a line
about orange. Pretty soon it is a
whole page of words, not lines.
Then another page. There should be
so much more, not of orange, of
words, of how terrible orange is
and life. Days go by. It is even in
prose, I am a real poet. My poem
is finished and I haven't mentioned
orange yet. It's twelve poems, I call
it ORANGES. And one day in a gallery
I see Mike's painting, called SARDINES.

THE DAY LADY DIED

It is 12:20 in New York a Friday
three days after Bastille day, yes
it is 1959 and I go get a shoeshine

because I will get off the 4:19 in Easthampton
at 7:15 and then go straight to dinner
and I don't know the people who will feed me

I walk up the muggy street beginning to sun
and have a hamburger and a malted and buy
an ugly NEW WORLD WRITING to see what the poets
in Ghana are doing these days
                              I go on to the bank
and Miss Stillwagon (first name Linda I once heard)
doesn't even look up my balance for once in her life
and in the GOLDEN GRIFFIN I get a little Verlaine
for Patsy with drawings by Bonnard although I do
think of Hesiod, trans. Richmond Lattimore or
Brendan Behan's new play or *Le Balcon* or *Les Nègres*
of Genet, but I don't, I stick with Verlaine
after practically going to sleep with quandariness

and for Mike I just stroll into the PARK LANE
Liquor Store and ask for a bottle of Strega and
then I go back where I came from to 6th Avenue
and the tobacconist in the Ziegfeld Theatre and
casually ask for a carton of Gauloises and a carton
of Picayunes, and a NEW YORK POST with her face on it

and I am sweating a lot by now and thinking of
leaning on the john door in the 5 SPOT
while she whispered a song along the keyboard
to Mal Waldron and everyone and I stopped breathing

STEPS

How funny you are today New York
like Ginger Rogers in *Swingtime*
and St. Bridget's steeple leaning a little to the left

here I have just jumped out of a bed full of V-days
(I got tired of D-days) and blue you there still
accepts me foolish and free
all I want is a room up there
and you in it

and even the traffic halt so thick is a way
for people to rub up against each other
and when their surgical appliances lock
they stay together
for the rest of the day (what a day)
I go by to check a slide and I say
that painting's not so blue

where's Lana Turner
she's out eating
and Garbo's backstage at the Met
everyone's taking their coat off
so they can show a rib-cage to the rib-watchers
and the park's full of dancers with their tights and shoes
in little bags
who are often mistaken for worker-outers at the West Side Y
why not
the Pittsburgh Pirates shout because they won
and in a sense we're all winning
we're alive

the apartment was vacated by a gay couple
who moved to the country for fun
they moved a day too soon
even the stabbings are helping the population explosion
though in the wrong country
and all those liars have left the U N
the Seagram Building's no longer rivalled in interest
not that we need liquor (we just like it)

and the little box is out on the sidewalk
next to the delicatessen
so the old man can sit on it and drink beer
and get knocked off it by his wife later in the day
while the sun is still shining

oh god it's wonderful
to get out of bed
and drink too much coffee
and smoke too many cigarettes
and love you so much

FRANK O'HARA

YESTERDAY DOWN AT THE CANAL

You say that everything is very simple and interesting
it makes me feel very wistful, like reading a great Russian novel
                                                            does
I am terribly bored
sometimes it is like seeing a bad movie
other days, more often, it's like having an acute disease of the
                                                            kidney
god knows it has nothing to do with the heart
nothing to do with people more interesting than myself
yak yak
that's an amusing thought
how can anyone be more amusing than oneself
how can anyone fail to be
can I borrow your forty-five
I only need one bullet preferably silver
if you can't be interesting at least you can be a legend
(but I hate all that crap)

POEM

Lana Turner has collapsed!
I was trotting along and suddenly
it started raining and snowing
and you said it was hailing
but hailing hits you on the head
hard so it was really snowing and
raining and I was in such a hurry
to meet you but the traffic
was acting exactly like the sky
and suddenly I see a headline
LANA TURNER HAS COLLAPSED!
there is no snow in Hollywood
there is no rain in California
I have been to lots of parties
and acted perfectly disgraceful
but I never actually collapsed
oh Lana Turner we love you get up

Mary Oliver

THE SWIMMING LESSON

Feeling the icy kick, the endless waves
Reaching around my life, I moved my arms
And coughed, and in the end saw land.

Somebody, I suppose,
Remembering the medieval maxim,
Had tossed me in,
Had wanted me to learn to swim,

Not knowing that none of us, who ever came back
From that long lonely fall and frenzied rising,
Ever learned anything at all
About swimming, but only
How to put off, one by one,
Dreams and pity, love and grace,—
How to survive in any place.

SLEEPING IN THE FOREST

I thought the earth
remembered me, she
took me back so tenderly, arranging
her dark skirts, her pockets
full of lichens and seeds. I slept
as never before, a stone
on the riverbed, nothing
between me and the white fire of the stars
but my thoughts, and they floated
light as moths among the branches
of the perfect trees. All night
I heard the small kingdoms breathing
around me, the insects, and the birds

who do their work in the darkness. All night
I rose and fell, as if in water, grappling
with a luminous doom. By morning
I had vanished at least a dozen times
into something better.

THE FISH

She climbs from the sea; moonlight
blazes the black rocks,
the surface razzle-dazzle
of sweet water
threading out of the tide. She
moves upstream, the flow
pressing against her;
she feels it, lets the hot
blade of her body pause,
drifts backward, whips awake. She
moves upstream; she is heavy;
deep in her belly
life that is to be
stirs like a million planets; she
moves upstream; when the waters
divide she follows
the fragrance spilling
from her old birth pond; she
sees the waterfalls—gleaming
stairways of stone,
water ripped and boiling
like white logs—and knows beyond
lies the green pond
rich with the shadows
of last year's swimmers where she
will nest her eggs and the fierce prince
quicken them; she flies
upstream—she arcs
in the long gown of her body, she leaps
into the walls of water,
she falls through like the torn
silvery half-drowned body

of any woman come to term, caught
    as mortality drives triumphantly toward
        immortality, the shaken bones like
            cages of fire.

MUSIC LESSONS

Sometimes, in the middle of the lesson,
we exchanged places. She would gaze a moment at her hands
spread over the keys; then the small house with its knickknacks,
its shut windows,

its photographs of her sons and the serious husband,
vanished as new shapes formed. Sound
became music, and music a white
scarp for the listener to climb

alone. I leaped rock over rock to the top
and found myself waiting, transformed,
and still she played, her eyes luminous and willful,
her pinned hair falling down—

forgetting me, the house, the neat green yard,
she fled in that lick of flame all tedious bonds:
supper, the duties of flesh and home,
the knife at the throat, the death in the metronome.

THE BLACK WALNUT TREE

My mother and I debate:
we could sell
the black walnut tree
to the lumberman,
and pay off the mortgage.
Likely some storm anyway
will churn down its dark boughs,
smashing the house. We talk

slowly, two women trying
in a difficult time to be wise.
Roots in the cellar drains,
I say, and she replies
that the leaves are getting heavier
every year, and the fruit
harder to gather away.
But something brighter than money
moves in our blood—an edge
sharp and quick as a trowel
that wants us to dig and sow.
So we talk, but we don't do
anything. That night I dream
of my fathers out of Bohemia
filling the blue fields
of fresh and generous Ohio
with leaves and vines and orchards.
What my mother and I both know
is that we'd crawl with shame
in the emptiness we'd made
in our own and our fathers' backyard.
So the black walnut tree
swings through another year
of sun and leaping winds,
of leaves and bounding fruit,
and, month after month, the whip-
crack of the mortgage.

STORM

The temperature
Cruises down, slides
Limply toward zero,

Meets it and crosses under
To the dark side
Of winter. Soon

I have to scrape frost away
To watch it withdrawing
Into itself, along the minuses,

All evening. Heaven
Help us! I say. But heaven
Is full of spitting snow,

And the deer lying
In the pine groves outside of town,
The foxes plunging home,

Even the crows, plump
As black rocks in the cold trees,
Are beginning to shiver. But they

Can bear the wrack of the storm. Patient
As stones or leaves or clumps of clay,
What saves them is not knowing they are mortal—

What saves them is thinking that dying
Is only floating away into
The life of the snow.

THE KITTEN

More amazed than anything
I took the perfectly black
stillborn kitten
with the one large eye
in the center of its small forehead
from the house cat's bed
and buried it in a field
behind the house.

I suppose I could have given it
to a museum,
I could have called the local
newspaper.

But instead I took it out into the field
and opened the earth
and put it back
saying, it was real,

saying, life is infinitely inventive,
saying, what other amazements
lie in the dark seed of the earth, yes,

I think I did right to go out alone
and give it back peacefully, and cover the place
with the reckless blossoms of weeds.

TASTING THE WILD GRAPES

The red beast
who lives in the side of these hills
won't come out for anything you have:
money or music. Still, there are moments
heavy with light and good luck. Walk
quietly under these tangled vines
and pay attention, and one morning
something will explode underfoot
like a branch of fire; one afternoon
something will flow down the hill
in plain view, a muscled sleeve the color
of all October! And forgetting
everything you will leap to name it
as though for the first time, your lit blood
rushing not to a word but a sound
small-boned, thin-faced, in a hurry,
lively as the dark thorns of the wild grapes
on the unsuspecting tongue!
The fox! The fox!

AN OLD WHOREHOUSE

We climbed through a broken window,
walked through every room.

Out of business for years,
the mattresses held only

rainwater, and one
woman's black shoe. Downstairs

spiders had wrapped up
the crystal chandelier.

A cracked cup lay in the sink.
But we were fourteen,

and no way dust could hide
the expected glamour from us,

or teach us anything.
We whispered, we imagined.

It would be years before
we'd learn how effortlessly

sin blooms, then softens,
like any bed of flowers.

UNIVERSITY HOSPITAL, BOSTON

The trees on the hospital lawn
are lush and thriving. They too
are getting the best of care,
like you, and the anonymous many,
in the clean rooms high above this city,
where day and night the doctors keep
arriving, where intricate machines
chart with cool devotion
the murmur of the blood,
the slow patching-up of bone,
the despair of the mind.

When I come to visit and we walk out
into the light of a summer day,
we sit under the trees—
buckeyes, a sycamore and one
black walnut brooding

high over a hedge of lilacs
as old as the red-brick building
behind them, the original
hospital built before the Civil War.
We sit on the lawn together, holding hands
while you tell me: you are better.

How many young men, I wonder,
came here, wheeled on cots off the slow trains
from the red and hideous battlefields
to lie all summer in the small and stuffy chambers
while doctors did what they could, longing
for tools still unimagined, medicines still unfound,
wisdoms still unguessed at, and how many died
staring at the leaves of the trees, blind
to the terrible effort around them to keep them alive?
I look into your eyes

which are sometimes green and sometimes gray,
and sometimes full of humor, but often not,
and tell myself, you are better,
because my life without you would be
a place of parched and broken trees.
Later, walking the corridors down to the street,
I turn and step inside an empty room.
Yesterday someone was here with a gasping face.
Now the bed is made all new,
the machines have been rolled away. The silence
continues, deep and neutral,
as I stand there, loving you.

IN BLACKWATER WOODS

Look, the trees
are turning
their own bodies
into pillars

MARY OLIVER

of light,
are giving off the rich
fragrance of cinnamon
and fulfillment,

the long tapers
of cattails
are bursting and floating away over
the blue shoulders

of the ponds,
and every pond,
no matter what its
name is, is

nameless now.
Every year
everything
I have ever learned

in my lifetime
leads back to this: the fires
and the black river of loss
whose other side

is salvation,
whose meaning
none of us will ever know.
To live in this world

you must be able
to do three things:
to love what is mortal;
to hold it

against your bones knowing
your own life depends on it;
and, when the time comes to let it go,
to let it go.

Charles Olson

MAXIMUS, TO HIMSELF

I have had to learn the simplest things
last. Which made for difficulties.
Even at sea I was slow, to get the hand out, or to cross
a wet deck.
       The sea was not, finally, my trade.
But even my trade, at it, I stood estranged
from that which was most familiar. Was delayed,
and not content with the man's argument
that such postponement
is now the nature of
obedience,

        that we are all late
        in a slow time,
        that we grow up many
        And the single
        is not easily
        known

It could be, though the sharpness (the *achiote*)
I note in others,
makes more sense
than my own distances. The agilities

        they show daily
        who do the world's
        businesses
        And who do nature's
        as I have no sense
        I have done either

I have made dialogues,
have discussed ancient texts,
have thrown what light I could, offered
what pleasures
doceat allows

CHARLES OLSON

But the known?
This, I have had to be given,
a life, love, and from one man
the world.

Tokens.
But sitting here
I look out as a wind
and water man, testing
And missing
some proof

I know the quarters
of the weather, where it comes from,
where it goes. But the stem of me,
this I took from their welcome,
or their rejection, of me

And my arrogance
was neither diminished
nor increased,
by the communication

2

It is undone business
I speak of, this morning,
with the sea
stretching out
from my feet

I, MAXIMUS OF GLOUCESTER, TO YOU

Off-shore, by islands hidden in the blood
jewels & miracles, I, Maximus
a metal hot from boiling water, tell you
what is a lance, who obeys the figures of
the present dance

CHARLES OLSON

1

the thing you're after
may lie around the bend
of the nest (second, time slain, the bird! the bird!

And there! (strong) thrust, the mast! flight
                    (of the bird
                    o kylix, o
                    Antony of Padua
                    sweep low, o bless

the roofs, the old ones, the gentle steep ones
on whose ridge-poles the gulls sit, from which they depart,

                            And the flake-racks
of my city!

2

love is form, and cannot be without
important substance (the weight
say, 58 carats each one of us, perforce
our goldsmith's scale

                  feather to feather added
                  (and what is mineral, what
                  is curling hair, the string
                  you carry in your nervous beak, these

                  make bulk, these, in the end, are
                  the sum

                  (o my lady of good voyage
                  in whose arm, whose left arm rests
no boy but a carefully carved wood, a painted face, a schooner!
a delicate mast, as bow-sprit for

                forwarding

3

the underpart is, though stemmed, uncertain
is, as sex is, as moneys are, facts!
facts, to be dealt with, as the sea is, the demand
that they be played by, that they only can be, that they must
be played by, said he, coldly, the
ear!

By ear, he sd.
But that which matters, that which insists, that which will last,
that! o my people, where shall you find it, how, where, where shall you
     listen
when all is become billboards, when, all, even silence, is spray-gunned?

when even our bird, my roofs,
cannot be heard

when even you, when sound itself is neoned in?

when, on the hill, over the water
where she who used to sing,
when the water glowed,
black, gold, the tide
outward, at evening

when bells came like boats
over the oil-slicks, milkweed
hulls

And a man slumped,
attentionless,
against pink shingles

o sea city)

4

one loves only form,
and form only comes
into existence when
the thing is born

born of yourself, born
of hay and cotton struts,
of street-pickings, wharves, weeds
you carry in, my bird

> of a bone of a fish
> of a straw, or will
> of a color, of a bell
> of yourself, torn

5

love is not easy
but how shall you know,
New England, now
that pejorocracy is here, how
that street-cars, o Oregon, twitter
in the afternoon, offend
a black-gold loin?

> how shall you strike,
> o swordsman, the blue-red back
> when, last night, your aim
> was mu-sick, mu-sick, mu-sick
> And not the cribbage game?

>> (o Gloucester-man,
>> weave
>> your birds and fingers
>> new, your roof-tops,
>> clean shit upon racks
>> sunned on
>> American
>> braid
>> with others like you, such
>> extricable surface
>> as faun and oral,
>> satyr lesbos vase

>> o kill kill kill kill kill
>> those
>> who advertise you
>> out)

6

in! in! the bow-sprit, bird, the beak
in, the bend is, in, goes in, the form
that which you make, what holds, which is
the law of object, strut after strut, what you are, what you must be, what
the force can throw up, can, right now hereinafter erect,
the mast, the mast, the tender
mast!

           The nest, I say, to you, I Maximus, say
           under the hand, as I see it, over the waters
           from this place where I am, where I hear,
           can still hear

           from where I carry you a feather
           as though, sharp, I picked up,
           in the afternoon delivered you
           a jewel,
                    it flashing more than a wing,
           than any old romantic thing,
           than memory, than place,
           than anything other than that which you carry

           than that which is,
           call it a nest, around the head of, call it
           the next second

           than that which you
           can do!

THE LIBRARIAN

The landscape (the landscape!) again: Gloucester,
the shore one of me is (duplicates), and from which
(from offshore, I, Maximus) am removed, observe.

In this night I moved on the territory with combinations
(new mixtures) of old and known personages: the leader,
my father, in an old guise, here selling books and manuscripts.

CHARLES OLSON

My thought was, as I looked in the window of his shop,
there should be materials here for Maximus, when, then,
I saw he was the young musician has been there (been before me)

before. It turned out it wasn't a shop, it was a loft (wharf-
house) in which, as he walked me around, a year ago
came back (I had been there before, with my wife and son,

I didn't remember, he presented me insinuations via
himself and his girl) both of whom I had known for years.
But never in Gloucester. I had moved them in, to my country.

His previous appearance had been in my parents' bedroom where I
found him intimate with my former wife: this boy
was now the Librarian of Gloucester, Massachusetts!

>   Black space,
>   old fish-house.
>   Motions
>   of ghosts.
>   I,
>   dogging
>   his steps.
>
>   He
>   (not my father,
>   by name himself
>   with his face
>   twisted
>   at birth)
>   possessed of knowledge
>   pretentious
>   giving me
>   what in the instant
>   I knew better of.
>
>   But the somber
>   place, the flooring
>   crude like a wharf's
>   and a barn's
>   space

I was struck by the fact I was in Gloucester, and that my daughter
was there—that I would see her! She was over the Cut. I
hadn't even connected her with my being there, that she was

here. That she was there (in the Promised Land—the Cut!
But there was this business, of poets,that all my Jews
were in the fish-house too, that the Librarian had made a party

I was to read. They were. There were many of them, slumped
around. It was not for me. I was outside. It was the Fort.
The Fort was in East Gloucester—old Gorton's Wharf, where the Library

was. It was a region of coal houses, bins. In one a gang
was beating someone to death, in a corner of the labyrinth
of fences. I could see their arms and shoulders whacking

down. But not the victim. I got out of there. But cops
tailed me along the Fort beach toward the Tavern

The places still
half-dark, mud,
coal-dust.

There is no light
east
of the Bridge

Only on the headland
toward the harbor
from Cressy's

have I seen it (once
when my daughter ran
out on a spit of sand

isn't even there.) Where
is Bristow? when does I-A
get me home? I am caught

in Gloucester. (What's buried
behind Lufkin's
Diner? Who is

Frank Moore?

CHARLES OLSON

MAXIMUS TO GLOUCESTER, LETTER 27 [WITHHELD]

I come back to the geography of it,
the land falling off to the left
where my father shot his scabby golf
and the rest of us played baseball
into the summer darkness until no flies
could be seen and we came home
to our various piazzas where the women
buzzed

To the left the land fell to the city,
to the right, it fell to the sea

I was so young my first memory
is of a tent spread to feed lobsters
to Rexall conventioneers, and my father,
a man for kicks, came out of the tent roaring
with a bread-knife in his teeth to take care of
a druggist they'd told him had made a pass at
my mother, she laughing, so sure, as round
as her face, Hines pink and apple,
under one of those frame hats women then

This, is no bare incoming
of novel abstract form, this

is no welter or the forms
of those events, this,

Greeks, is the stopping
of the battle

            It is the imposing
of all those antecedent predecessions, the precessions

of me, the generation of those facts
which are my words, it is coming

from all that I no longer am, yet am,
the slow westward motion of

more than I am

There is no strict personal order

for my inheritance.

         No Greek will be able

to discriminate my body.

        An American

is a complex of occasions,

themselves a geometry

of spatial nature.

      I have this sense,

that I am one

with my skin

       Plus this—plus this:

that forever the geography

which leans in

on me I compell

backwards I compell Gloucester

to yield, to

change

    Polis

is this

A LATER NOTE ON
LETTER #15

In English the poetics became meubles—furniture—
thereafter (after 1630

& Descartes was the value

until Whitehead, who cleared out the gunk
by getting the universe in (as against man alone

& that concept of history (not Herodotus's,
which was a verb, to find out for yourself:
'istorin, which makes any one's acts a finding out for him or her
self, in other words restores the traum: that we act somewhere

at least by seizure, that the objective (example Thucidides, or
the latest finest tape-recorder, or any form of record on the spot

—live television or what—is a lie

as against what we know went on, the dream: the dream being
self-action with Whitehead's important corollary: that no event

is not penetrated, in intersection or collision with, an eternal
event

        The poetics of such a situation
are yet to be found out

MOONSET, GLOUCESTER,
DECEMBER 1, 1957, 1:58 AM

Goodbye red moon
In that color you set
west of the Cut I should imagine
forever Mother

After 47 years this month
a Monday at 9 AM
you set I rise I hope
a free thing as probably
what you more were Not
the suffering one you sold
sowed me on Rise
Mother from off me
God damn you God damn me my
misunderstanding of you

I can die now I just begun to live

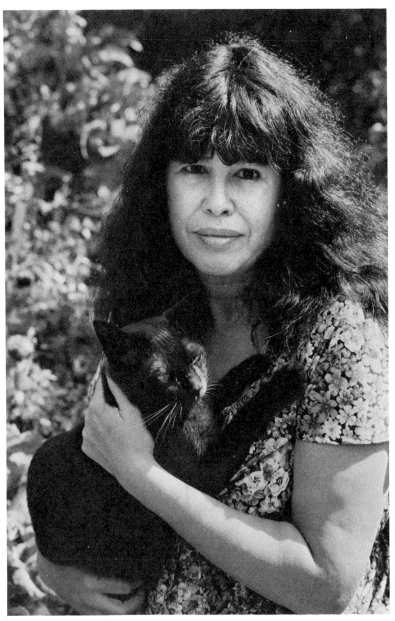

Marge Piercy

A WORK OF ARTIFICE

The bonsai tree
in the attractive pot
could have grown eighty feet tall
on the side of a mountain
till split by lightning.
But a gardener
carefully pruned it.
It is nine inches high.
Every day as he
whittles back the branches
the gardener croons,
It is your nature
to be small and cozy,
domestic and weak;
how lucky, little tree,
to have a pot to grow in.
With living creatures
one must begin very early
to dwarf their growth:
the bound feet,
the crippled brain,
the hair in curlers,
the hands you
love to touch.

THE SKYSCRAPERS OF THE FINANCIAL DISTRICT
DANCE WITH GASMAN

The skyscrapers are dancing by the river,
they are leaping over their reflections
their lightning bright zigzag and beady reflections

jagged and shattered on East River.
With voices shrill as children's whistles they hop
while the safes pop open like corn
and the files come whizzing through the air
to snow on the streets that lie throbbing,
eels copulating in heaps.
Ticker tape hangs in garlands from the wagging streetlamps.
Standard Oil and General Foods have amalgamated
and Dupont, Schenley and AT&T lie down together.
It does not matter, don't hope, it does not matter.
In the morning the buildings stand smooth and shaven and straight
and all goes on whirring and ticking.
Money is reticulated and stronger than steel or stone or vision,
though sometimes at night
the skyscrapers bow and lean and leap under no moon.

THE FRIEND

We sat across the table.
he said, cut off your hands.
they are always poking at things.
they might touch me.
I said yes.

Food grew cold on the table.
he said, burn your body.
it is not clean and smells like sex.
it rubs my mind sore.
I said yes.

I love you, I said.
That's very nice, he said
I like to be loved,
that makes me happy.
Have you cut off your hands yet?

MARGE PIERCY

BARBIE DOLL

This girlchild was born as usual
and presented dolls that did pee-pee
and miniature GE stoves and irons
and wee lipsticks the color of cherry candy.
Then in the magic of puberty, a classmate said:
You have a great big nose and fat legs.

She was healthy, tested intelligent,
possessed strong arms and back,
abundant sexual drive and manual dexterity.
She went to and fro apologizing.
Everyone saw a fat nose on thick legs.

She was advised to play coy,
exhorted to come on hearty,
exercise, diet, smile and wheedle.
Her good nature wore out
like a fan belt.
So she cut off her nose and her legs
and offered them up.

In the casket displayed on satin she lay
with the undertaker's cosmetics painted on,
a turned-up putty nose,
dressed in a pink and white nightie.
Doesn't she look pretty? everyone said.
Consummation at last.
To every woman a happy ending.

TO BE OF USE

The people I love the best
jump into work head first
without dallying in the shallows

and swim off with sure strokes almost out of sight.
They seem to become natives of that element,
the black sleek heads of seals
bouncing like half-submerged balls.

I love people who harness themselves, an ox to a heavy cart,
who pull like water buffalo, with massive patience,
who strain in the mud and the muck to move things forward,
who do what has to be done, again and again.

I want to be with people who submerge
in the task, who go into the fields to harvest
and work in a row and pass the bags along,
who are not parlor generals and field deserters
but move in a common rhythm
when the food must come in or the fire be put out.

The work of the world is common as mud.
Botched, it smears the hands, crumbles to dust.
But the thing worth doing well done
has a shape that satisfies, clean and evident.
Greek amphoras for wine or oil,
Hopi vases that held corn, are put in museums
but you know they were made to be used.
The pitcher cries for water to carry
and a person for work that is real.

THE LOVE OF LETTUCE

With a pale green curly
lust I gloat over it nestled
there on the wet earth
(oakleaf, buttercrunch, ruby, cos)
like so many nests
waiting for birds
who lay hard boiled eggs.

The first green eyes
of the mustard, the frail
wands of carrots, the fat

thrust of the peas: all
are precious as I kneel
in the mud weeding
and the thinnings go into the salad.

The garden with crooked
wandering rows dug
by the three of us
drunk with sunshine has
an intricate pattern emerging
like the back of a rug.
The tender seedlings

raise their pinheads
with the cap of seed stuck on.
Cruel and smiling with sharp
teeth is the love of lettuce.
You grow out of last year's
composted dinner and you
will end in my hot mouth.

YOU ASK WHY SOMETIMES I SAY STOP

You ask why sometimes I say stop
why sometimes I cry no
while I shake with pleasure.
What do I fear, you ask,
why don't I always want to come
and come again to that molten
deep sea center where the nerves
fuse open and the brain
and body shine with a black wordless light
fluorescent and heaving like plankton.

If you turn over the old refuse
of sexual slang, the worn buttons
of language, you find men
talk of spending and women
of dying.

You come in a torrent and ease
into limpness. Pleasure takes me
farther and farther from shore
in a series of breakers, each
towering higher before it
crashes and spills flat.

I am open then as a palm held out,
open as a sunflower, without
crust, without shelter, without
skin, hideless and unhidden.
How can I let you ride
so far into me and not fear?

Helpless as a burning city,
how can I ignore that the extremes
of pleasure are fire storms
that leave a vacuum into which
dangerous feelings (tenderness,
affection, l o v e) may rush
like gale force winds.

CROWS

They give me a bad
reputation, those swart rowers
through the air, heavy winged
and heavy voiced, brass tipped.
Before us they lived here
in the tallest pine. Shortly
after coming I walked in
on a ceremony, the crows
were singing secretly
and beautifully a ritual.
They divebombed me. To make
peace I brought a sacrifice,
the remains of a leg
of lamb. Since then
we have had truce.

Smart, ancient, rowdy and far-
sighted, they use our land
as sanctuary for raiding
where men shoot at them.

They come down, settling like
unwieldy cargo jets, to the bird
food, scattering the
cardinals, the juncos. *God
they're big, I've never seen
them so near a house,*
the guest says. We look
at each other, the crows
and me. Outside
they allow my slow approach.
They do not touch our crops
even in the far garden
in the bottomland. I'm aware
women have been burned
for less. I stand
under the oldest white oak
whose arms coil fat as pythons
and scream at the hunters
driving them back
with black hair coarse and streaming:
Caw! Caw!

CATS LIKE ANGELS

Cats like angels are supposed to be thin;
pigs like cherubs are supposed to be fat.
People are mostly in between, a knob
of bone sticking out in the knee you might
like to pad, a dollop of flab hanging
over the belt. You punish yourself,
one of those rubber balls kids have
that come bouncing back off their own
paddles, rebounding on the same slab.
You want to be slender and seamless
as a bolt.

MARGE PIERCY

When I was a girl
I loved spiny men with ascetic grimaces
all elbows and words and cartilage
ribbed like cast up fog-grey hulls,
faces to cut the eyes blind
on the glittering blade, chins
of Aegean prows bent on piracy.

Now I look for men whose easy bellies
show a love for the flesh and the table,
men who will come in the kitchen
and sit, who don't think peeling potatoes
makes their penis shrink; men with broad
fingers and purple figgy balls,
men with rumpled furrows and the slightly
messed look at ease of beds recently
well used.
            We are not all supposed
to look like undernourished fourteen year
old boys, no matter what the fashions
ordain. You are built to pull a cart,
to lift a heavy load and bear it,
to haul up the long slope, and so
am I, peasant bodies, earthy, solid
shapely dark glazed clay pots that can
stand on the fire. When we put our
bellies together we do not clatter
but bounce on the good upholstery.

DIGGING IN

This fall you will taste carrots
you planted, you thinned, you mulched,
you weeded and watered. You don't
know yet they will taste like yours,
not others, not mine.
This earth is yours as you love it.

MARGE PIERCY

We drink the water of this hill
and give our garbage to its soil.
We haul thatch for it and seaweed.
Out of it rise supper and roses
for the bedroom and herbs
for your next cold.

Your flesh grows out of this hill
like the maple trees. Its sweetness
is baked by this sun. Your eyes
have taken in sea and the light leaves
of the locust and the dark bristles
of the pine.

When we work in the garden you say
that now it feels sexual, the plants
pushing through us, the shivering
of the leaves. As we make love
later the oaks bend over us,
the hill listens.

The cats come and sit on the foot
of the bed to watch us.
Afterwards they purr.
The tomatoes grow faster and the beans.
You are learning to live in circles
as well as straight lines.

Sylvia Plath

THE COLOSSUS

I shall never get you put together entirely,
Pieced, glued, and properly jointed.
Mule-bray, pig-grunt and bawdy cackles
Proceed from your great lips.
It's worse than a barnyard.

Perhaps you consider yourself an oracle,
Mouthpiece of the dead, or of some god or other.
Thirty years now I have labored
To dredge the silt from your throat.
I am none the wiser.

Scaling little ladders with gluepots and pails of lysol
I crawl like an ant in mourning
Over the weedy acres of your brow
To mend the immense skull plates and clear
The bald, white tumuli of your eyes.

A blue sky out of the Oresteia
Arches above us. O father, all by yourself
You are pithy and historical as the Roman Forum.
I open my lunch on a hill of black cypress.
Your fluted bones and acanthine hair are littered

In their old anarchy to the horizon-line.
It would take more than a lightning-stroke
To create such a ruin.
Nights, I squat in the cornucopia
Of your left ear, out of the wind,

Counting the red stars and those of plum-color.
The sun rises under the pillar of your tongue.
My hours are married to shadow.
No longer do I listen for the scrape of a keel
On the blank stones of the landing.

SYLVIA PLATH

DADDY

You do not do, you do not do
Any more, black shoe
In which I have lived like a foot
For thirty years, poor and white,
Barely daring to breathe or Achoo.

Daddy, I have had to kill you.
You died before I had time——
Marble-heavy, a bag full of God,
Ghastly statue with one grey toe
Big as a Frisco seal

And a head in the freakish Atlantic
Where it pours bean green over blue
In the waters off beautiful Nauset.
I used to pray to recover you.
Ach, du.

In the German tongue, in the Polish town
Scraped flat by the roller
Of wars, wars, wars.
But the name of the town is common.
My Polack friend

Says there are a dozen or two.
So I never could tell where you
Put your foot, your root,
I never could talk to you.
The tongue stuck in my jaw.

It stuck in a barb wire snare.
Ich, ich, ich, ich,
I could hardly speak.
I thought every German was you.
And the language obscene

An engine, an engine
Chuffing me off like a Jew.
A Jew to Dachau, Auschwitz, Belsen.
I began to talk like a Jew.
I think I may well be a Jew.

The snows of the Tyrol, the clear beer of Vienna
Are not very pure or true.
With my gypsy ancestress and my weird luck
And my Taroc pack and my Taroc pack
I may be a bit of a Jew.

I have always been scared of *you*,
With your Luftwaffe, your gobbledygoo.
And your neat moustache
And your Aryan eye, bright blue.
Panzer-man, panzer-man, O You——

Not God but a swastika
So black no sky could squeak through.
Every woman adores a Fascist,
The boot in the face, the brute
Brute heart of a brute like you.

You stand at the blackboard, daddy,
In the picture I have of you,
A cleft in your chin instead of your foot
But no less a devil for that, no not
Any less the black man who

Bit my pretty red heart in two.
I was ten when they buried you.
At twenty I tried to die
And get back, back, back to you.
I thought even the bones would do.

But they pulled me out of the sack,
And they stuck me together with glue.
And then I knew what to do.
I made a model of you,
A man in black with a Meinkampf look

And a love of the rack and the screw.
And I said I do, I do.
So daddy, I'm finally through.
The black telephone's off at the root,
The voices just can't worm through.

If I've killed one man, I've killed two——
The vampire who said he was you

And drank my blood for a year,
Seven years, if you want to know.
Daddy, you can lie back now.

There's a stake in your fat black heart
And the villagers never liked you.
They are dancing and stamping on you.
They always *knew* it was you.
Daddy, daddy, you bastard, I'm through.

THE MUNICH MANNEQUINS

Perfection is terrible, it cannot have children.
Cold as snow breath, it tamps the womb

Where the yew trees blow like hydras,
The tree of life and the tree of life

Unloosing their moons, month after month, to no purpose.
The blood flood is the flood of love,

The absolute sacrifice.
It means: no more idols but me,

Me and you.
So, in their sulphur loveliness, in their smiles

These mannequins lean tonight
In Munich, morgue between Paris and Rome,

Naked and bald in their furs,
Orange lollies on silver sticks,

Intolerable, without mind.
The snow drops its pieces of darkness,

Nobody's about. In the hotels
Hands will be opening doors and setting

Down shoes for a polish of carbon
Into which broad toes will go tomorrow.

O the domesticity of these windows,
The baby lace, the green-leaved confectionery,

The thick Germans slumbering in their bottomless Stolz.
And the black phones on hooks

Glittering
Glittering and digesting

Voicelessness. The snow has no voice.

MARY'S SONG

The Sunday lamb cracks in its fat.
The fat
Sacrifices its opacity. . . .

A window, holy gold.
The fire makes it precious,
The same fire

Melting the tallow heretics,
Ousting the Jews.
Their thick palls float

Over the cicatrix of Poland, burnt-out
Germany.
They do not die.

Grey birds obsess my heart,
Mouth-ash, ash of eye.
They settle. On the high

Precipice
That emptied one man into space
The ovens glowed like heavens, incandescent.

It is a heart,
This holocaust I walk in,
O golden child the world will kill and eat.

SYLVIA PLATH

NICK AND THE CANDLESTICK

I am a miner. The light burns blue.
Waxy stalactites
Drip and thicken, tears

The earthen womb
Exudes from its dead boredom.
Black bat airs

Wrap me, raggy shawls,
Cold homicides.
They weld to me like plums.

Old cave of calcium
Icicles, old echoer.
Even the newts are white,

Those holy Joes.
And the fish, the fish——
Christ! They are panes of ice,

A vice of knives,
A piranha
Religion, drinking

Its first communion out of my live toes.
The candle
Gulps and recovers its small altitude,

Its yellows hearten.
O love, how did you get here?
O embryo

Remembering, even in sleep,
Your crossed position.
The blood blooms clean

In you, ruby.
The pain
You wake to is not yours.

Love, love,
I have hung our cave with roses.
With soft rugs——

The last of Victoriana.
Let the stars
Plummet to their dark address,

Let the mercuric
Atoms that cripple drip
Into the terrible well,

You are the one
Solid the spaces lean on, envious.
You are the baby in the barn.

LADY LAZARUS

I have done it again.
One year in every ten
I manage it——

A sort of walking miracle, my skin
Bright as a Nazi lampshade,
My right foot

A paperweight,
My face a featureless, fine
Jew linen.

Peel off the napkin
O my enemy.
Do I terrify?——

The nose, the eye pits, the full set of teeth?
The sour breath
Will vanish in a day.

Soon, soon the flesh
The grave cave ate will be
At home on me

And I a smiling woman.
I am only thirty.
And like the cat I have nine times to die.

This is Number Three.
What a trash
To annihilate each decade.

What a million filaments.
The peanut-crunching crowd
Shoves in to see

Them unwrap me hand and foot——
The big strip tease.
Gentleman, ladies,

These are my hands,
My knees.
I may be skin and bone,

Nevertheless, I am the same, identical woman.
The first time it happened I was ten.
It was an accident.

The second time I meant
To last it out and not come back at all.
I rocked shut

As a seashell.
They had to call and call
And pick the worms off me like sticky pearls.

Dying
Is an art, like everything else.
I do it exceptionally well.

I do it so it feels like hell.
I do it so it feels real.
I guess you could say I've a call.

It's easy enough to do it in a cell.
It's easy enough to do it and stay put.
It's the theatrical

Comeback in broad day
To the same place, the same face, the same brute
Amused shout:

"A miracle!"
That knocks me out.
There is a charge

For the eyeing of my scars, there is a charge
For the hearing of my heart——
It really goes.

And there is a charge, a very large charge,
For a word or a touch
Or a bit of blood

Or a piece of my hair or my clothes.
So, so, Herr Doktor.
So, Herr Enemy.

I am your opus,
I am your valuable,
The pure gold baby

That melts to a shriek.
I turn and burn.
Do not think I underestimate your great concern.

Ash, ash—
You poke and stir.
Flesh, bone, there is nothing there——

A cake of soap,
A wedding ring,
A gold filling.

Herr God, Herr Lucifer,
Beware
Beware.

Out of the ash
I rise with my red hair
And I eat men like air.

CUT

for Susan O'Neill Roe

What a thrill——
My thumb instead of an onion.
The top quite gone
Except for a sort of a hinge

Of skin,
A flap like a hat,
Dead white.
Then that red plush.

Little pilgrim,
The Indian's axed your scalp.
Your turkey wattle
Carpet rolls

Straight from the heart.
I step on it,
Clutching my bottle
Of pink fizz.

A celebration, this is.
Out of a gap
A million soldiers run,
Redcoats, every one.

Whose side are they on?
O my
Homunculus, I am ill.
I have taken a pill to kill

The thin
Papery feeling.
Saboteur,
Kamikaze man——

The stain on your
Gauze Ku Klux Klan
Babushka
Darkens and tarnishes and when

The balled
Pulp of your heart
Confronts its small
Mill of silence

How you jump——
Trepanned veteran,
Dirty girl,
Thumb stump.

WINTER TREES

The wet dawn inks are doing their blue dissolve.
On their blotter of fog the trees
Seem a botanical drawing.
Memories growing, ring on ring,
A series of weddings.

Knowing neither abortions nor bitchery,
Truer than women,
They seed so effortlessly!
Tasting the winds, that are footless,
Waist-deep in history.

Full of wings, otherworldliness.
In this, they are Ledas.
O mother of leaves and sweetness
Who are these pietas?
The shadows of ringdoves chanting, but easing nothing.

CROSSING THE WATER

Black lake, black boat, two black, cut-paper people.
Where do the black trees go that drink here?
Their shadows must cover Canada.

A little light is filtering from the water flowers.
Their leaves do not wish us to hurry:
They are round and flat and full of dark advice.

Cold worlds shake from the oar.
The spirit of blackness is in us, it is in the fishes.
A snag is lifting a valedictory, pale hand;

Stars open among the lilies.
Are you not blinded by such expressionless sirens?
This is the silence of astounded souls.

WITCH BURNING

In the marketplace they are piling the dry sticks.
A thicket of shadows is a poor coat. I inhabit
The wax image of myself, a doll's body.
Sickness begins here: I am a dartboard for witches.
Only the devil can eat the devil out.
In the month of red leaves I climb to a bed of fire.

It is easy to blame the dark: the mouth of a door,
The cellar's belly. They've blown my sparkler out.
A black-sharded lady keeps me in a parrot cage.
What large eyes the dead have!
I am intimate with a hairy spirit.
Smoke wheels from the beak of this empty jar.

If I am a little one, I can do no harm.
If I don't move about, I'll knock nothing over. So I said,
Sitting under a potlid, tiny and inert as a rice grain.
They are turning the burners up, ring after ring.
We are full of starch, my small white fellows. We grow.
It hurts at first. The red tongues will teach the truth.

Mother of beetles, only unclench your hand:
I'll fly through the candle's mouth like a singeless moth.
Give me back my shape. I am ready to construe the days
I coupled with dust in the shadow of a stone.
My ankles brighten. Brightness ascends my thighs.
I am lost, I am lost, in the robes of all this light.

BRASÍLIA

Will they occur,
These people with torsos of steel
Winged elbows and eyeholes

Awaiting masses
Of cloud to give them expression,
These super-people!—

And my baby a nail
Driven in, driven in.
He shrieks in his grease,

Bones nosing for distances.
And I, nearly extinct,
His three teeth cutting

Themselves on my thumb—
And the star,
The old story.

In the lane I meet sheep and wagons,
Red earth, motherly blood.
O You who eat

People like light rays, leave
This one
Mirror safe, unredeemed

By the dove's annihilation,
The glory
The power, the glory.

Adrienne Rich

AUNT JENNIFER'S TIGERS

Aunt Jennifer's tigers prance across a screen,
Bright topaz denizens of a world of green.
They do not fear the men beneath the tree;
They pace in sleek chivalric certainty.

Aunt Jennifer's fingers fluttering through her wool
Find even the ivory needle hard to pull.
The massive weight of Uncle's wedding band
Sits heavily upon Aunt Jennifer's hand.

When Aunt is dead, her terrified hands will lie
Still ringed with ordeals she was mastered by.
The tigers in the panel that she made
Will go on prancing, proud and unafraid.

NOVEMBER 1968

Stripped
you're beginning to float free
up through the smoke of brushfires
and incinerators
the unleafed branches won't hold you
nor the radar aerials

You're what the autumn knew would happen
after the last collapse
of primary color
once the last absolutes were torn to pieces
you could begin

How you broke open, what sheathed you
until this moment
I know nothing about it
my ignorance of you amazes me
now that I watch you
starting to give yourself away
to the wind

1968

PLANETARIUM

Thinking of Caroline Herschel (1750–1848)
astronomer, sister of William; and others.

A woman in the shape of a monster
a monster in the shape of a woman
the skies are full of them

a woman   'in the snow
among the Clocks and instruments
or measuring the ground with poles'

in her 98 years to discover
8 comets

she whom the moon ruled
like us
levitating into the night sky
riding the polished lenses

Galaxies of women, there
doing penance for impetuousness
ribs chilled
in those spaces   of the mind

An eye,

        'virile, precise and absolutely certain'
        from the mad webs of Uranusborg

                                    encountering the NOVA

ADRIENNE RICH

every impulse of light exploding
from the core
as life flies out of us

    Tycho whispering at last
    'Let me not seem to have lived in vain'

What we see, we see
and seeing is changing

the light that shrivels a mountain
and leaves a man alive

Heartbeat of the pulsar
heart sweating through my body

The radio impulse
pouring in from Taurus

    I am bombarded yet   I stand

I have been standing all my life in the
direct path of a battery of signals
the most accurately transmitted most
untranslatable language in the universe
I am a galactic cloud so deep   so invo-
luted that a light wave could take 15
years to travel through me   And has
taken   I am an instrument in the shape
of a woman trying to translate pulsations
into images   for the relief of the body
and the reconstruction of the mind.

1968

DIVING INTO THE WRECK

First having read the book of myths,
and loaded the camera,
and checked the edge of the knife-blade,
I put on

the body-armor of black rubber
the absurd flippers
the grave and awkward mask.
I am having to do this
not like Cousteau with his
assiduous team
aboard the sun-flooded schooner
but here alone.

There is a ladder.
The ladder is always there
hanging innocently
close to the side of the schooner.
We know what it is for,
we who have used it.
Otherwise
it's a piece of maritime floss
some sundry equipment.

I go down.
Rung after rung and still
the oxygen immerses me
the blue light
the clear atoms
of our human air.
I go down.
My flippers cripple me,
I crawl like an insect down the ladder
and there is no one
to tell me when the ocean
will begin.

First the air is blue and then
it is bluer and then green and then
black I am blacking out and yet
my mask is powerful
it pumps my blood with power
the sea is another story
the sea is not a question of power
I have to learn alone
to turn my body without force
in the deep element.

ADRIENNE RICH

And now: it is easy to forget
what I came for
among so many who have always
lived here
swaying their crenellated fans
between the reefs
and besides
you breathe differently down here.

I came to explore the wreck.
The words are purposes.
The words are maps.
I came to see the damage that was done
and the treasures that prevail.
I stroke the beam of my lamp
slowly along the flank
of something more permanent
than fish or weed

the thing I came for:
the wreck and not the story of the wreck
the thing itself and not the myth
the drowned face always staring
toward the sun
the evidence of damage
worn by salt and sway into this threadbare beauty
the ribs of the disaster
curving their assertion
among the tentative haunters.

This is the place.
And I am here, the mermaid whose dark hair
streams black, the merman in his armored body
We circle silently
about the wreck
we dive into the hold.
I am she: I am he

whose drowned face sleeps with open eyes
whose breasts still bear the stress
whose silver, copper, vermeil cargo lies
obscurely inside barrels

half-wedged and left to rot
we are the half-destroyed instruments
that once held to a course
the water-eaten log
the fouled compass

We are, I am, you are
by cowardice or courage
the one who find our way
back to this scene
carrying a knife, a camera
a book of myths
in which
our names do not appear.

1972

AUGUST

Two horses in yellow light
eating windfall apples under a tree

as summer tears apart   milkweeds stagger
and grasses grow more ragged

They say there are ions in the sun
neutralizing magnetic fields on earth

Some way to explain
what this week has been, and the one before it!

If I am flesh sunning on rock
if I am brain burning in fluorescent light

if I am dream like a wire with fire
throbbing along it

if I am death to man
I have to know it

His mind is too simple, I cannot go on
sharing his nightmares

My own are becoming clearer, they open
into prehistory

which looks like a village lit with blood
where all the fathers are crying: *My son is mine!*

1972

SPLITTINGS

1

My body opens over San Francisco like the day-
light raining down   each pore crying the change of light
I am not with her   I have been waking off and on
all night to that pain   not simply absence but
the presence of the past   destructive
to living here and now   Yet if I could instruct
myself, if we could learn to learn from pain
even as it grasps us   if the mind, the mind that lives
in this body could refuse   to let itself be crushed
in that grasp   it would loosen   Pain would have to stand
off from me and listen   its dark breath still on me
but the mind could begin to speak to pain
and pain would have to answer:

                          We are older now
we have met before   these are my hands before your eyes
my figure blotting out   all that is not mine
I am the pain of division   creator of divisions
it is I who blot your lover from you
and not the time-zones nor the miles
It is not separation calls me forth   but I
who am separation   And remember
I have no existence   apart from you

2

I believe I am choosing something new
not to suffer uselessly   yet still to feel
Does the infant memorize the body of the mother
and create her in absence?   or simply cry
primordial loneliness?   does the bed of the stream
once diverted   mourning   remember wetness?

But we, we live so much in these
configurations of the past   I choose
to separate her   from my past we have not shared
I choose not to suffer uselessly
to detect primordial pain as it stalks toward me
flashing its bleak torch in my eyes   blotting out
her particular being   the details of her love
I will not be divided   from her or from myself
by myths of separation
while her mind and body in Manhattan are more with me
than the smell of eucalyptus coolly burning   on these hills

3

The world tells me I am its creature
I am raked by eyes   brushed by hands
I want to crawl into her for refuge   lay my head
in the space   between her breast and shoulder
abnegating power for love
as women have done   or hiding
from power in her love   like a man
I refuse these givens   the splitting
between love and action   I am choosing
not to suffer uselessly   and not to use her
I choose to love   this time   for once
with all my intelligence

1974

ADRIENNE RICH

INTEGRITY

the quality or state of being complete; unbroken condition; entirety

— *Webster*

A wild patience has taken me this far

as if I had to bring to shore
a boat with a spasmodic outboard motor
old sweaters, nets, spray-mottled books
tossed in the prow
some kind of sun burning my shoulder-blades.
Splashing the oarlocks. Burning through.
Your fore-arms can get scalded, licked with pain
in a sun blotted like unspoken anger
behind a casual mist.

The length of daylight
this far north, in this
forty-ninth year of my life
is critical.

The light is critical: of me, of this
long-dreamed, involuntary landing
on the arm of an inland sea.
The glitter of the shoal
depleting into shadow
I recognize: the stand of pines
violet-black really, green in the old postcard
but really I have nothing but myself
to go by; nothing
stands in the realm of pure necessity
except what my hands can hold.

Nothing but myself? . . . My selves.
After so long, this answer.

As if I had always known
I steer the boat in, simply.
The motor dying on the pebbles
cicadas taking up the hum
dropped in the silence.

Anger and tenderness: my selves.
And now I can believe they breathe in me
as angels, not polarities.
Anger and tenderness: the spider's genius
to spin and weave in the same action
from her own body, anywhere —
even from a broken web.

The cabin in the stand of pines
is still for sale. I know this. Know the print
of the last foot, the hand that slammed and locked that door,
then stopped to wreathe the rain-smashed clematis
back on the trellis
for no one's sake except its own.
I know the chart nailed to the wallboards
the icy kettle squatting on the burner.
The hands that hammered in those nails
emptied that kettle one last time
are these two hands
and they have caught the baby leaping
from between trembling legs
and they have worked the vacuum aspirator
and stroked the sweated temples
and steered the boat here through this hot
misblotted sunlight, critical light
imperceptibly scalding
the skin these hands will also salve.

1978

FOR THE RECORD

The clouds and the stars didn't wage this war
the brooks gave no information
if the mountain spewed stones of fire into the river

it was not taking sides
the raindrop faintly swaying under the leaf
had no political opinions

and if here or there a house
filled with backed-up raw sewage
or poisoned those who lived there
with slow fumes, over years
the houses were not at war
nor did the tinned-up buildings

intend to refuse shelter
to homeless old women and roaming children
they had no policy to keep them roaming
or dying, no, the cities were not the problem
the bridges were non-partisan
the freeways burned, but not with hatred

Even the miles of barbed-wire
stretched around crouching temporary huts
designed to keep the unwanted
at a safe distance, out of sight
even the boards that had to absorb
year upon year, so many human sounds

so many depths of vomit, tears
slow-soaking blood
had not offered themselves for this
The trees didn't volunteer to be cut into boards
nor the thorns for tearing flesh
Look around at all of it

and ask whose signature
is stamped on the orders, traced
in the corner of the building plans
Ask where the illiterate, big-bellied
women were, the drunks and crazies,
the ones you fear most of all: ask where you were.

1983

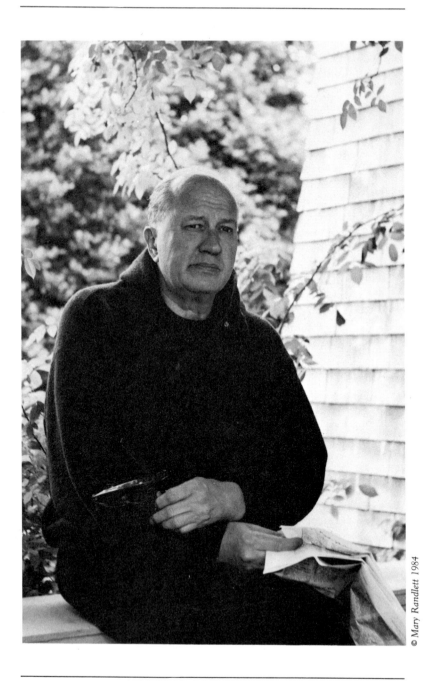

Theodore Roethke

THE PREMONITION

Walking this field I remember
Days of another summer.
Oh that was long ago! I kept
Close to the heels of my father,
Matching his stride with half-steps
Until we came to a river.
He dipped his hand in the shallow:
Water ran over and under
Hair on a narrow wrist bone;
His image kept following after,—
Flashed with the sun in the ripple.
But when he stood up, that face
Was lost in a maze of water.

CUTTINGS

(later)

This urge, wrestle, resurrection of dry sticks,
Cut stems struggling to put down feet,
What saint strained so much,
Rose on such lopped limbs to a new life?

I can hear, underground, that sucking and sobbing,
In my veins, in my bones I feel it,—
The small waters seeping upward,
The tight grains parting at last.
When sprouts break out,
Slippery as fish,
I quail, lean to beginnings, sheath-wet.

THEODORE ROETHKE

FORCING HOUSE

Vines tougher than wrists
And rubbery shoots,
Scums, mildews, smuts along stems,
Great cannas or delicate cyclamen tips,—
All pulse with the knocking pipes
That drip and sweat,
Sweat and drip,
Swelling the roots with steam and stench,
Shooting up lime and dung and ground bones,—
Fifty summers in motion at once,
As the live heat billows from pipes and pots.

MY PAPA'S WALTZ

The whiskey on your breath
Could make a small boy dizzy;
But I hung on like death:
Such waltzing was not easy.

We romped until the pans
Slid from the kitchen shelf;
My mother's countenance
Could not unfrown itself.

The hand that held my wrist
Was battered on one knuckle;
At every step you missed
My right ear scraped a buckle.

You beat time on my head
With a palm caked hard by dirt,
Then waltzed me off to bed
Still clinging to your shirt.

THEODORE ROETHKE

ELEGY FOR JANE

My Student, Thrown by a Horse

I remember the neckcurls, limp and damp as tendrils;
And her quick look, a sidelong pickerel smile;
And how, once startled into talk, the light syllables leaped for her,
And she balanced in the delight of her thought,
A wren, happy, tail into the wind,
Her song trembling the twigs and small branches.
The shade sang with her;
The leaves, their whispers turned to kissing;
And the mold sang in the bleached valleys under the rose.

Oh, when she was sad, she cast herself down into such a pure depth,
Even a father could not find her:
Scraping her cheek against straw;
Stirring the clearest water.

My sparrow, you are not here,
Waiting like a fern, making a spiny shadow.
The sides of wet stones cannot console me,
Nor the moss, wound with the last light.

If only I could nudge you from this sleep,
My maimed darling, my skittery pigeon.
Over this damp grave I speak the words of my love:
I, with no rights in this matter,
Neither father nor lover.

THE WAKING

I wake to sleep, and take my waking slow.
I feel my fate in what I cannot fear.
I learn by going where I have to go.

We think by feeling. What is there to know?
I hear my being dance from ear to ear.
I wake to sleep, and take my waking slow.

Of those so close beside me, which are you?
God bless the Ground! I shall walk softly there,
And learn by going where I have to go.

Light takes the Tree; but who can tell us how?
The lowly worm climbs up a winding stair;
I wake to sleep, and take my waking slow.

Great Nature has another thing to do
To you and me; so take the lively air,
And, lovely, learn by going where to go.

This shaking keeps me steady. I should know.
What falls away is always. And is near.
I wake to sleep, and take my waking slow.
I learn by going where I have to go.

I KNEW A WOMAN

I knew a woman, lovely in her bones,
When small birds sighed, she would sigh back at them;
Ah, when she moved, she moved more ways than one:
The shapes a bright container can contain!
Of her choice virtues only gods should speak,
Or English poets who grew up on Greek
(I'd have them sing in chorus, cheek to cheek).

How well her wishes went! She stroked my chin,
She taught me Turn, and Counter-turn, and Stand;
She taught me Touch, that undulant white skin;
I nibbled meekly from her proffered hand;
She was the sickle; I, poor I, the rake,
Coming behind her for her pretty sake
(But what prodigious mowing we did make).

THEODORE ROETHKE

Love likes a gander, and adores a goose:
Her full lips pursed, the errant note to seize;
She played it quick, she played it light and loose;
My eyes, they dazzled at her flowing knees;
Her several parts could keep a pure repose,
Or one hip quiver with a mobile nose
(She moved in circles, and those circles moved).

Let seed be grass, and grass turn into hay:
I'm martyr to a motion not my own;
What's freedom for? To know eternity.
I swear she cast a shadow white as stone.
But who would count eternity in days?
These old bones live to learn her wanton ways:
(I measure time by how a body sways).

MEDITATION AT OYSTER RIVER

1

Over the low, barnacled, elephant-colored rocks,
Come the first tide-ripples, moving, almost without sound, toward me,
Running along the narrow furrows of the shore, the rows of dead clam
    shells;
Then a runnel behind me, creeping closer,
Alive with tiny striped fish, and young crabs climbing in and out of the
    water.

No sound from the bay. No violence.
Even the gulls quiet on the far rocks,
Silent, in the deepening light,
Their cat-mewing over,
Their child-whimpering.

At last one long undulant ripple,
Blue-black from where I am sitting,
Makes almost a wave over a barrier of small stones,

Slapping lightly against a sunken log.
I dabble my toes in the brackish foam sliding forward,
Then retire to a rock higher up on the cliff-side.
The wind slackens, light as a moth fanning a stone:
A twilight wind, light as a child's breath
Turning not a leaf, not a ripple.
The dew revives on the beach-grass;
The salt-soaked wood of a fire crackles;
A fish raven turns on its perch (a dead tree in the rivermouth),
Its wings catching a last glint of the reflected sunlight.

2

The self persists like a dying star,
In sleep, afraid. Death's face rises afresh,
Among the shy beasts, the deer at the salt-lick,
The doe with its sloped shoulders loping across the highway,
The young snake, poised in green leaves, waiting for its fly,
The hummingbird, whirring from quince-blossom to morning-glory—
With these I would be.
And with water: the waves coming forward, without cessation,
The waves, altered by sand-bars, beds of kelp, miscellaneous driftwood,
Topped by cross-winds, tugged at by sinuous undercurrents
The tide rustling in, sliding between the ridges of stone,
The tongues of water, creeping in, quietly.

3

In this hour,
In this first heaven of knowing,
The flesh takes on the pure poise of the spirit,
Acquires, for a time, the sandpiper's insouciance,
The hummingbird's surety, the kingfisher's cunning—
I shift on my rock, and I think:
Of the first trembling of a Michigan brook in April,
Over a lip of stone, the tiny rivulet;
And that wrist-thick cascade tumbling from a cleft rock,
Its spray holding a double rain-bow in early morning,
Small enough to be taken in, embraced, by two arms,—
Or the Tittebawasee, in the time between winter and spring,

When the ice melts along the edges in early afternoon.
And the midchannel begins cracking and heaving from the pressure
     beneath,
The ice piling high against the iron-bound spiles,
Gleaming, freezing hard again, creaking at midnight—
And I long for the blast of dynamite,
The sudden sucking roar as the culvert loosens its debris of branches and
     sticks,
Welter of tin cans, pails, old bird nests, a child's shoe riding a log,
As the piled ice breaks away from the battered spiles,
And the whole river begins to move forward, its bridges shaking.

4

Now, in this waning of light,
I rock with the motion of morning;
In the cradle of all that is,
I'm lulled into half-sleep
By the lapping of water,
Cries of the sandpiper.
Water's my will, and my way,
And the spirit runs, intermittently,
In and out of the small waves,
Runs with the intrepid shorebirds—
How graceful the small before danger!

In the first of the moon,
All's a scattering,
A shining.

IN A DARK TIME

In a dark time, the eye begins to see,
I meet my shadow in the deepening shade;
I hear my echo in the echoing wood—
A lord of nature weeping to a tree.
I live between the heron and the wren,
Beasts of the hill and serpents of the den.

What's madness but nobility of soul
At odds with circumstance? The day's on fire!
I know the purity of pure despair,
My shadow pinned against a sweating wall.
That place among the rocks—is it a cave,
Or winding path? The edge is what I have.

A steady storm of correspondences!
A night flowing with birds, a ragged moon,
And in broad day the midnight come again!
A man goes far to find out what he is—
Death of the self in a long, tearless night,
All natural shapes blazing unnatural light.

Dark, dark my light, and darker my desire.
My soul, like some heat-maddened summer fly,
Keeps buzzing at the sill. Which I is I?
A fallen man, I climb out of my fear.
The mind enters itself, and God the mind,
And one is One, free in the tearing wind.

IN EVENING AIR

1

A dark theme keeps me here,
Though summer blazes in the vireo's eye.
Who would be half possessed
By his own nakedness?
Waking's my care—
I'll make a broken music, or I'll die.

2

Ye littles, lie more close!
Make me, O Lord, a last, a simple thing
Time cannot overwhelm.
Once I transcended time:
A bud broke to a rose,
And I rose from a last diminishing.

3

I look down the far light
And I behold the dark side of a tree
Far down a billowing plain,
And when I look again,
It's lost upon the night—
Night I embrace, a dear proximity.

4

I stand by a low fire
Counting the wisps of flame, and I watch how
Light shifts upon the wall.
I bid stillness be still.
I see, in evening air,
How slowly dark comes down on what we do.

Anne Sexton

HER KIND

I have gone out, a possessed witch,
haunting the black air, braver at night;
dreaming evil, I have done my hitch
over the plain houses, light by light:
lonely thing, twelve-fingered, out of mind.
A woman like that is not a woman, quite.
I have been her kind.

I have found the warm caves in the woods,
filled them with skillets, carvings, shelves,
closets, silks, innumerable goods;
fixed the suppers for the worms and the elves:
whining, rearranging the disaligned.
A woman like that is misunderstood.
I have been her kind.

I have ridden in your cart, driver,
waved my nude arms at villages going by,
learning the last bright routes, survivor
where your flames still bite my thigh
and my ribs crack where your wheels wind.
A woman like that is not ashamed to die.
I have been her kind.

WITH MERCY FOR THE GREEDY

*For my friend, Ruth, who urges me to make an
appointment for the Sacrament of Confession*

Concerning your letter in which you ask
me to call a priest and in which you ask
me to wear The Cross that you enclose;
your own cross,
your dog-bitten cross,

no larger than a thumb,
small and wooden, no thorns, this rose—

I pray to its shadow,
that gray place
where it lies on your letter . . . deep, deep.
I detest my sins and I try to believe
in The Cross. I touch its tender hips, its dark jawed face,
its solid neck, its brown sleep.

True. There is
a beautiful Jesus.
He is frozen to his bones like a chunk of beef.
How desperately he wanted to pull his arms in!
How desperately I touch his vertical and horizontal axes!
But I can't. Need is not quite belief.

All morning long
I have worn
your cross, hung with package string around my throat.
It tapped me lightly as a child's heart might,
tapping secondhand, softly waiting to be born.
Ruth, I cherish the letter you wrote.

My friend, my friend, I was born
doing reference work in sin, and born
confessing it. This is what poems are:
with mercy
for the greedy,
they are the tongue's wrangle,
the world's pottage, the rat's star.

THE ABORTION

Somebody who should have been born
is gone.

Just as the earth puckered its mouth,
each bud puffing out from its knot,
I changed my shoes, and then drove south.

ANNE SEXTON

Up past the Blue Mountains, where
Pennsylvania humps on endlessly,
wearing, like a crayoned cat, its green hair,

its roads sunken in like a gray washboard;
where, in truth, the ground cracks evilly,
a dark socket from which the coal has poured,

Somebody who should have been born
is gone.

the grass as bristly and stout as chives,
and me wondering when the ground would break,
and me wondering how anything fragile survives;

up in Pennsylvania, I met a little man,
not Rumpelstiltskin, at all, at all . . .
he took the fullness that love began.

Returning north, even the sky grew thin
like a high window looking nowhere.
The road was as flat as a sheet of tin.

Somebody who should have been born
is gone.

Yes, woman, such logic will lead
to loss without death. Or say what you meant,
you coward . . . this baby that I bleed.

MAN AND WIFE

To speke of wo
that is in mariage . . .

We are not lovers.
We do not even know each other.
We look alike
but we have nothing to say.
We are like pigeons . . .

that pair who came to the suburbs
by mistake,
forsaking Boston where they bumped
their small heads against a blind wall,
having worn out the fruit stalls in the North End,
the amethyst windows of Louisburg Square,
the seats on the Common
And the traffic that kept stamping
and stamping.

Now there is green rain for everyone
as common as eyewash.
Now they are together
like strangers in a two-seater outhouse,
eating and squatting together.
They have teeth and knees
but they do not speak.
A soldier is forced to stay with a soldier
because they share the same dirt
and the same blows.

They are exiles
soiled by the same sweat and the drunkard's dream.
As it is they can only hang on,
their red claws wound like bracelets
around the same limb.
Even their song is not a sure thing.
It is not a language;
it is a kind of breathing.
They are two asthmatics
whose breath sobs in and out
through a small fuzzy pipe.

Like them
we neither talk nor clear our throats.
Oh darling,
we gasp in unison beside our window pane,

drunk on the drunkard's dream.
Like them
we can only hang on.

But they would pierce our heart
if they could only fly the distance.

IN CELEBRATION OF MY UTERUS

Everyone in me is a bird.
I am beating all my wings.
They wanted to cut you out
but they will not.
They said you were immeasurably empty
but you are not.
They said you were sick unto dying
but they were wrong.
You are singing like a school girl.
You are not torn.

Sweet weight,
in celebration of the woman I am
and of the soul of the woman I am
and of the central creature and its delight
I sing for you. I dare to live.

Hello, spirit. Hello, cup.
Fasten, cover. Cover that does contain.
Hello to the soil of the fields.
Welcome, roots.

Each cell has a life.
There is enough here to please a nation.
It is enough that the populace own these goods.

Any person, any commonwealth would say of it,
"It is good this year that we may plant again
and think forward to a harvest.
A blight had been forecast and has been cast out."
Many women are singing together of this:
one is in a shoe factory cursing the machine,
one is at the aquarium tending a seal,
one is dull at the wheel of her Ford,
one is at the toll gate collecting,
one is tying the cord of a calf in Arizona,
one is straddling a cello in Russia,
one is shifting pots on the stove in Egypt,
one is painting her bedroom walls moon color,
one is dying but remembering a breakfast,
one is stretching on her mat in Thailand,
one is wiping the ass of her child,
one is staring out the window of a train
in the middle of Wyoming and one is
anywhere and some are everywhere and all
seem to be singing, although some can not
sing a note.

Sweet weight,
in celebration of the woman I am
let me carry a ten-foot scarf,
let me drum for the nineteen-year-olds,
let me carry bowls for the offering
(if that is my part).
Let me study the cardiovascular tissue,
let me examine the angular distance of meteors,
let me suck on the stems of flowers
(if that is my part).
Let me make certain tribal figures
(if that is my part).
For this thing the body needs
let me sing
for the supper,
for the kissing,
for the correct
yes.

ANNE SEXTON

US

I was wrapped in black
fur and white fur and
you undid me and then
you placed me in gold light
and then you crowned me,
while snow fell outside
the door in diagonal darts.
While a ten-inch snow
came down like stars
in small calcium fragments,
we were in our own bodies
(that room that will bury us)
and you were in my body
(that room that will outlive us)
and at first I rubbed your
feet dry with a towel
because I was your slave
and then you called me princess.
Princess!

Oh then
I stood up in my gold skin
and I beat down the psalms
and I beat down the clothes
and you undid the bridle
and you undid the reins
and I undid the buttons,
the bones, the confusions,
the New England postcards,
the January ten o'clock night,
and we rose up like wheat,
acre after acre of gold,
and we harvested,
we harvested.

ANNE SEXTON

THE FURY OF COCKS

There they are
drooping over the breakfast plates,
angel-like,
folding in their sad wing,
animal sad,
and only the night before
there they were
playing the banjo.
Once more the day's light comes
with its immense sun,
its mother trucks,
its engines of amputation.
Whereas last night
the cock knew its way home,
as stiff as a hammer,
battering in with all
its awful power.
That theater.
Today it is tender,
a small bird,
as soft as a baby's hand.
She is the house.
He is the steeple.
When they fuck they are God.
When they break away they are God.
When they snore they are God.
In the morning they butter the toast.
They don't say much.
They are still God.
All the cocks of the world are God,
blooming, blooming, blooming
into the sweet blood of woman.

ANNE SEXTON

ROWING

A story, a story!
(Let it go. Let it come.)
I was stamped out like a Plymouth fender
into this world.
First came the crib
with its glacial bars.
Then dolls
and the devotion to their plastic mouths.
Then there was school,
the little straight rows of chairs,
blotting my name over and over,
but undersea all the time,
a stranger whose elbows wouldn't work.
Then there was life
with its cruel houses
and people who seldom touched—
though touch is all—
but I grew,
like a pig in a trenchcoat I grew,
and then there were many strange apparitions,
the nagging rain, the sun turning into poison
and all of that, saws working through my heart,
but I grew, I grew,
and God was there like an island I had not rowed to,
still ignorant of Him, my arms and my legs worked,
and I grew, I grew,
I wore rubies and bought tomatoes
and now, in my middle age,
about nineteen in the head I'd say,
I am rowing, I am rowing
though the oarlocks stick and are rusty

and the sea blinks and rolls
like a worried eyeball,
but I am rowing, I am rowing,
though the wind pushes me back
and I know that that island will not be perfect,
it will have the flaws of life,
the absurdities of the dinner table,
but there will be a door
and I will open it
and I will get rid of the rat inside of me,
the gnawing pestilential rat.
God will take it with his two hands
and embrace it.

As the African says:
This is my tale which I have told,
if it be sweet, if it be not sweet,
take somewhere else and let some return to me.
This story ends with me still rowing.

TWO HANDS

From the sea came a hand,
ignorant as a penny,
troubled with the salt of its mother,
mute with the silence of the fishes,
quick with the altars of the tides,
and God reached out of His mouth
and called it man.
Up came the other hand
and God called it woman.
The hands applauded.
And this was no sin.
It was as it was meant to be.

I see them roaming the streets:
Levi complaining about his mattress,
Sarah studying a beetle,
Mandrake holding his coffee mug,

ANNE SEXTON

Sally playing the drum at a football game,
John closing the eyes of the dying woman,
and some who are in prison,
even the prison of their bodies,
as Christ was prisoned in His body
until the triumph came.

Unwind, hands,
you angel webs,
unwind like the coil of a jumping jack,
cup together and let yourselves fill up with sun
and applaud, world,
applaud.

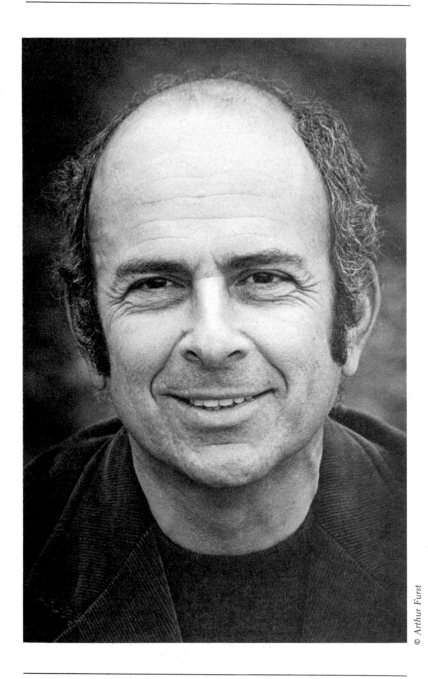

Louis Simpson

TO THE WESTERN WORLD

A siren sang, and Europe turned away
From the high castle and the shepherd's crook.
Three caravels went sailing to Cathay
On the strange ocean, and the captains shook
Their banners out across the Mexique Bay.

And in our early days we did the same.
Remembering our fathers in their wreck
We crossed the sea from Palos where they came
And saw, enormous to the little deck,
A shore in silence waiting for a name.

The treasures of Cathay were never found.
In this America, this wilderness
Where the axe echoes with a lonely sound,
The generations labor to possess
And grave by grave we civilize the ground.

HOT NIGHT ON WATER STREET

A hot midsummer night on Water Street—
The boys in jeans were combing their blond hair,
Watching the girls go by on tired feet;
And an old woman with a witch's stare
Cried "Praise the Lord!" She vanished on a bus
With hissing air brakes, like an incubus.

Three hardware stores, a barbershop, a bar,
A movie playing Westerns—where I went
To see a dream of horses called *The Star*. . . .
Some day, when this uncertain continent
Is marble, and men ask what was the good
We lived by, dust may whisper "Hollywood."

LOUIS SIMPSON

Then back along the river bank on foot
By moonlight. . . . On the West Virginia side
An owlish train began to huff and hoot;
It seemed to know of something that had died.
I didn't linger—sometimes when I travel
I think I'm being followed by the Devil.

At the newsstand in the lobby, a cigar
Was talkative: "Since I've been in this town
I've seen one likely woman, and a car
As she was crossing Main Street knocked her down."
I was a stranger here myself, I said,
And bought the *New York Times*, and went to bed.

IN THE SUBURBS

There's no way out.
You were born to waste your life.
You were born to this middleclass life

As others before you
Were born to walk in procession
To the temple, singing.

WALT WHITMAN AT BEAR MOUNTAIN

"*. . . life which does not give the preference to any other life, of any previous period, which therefore prefers its own existence . . .*"

Ortega y Gasset

Neither on horseback nor seated,
But like himself, squarely on two feet,
The poet of death and lilacs
Loafs by the footpath. Even the bronze looks alive
Where it is folded like cloth. And he seems friendly.

"Where is the Mississippi panorama
And the girl who played the piano?
Where are you, Walt?
The Open Road goes to the used-car lot.

"Where is the nation you promised?
These houses built of wood sustain
Colossal snows,
And the light above the street is sick to death.

"As for the people—see how they neglect you!
Only a poet pauses to read the inscription."

"I am here," he answered.
"It seems you have found me out.
Yet, did I not warn you that it was Myself
I advertised? Were my words not sufficiently plain?

"I gave no prescriptions,
And those who have taken my moods for prophecies
Mistake the matter."
Then, vastly amused—"Why do you reproach me?
I freely confess I am wholly disreputable.
Yet I am happy, because you have found me out."

A crocodile in wrinkled metal loafing . . .

Then all the realtors,
Pickpockets, salesmen, and the actors performing
Official scenarios,
Turned a deaf ear, for they had contracted
American dreams.

But the man who keeps a store on a lonely road,
And the housewife who knows she's dumb,
And the earth, are relieved.

All that grave weight of America
Cancelled! Like Greece and Rome.
The future in ruins!

The castles, the prisons, the cathedrals
Unbuilding, and roses
Blossoming from the stones that are not there . . .

The clouds are lifting from the high Sierras,
The Bay mists clearing.
And the angel in the gate, the flowering plum,
Dances like Italy, imagining red.

AMERICAN POETRY

Whatever it is, it must have
A stomach that can digest
Rubber, coal, uranium, moons, poems.

Like the shark, it contains a shoe.
It must swim for miles through the desert
Uttering cries that are almost human.

AFTER MIDNIGHT

The dark streets are deserted,
With only a drugstore glowing
Softly, like a sleeping body;

With one white, naked bulb
In the back, that shines
On suicides and abortions.

Who lives in these dark houses?
I am suddenly aware
I might live here myself.

The garage man returns
And puts the change in my hand,
Counting the singles carefully.

LOUIS SIMPSON

LUMINOUS NIGHT

I love the dark race of poets,
And yet there is also happiness.
Happiness . . .

If I can stand it, I can stand anything.
Luminous night, let fall your pearls!
Wind, toss the sodden boughs!

Then let the birch trees shine
Like crystal. Light the boughs!
We can live here, Cristina,

We can live here,
In this house, among these trees,
This world so many have left.

AMERICAN DREAMS

In dreams my life came toward me,
my loves that were slender as gazelles.
But America also dreams. . . .
Dream, you are flying over Russia,
dream, you are falling in Asia.

As I look down the street
on a typical sunny day in California
it is my house that is burning
and my dear ones that lie in the gutter
as the American army enters.

Every day I wake far away
from my life, in a foreign country.
These people are speaking a strange language.
It is strange to me
and strange, I think, even to themselves.

PORT JEFFERSON

My whole life coming to this place,
and understanding it better
maybe for having been born
offshore, and at an early age
left to my own support . . .

I have come where sea and wind,
wave and leaf, are one sighing,
where the house strains at an anchor
and the salt-rose clings and clambers
on the humorous grave.

This is the place, Camerado,
that hides the sea-bird's nest.
Listening to the distant voices
in summer, a murmur of the sea,
I seem to remember everything.

THE SILENT PIANO

We have lived like civilized people.
O ruins, traditions!

And we have seen the barbarians,
breakers of sculpture and glass.

And now we talk of 'the inner life',
and I ask myself, where is it?

Not here, in these streets and houses,
so I think it must be found

in indolence, pure indolence,
an ocean of darkness,

in silence, an arm of the moon,
a hand that enters slowly.

*

I am reminded of a story
Camus tells, of a man in prison camp.

He had carved a piano keyboard
with a nail on a piece of wood.

And sat there playing the piano.
This music was made entirely of silence.

SACRED OBJECTS

I am taking part in a great experiment—
whether writers can live peacefully in the suburbs
and not be bored to death.

As Whitman said, an American muse
installed amid the kitchen ware.
And we have wonderful household appliances . . .
now tell me about the poets.

Where are your children, Lucina?
Since Eliot died and Pound
has become . . . an authority,
chef d'école au lieu d'être tout de go,

I have been listening to the whispers
of U.S. Steel and Anaconda:
'In a little while it will stiffen . . .
blown into the road,

drifting with the foam of chemicals.'

2

The light that shines through the *Leaves*
is clear: 'to form individuals.'

A swamp where the seabirds brood.
When the psyche is still and the soul does nothing,
a Sound, with shining tidal pools and channels.

And the kingdom is within you . . .
the hills and all the streams
running west to the Mississippi.
There the roads are lined with timothy
and the clouds are tangled with the haystacks.

Your loves are a line of birch trees.
When the wind flattens the grass, it
shines, and a butterfly
writes dark lines on the air.

There are your sacred objects,
the wings and gazing eyes
of the life you really have.

3

Where then shall we meet?

                    Where you left me.

At the drive-in restaurant . . .
the fields on either side covered with stubble,
an odor of gasoline and burning asphalt,
glare on tinted glass, chrome-plated hubcaps and bumpers.

I came out, wiping my hands
on my apron, to take your orders.
Thin hands, streaked with mustard,

give us a hot-dog,
give us a Pepsi-Cola.

Listening to the monotonous grasshoppers
for years I have concentrated on the moment.

And at night when the passing headlights hurl
shadows flitting across the wall,
I sit in a window, combing my hair
day in day out.

AS A MAN WALKS

It's a strange country,
strange for me to have come to.
Cattle standing in a field,
sheep that are motionless
as stones,
the sun sinking in a pile of clouds,
and the eternal flies
getting in your ears and eyes...

I suppose you have become accustomed.
Mrs. Scully was in her kitchen
entertaining two friends
when one said, "Isn't that a snake?"
and pointed. Sure enough
one was sliding around the divider.
She reached for something, the rolling pin,
and stunned it. Then finished it off
with a hammer.

The green-hide and stringy-bark Australian...
my candidate for survival
in the event of fire, flood,
or nuclear explosion.

As a man walks he creates the road he walks on.
All of my life in America
I must have been reeling out of myself
this red dirt, gravel road.

Three boys seated on motorcycles
conferring...

A little further on,
a beaten-up Holden parked off the road
with two men inside passing the bottle.
Dark-skinned...maybe they are aboriginal.

I might have been content to live
in Belle Terre, among houses and lawns,
but inside me are gum trees,
and magpies, cackling and whistling,
and a bush-roaming kangaroo.

PHYSICAL UNIVERSE

He woke at five and, unable
to go back to sleep,
went downstairs.

A book was lying on the table
where his son had done his homework.
He took it into the kitchen,
made coffee, poured himself a cup,
and settled down to read.

"There was a local eddy in the swirling gas
of the primordial galaxy,
and a cloud was formed, the protosun,
as wide as the present solar system.

LOUIS SIMPSON

This contracted. Some of the gas
formed a diffuse, spherical nebula,
a thin disk, that cooled and flattened.
Pulled one way by its own gravity,
the other way by the sun,
it broke, forming smaller clouds,
the protoplanets. Earth
was 2000 times as wide as it is now."

The earth was without form, and void,
and darkness was upon the face of the deep.

*

"Then the sun began to shine,
dispelling the gases and vapors,
shrinking the planets, melting earth,
separating iron and silicate
to form the core and mantle.
Continents appeared..."
history, civilisation,
the discovery of America
and the settling of Green Harbor,
bringing us to Tuesday, the seventh of July.

Tuesday, the day they pick up the garbage!
He leaped into action,
took the garbage bag out of its container,
tied it with a twist of wire,
and carried it out to the tool-shed,
taking care not to let the screen-door slam,
and put it in the large garbage-can
that was three-quarters full.
He kept it in the tool-shed so the raccoons
couldn't get at it.

He carried the can out to the road,
then went back into the house
and walked around, picking up newspapers
and fliers for: "Thompson Seedless Grapes,
California's finest sweet eating";

"Scott Bathroom Tissue";

"Legislative report from Senator Ken LaValle."

He put all this paper in a box,
and emptied the waste baskets in the two
downstairs bathrooms,
and the basket in the study.

He carried the box out to the road,
taking care not to let the screen-door slam,
and placed the box next to the garbage.

Now let the garbage men come!

*

He went back upstairs.
Susan said, "Did you put out the garbage?"
But her eyes were closed.
She was sleeping, yet could speak in her sleep,
ask a question, even answer one.

"Yes," he said, and climbed into bed.
She turned around to face him,
with her eyes still closed.

He thought, perhaps she's an oracle,
speaking from the Collective Unconscious.
He said to her, "Do you agree with Darwin
that people and monkeys have a common ancestor?
Or should we stick to the Bible?"

She said, "Did you take out the garbage?"

LOUIS SIMPSON

"Yes," he said, for the second time.
Then thought about it. Her answer
had something in it of the sublime.
Like a *koan*...the kind of irrelevance
a Zen-master says to the disciple
who is asking riddles of the universe.

He put his arm around her,
and she continued to breathe evenly
from the depths of sleep.

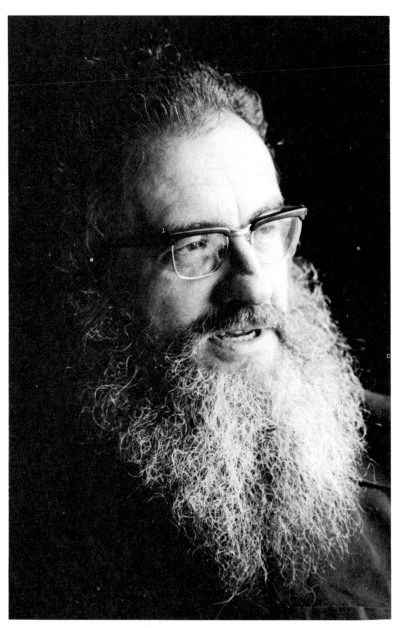

W. D. Snodgrass

APRIL INVENTORY

The green catalpa tree has turned
All white; the cherry blooms once more.
In one whole year I haven't learned
A blessed thing they pay you for.
The blossoms snow down in my hair;
The trees and I will soon be bare.

The trees have more than I to spare.
The sleek, expensive girls I teach,
Younger and pinker every year,
Bloom gradually out of reach.
The pear tree lets its petals drop
Like dandruff on a tabletop.

The girls have grown so young by now
I have to nudge myself to stare.
This year they smile and mind me how
My teeth are falling with my hair.
In thirty years I may not get
Younger, shrewder, or out of debt.

The tenth time, just a year ago,
I made myself a little list
Of all the things I'd ought to know,
Then told my parents, analyst,
And everyone who's trusted me
I'd be substantial, presently.

I haven't read one book about
A book or memorized one plot.
Or found a mind I did not doubt.
I learned one date. And then forgot.
And one by one the solid scholars
Get the degrees, the jobs, the dollars.

And smile above their starchy collars.
I taught my classes Whitehead's notions;
One lovely girl, a song of Mahler's.
Lacking a source-book or promotions,
I showed one child the colors of
A luna moth and how to love.

I taught myself to name my name,
To bark back, loosen love and crying;
To ease my woman so she came,
To ease an old man who was dying.
I have not learned how often I
Can win, can love, but choose to die.

I have not learned there is a lie
Love shall be blonder, slimmer, younger;
That my equivocating eye
Loves only by my body's hunger;
That I have forces, true to feel,
Or that the lovely world is real.

While scholars speak authority
And wear their ulcers on their sleeves,
My eyes in spectacles shall see
These trees procure and spend their leaves.
There is a value underneath
The gold and silver in my teeth.

Though trees turn bare and girls turn wives,
We shall afford our costly seasons;
There is a gentleness survives
That will outspeak and has its reasons.
There is a loveliness exists,
Preserves us, not for specialists.

from **HEART'S NEEDLE**

6

Easter has come around
again; the river is rising
over the thawed ground

and the banksides. When you come you bring
　　an egg dyed lavender.
　We shout along our bank to hear
our voices returning from the hills to meet us.
　　We need the landscape to repeat us.

　　You lived on this bank first.
　While nine months filled your term, we knew
　　how your lungs, immersed
in the womb, miraculously grew
　　their useless folds till
the fierce, cold air rushed in to fill
them out like bushes thick with leaves. You took your hour,
　　caught breath, and cried with your full lung power.

　　Over the stagnant bight
we see the hungry bank swallow
　　flaunting his free flight
still; we sink in mud to follow
　　the killdeer from the grass
that hides her nest. That March there was
rain; the rivers rose; you could hear killdeers flying
　　all night over the mudflats crying.

　　You bring back how the red-
winged blackbird shrieked, slapping frail wings,
　　diving at my head—
I saw where her tough nest, cradled, swings
　　in tall reeds that must sway
with the winds blowing every way.
If you recall much, you recall this place. You still
　　live nearby—on the opposite hill.

　　After the sharp windstorm
of July Fourth, all that summer
　　through the gentle, warm
afternoons, we heard great chain saws chirr
　　like iron locusts. Crews
of roughneck boys swarmed to cut loose
branches wrenched in the shattering wind, to hack free
　　all the torn limbs that could sap the tree.

In the debris lay
starlings, dead. Near the park's birdrun
we surprised one day
a proud, tan-spatted, buff-brown pigeon.
In my hands she flapped so
fearfully that I let her go.
Her keeper came. And we helped snarl her in a net.
You bring things I'd as soon forget.

You raise into my head
a Fall night that I came once more
to sit on your bed;
sweat beads stood out on your arms and fore-
head and you wheezed for breath,
for help, like some child caught beneath
its comfortable woolly blankets, drowning there.
Your lungs caught and would not take the air.

Of all things, only we
have power to choose that we should die;
nothing else is free
in this world to refuse it. Yet I,
who say this, could not raise
myself from bed how many days
to the thieving world. Child, I have another wife,
another child. We try to choose our life.

THE MOTHER

She stands in the dead center like a star;
They form around her like her satellites
Taking her energies, her heat, light
And massive attraction on their paths, however far.

Born of her own flesh; still, she feels them drawn
Into the outer cold by dark forces;
They are in love with suffering and perversion,
With the community of pain. Thinking them gone,

Out of her reach, she is consoled by evil
In neighbors, children, the world she cannot change,
That lightless universe where they range
Out of the comforts of her disapproval.

If evil did not exist, she would create it
To die in righteousness, her martyrdom
To that sweet dominion they have bolted from.
Then, at last, she can think that she is hated

And is content. Things can decay, break,
Spoil themselves; who cares? She'll gather the debris
With loving tenderness to give them; she
Will weave a labyrinth of waste, wreckage

And hocus-pocus; leave free no fault
Or cornerhole outside those lines of force
Where she and only she can thread a course.
All else in her grasp grows clogged and halts.

Till one by one, the areas of her brain
Switch off and she has filled all empty spaces;
Now she hallucinates in their right places
Their after-images, reversed and faint.

And the drawn strands of love, spun in her mind,
Turn dark and cluttered, precariously hung
With the black shapes of her mates, her sapless young,
Where she moves by habit, hungering and blind.

VIEWING THE BODY

Flowers like a gangster's funeral;
    Eyeshadow like a whore.
They all say isn't she beautiful.
    She, who never wore

Lipstick or such a dress,
    Never got taken out,

Was scarcely looked at, much less
    Wanted or talked about;

Who, gray as a mouse, crept
    The dark halls at her mother's
Or snuggled, soft, and slept
    Alone in the dim bedcovers.

Today at last she holds
    All eyes and a place of honor
Till the obscene red folds
    Of satin close down on her.

DISPOSAL

The unworn long gown, meant for dances
She would have scarcely dared attend,
Is fobbed off on a friend—
Who can't help wondering if it's spoiled
But thinks, well, she can take her chances.

We roll her spoons up like old plans
Or failed securities, seal their case,
They lay them back. One lace
Nightthing lies in the chest, unsoiled
By wear, untouched by human hands.

We don't dare burn those cancelled patterns
And markdowns that she actually wore,
Yet who do we know so poor
They'd take them? Spared all need, all passion,
Saved from loss, she lies boxed in satins

Like a pair of party shoes
That seemed to never find a taker;
We send back to its maker
A life somehow gone out of fashion
But still too good to use.

A FLAT ONE

Old Fritz, on this rotating bed
For seven wasted months you lay
Unfit to move, shrunken, gray,
No good to yourself or anyone
But to be babied—changed and bathed and fed.
     At long last, that's all done.

Before each meal, twice every night,
We set pads on your bedsores, shut
Your catheter tube off, then brought
The second canvas-and-black-iron
Bedframe and clamped you in between them, tight,
     Scared, so we could turn

You over. We washed you, covered you,
Cut up each bite of meat you ate;
We watched your lean jaws masticate
As ravenously your useless food
As thieves at hard labor in their chains chew
     Or insects in the wood.

Such pious sacrifice to give
You all you could demand of pain:
Receive this haddock's body, slain
For you, old tyrant; take this blood
Of a tomato, shed that you might live.
     You had that costly food.

You seem to be all finished, so
We'll plug your old recalcitrant anus
And tie up your discouraged penis
In a great, snow-white bow of gauze.
We wrap you, pin you, and cart you down below,
     Below, below, because

Your credit has finally run out.
On our steel table, trussed and carved,
You'll find this world's hardworking, starved

Teeth working in your precious skin.
The earth turns, in the end, by turn about
    And opens to take you in.

    Seven months gone down the drain; thank God
    That's through. Throw out the four-by-fours,
    Swabsticks, the thick salve for bedsores,
    Throw out the diaper pads and drug
Containers, pile the bedclothes in a wad,
        And rinse the cider jug

    Half-filled with the last urine. Then
    Empty out the cotton cans,
    Autoclave the bowls and spit pans,
    Unhook the pumps and all the red
Tubes—catheter, suction, oxygen;
        Next, wash the empty bed.

    —All this Dark Age machinery
    On which we had tormented you
    To life. Last, we collect the few
    Belongings: snapshots, some odd bills,
Your mail, and half a pack of Luckies we
        Won't light you after meals.

    Old man, these seven months you've lain
    Determined—not that you would live—
    Just to not die. No one would give
    You one chance you could ever wake
From that first night, much less go well again,
        Much less go home and make

    Your living; how could you hope to find
    A place for yourself in all creation?—
    Pain was your only occupation.
    And pain that should content and will
A man to give it up, nerved you to grind
        Your clenched teeth, breathing, till

    Your skin broke down, your calves went flat
    And your legs lost all sensation. Still,
    You took enough morphine to kill

W. D. SNODGRASS

A strong man. Finally, nitrogen
Mustard: you could last two months after that;
       It would kill you then.

Even then you wouldn't quit.
Old soldier, yet you must have known
Inside the animal had grown
Sick of the world, made up its mind
To stop. Your mind ground on its separate
       Way, merciless and blind,

Into these last weeks when the breath
Would only come in fits and starts
That puffed out your sections like the parts
Of some enormous, damaged bug.
You waited, not for life, not for your death,
       Just for the deadening drug

That made your life seem bearable.
You still whispered you would not die.
Yet in the nights I heard you cry
Like a whipped child; in fierce old age
You whimpered, tears stood on your gun-metal
       Blue cheeks shaking with rage

And terror. So much pain would fill
Your room that when I left I'd pray
That if I came back the next day
I'd find you gone. You stayed for me—
Nailed to your own rapacious, stiff self-will.
       You've shook loose, finally.

They'd say this was a worthwhile job
Unless they tried it. It is mad
To throw our good lives after bad;
Waste time, drugs, and our minds, while strong
Men starve. How many young men did we rob
       To keep you hanging on?

I can't think we did *you* much good.
Well, when you died, none of us wept.
You killed for us, and so we kept

You, because we need to earn our pay.
No. We'd still have to help you try. We would
Have killed for you today.

"AFTER EXPERIENCE TAUGHT ME..."

After experience taught me that all the ordinary
Surroundings of social life are futile and vain;

I'm going to show you something very
Ugly: someday, it might save your life.

Seeing that none of the things I feared contain
In themselves anything either good or bad

What if you get caught without a knife;
Nothing—even a loop of piano wire;

Excepting only in the effect they had
Upon my mind, I resolved to inquire

Take the first two fingers of this hand;
Fork them out—kind of a "V for Victory"—

Whether there might be something whose discovery
Would grant me supreme, unending happiness.

And jam them into the eyes of your enemy.
You have to do this hard. Very hard. Then press

No virtue can be thought to have priority
Over this endeavor to preserve one's being.

Both fingers down around the cheekbone
And setting your foot high into the chest

No man can desire to act rightly, to be blessed,
To live rightly, without simultaneously

W. D. SNODGRASS

You must call up every strength you own
And you can rip off the whole facial mask.

Wishing to be, to act, to live. He must ask
First, in other words, to actually exist.

And you, whiner, who wastes your time
Dawdling over the remorseless earth,
What evil, what unspeakable crime
Have you made your life worth?

from THE FÜHRER BUNKER

Eva Braun

—22 April, 1945.

(Hitler's mistress received no public recognition and often felt badly neglected.
Her small revenges included singing American songs, her favorite being "Tea for
Two." Having chosen to die with him in the bunker, she appeared quite serene
during the last days.)

Tea for two
And two for tea

I ought to feel ashamed
Feeling such joy. Behaving like a spoiled child!
So fulfilled. This is a very serious matter.
All of them have come here to die. And they grieve.
I have come here to die. If this is dying,
Why else did I ever live?

Me for you
And you for me

We ought never to flaunt our good luck
In the face of anyone less fortunate—
These live fools mourning already
For their own deaths; these dead fools
Who believe they can go on living . . .

And you for me
    Alone.

    Who out of all of them, officers, ministers,
    These liars that despise me, these empty
    Women that envy me—so they hate me—
    Who else of them dares to disobey Him
    As I dared? I have defied Him to His face
    And He has honored me.

                  We will raise
                    A family

    They sneer at me—at my worrying about
    Frau Goebbels' children, that I make fairytales
    For them, that we play at war. Is our war
    More lost if I console these poor trapped rabbits?
    These children He would not give me . . .

A boy for you
A girl for me

    They sneer that I should bring
    Fine furniture down this dank hole. Speer
    Built this bed for me. Where I have slept
    Beside our Chief. Who else should have it?
    My furs, my best dress to my little sister—
    They would sneer even at this; yet
    What else can I give her?

                Can't you see
            How happy we would be?

            Or to the baby
    She will bear Fegelein? Lechering dolt!
    Well, I have given her her wedding
    As if it was my own. And she will have
    My diamonds, my watch. The little things you
    Count on, things that see you through your
    Missing life, the life that stood you up.

W. D. SNODGRASS

Nobody near us
To see us or hear us

> I have it all. They are all gone, the others—
> The Valkyrie; and the old rich bitch Bechstein;
> Geli above all. No, the screaming mobs above all.
> They are all gone now; He has left them all.
> No one but me and the love-struck secretaries—
> Traudl, Daran—who gave up years ago.

> > *No friends or relations*
> > *On weekend vacations*

> That I, I above all, am chosen—even I
> Must find that strange. I who was always
> Disobedient, rebellious—smoked in the dining car,
> Wore rouge whenever he said I shouldn't.
> When he ordered that poor Chancellor Schussnig
> Was to starve, I sent in food.

We won't have it known, dear,
That we own a telephone, dear.

> I who joined the Party, I who took Him
> For my lover just to spite my old stiff father—
> Den Alten Fritz!—and those stupid nuns.
> I ran my teachers crazy, and my mother—I
> Held out even when she stuck my head in water.
> He shall have none but me.

> > *Day will break*
> > *And you will wake*

> We cannot make it through another month;
> We follow the battles now on a subway map.
> Even if the Russians pulled back—
> His hand trembles, the whole left side
> Staggers. His marvellous eyes are failing.
> We go out to the sunlight less each day. We live
> Like flies sucked up in a sweeper bag.

W. D. SNODGRASS

And start to bake
  A sugar cake

He forbade me to leave Berchtesgaden,
Forbade me to come here. I tricked
My keepers, stole my own car, my driver Jung.
He tried to scold me; He was too
Proud of me. Today He ordered me to leave,
To go back to the mountain. I refused.
I have refused to save my own life and He,
In public, He kissed me on the mouth.

  For me to take
  For all the boys to see.

Once more I have won, won out over Him
Who spoke one word and whole populations vanished.
Until today, in public, we were good friends.
He is mine. No doubt
I did only what He wanted; no doubt
I should resent that. In the face
Of such fulfillment? In the face
Of so much joy?

  Picture you
  Upon my knee;
  Tea for two
  And two for tea . . .

Dr. Joseph Goebbels

—*1 May, 1945; 1800 hours.*

(*The day after Hitler's death, Goebbels and his wife climbed the steps into the garden where both committed suicide.*)

Say goodbye to the help, the ranks
Of Stalin-bait. Give too much thanks
To Naumann—Magda's lover: we

Thank him for *all* his loyalty.
Schwaegermann; Rach. After a while
Turn back to them with a sad smile:
We'll save them trouble—no one cares
Just now to carry us upstairs.

Turn away; check your manicure;
Pull on your gloves. Take time; make sure
The hat brim curves though the hat's straight.
Give her your arm. Let the fools wait;
They act like they've someplace to go.
Take the stairs, now. Self-control. Slow.
A slight limp; just enough to see,
Pass on, and infect history.

The rest is silence. Left like sperm
In a stranger's gut, waiting its term,
Each thought, each step lies; the roots spread.
They'll believe in us when we're dead.
When we took "Red Berlin" we found
We always worked best underground.
So; the vile body turns to spirit
That speaks soundlessly. They'll hear it.

OLD APPLE TREES

Like battered old millhands, they stand in the orchard—
Like drunk legionnaires, heaving themselves up,
Lurching to attention. Not one of them wobbles
The same way as another. Uniforms won't fit them—
All those cramps, humps, bulges. Here, a limb's gone;
There, rain and corruption have eaten the whole core.
They've all grown too tall, too thick, or too something.
Like men bent too long over desks, engines, benches,
Or bent under mailsacks, under loss.
They've seen too much history and bad weather, grown
Around rocks, into high winds, diseases, grown
Too long to be wilful, too long to be changed.

W. D. SNODGRASS

Oh, I could replant, bulldoze the lot,
Get nursery stock, all the latest ornamentals,
Make the whole place look like a suburb,
Each limb sleek as a teeny bopper's — pink
To the very crotch — each trunk smoothed, ideal
As the fantasy life of an adman.
We might just own the Arboreal Muscle Beach:
Each tree disguised as its neighbor. Or each disguised
As if not its neighbor — each doing its own thing
Like executives' children.

                              At least I could prune,
At least I should trim the dead wood; fill holes
Where rain collects and decay starts. Well, I should;
I should. There's a red squirrel nests here someplace.
I live in the hope of hearing one saw-whet owl.
Then, too, they're right about Spring. Bees hum
Through these branches like lascivious intentions. The white
Petals drift down, sift across the ground; this air's so rich
No man should come here except on a working pass;
No man should leave here without going to confession.
All Fall, apples nearly crack the boughs;
They hang here red as candles in the
White oncoming snow.

Tonight we'll drive down to the bad part of town
To the New Hungarian Bar or the Klub Polski,
To the Old Hellas where we'll eat the new spring lamb;
Drink good *mavrodaphne*, say, at the Laikon Bar,
Send drinks to the dancers, those meatcutters and laborers
Who move in their native dances, the archaic forms.
Maybe we'll still find our old crone selling chestnuts,
Whose toothless gums can spit out fifteen languages,
Who turns, there, late at night, in the center of the floor,
Her ancient dry hips wheeling their slow, slow *tsamikos*;
We'll stomp under the tables, whistle, we'll all hiss
Till even the belly dancer leaves, disgraced.

We'll drive back, lushed and vacant, in the first dawn;
Out of the light gray mists may rise our flowering
Orchard, the rough trunks holding their formations
Like elders of Colonus, the old men of Thebes
Tossing their white hair, almost whispering,

W. D. SNODGRASS

Soon, each one of us will be taken
By dark powers under this ground
That drove us here, that warped us.
Not one of us got it his own way.
Nothing like any one of us
Will be seen again, forever.
Each of us held some noble shape in mind.
It seemed better that we kept alive.

Gary Snyder

RIPRAP

Lay down these words
Before your mind like rocks.
           placed solid, by hands
In choice of place, set
Before the body of the mind
           in space and time:
Solidity of bark, leaf, or wall
           riprap of things:
Cobble of milky way,
           straying planets,
These poems, people,
           lost ponies with
Dragging saddles—
           and rocky sure-foot trails.
The worlds like an endless
           four-dimensional
Game of Go.
           ants and pebbles
In the thin loam, each rock a word
           a creek-washed stone
Granite: ingrained
           with torment of fire and weight
Crystal and sediment linked hot
           all change, in thoughts,
As well as things.

MILTON BY FIRELIGHT

"O hell, what do mine eyes
           with grief behold?"
Working with an old
Singlejack miner, who can sense

GARY SNYDER

The vein and cleavage
In the very guts of rock, can
Blast granite, build
Switchbacks that last for years
Under the beat of snow, thaw, mule-hooves.
What use, Milton, a silly story
Of our lost general parents,
                    eaters of fruit?

The Indian, the chainsaw boy,
And a string of six mules
Came riding down to camp
Hungry for tomatoes and green apples.
Sleeping in saddle-blankets
Under a bright night-sky
Han River slantwise by morning.
Jays squall
Coffee boils

In ten thousand years the Sierras
Will be dry and dead, home of the scorpion.
Ice-scratched slabs and bent trees.

No paradise, no fall,
Only the weathering land
The wheeling sky,
Man, with his Satan
Scouring the chaos of the mind.
Oh Hell!

Fire down
Too dark to read, miles from a road
The bell-mare clangs in the meadow
That packed dirt for a fill-in
Scrambling through loose rocks
On an old trail
All of a summer's day.

Piute Creek, August 1955

HAY FOR THE HORSES

He had driven half the night
From far down San Joaquin
Through Mariposa, up the
Dangerous mountain roads,
And pulled in at eight a.m.
With his big truckload of hay
        behind the barn.
With winch and ropes and hooks
We stacked the bales up clean
To splintery redwood rafters
High in the dark, flecks of alfalfa
Whirling through shingle-cracks of light,
Itch of haydust in the
        sweaty shirt and shoes.
At lunchtime under Black oak
Out in the hot corral,
—The old mare nosing lunchpails,
Grasshoppers crackling in the weeds—
"I'm sixty-eight" he said,
"I first bucked hay when I was seventeen.
I thought, that day I started,
I sure would hate to do this all my life.
And dammit, that's just what
I've gone and done."

VAPOR TRAILS

Twin streaks twice higher than cumulus,
Precise plane icetracks in the vertical blue
Cloud-flaked light-shot shadow-arcing
Field of all future war, edging off to space.

GARY SNYDER

Young expert U.S. pilots waiting
The day of criss-cross rockets
And white blossoming smoke of bomb,
The air world torn and staggered for these
Specks of brushy land and ant-hill towns—

    I stumble on the cobble rockpath,
Passing through temples,
Watching for two-leaf pine
      —spotting that design.

SONG OF THE TASTE

    Eating the living germs of grasses
    Eating the ova of large birds

      the fleshy sweetness packed
      around the sperm of swaying trees

    The muscles of the flanks and thighs of
        soft-voiced cows
      the bounce in the lamb's leap
      the swish in the ox's tail

    Eating roots grown swoll
        inside the soil

    Drawing on life of living
      clustered points of light spun
        out of space
    hidden in the grape.

    Eating each other's seed
        eating
    ah, each other.

    Kissing the lover in the mouth of bread:
      lip to lip.

GARY SNYDER

I WENT INTO THE MAVERICK BAR

I went into the Maverick Bar
In Farmington, New Mexico.
And drank double shots of bourbon
                                backed with beer.
My long hair was tucked up under a cap
I'd left the earring in the car.

Two cowboys did horseplay
                        by the pool tables,
A waitress asked us
                        where are you from?
a country-and-western band began to play
"We don't smoke Marijuana in Muskokie"
And with the next song,
                        a couple began to dance.

They held each other like in High School dances
                        in the fifties;
I recalled when I worked in the woods
                        and the bars of Madras, Oregon.
That short-haired joy and roughness—
                        America—your stupidity.
I could almost love you again.

We left—onto the freeway shoulders—
                        under the tough old stars—
In the shadow of bluffs
                        I came back to myself,
To the real work, to
                        "What is to be done."

THE BATH

Washing Kai in the sauna,
The kerosene lantern set on a box
        outside the ground-level window,

GARY SNYDER

Lights up the edge of the iron stove and the
    washtub down on the slab
Steaming air and crackle of waterdrops
    brushed by on the pile of rocks on top
He stands in warm water
Soap all over the smooth of his thigh and stomach
    "Gary don't soap my hair!"
    —his eye-sting fear—
    the soapy hand feeling
    through and around the globes and curves of his body
    up in the crotch,
And washing-tickling out the scrotum, little anus,
    his penis curving up and getting hard
    as I pull back skin and try to wash it
Laughing and jumping, flinging arms around,
    I squat all naked too,
                is this our body?

Sweating and panting in the stove-steam hot-stone
    cedar-planking wooden bucket water-splashing
    kerosene lantern-flicker wind-in-the-pines-out
    sierra forest ridges night—
Masa comes in, letting fresh cool air
    sweep down from the door
    a deep sweet breath
And she tips him over gripping neatly, one knee down
    her hair falling hiding one whole side of
    shoulder, breast, and belly,
Washes deftly Kai's head-hair
    as he gets mad and yells—
The body of my lady, the winding valley spine,
    the space between the thighs I reach through,
    cup her curving vulva arch and hold it from behind,
    a soapy tickle   a hand of grail
The gates of Awe
That open back a turning double-mirror world of
    wombs in wombs, in rings,
    that start in music,
                is this our body?

GARY SNYDER

The hidden place of seed
The veins net flow across the ribs, that gathers
    milk and peaks up in a nipple—fits
    our mouth—
The sucking milk from this our body sends through
    jolts of light; the son, the father,
    sharing mother's joy
That brings a softness to the flower of the awesome
    open curling lotus gate I cup and kiss
As Kai laughs at his mother's breast he now is weaned
    from, we
    wash each other,
                     this our body

Kai's little scrotum up close to his groin,
    the seed still tucked away, that moved from us to him
In flows that lifted with the same joys forces
    as his nursing Masa later,
    playing with her breast,
Or me within her,
Or him emerging,
                     this is our body:

Clean, and rinsed, and sweating more, we stretch
    out on the redwood benches hearts all beating
Quiet to the simmer of the stove,
    the scent of cedar
And then turn over,
    murmuring gossip of the grasses,
    talking firewood,
Wondering how Gen's napping, how to bring him in
    soon wash him too—
These boys who love their mother
    who loves men, who passes on
    her sons to other women;

The cloud across the sky. The windy pines.
    the trickle gurgle in the swampy meadow

    this is our body.

Fire inside and boiling water on the stove
We sigh and slide ourselves down from the benches
    wrap the babies, step outside,

black night & all the stars.

Pour cold water on the back and thighs
Go in the house—stand steaming by the center fire
Kai scampers on the sheepskin
Gen standing hanging on and shouting,

"Bao! bao! bao! bao! bao!"

This is our body. Drawn up crosslegged by the flames
    drinking icy water
      hugging babies, kissing bellies,

Laughing on the Great Earth

Come out from the bath.

AS FOR POETS

    As for poets
    The Earth Poets
    Who write small poems,
    Need help from no man.

    The Air Poets
    Play out the swiftest gales
    And sometimes loll in the eddies.
    Poem after poem,
    Curling back on the same thrust.

    At fifty below
    Fuel oil won't flow
    And propane stays in the tank.
    Fire Poets
    Burn at absolute zero
    Fossil love pumped back up.

GARY SNYDER

The first
Water Poet
Stayed down six years.
He was covered with seaweed.
The life in his poem
Left millions of tiny
Different tracks
Criss-crossing through the mud.

With the Sun and Moon
In his belly,
The Space Poet
Sleeps.
No end to the sky—
But his poems,
Like wild geese,
Fly off the edge.

A Mind Poet
Stays in the house.
The house is empty
And it has no walls.
The poem
Is seen from all sides,
Everywhere,
At once.

SOY SAUCE

for Bruce Boyd and Holly Tornheim

Standing on a stepladder
        up under hot ceiling
tacking on wire net for plaster,
a day's work helping Bruce and Holly on their house,
I catch a sour salt smell and come back
        down the ladder.

"Deer lick it nights" she says,
and shows me the frame of the window she's planing,
clear redwood, but dark, with a smell.

GARY SNYDER

"Scored a broken-up, two-thousand-gallon redwood
soy sauce tank from a company went out of business
down near San Jose."

Out in the yard the staves are stacked:
I lean over, sniff them, ah! it's like Shinshu miso,
the darker saltier miso paste of the Nagano
uplands, central main island, Japan —
it's like Shinshu pickles!

I see in mind my friend Shimizu Yasushi and me,
one October years ago, trudging through days of snow
crossing the Japan Alps and descending
the last night, to a farmhouse,
taking a late hot bath in the dark — and eating
        a bowl of chill miso radish pickles,
        nothing ever so good!

Back here, hot summer sunshine dusty yard,
        hammer in hand.

But I know how it tastes
        to lick those window frames
        in the dark,
                the deer.

AXE HANDLES

One afternoon the last week in April
Showing Kai how to throw a hatchet
One-half turn and it sticks in a stump.
He recalls the hatchet-head
Without a handle, in the shop
And go gets it, and wants it for his own.
A broken-off axe handle behind the door
Is long enough for a hatchet,
We cut it to length and take it
With the hatchet head
And working hatchet, to the wood block.
There I begin to shape the old handle

GARY SNYDER

With the hatchet, and the phrase
First learned from Ezra Pound
Rings in my ears!
"When making an axe handle
         the pattern is not far off."
And I say this to Kai
"Look: We'll shape the handle
By checking the handle
Of the axe we cut with—"
And he sees. And I hear it again:
It's in Lu Ji's *Wên Fu,* fourth century
A.D. "Essay on Literature"—in the
Preface: "In making the handle
Of an axe
By cutting wood with an axe
The model is indeed near at hand."
My teacher Shih-hsiang Chen
Translated that and taught it years ago
And I see: Pound was an axe,
Chen was an axe, I am an axe
And my son a handle, soon
To be shaping again, model
And tool, craft of culture,
How we go on.

William Stafford

AT THE BOMB TESTING SITE

At noon in the desert a panting lizard
waited for history, its elbows tense,
watching the curve of a particular road
as if something might happen.

It was looking at something farther off
than people could see, an important scene
acted in stone for little selves
at the flute end of consequences.

There was just a continent without much on it
under a sky that never cared less.
Ready for a change, the elbows waited.
The hands gripped hard on the desert.

TRAVELING THROUGH THE DARK

Traveling through the dark I found a deer
dead on the edge of the Wilson River road.
It is usually best to roll them into the canyon:
that road is narrow; to swerve might make more dead.

By glow of the tail-light I stumbled back of the car
and stood by the heap, a doe, a recent killing;
she had stiffened already, almost cold.
I dragged her off; she was large in the belly.

My fingers touching her side brought me the reason—
her side was warm; her fawn lay there waiting,
alive, still, never to be born.
Beside that mountain road I hesitated.

The car aimed ahead its lowered parking lights;
under the hood purred the steady engine.
I stood in the glare of the warm exhaust turning red;
around our group I could hear the wilderness listen.

I thought hard for us all—my only swerving—,
then pushed her over the edge into the river.

VOCATION

This dream the world is having about itself
includes a trace on the plains of the Oregon trail,
a groove in the grass my father showed us all
one day while meadowlarks were trying to tell
something better about to happen.

I dreamed the trace to the mountains, over the hills,
and there a girl who belonged wherever she was.
But then my mother called us back to the car:
she was afraid; she always blamed the place,
the time, anything my father planned.

Now both of my parents, the long line through the plain,
the meadowlarks, the sky, the world's whole dream
remain, and I hear him say while I stand between the two,
helpless, both of them part of me:
"Your job is to find what the world is trying to be."

MY FATHER: OCTOBER 1942

He picks up what he thinks is
a road map, and it is
his death: he holds it easily, and
nothing can take it from his firm hand.
The pulse in his thumb on the map
says, "1:19 P.M. next Tuesday, at
this intersection." And an ambulance
begins to throb while his face looks tired.

Any time anyone may pick up something
so right that he can't put it down:
that is the problem for all who travel—they
fatally own whatever is really theirs,
and that is the inner thread, the lock,
what can hold. If it is to be, nothing breaks
it. Millions of observers guess all the
time, but each person, once, can say, "Sure."

Then he's no longer an observer. He isn't right,
or wrong. He just wins or loses.

ACROSS KANSAS

My family slept those level miles
but like a bell rung deep till dawn
I drove down an aisle of sound,
nothing real but in the bell,
past the town where I was born.

Once you cross a land like that
you own your face more: what the light
struck told a self; every rock
denied all the rest of the world.
We stopped at Sharon Springs and ate—

My state still dark, my dream too long to tell.

A FAMILY TURN

All her Kamikaze friends admired my aunt,
their leader, charmed in vinegar,
a woman who could blaze with such white blasts
as Lawrence's that lit Arabia.
Her mean opinions bent her hatpins.

We'd take a ride in her old car
that ripped like Sherman through society:

Main Street's oases sheltered no one
when she pulled up at Thirty-first
and whirled that Ford for another charge.

We swept headlines from under rugs, names
all over town, which I learned her way, by heart,
and blazed with love that burns because it's real.
With a turn that's our family's own,
she'd say, "Our town is not the same"—

Pause—"And it's never been."

AN INTRODUCTION TO SOME POEMS

Look: no one ever promised for sure
that we would sing. We have decided
to moan. In a strange dance that
we don't understand till we do it, we
have to carry on.

Just as in sleep you have to dream
the exact dream to round out your life,
so we have to live that dream into stories
and hold them close at you, close at the
edge we share, to be right.

We find it an awful thing to meet people,
serious or not, who have turned into vacant
effective people, so far lost that they
won't believe their own feelings
enough to follow them out.

The authentic is a line from one thing
along to the next; it interests us.
Strangely, it relates to what works,
but is not quite the same. It never
swerves for revenge,

Or profit, or fame: it holds
together something more than the world,

this line. And we are your wavery
efforts at following it. Are you coming?
Good: now it is time.

REPORT FROM A FAR PLACE

Making these word things to
step on across the world, I
could call them snowshoes.

They creak, sag, bend, but
hold, over the great deep cold,
and they turn up at the toes.

In war or city or camp
they could save your life;
you can muse them by the fire.

Be careful, though: they
burn, or don't burn, in their own
strange way, when you say them.

THE STICK IN THE FOREST

A stick in the forest that pointed
where the center of the universe is
broke in the wind that started
its exact note of mourning
when Buddha's mother died.

Around us then a new crystal
began to form itself, and men—
awakened by what happened—
held precious whatever breathed:
we are all gestures that the world makes.

"Be, be," Buddha said.

WILLIAM STAFFORD

TEMPORARY FACTS

That look you had, Agnes, was a temporary fact.
Probably by now Time has it back.
From spiral nebulae I call it here now.

Through the trance of high school you pass along
          the hall.
Lockers clang the hours; you pass windows.
A Christmas candle shines on your hair.

On spellbound evenings you call your brother home,
coming toward the streetlight through shadows
          of the elm.
Shadows touch your mouth when you say a name.

All of these things were temporary facts.
Only for an instant Time gives them back.
In spiral nebulae a shadow goes on.

ASSURANCE

You will never be alone, you hear so deep
a sound when autumn comes. Yellow
pulls across the hills and thrums,
or the silence after lightning before it says
its names—and then the clouds' wide-mouthed
apologies. You were aimed from birth:
you will never be alone. Rain
will come, a gutter filled, an Amazon,
long aisles—you never heard so deep a sound,
moss on rock, and years. You turn your head—
that's what the silence meant: *you're not alone.*
The whole wide world pours down.

WILLIAM STAFFORD

A CERTAIN BEND

A certain bend in the road, swayed willows
beyond a fence, and a flat farmyard
waiting—we come around and that instant
freezes: years later I remember.
Why? Why did a lifetime pass, two wars,
a family move and scatter, the country
skid where it is—and only now
that scene return? I put my teacup
down here to hold it all steady. Was that
the day I became the person I am?
Father, you should have held my face
in your hands and stared into my eyes. That farmyard
or one like it could be ours, in Kansas, or
Alaska, or anywhere. You would be there
now, I would hold out my hand
for whatever came, and the willows would bend
still in that picture we saw that day.

ODE TO GARLIC

Sudden, it comes for you
in the cave of yourself where you know
and are lifted by important events.

Say you are dining and it happens:
soaring like an eagle, you are
pierced by a message from the midst of life:

Memory—what holds the days together—touches
your tongue. It is from deep in the earth
and it reaches out kindly, saying, "Hello, Old Friend."

It makes us alike, all offspring of powerful
forces, part of one great embrace of democracy,
united across every boundary.

You walk out generously, giving it back
in a graceful wave, what you've been given.
Like a child again, you breathe on the world, and it shines.

ANSWERERS

There are songs too wide for sound. There are quiet
places where something stopped a long time
ago and the days began to open
their mouths toward nothing but the sky. We live
in place of the many who stir only
if we listen, only because the living
live and call out. I am ready
as all of us are who wake at night:
we become rooms for whatever almost
is. It speaks in us, trying. And even if
only by a note like this, we answer.

THINGS THAT HAPPEN
WHERE THERE AREN'T ANY PEOPLE

It's cold on Lakeside Road
with no one traveling. At its turn
on the hill an old sign sags and
finally goes down. The traveler rain
walks back and forth over its victim
flat on the mud.

You don't have to have any people when
sunlight stands on the rocks or gloom
comes following the great dragged clouds
over a huddle of hills. Plenty of
things happen in deserted places, maybe

WILLIAM STAFFORD

dust counting millions of its little worlds
or the slow arrival of deep dark.

And out there in the country a rock has been
waiting to be mentioned for thousands of years.
Every day its shadow leans, crouches,
then walks away eastward in one measured stride
exactly right for its way of being. To reach
for that rock we have the same reasons
that explorers always have for their journeys:
because it is far, because there aren't any people.

THE EARLY ONES

They kept it all level. And low. Even
little stones they swept away. They went on
for miles, a bend at a hill, then a bend
back. Around them birch forest mostly
or openings for lakes, and a few hidden lakes.

They carved on the rocks—these are what stay,
hardly worn at all if sheltered, some
broken and all of them gray, that distant
gray that clouds have, or storms that moan
at the coast. They carved and went away.

Level and low. And the carved things. And one
more thing: when you look around and listen,
the last thing is there. You hear it wait.
Because they were early and quiet, and because
of that last bend, and because of the gray—

There is something left. We'll find it some day.

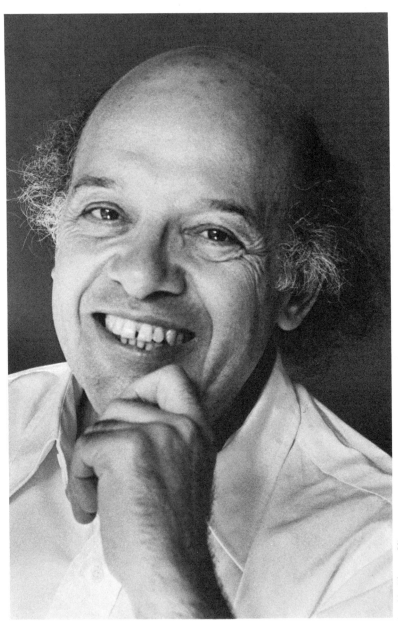

Gerald Stern

IN CARPENTER'S WOODS

This is a corner of heaven here,
the moss growing under the leaves,
the rocks cropping up like small graves under the trees,
the old giants rotting in the shade.
I used to come here every Sunday
to stand on the bridge and look at the bird-watchers.
Once I made love in the dead brush
and slept impaled on the thorns, too tired to move;
once I gave myself up to the *New York Times*
and buried myself in sections a whole afternoon;
once I played football with the radicals
while the sun and the rain fought for control.
      At the bottom of the hill where the trees give way to grass
a creek runs through a silent picnic ground
almost a mile away from any access.
Here the neighborhood dogs broke into their runs
at the first threat of authority.
Here the exhibitionists came out in the open
after the long morning with the squirrels and flickers.
Here the Jehovah's Witnesses lay down their arms
and gathered quietly around the tables.
—Without knowing the name or the reason
I gave myself up to vertigo;
I lay for hours with my eyes closed listening to the great sounds
coming in from Germantown;
I loved the ground so much that I had to hold on to the grass for balance.
      I can tell you that where those two girls go carefully over the stones,
and where that civilized man and his son
pick up loose wood for the fireplace
was, for three years, my refuge.
I can tell you that I have spent half a lifetime hunting for relief,
that in the simplest locations, in libraries,

in drug stores, in bus stations—
as well as under stone bridges and on hillsides—
I have found places to wait and think.
I tell you that world is as large as the one you sigh and tremble over;
that it is also invulnerable and intricate and pleasurable;
that it has a serious history;
that it was always there, from the beginning.

AT BICKFORD'S

You should understand that I use my body now for everything
whereas formerly I kept it away from higher regions.
My clothes are in a stack over against the orange pine cupboard
and my hair is lying in little piles on the kitchen floor.
I am finally ready for the happiness I spent my youth arguing and
        fighting against.
    Twenty years ago—walking on Broadway—
I crashed into Shaddai and his eagles.
My great specialty was darkness then
and radiant sexual energy.
Now when light drips on me I walk around without tears.
—Before long I am going to live again on four dollars a day
in the little blocks between 96th and 116th.
I am going to follow the thin line of obedience
between George's Restaurant and Salter's Books.
There is just so much feeling left in me for my old ghost
and I will spend it all in one last outburst of charity.
I will give him money; I will listen to his poems;
I will pity his marriage.
—After that I will drift off again to Bickford's
and spend my life in the cracked cups and the corn muffins.
I will lose half my hatred
at the round tables
and let any beliefs that want to overtake me.
On lucky afternoons the sun will break through the thick glass
and rest like a hand on my forehead.
I will sit and read in my chair;
I will wave from my window.

GERALD STERN

THE CEMETERY OF ORANGE TREES IN CRETE

In Crete the old orange trees are cut back until they are stumps,
with little leaves coming out again from the butchered arms.
They are painted white and stand there in long straight rows
like the white gravestones at Gettysburg and Manassas.
    I first came across them on the bus ride to Omalos
as we began our climb through the empty mountains,
thinking of the beauty and exhaustion that lay ahead.
They are mementos of my journey south, the renewal
of my youth, green leaves growing out of my neck,
my shoulders flowering again with small blossoms,
my body painted white, my hands joining
the other hands on the hill, my white heart remembering
the violence and sorrow that gave us our life again.

THE WAR AGAINST THE JEWS

Look how peaceful these wooden figures are, going to their death.
How happy they were to go instead of me.
They love to march back and forth under the iron clock.
One tips his hat endlessly to a mother and her three children.
One dries his tears in front of the water fountain.
They bump their heads as they bend down to drink.

Over there a German soldier is blowing his whistle.
He was carved while he still could remember his mother's garden.
How glad he was to go to Poland.
How young he felt in his first pair of boots.

I would give anything to bring them back:
to let them sit again on the polished benches;
to let them see the great glass roof again;
to rush through the noisy crowd screaming
"Stop! It's a dream! It's a dream!
Go back to your shuls. Go back to your mother's garden.
O wooden figures, go back, go back."

GERALD STERN

LORD, FORGIVE A SPIRIT

So what shall we do about this angel,
growing dizzy every time he climbs a ladder,
crying over his old poems.
I walk out into the garden and there he is,
watering the lilies and studying the digitalis.
He is talking to his own invisible heart;
he is leaking blood.
    The sun shines on him all day long
as he wanders from bush to bush.
His eyes flash with fire, his eyelashes blaze and
his skin shines like brass,
but he trips in the dirt just like any gardener, or grieving poet.
    I watch him walk beside the cactus;
I watch him kneel in front of the wet horsetails;
I touch his lips.
I write all day. I sit beside him all
day long and write the garbled words.
I sit in the sun and fill a whole new book
with scrawls and symbols.
I watch the sky as he talks about the gold leaf
and the half-forgotten ruins; I watch the words
drift from his mouth like clouds.
I watch the colors change from orange to red
to pink as he tries to remember his old words—
his old songs, his first human songs—
lost somewhere in the broken glass and the cinders,
a foot below the soft nails and the hinges.

THE SHIRT POEM

It is ten years since I have seen these shirts
screaming from their hangers, crying for blood and money.
They shake their empty arms
and grow stiff as they wait for the light to come.
I open the door an inch at a time to let them out
and start candles all over the room to soothe them.

GERALD STERN

—Gone is sweetness in that closet, gone is the dream
of brotherhood, the affectionate meeting
of thinkers and workers inside a rented hall.
Gone are the folding chairs, gone forever
the sacred locking of elbows under the two flags.

On Sunday night they used to sing for hours
before the speeches. Once the rabbis joined them
and religion and economics were finally combined in exile.
"Death is a defect," they sang, and threw their hats
on the floor. "We will save nature from death,"
they shouted, and ended up dancing on the small stage,
the dark crows and the speckled doves finally arm in arm.

They will never come back—in a thousand years;
it is not like bringing a forest back, putting a truckload
of nitrogen in the soil, burning some brush,
planting seedlings, measuring distance—
these are people, whose secret habits we no longer know,
how they tore their bread and what designs they made on the tablecloth,
what they thought about as they stared through the warped glass,
what the melting ice meant to them.

Poor dead ones! Forgive me for the peace I feel as I walk out
to the mailbox. Forgive me for the rich life I lead.
Forgive me for the enormous budget and the bureaucracy and the
    permanent army.
When I come home from New York City I stand outside
for twenty minutes and look out at the lights.
Upstairs the shirts are howling and snapping,
marching back and forth in front of the silver radiator.
In a minute I will be up there closing doors
and turning on lamps.
I will take the papers out of my coat pocket
and put them in their slots.
I will think of you with your own papers and your rubber bands.
What is my life if not a substitute for yours,
and my dream a substitute for your dream?
Lord, how it has changed, how we have
made ourselves strange, how embarrassing the words
sound to us, how clumsy and half-hearted we are.

I want to write it down before it's forgotten,
how we lived, what we believed in;
most of all to remember the giants
and how they walked, always with white hair,
always with long white hair hanging down over their collars,
always with red faces, always bowing and listening,
their heads floating as they moved through the small crowd.

Outside the wind is blowing
and the snow is piling up against the pillars.
I could go back in a minute to the synagogue in Beechview
or the Carnegie Library on the North Side.
I could turn and shake hands with the tiny man
sitting beside me and wish him peace.
I could stand in front and watch the stained-glass
window rattle in its frame and the guest speaker
climb into the back seat of his car.

I am writing about the past because there was
still affection left then, and other sorrows;
because I believed my white silk scarf could save me,
and my all-day walks;
because when I opened my window the smell
of snow made me tremble with pleasure;
because I was a head taller than the tiny man sitting next to me;
because I was always the youngest;
because I believed in Shelley;
because I carried my entire memory along with me in the summer;
because I stared at the old men with loving eyes;
because I studied their fallen shoulders and their huge hands;
because I found relief only in my drawings;
because I knew the color and texture of every rug and every chair
and every lampshade in my first house.

Give this to Rabbi Kook who always arrived
with his clothes on fire and stood between the mourners,
singing songs against death in all three languages
at the crowded wall, in the dark sunlight.

And give this to Malatesta who believed in
the perfect world and lived in it as he moved
from country to country, for sixty years, tasting the

GERALD STERN

bread, tasting the meat, always working,
cursing the Church, cursing the State,
seeing through everything, always seeing the heart
and what it wanted, the beautiful cramped heart.

My shirts are fine. They dance
by themselves along the river
and bleed a little as they fall down on the dirty glass.
If they had knees they would try to
crawl back up the hill and stop the trucks
or march back and forth singing their swamp songs.
They see me coming and fly up to the roof;
they are like prehistoric birds,
half leaping, half sailing by.
They scream with cold, they break through the hall window
and knock over baskets and push open doors
until they stand there in place, in back of the neckties,
beside the cold plaster, in the dust
above the abandoned shoes, weeping in silence,
moaning in exhaustion,
getting ready again to live in darkness.

DAYS OF 1978

This is the only thing that clarifies my life,
this beautiful old living room
with the pink walls and the mohair sofa.
I walk out every night singing
a little song from Gus Williams or W. C. Handy.
I throw my yellow scarf around my neck
and pull my cap down over my eyes.
Even here I am dressed up,
walking through the light flakes and the ice puddles.
—Tonight I will think about Cavafy
and the way he wept on his satin pillow,
remembering the days of 1903.
I will compare my life to his:
the sorrows of Alexandria,
the lights on the river;

the dead kings returning to Syria,
the soap in my bath.
—Later I will lie on my own pillow
with the window open and the blinds up,
weeping a little myself at the thick blankets
and the smoking candles
and the stack of books,
a new sweetness and clarity beginning
to monopolize my own memory.

SONG

There's nothing in this gardenous world more delightful
than blossoms lying where they fall,
soldiers sprawled from one ravine to another,
lovers under a bloody window.

I look up through the branches
dreaming of fate.
My old enemy the blue sky is above me.
My old enemy the hawk
is moving slowly through the string of white clouds.

One day I will wake up at dawn
and philosophize about my state
as I get ready.
I will put on my heavy shirt
and think of the long and bitter day ahead.

It will take hours to know
whether I will live or die,
which car to get ready,
which woods to pass by,
which animal to ride over,
which bridge to cross on the way.

I love the sight of me
rolled over on the ground.
I love being pierced through the heart,

GERALD STERN

half a man, half a flower,
reaching my hand out, turning my palm away,
one of the many pink and white blossoms,
one of the many on the brutal lawn.

WEEPING AND WAILING

I like the way my little harp makes trees
leap, how putting the metal between my teeth
makes half the animals in my back yard quiver,
how plucking the sweet tongue makes the stars
live together in love and ecstasy.

I bend my face and cock my head. My eyes
are open wide listening to the sound.
My hand goes up and down like a humming bird.
My mouth is opening and closing, I am singing
in harmony, I am weeping and wailing.

ROMANCE

After thirty years
I am still listening to the pipes,
I am still enchanted
with the singing and moaning of the dry boards.

I am lying there night after night
thinking of water.
I am joining palms, or whistling Mozart
and early Yeats.

I am living without savagery,
stretching my body and turning on my left side
for music,
humming to myself and turning on my right side
for words.

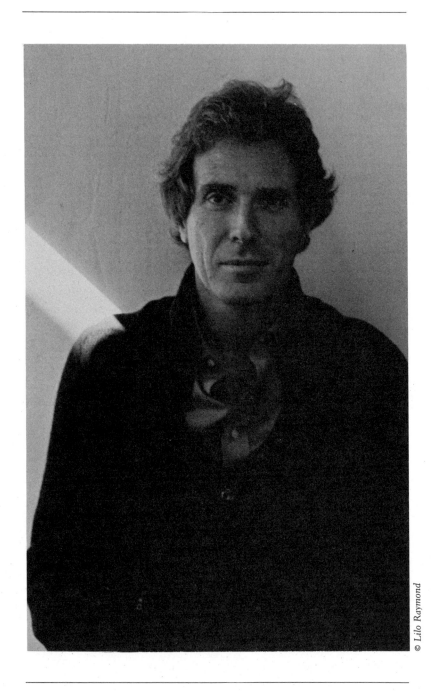

Mark Strand

SLEEPING WITH ONE EYE OPEN

Unmoved by what the wind does,
The windows
Are not rattled, nor do the various
Areas
Of the house make their usual racket—
Creak at
The joints, trusses and studs.
Instead,
They are still. And the maples,
Able
At times to raise havoc,
Evoke
Not a sound from their branches'
Clutches.
It's my night to be rattled,
Saddled
With spooks. Even the half-moon
(Half man,
Half dark), on the horizon,
Lies on
Its side casting a fishy light
Which alights
On my floor, lavishly lording
Its morbid
Look over me. Oh, I feel dead,
Folded
Away in my blankets for good, and
Forgotten.
My room is clammy and cold,
Moonhandled
And weird. The shivers
Wash over
Me, shaking my bones, my loose ends
Loosen,

And I lie sleeping with one eye open,
Hoping
That nothing, nothing will happen.

OLD PEOPLE ON THE NURSING HOME PORCH

Able at last to stop
And recall the days it took
To get them here, they sit
On the porch in rockers
Letting the faded light
Of afternoon carry them off

I see them moving back
And forth over the dullness
Of the past, covering ground
They did not know was there,
And ending up with nothing
Save what might have been.

And so they sit, gazing
Out between the trees
Until in all that vacant
Wash of sky, the wasted
Vision of each one
Comes down to earth again.

It is too late to travel
Or even find a reason
To make it seem worthwhile.
Already now, the evening
Reaches out to take
The aging world away.

And soon the dark will come,
And these tired elders feel
The need to go indoors
Where each will lie alone
In the deep and sheepless
Pastures of a long sleep.

MARK STRAND

KEEPING THINGS WHOLE

In a field
I am the absence
of field.
This is
always the case.
Wherever I am
I am what is missing.

When I walk
I part the air
and always
the air moves in
to fill the spaces
where my body's been.

We all have reasons
for moving.
I move
to keep things whole.

THE MAILMAN

It is midnight.
He comes up the walk
and knocks at the door.
I rush to greet him.
He stands there weeping,
shaking a letter at me.
He tells me it contains
terrible personal news.
He falls to his knees.
"Forgive me! Forgive me!" he pleads.

I ask him inside.
He wipes his eyes.
His dark blue suit
is like an inkstain

on my crimson couch.
Helpless, nervous, small,
he curls up like a ball
and sleeps while I compose
more letters to myself
in the same vein:

"You shall live
by inflicting pain.
You shall forgive."

EATING POETRY

Ink runs from the corners of my mouth.
There is no happiness like mine.
I have been eating poetry.

The librarian does not believe what she sees.
Her eyes are sad
and she walks with her hands in her dress.

The poems are gone.
The light is dim.
The dogs are on the basement stairs and coming up.

Their eyeballs roll,
their blond legs burn like brush.
The poor librarian begins to stamp her feet and weep.

She does not understand.
When I get on my knees and lick her hand,
she screams.

I am a new man.
I snarl at her and bark.
I romp with joy in the bookish dark.

MARK STRAND

THE SLEEP

There is the sleep of my tongue
speaking a language I can never remember—
words that enter the sleep of words
once they are spoken.

There is the sleep of one moment
inside the next, lengthening the night,
and the sleep of the window
turning the tall sleep of trees into glass.

The sleep of novels as they are read is soundless
like the sleep of dresses on the warm bodies of women.
And the sleep of thunder gathering dust on sunny days
and the sleep of ashes long after.

The sleep of wind has been known to fill the sky.
The long sleep of air locked in the lungs of the dead.
The sleep of a room with someone inside it.
Even the wooden sleep of the moon is possible.

And there is the sleep that demands I lie down
and be fitted to the dark that comes upon me
like another skin in which I shall never be found,
out of which I shall never appear.

THE ONE SONG

I prefer to sit all day
like a sack in a chair
and to lie all night
like a stone in my bed.

When food comes
I open my mouth.
When sleep comes
I close my eyes.

My body sings
only one song;
the wind turns
gray in my arms.

Flowers bloom.
Flowers die.
More is less.
I long for more.

THE GARDEN

for Robert Penn Warren

It shines in the garden,
in the white foliage of the chestnut tree,
in the brim of my father's hat
as he walks on the gravel.

In the garden suspended in time
my mother sits in a redwood chair;
light fills the sky,
the folds of her dress,
the roses tangled beside her.

And when my father bends
to whisper in her ear,
when they rise to leave
and the swallows dart
and the moon and stars
have drifted off together, it shines.

Even as you lean over this page,
late and alone, it shines; even now
in the moment before it disappears.

SHOOTING WHALES

for Judith and Leon Major

When the shoals of plankton
swarmed into St. Margaret's Bay,
turning the beaches pink,
we saw from our place on the hill
the sperm whales feeding,
fouling the nets
in their play,
and breaching clean
so the humps of their backs
rose over the wide sea meadows.

Day after day
we waited inside
for the rotting plankton to disappear.
The smell stilled even the wind,
and the oxen looked stunned,
pulling hay on the slope
of our hill.
But the plankton kept coming in
and the whales would not go.

That's when the shooting began.
The fishermen got in their boats
and went after the whales,
and my father and uncle
and we children went, too.
The froth of our wake sank fast
in the wind-shaken water.

The whales surfaced close by.
Their foreheads were huge,
the doors of their faces were closed.
Before sounding, they lifted
their flukes into the air
and brought them down hard.
They beat the sea into foam,
and the path that they made
shone after them.

Though I did not see their eyes,
I imagined they were
like the eyes of mourning,
glazed with rheum,
watching us, sweeping along
under the darkening sheets of salt.

When we cut our engine and waited
for the whales to surface again,
the sun was setting,
turning the rock-strewn barrens a gaudy salmon.
A cold wind flailed at our skin.
When finally the sun went down
and it seemed like the whales had gone,
my uncle, no longer afraid,
shot aimlessly into the sky.

Three miles out
in the rolling dark
under the moon's astonished eyes,
our engine would not start
and we headed home in the dinghy.
And my father, hunched over the oars,
brought us in. I watched him,
rapt in his effort, rowing against the tide,
his blond hair glistening with salt.
I saw the slick spillage of moonlight
being blown over his shoulders,
and the sea and spindrift
suddenly silver.

He did not speak the entire way.
At midnight
when I went to bed,
I imagined the whales
moving beneath me,
sliding over the weed-covered hills of the deep;
they knew where I was;
they were luring me
downward and downward
into the murmurous
waters of sleep.

MARK STRAND

ALWAYS

for Charles Simic

Always so late in the day
in their rumpled clothes, sitting
around a table lit by a single bulb,
the great forgetters were hard at work.
They tilted their heads to one side, closing their eyes.
Then a house disappeared and a man in his yard
with all his flowers in a row.
The moon was next to go.
The great forgetters wrinkled their brows.
Then Florida went and San Francisco
where tugs and barges leave
small gleaming scars across the Bay.
One of the great forgetters struck a match.
Gone were the harps of beaded lights
that vault the rivers of New York.
Another filled his glass
and that was it for crowds at evening
under sulphur yellow streetlamps coming on.
And afterwards Bulgaria was gone, and then Japan.
'Where will it end?' one of them said.
'Such difficult work, pursuing the fate
of everything known,' said another.
'Yes,' said a third, 'down to the last stone,
and only the cold zero of perfection
left for the imagination.'
The great forgetters slouched in their chairs.
Suddenly Asia was gone, and the evening star
and the common sorrows of the sun.
One of them yawned. Another coughed.
The last one gazed at the window:
not a cloud, not a tree,
the blaze of promise everywhere.

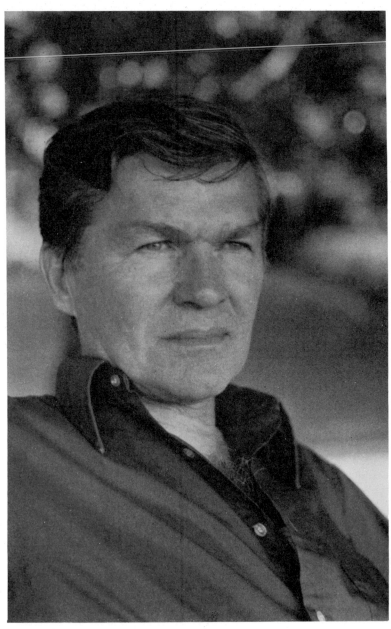

Lucien Stryk

AWAKENING

Homage to Hakuin, Zen Master, 1685–1768

I

Shoichi brushed the black
on thick.
His circle held a poem
like buds
above a flowering bowl.

Since the moment of my
pointing,
this bowl, an "earth device,"
holds
nothing but the dawn.

II

A freeze last night, the window's
laced ice flowers, a meadow drifting
from the glacier's side. I think of Hakuin:

"Freezing in an icefield, stretched
thousands of miles in all directions,
I was alone, transparent, and could not move."

Legs cramped, mind pointing
like a torch, I cannot see beyond
the frost, out nor in. And do not move.

III

I balance the round stone
          in my palm,
turn it full circle,

slowly, in the late sun,
          spring to now.
Severe compression,

like a troubled head,
          stings my hand.
It falls. A small dust rises.

IV

Beyond the sycamore
dark air moves
westward —

smoke, cloud, something
wanting a name.
Across the window,

my gathered breath,
I trace
a simple word.

V

My daughter gathers shells
where thirty years before
I'd turned them over, marveling.

I take them from her,
make, at her command,
the universe. Hands clasped,

marking the limits of
a world, we watch till sundown
planets whirling in the sand.

VI

Softness everywhere,
snow a smear,
air a gray sack.

Time. Place. Thing.
Felt between
skin and bone, flesh.

VII

I write in the dark again,
rather by dusk-light,
and what I love about

this hour is the way the trees
are taken, one by one,
into the great wash of darkness.

At this hour I am always happy,
ready to be taken myself,
fully aware.

TO A JAPANESE POET

You stood frozen there,
One hand gripping my arm,
In the other your lunchbasket,

And when I turned
To look into your face,
It was like witnessing a birth.

When the poem came,
Your fingers loosened and you
Spoke the dozen words as if
Directing one who'd
Lost his way upon
A mountain path, the night descending.

Finally we went to join
The others, but you were not the same.
All that brilliant autumn day
You avoided me
As if I'd surprised you
In some intimacy, as if my being

Near had suddenly
Cut us off. Later, when I mentioned
A hurt no memory of scarlet leaves
Could ease, you laughed
And said, "Why should you
Have felt badly? We had an enjoyable outing."

THE CANNERY

In summer this town is full of rebels
Come up from Tennessee to shell the peas.

And wetbacks roam the supermarts, making
A Tijuana of the drab main street.

The Swedes and Poles who work at Wurlitzer,
And can't stand music, are all dug in:

Doors are bolted, their pretty children warned,
Where they wait for the autumnal peace.

At night the cannery's like a train,
A runaway, cans flung up like clinkers.

Sometimes on an evening hot as Southland
When even fear won't keep the windows down,

One hears the drawl of Tennessee, the quick
Laugh of Mexico in the empty streets.

SUMMER

My neighbor frets about his lawn,
and he has reasons —
dandelions, crabgrass, a passing dog.

He scowls up at my maple, rake
clogged and trembling,
as its seeds spin down —

not angels, moths, but paratroopers
carried by the wind,
planting barricades along his eaves.

He's on the ladder now, scaring
the nibbling squirrels,
scattering starlings with his water hose.

Thank God his aim is bad
or he'd have drowned
or B-B gunned the lot. Now he

shakes a fist of seeds at me
where I sit poeming
my dandelions, crabgrass and a passing dog.

I like my neighbor, in his way
he cares for me. Look what
I've given him — something to feel superior to.

LUCIEN STRYK

LETTER TO JEAN-PAUL BAUDOT, AT CHRISTMAS

Friend, on this sunny day, snow sparkling
everywhere, I think of you once more,
how many years ago, a child Resistance

fighter trapped by Nazis in a cave
with fifteen others, left to die, you became
a cannibal. Saved by Americans,

the taste of a dead comrade's flesh foul
in your mouth, you fell onto the snow
of the Haute Savoie and gorged to purge yourself,

somehow to start again. Each winter since
you were reminded, vomiting for days.
Each winter since you told me at the Mabillon,

I see you on the first snow of the year
spreadeagled, face buried in that stench.
I write once more, Jean-Paul, though you don't

answer, because I must: today men do far worse.
Yours in hope of peace, for all of us,
before the coming of another snow.

FARMER

Seasons waiting the miracle,
dawn after dawn framing
the landscape in his eyes:

bound tight as wheat, packed
hard as dirt. Made shrewd
by soil and weather, through

the channel of his bones
shift ways of animals,
their matings twist his dreams.

While night-fields quicken,
shadows slanting right, then left
across the moonlit furrows,

he shelters in the farmhouse
merged with trees, a skin of wood,
as much the earth's as his.

CHERRIES

After Chekhov

Because I sit eating cherries
which I did not pick
a girl goes bad under

the elevator tracks, will
never be whole again.
Because I want the full bag,

grasping, twenty-five children
cry for food. Gorging,
I've none to offer. I want

to care, I mean to, but not
yet, a dozen cherries
rattling at the bottom of my bag.

One by one I lift them to
my mouth, slowly break
their skin — twelve nations

bleed. Because I love, because
I need cherries, I
cannot help them. My happiness,

bought cheap, must last forever.

EXTERMINATOR

Phone vibrates all winter. The
exterminator cringes—
yet another squeal, demanding

he come fast. He plays at cat
and mouse, stalling them hours,
days. Then pocketing thick

gloves, flashlight, steelwool,
poison, he enters musty corners,
sets dry traps, pours tempting

pellets into little paper boats,
launches them here and there.
As he stuffs holes, he contemplates

the toughness of a world which
outlaws creatures he had learned
to love: starved from frozen

corn-stripped fields, small wonder
they outsmart those who grudge them
a few crumbs, a little warmth. The

exterminator does his job, takes his
money, leaves. In the long run of
things, he knows who will survive.

LUCIEN STRYK

WATCHING WAR MOVIES

Always the same: watching
World War II movies on TV,
landing barges bursting onto

islands, my skin crawls—
heat, dust—the scorpion
bites again. How I deceived

myself. Certain my role would
not make me killer, my unarmed
body called down fire from

scarred hills. As life took
life, blood coursed into
one stream. I knew one day,

the madness stopped, I'd make
my pilgrimage to temples,
gardens, serene masters of

a Way which pain was bonding.
Atoms fuse, a mushroom cloud,
the movie ends. But I still

stumble under camouflage, near
books of tranquil Buddhas by the
screen. The war goes on and on.

JUGGLER

Someone with skill juggles
three worlds together,
rainbow, miraculous arc.

LUCIEN STRYK

Something compels a fourth,
widening the circle. Five,
six float in the charged

steep of his mind: soon
others whirl his wrist.
Seven, eight—now he's on

his toes, up, up, rising
with the music of the
spheres. Still unsatisfied,

risks the lot, down on his
knees. He dare not drop one.
Our lives depend on it.

DAWN

Five a.m., and I've been
up for hours. My lamp,
false star, holds back

the dark. In the next
room my wife guards our
closeness deep in dream.

I love this sleeplessness,
cloistered unbroken
hours over a spotless page,

the book with all the
answers on the shelf. I
doodle on one, thumb

through the other, now
and then. This hour, it
makes no difference.

I sit back, let thoughts
come as they may. Who
knows, before dawn rides

the oak across the way,
the book may jostle just a
bit, the paper bear a poem.

Richard Wilbur

ADVICE TO A PROPHET

When you come, as you soon must, to the streets of our city,
Mad-eyed from stating the obvious,
Not proclaiming our fall but begging us
In God's name to have self-pity,

Spare us all word of the weapons, their force and range,
The long numbers that rocket the mind;
Our slow, unreckoning hearts will be left behind,
Unable to fear what is too strange.

Nor shall you scare us with talk of the death of the race.
How should we dream of this place without us?—
The sun mere fire, the leaves untroubled about us,
A stone look on the stone's face?

Speak of the world's own change. Though we cannot conceive
Of an undreamt thing, we know to our cost
How the dreamt cloud crumbles, the vines are blackened by frost,
How the view alters. We could believe,

If you told us so, that the white-tailed deer will slip
Into perfect shade, grown perfectly shy,
The lark avoid the reaches of our eye,
The jack-pine lose its knuckled grip

On the cold ledge, and every torrent burn
As Xanthus once, its gliding trout
Stunned in a twinkling. What should we be without
The dolphin's arc, the dove's return,

These things in which we have seen ourselves and spoken?
Ask us, prophet, how we shall call
Our natures forth when that live tongue is all
Dispelled, that glass obscured or broken

In which we have said the rose of our love and the clean
Horse of our courage, in which beheld
The singing locust of the soul unshelled,
And all we mean or wish to mean.

Ask us, ask us whether with the worldless rose
Our hearts shall fail us; come demanding
Whether there shall be lofty or long standing
When the bronze annals of the oak-tree close.

LOVE CALLS US TO THE THINGS OF THIS WORLD

The eyes open to a cry of pulleys,
And spirited from sleep, the astounded soul
Hangs for a moment bodiless and simple
As false dawn.
                Outside the open window
The morning air is all awash with angels.

Some are in bed-sheets, some are in blouses,
Some are in smocks: but truly there they are.
Now they are rising together in calm swells
Of halcyon feeling, filling whatever they wear
With the deep joy of their impersonal breathing;

Now they are flying in place, conveying
The terrible speed of their omnipresence, moving
And staying like white water; and now of a sudden
They swoon down into so rapt a quiet
That nobody seems to be there.
                     The soul shrinks

From all that it is about to remember,
From the punctual rape of every blessèd day,
And cries,

"Oh, let there be nothing on earth but laundry,
Nothing but rosy hands in the rising steam
And clear dances done in the sight of heaven."

Yet, as the sun acknowledges
With a warm look the world's hunks and colors,
The soul descends once more in bitter love
To accept the waking body, saying now
In a changed voice as the man yawns and rises,

"Bring them down from their ruddy gallows.
Let there be clean linen for the backs of thieves;
Let lovers go fresh and sweet to be undone,
And the heaviest nuns walk in a pure floating
Of dark habits,
              keeping their difficult balance."

ON THE EYES OF AN SS OFFICER

I think of Amundsen, enormously bit
By arch-dark flurries on the ice plateaus,
An amorist of violent virgin snows
At the cold end of the world's spit.

Or a Bombay saint asquat in the market place,
Eyes gone from staring the sun over the sky,
Who still dead-reckons that acetylene eye,
An eclipsed mind in a blind face.

But this one's iced or ashen eyes devise,
Foul purities, in flesh their wilderness,
Their fire; I ask my makeshift God of this
My opulent bric-a-brac earth to damn his eyes.

RICHARD WILBUR

YEAR'S END

Now winter downs the dying of the year,
And night is all a settlement of snow;
From the soft street the rooms of houses show
A gathered light, a shapen atmosphere,
Like frozen-over lakes whose ice is thin
And still allows some stirring down within.

I've known the wind by water banks to shake
The late leaves down, which frozen where they fell
And held in ice as dancers in a spell
Fluttered all winter long into a lake;
Graved on the dark in gestures of descent,
They seemed their own most perfect monument.

There was perfection in the death of ferns
Which laid their fragile cheeks against the stone
A million years. Great mammoths overthrown
Composedly have made their long sojourns,
Like palaces of patience, in the gray
And changeless lands of ice. And at Pompeii

The little dog lay curled and did not rise
But slept the deeper as the ashes rose
And found the people incomplete, and froze
The random hands, the loose unready eyes
Of men expecting yet another sun
To do the shapely thing they had not done.

These sudden ends of time must give us pause.
We fray into the future, rarely wrought
Save in the tapestries of afterthought.
More time, more time. Barrages of applause
Come muffled from a buried radio.
The New-year bells are wrangling with the snow.

RICHARD WILBUR

A BAROQUE WALL-FOUNTAIN
IN THE VILLA SCIARRA

for Dore and Adja

Under the bronze crown
Too big for the head of the stone cherub whose feet
    A serpent has begun to eat,
Sweet water brims a cockle and braids down

    Past spattered mosses, breaks
On the tipped edge of a second shell, and fills
    The massive third below. It spills
In threads then from the scalloped rim, and makes

    A scrim or summery tent
For a faun-ménage and their familiar goose.
    Happy in all that ragged, loose
Collapse of water, its effortless descent

    And flatteries of spray,
The stocky god upholds the shell with ease,
    Watching, about his shaggy knees,
The goatish innocence of his babes at play;

    His fauness all the while
Leans forward, slightly, into a clambering mesh
    Of water-lights, her sparkling flesh
In a saecular ecstasy, her blinded smile

    Bent on the sand floor
Of the trefoil pool, where ripple-shadows come
    And go in swift reticulum,
More addling to the eye than wine, and more

    Interminable to thought
Than pleasure's calculus. Yet since this all
    Is pleasure, flash, and waterfall,
Must it not be too simple? Are we not

More intricately expressed
In the plain fountains that Maderna set
 Before St. Peter's—the main jet
Struggling aloft until it seems at rest

 In the act of rising, until
The very wish of water is reversed,
 That heaviness borne up to burst
In a clear, high, cavorting head, to fill

 With blaze, and then in gauze
Delays, in a gnatlike shimmering, in a fine
 Illumined version of itself, decline,
And patter on the stones its own applause?

 If that is what men are
Or should be, if those water-saints display
 The pattern of our areté,
What of these showered fauns in their bizarre,

 Spangled, and plunging house?
They are at rest in fulness of desire
 For what is given, they do not tire
Of the smart of the sun, the pleasant water-douse

 And riddled pool below,
Reproving our disgust and our ennui
 With humble insatiety.
Francis, perhaps, who lay in sister snow

 Before the wealthy gate
Freezing and praising, might have seen in this
 No trifle, but a shade of bliss—
That land of tolerable flowers, that state

 As near and far as grass
Where eyes become the sunlight, and the hand
 Is worthy of water: the dreamt land
Toward which all hungers leap, all pleasures pass.

RICHARD WILBUR

POTATO

for André du Bouchet

An underground grower, blind and a common brown;
Got a misshapen look, it's nudged where it could;
Simple as soil yet crowded as earth with all.

Cut open raw, it looses a cool clean stench,
Mineral acid seeping from pores of prest meal;
It is like breaching a strangely refreshing tomb:

Therein the taste of first stones, the hands of dead slaves,
Waters men drank in the earliest frightful woods,
Flint chips, and peat, and the cinders of buried camps.

Scrubbed under faucet water the planet skin
Polishes yellow, but tears to the plain insides;
Parching, the white's blue-hearted like hungry hands.

All of the cold dark kitchens, and war-frozen gray
Evening at window; I remember so many
Peeling potatoes quietly into chipt pails.

"It was potatoes saved us, they kept us alive."
Then they had something to say akin to praise
For the mean earth-apples, too common to cherish or steal.

Times being hard, the Sikh and the Senegalese,
Hobo and Okie, the body of Jesus the Jew,
Vestigial virtues, are eaten; we shall survive.

What has not lost its savor shall hold us up,
And we are praising what saves us, what fills the need.
(Soon there'll be packets again, with Algerian fruits.)

Oh, it will not bear polish, the ancient potato,
Needn't be nourished by Caesars, will blow anywhere,
Hidden by nature, counted-on, stubborn and blind.

You may have noticed the bush that it pushes to air,
Comical-delicate, sometimes with second-rate flowers
Awkward and milky and beautiful only to hunger.

A DUBIOUS NIGHT

A bell diphthonging in an atmosphere
Of shying night air summons some to prayer
Down in the town, two deep lone miles from here,

Yet wallows faint or sudden everywhere,
In every ear, as if the twist wind wrung
Some ten years' tangled echoes from the air.

What kyries it says are mauled among
The queer elisions of the mist and murk,
Of lights and shapes; the senses were unstrung,

Except that one star's synecdochic smirk
Burns steadily to me, that nothing's odd
And firm as ever is the masterwork.

I weary of the confidence of God.

PRAISE IN SUMMER

Obscurely yet most surely called to praise,
As sometimes summer calls us all, I said
The hills are heavens full of branching ways
Where star-nosed moles fly overhead the dead;
I said the trees are mines in air, I said
See how the sparrow burrows in the sky!
And then I wondered why this mad *instead*
Perverts our praise to uncreation, why
Such savor's in this wrenching things awry.
Does sense so stale that it must needs derange
The world to know it? To a praiseful eye

RICHARD WILBUR

Should it not be enough of fresh and strange
That trees grow green, and moles can course in clay,
And sparrows sweep the ceiling of our day?

COTTAGE STREET, 1953

Framed in her phoenix fire-screen, Edna Ward
Bends to the tray of Canton, pouring tea
For frightened Mrs. Plath; then, turning toward
The pale, slumped daughter, and my wife, and me,

Asks if we would prefer it weak or strong.
Will we have milk or lemon, she enquires?
The visit seems already strained and long.
Each in his turn, we tell her our desires.

It is my office to exemplify
The published poet in his happiness,
Thus cheering Sylvia, who has wished to die;
But half-ashamed, and impotent to bless,

I am a stupid life-guard who has found,
Swept to his shallows by the tide, a girl
Who, far from shore, has been immensely drowned,
And stares through water now with eyes of pearl.

How large is her refusal; and how slight
The genteel chat whereby we recommend
Life, of a summer afternoon, despite
The brewing dusk which hints that it may end.

And Edna Ward shall die in fifteen years,
After her eight-and-eighty summers of
Such grace and courage as permit no tears,
The thin hand reaching out, the last word *love*,

Outliving Sylvia who, condemned to live,
Shall study for a decade, as she must,
To state at last her brilliant negative
In poems free and helpless and unjust.

RICHARD WILBUR

THE WRITER

In her room at the prow of the house
Where light breaks, and the windows are tossed with linden,
My daughter is writing a story.

I pause in the stairwell, hearing
From her shut door a commotion of typewriter-keys
Like a chain hauled over a gunwale.

Young as she is, the stuff
Of her life is a great cargo, and some of it heavy:
I wish her a lucky passage.

But now it is she who pauses,
As if to reject my thought and its easy figure.
A stillness greatens, in which

The whole house seems to be thinking,
And then she is at it again with a bunched clamor
Of strokes, and again is silent.

I remember the dazed starling
Which was trapped in that very room, two years ago;
How we stole in, lifted a sash

And retreated, not to affright it;
And how for a helpless hour, through the crack of the door,
We watched the sleek, wild, dark

And iridescent creature
Batter against the brilliance, drop like a glove
To the hard floor, or the desk-top,

And wait then, humped and bloody,
For the wits to try it again; and how our spirits
Rose when, suddenly sure,

It lifted off from a chair-back,
Beating a smooth course for the right window
And clearing the sill of the world.

RICHARD WILBUR

It is always a matter, my darling,
Of life or death, as I had forgotten. I wish
What I wished you before, but harder.

HAMLEN BROOK

At the alder-darkened brink
Where the stream slows to a lucid jet
I lean to the water, dinting its top with sweat,
And see, before I can drink,

A startled inchling trout
Of spotted near-transparency,
Trawling a shadow solider than he.
He swerves now, darting out

To where, in a flicked slew
Of sparks and glittering silt, he weaves
Through stream-bed rocks, disturbing foundered leaves,
And butts then out of view

Beneath a sliding glass
Crazed by the skimming of a brace
Of burnished dragon-flies across its face,
In which deep cloudlets pass

And a white precipice
Of mirrored birch-trees plunges down
Toward where the azures of the zenith drown.
How shall I drink all this?

Joy's trick is to supply
Dry lips with what can cool and slake,
Leaving them dumbstruck also with an ache
Nothing can satisfy.

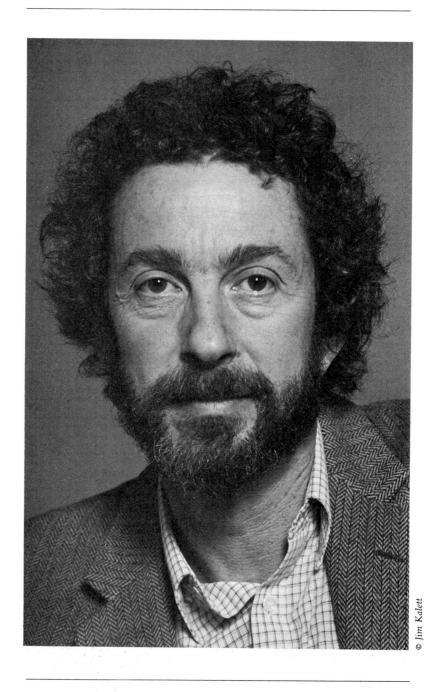

C. K. Williams

IT IS THIS WAY WITH MEN

They are pounded into the earth
like nails; move an inch,
they are driven down again.
The earth is sore with them.
It is a spiny fruit
that has lost hope
of being raised and eaten.
It can only ripen and ripen.
And men, they too are wounded.
They too are sifted from their loss
and are without hope. The core
softens. The pure flesh softens
and melts. There are thorns, there
are the dark seeds, and they end.

PATIENCE IS WHEN YOU STOP WAITING

I stand on the first step under the torn mouths of hours
in a new suit. Terrified of the arched webs and the dust,
of my speech, my own hair slicked with its thin pride,
I jut like a thorn; I turn, my pain turns and closes.

Tell me again about silence. Tell me I won't,
not ever, hear the cold men whispering in my pores
or the mothers and fathers who scream in the bedroom
and throw boxes of money between them and kiss.

At the window, faces hover against the soft glow
like names. If I cry out, it will forget me and go;
if I don't, nothing begins again. Tell me
about mercy again, how she rides in eternity's arms

in the drifts and the dreams come. The night is dying.
Wisely it thinks of death as a thing born of desire.
Gently it opens its sharp ribs and bites through
and holds me. Tell me about my life again, where it is now.

THEN THE BROTHER OF THE WIND

there's no such thing as death everybody
knows that also
nothing in the world that can batter you
and hang you on a fencepost like a towel

and no such thing as love that stays inside
getting thicker and heavier falling
into the middle one seed
that weighs more than the universe

and no angels either
and even if there were even if we hadn't laughed
the second heart out and made the second brain
have whole wars happening inside it like bacteria

and if they were made out of tin cans like shacks
in rio and rubber tires like crete sandals
and were all the same place rags in ratholes
in harlem rags sticking to burned faces in bengal

we'd still break like motors
and slip out of them anyway like penises
onto the damp thigh
and have to begin over

THEY WARNED HIM THEN THEY THREW HIM AWAY

there's somebody who's dying
to eat god
when the name happens

the juices leap from the bottom of his mouth like waves
he almost falls over with lightheadedness
nobody has ever been this hungry before
you might know people who've never had anything
but teaspoons of rice or shreds
from the shin of an ape well that's nothing
you should know what this person would do
he'd pull handfuls of hair out of his children
and shove them down
he'd squeeze the docile bud in his wife
until it screamed
if you told him god lived in his own penis
he'd bite into it
and tear like a carnivore
this is how men renounce
this is how we obliterate
one morning near the end he'll climb into the fire
and look back at himself
what was dark will be light
what was song will be roaring
and the worst thing is you'll still want this
beyond measure you'll still want this
believe me
you should know this

SPIT

... then the son of the "superior race" began to spit into the Rabbi's mouth so that the Rabbi could continue to spit on the Torah ...

The Black Book

After this much time, it's still impossible. The SS man with his stiff hair and
    his uniform;
the Rabbi, probably in a torn overcoat, probably with a stained beard the
    other would be clutching;
the Torah, God's word, on the altar, the letters blurring under the blended
    phlegm;
the Rabbi's parched mouth, the SS man perfectly absorbed, obsessed with
    perfect humiliation.

C. K. WILLIAMS

So many years and what is there to say still about the soldiers waiting
 impatiently in the snow,
about the one stamping his feet, thinking, "Kill him! Get it over with!"
while back there the lips of the Rabbi and the other would have brushed
and if time had stopped you would have thought they were lovers,
so lightly kissing, the sharp, luger hand under the dear chin,
the eyes furled slightly and then when it started again the eyelashes of both
 of them
shyly fluttering as wonderfully as the pulse of a baby.
Maybe we don't have to speak of it at all, it's still the same.
War, that happens and stops happening but is always somehow right there,
 twisting and hardening us;
then what we make of God—words, spit, degradation, murder, shame; every
 conceivable torment.
All these ways to live that have something to do with how we live
and that we're almost ashamed to use as metaphors for what goes on in us
but that we do anyway, so that love is battle and we watch ourselves in love
become maddened with pride and incompletion, and God is what it is when
 we're alone
wrestling with solitude and everything speaking in our souls turns against us
 like His fury
and just facing another person, there is so much terror and hatred that yes,
spitting in someone's mouth, trying to make him defile his own meaning,
would signify the struggle to survive each other and what we'll enact to
 accomplish it.

There's another legend.
It's about Moses, that when they first brought him as a child before Pharaoh,
the king tested him by putting a diamond and a live coal in front of him
and Moses picked up the red ember and popped it into his mouth
so for the rest of his life he was tongue-tied and Aaron had to speak for him.
What must his scarred tongue have felt like in his mouth?
It must have been like always carrying something there that weighed too
 much,
something leathery and dead whose greatest gravity was to loll out like an
 ox's,
and when it moved, it must have been like a thick embryo slowly coming
 alive,

butting itself against the inner sides of his teeth and cheeks.

And when God burned in the bush, how could he not cleave to him?

How could he not know that all of us were on fire and that every word we
said would burn forever,

in pain, unquenchably, and that God knew it, too, and would say nothing
Himself ever again beyond this,

ever, but would only live in the flesh that we use like firewood,

in all the caves of the body, the gut cave, the speech cave:

He would slobber and howl like something just barely a man that beats itself
again and again onto the dark,

moist walls away from the light, away from whatever would be light for this
last eternity.

"Now therefore go," He said, "and I will be with thy mouth."

THE GAS STATION

This is before I'd read Nietzsche. Before Kant or Kierkegaard, even before
Whitman and Yeats.

I don't think there were three words in my head yet. I knew, perhaps, that
I should suffer,

I can remember I almost cried for this or for that, nothing special, nothing
to speak of.

Probably I was mad with grief for the loss of my childhood, but I wouldn't
have known that.

It's dawn. A gas station. Route twenty-two. I remember exactly: route
twenty-two curved,

there was a squat, striped concrete divider they'd put in after a plague of
collisions.

The gas station? Texaco, Esso—I don't know. They were just words anyway
then, just what their signs said.

I wouldn't have understood the first thing about monopoly or imperialist or
oppression.

It's dawn. It's so late. Even then, when I was never tired, I'm just holding on.

Slumped on my friend's shoulder, I watch the relentless, wordless misery of
the route twenty-two sky

that seems to be filming my face with a grainy oil I keep trying to rub off or in.

Why are we here? Because one of my friends, in the men's room over there, has blue balls.

He has to jerk off. I don't know what that means, "blue balls," or why he has to do that—

it must be important to have to stop here after this long night, but I don't ask.

I'm just trying, I think, to keep my head as empty as I can for as long as I can.

One of my other friends is asleep. He's so ugly, his mouth hanging, slack and wet.

Another—I'll never see this one again—stares from the window as though he were frightened.

Here's what we've done. We were in Times Square, a pimp found us, corralled us, led us somewhere,

down a dark street, another dark street, up dark stairs, dark hall, dark apartment,

where his whore, his girl or his wife or his mother for all I know dragged herself from her sleep,

propped herself on an elbow, gazed into the dark hall and agreed, for two dollars each, to take care of us.

Take care of us. Some of the words that come through me now seem to stay, to hook in.

My friend in the bathroom is taking so long. The filthy sky must be starting to lighten.

It took me a long time, too, with the woman, I mean. Did I mention that she, the woman, the whore or mother,

was having her time and all she would deign do was to blow us? Did I say that? Deign? Blow?

What a joy, though, the idea was in those days. Blown! What a thing to tell the next day.

She only deigned, though, no more. She was like a machine. When I lift her back to me now,

there's nothing there but that dark, curly head, working, a machine, up and down, and now,

Freud, Marx, Fathers, tell me, what am I, doing this, telling this, on her, on myself,

hammering it down, cementing it, sealing it in, but a machine, too! *Why am I doing this?*

I still haven't read Augustine. I don't understand Chomsky that well. Should
I?

My friend at last comes back. Maybe the right words were there all along.
Complicity. Wonder.

How pure we were then, before Rimbaud, before Blake. *Grace. Love. Take
care of us. Please.*

TAR

The first morning of Three Mile Island: those first disquieting, uncertain,
mystifying hours.

All morning a crew of workmen have been tearing the old decrepit roof off
our building,

and all morning, trying to distract myself, I've been wandering out to watch
them

as they hack away the leaden layers of asbestos paper and disassemble the
disintegrating drains.

After half a night of listening to the news, wondering how to know a
hundred miles downwind

if and when to make a run for it and where, then a coming bolt awake at
seven

when the roofers we've been waiting for since winter sent their ladders
shrieking up our wall,

we still know less than nothing: the utility company continues making little
of the accident,

the slick federal spokesmen still have their evasions in some semblance of
order.

Surely we suspect now we're being lied to, but in the meantime, there are
the roofers,

setting winch-frames, sledging rounds of tar apart, and there I am, on the
curb across, gawking.

I never realized what brutal work it is, how matter-of-factly and harrowingly
dangerous.

The ladders flex and quiver, things skid from the edge, the materials are
bulky and recalcitrant.

When the rusty, antique nails are levered out, their heads pull off; the under-
roofing crumbles.
Even the battered little furnace, roaring along as patient as a donkey, chokes
and clogs,
a dense, malignant smoke shoots up, and someone has to fiddle with a cock,
then hammer it,
before the gush and stench will deintensify, the dark, Dantean broth wearily
subside.
In its crucible, the stuff looks bland, like licorice, spill it, though, on your
boots or coveralls,
it sears, and everything is permeated with it, the furnace gunked with burst
and half-burst bubbles,
the men themselves so completely slashed and mucked they seem almost
from another realm, like trolls.
When they take their break, they leave their brooms standing at attention
in the asphalt pails,
work gloves clinging like Brer Rabbit to the bitten shafts, and they slouch
along the precipitous lip,
the enormous sky behind them, the heavy noontime air alive with shimmers
and mirages.

Sometime in the afternoon I had to go inside: the advent of our vigil was
upon us.
However much we didn't want to, however little we would do about it, we'd
understood:
we were going to perish of all this, if not now, then soon, if not soon, then
someday.
Someday, some final generation, hysterically aswarm beneath an
atmosphere as unrelenting as rock,
would rue us all, anathematize our earthly comforts, curse our surfeits and
submissions.
I think I know, though I might rather not, why my roofers stay so clear to
me and why the rest,
the terror of that time, the reflexive disbelief and distancing, all we should
hold on to, dims so.
I remember the president in his absurd protective booties, looking absolutely
unafraid, the fool.
I remember a woman on the front page glaring across the misty
Susquehanna at those looming stacks.
But, more vividly, the men, silvered with glitter from the shingles, clinging
like starlings beneath the eaves.

Even the leftover carats of tar in the gutter, so black they seemed to suck the light out of the air.

By nightfall kids had come across them: every sidewalk on the block was scribbled with obscenities and hearts.

FROM MY WINDOW

Spring: the first morning when that one true block of sweet, laminar, complex scent arrives

from somewhere west and I keep coming to lean on the sill, glorying in the end of the wretched winter.

The scabby-barked sycamores ringing the empty lot across the way are budded—I hadn't noticed—

and the thick spikes of the unlikely urban crocuses have already broken the gritty soil.

Up the street, some surveyors with tripods are waving each other left and right the way they do.

A girl in a gym suit jogged by a while ago, some kids passed, playing hooky, I imagine,

and now the paraplegic Vietnam vet who lives in a half-converted warehouse down the block

and the friend who stays with him and seems to help him out come weaving towards me,

their battered wheelchair lurching uncertainly from one edge of the sidewalk to the other.

I know where they're going—to the "Legion": once, when I was putting something out, they stopped,

both drunk that time, too, both reeking—it wasn't ten o'clock—and we chatted for a bit.

I don't know how they stay alive—on benefits most likely. I wonder if they're lovers?

They don't look it. Right now, in fact, they look a wreck, careening haphazardly along,

contriving, as they reach beneath me, to dip a wheel from the curb so that the chair skewers, teeters,

tips, and they both tumble, the one slowly, almost gracefully sliding in stages from his seat,

his expression hardly marking it, the other staggering over him, spinning heavily down,

to lie on the asphalt, his mouth working, his feet shoving weakly and
    fruitlessly against the curb.
In the storefront office on the corner, Reed and Son, Real Estate, have come
    to see the show.
Gazing through the golden letters of their name, they're not, at least, thank
    god, laughing.
Now the buddy, grabbing at a hydrant, gets himself erect and stands there
    for a moment, panting.
Now he has to lift the other one, who lies utterly still, a forearm shielding
    his eyes from the sun.
He hauls him partly upright, then hefts him almost all the way into the chair
    but a dangling foot
catches a support-plate, jerking everything around so that he has to put him
    down,
set the chair to rights and hoist him again and as he does he jerks the grimy
    jeans right off him.
No drawers, shrunken, blotchy thighs: under the thick, white coils of belly
    blubber,
the poor, blunt pud, tiny, terrified, retracted, is almost invisible in the sparse
    genital hair,
then his friend pulls his pants up, he slumps wholly back as though he were,
    at last, to be let be,
and the friend leans against the cyclone fence, suddenly staring up at me as
    though he'd known,
all along, that I was watching and I can't help wondering if he knows that
    in the winter, too,
I watched, the night he went out to the lot and walked, paced rather, almost
    ran, for how many hours.
It was snowing, the city in that holy silence, the last we have, when the storm
    takes hold,
and he was making patterns that I thought at first were circles then realized
    made a figure eight,
what must have been to him a perfect symmetry but which, from where I
    was, shivered, bent,
and lay on its side: a warped, unclear infinity, slowly, as the snow came
    faster, going out.
Over and over again, his head lowered to the task, he slogged the path he'd
    blazed,
but the race was lost, his prints were filling faster than he made them now
    and I looked away,
up across the skeletal trees to the tall center city buildings, some, though it
    was midnight,

with all their offices still gleaming, their scarlet warning-beacons signalling
    erratically
against the thickening flakes, their smoldering auras softening portions of
    the dim, milky sky.
In the morning, nothing: every trace of him effaced, all the field pure white,
its surface glittering, the dawn, glancing from its glaze, oblique, relentless,
    unadorned.

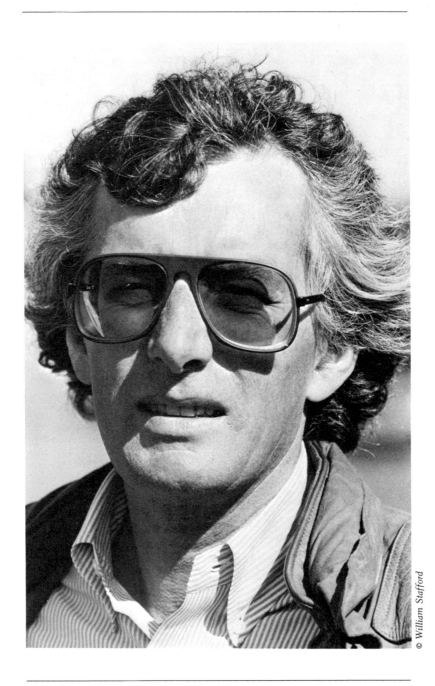

Charles Wright

THE NEW POEM

It will not resemble the sea.
It will not have dirt on its thick hands
It will not be part of the weather.

It will not reveal its name.
It will not have dreams you can count on.
It will not be photogenic.

It will not attend our sorrow.
It will not console our children.
It will not be able to help us.

BLACKWATER MOUNTAIN

That time of evening, weightless and disparate,
When the loon cries, when the small bass
Jostle the lake's reflections, when
The green of the oak begins
To open its robes to the dark, the green
Of water to offer itself to the flames,
When lily and lily pad
Husband the last light
Which flares like a white disease, then disappears:
This is what I remember. And this:

The slap of the jacklight on the cove;
The freeze-frame of ducks
Below us; your shots; the wounded flop
And skid of one bird to the thick brush;
The moon of your face in the fire's glow;

The cold; the darkness. Young,
Wanting approval, what else could I do?
And did, for two hours, waist-deep in the lake,
The thicket as black as death,
Without success or reprieve, try.

The stars over Blackwater Mountain
Still dangle and flash like hooks, and ducks
Coast on the evening water;
The foliage is like applause.
I stand where we stood before and aim
My flashlight down to the lake. A black duck
Explodes to my right, hangs, and is gone.
He shows me the way to you;
He shows me the way to a different fire
Where you, black moon, warm your hands.

NIGHTDREAM

Each day is an iceberg,
Dragging its chill paunch underfoot;
Each night is a tree to hang from,
The wooden knife, the mud rope
You scratch your initials on—
Panoply, panoply.

Up and up from his green grave, your father
Wheels in the wind, split scrap of smoke;
Under him stretch, in one file, Bob's Valley, Bald Knob,
The infinite rectitude
Of all that is past: Ouachita,
Ocoee, the slow slide of the Arkansas.

Listen, the old roads are taking flight;
Like bits of string, they, too,
Rise in the pendulous sky,
Whispering, whispering:
Echo has turned a deaf ear,
The wayside is full of leaves.

Your mother floats from her bed
In slow-motion, her loose gown like a fog
Approaching, offering
Meat; across the room, a hand
Again and again
Rises and falls back, clenching, unclenching.

The chambers you've reached, the stones touched,
All stall and worm to a dot;
Sirens drain through the night; lights
Flick and release; the fields, the wet stumps,
Shed their hair and retire;
The bedroom becomes a rose:

(In Kingsport, beneath the trees,
A Captain is singing Dixie; sons
Dance in their gold suits, clapping their hands;
And mothers and fathers, each
In a soft hat, fill
With dust-dolls their long boxes).

SNOW

If we, as we are, are dust, and dust, as it will, rises,
Then we will rise, and recongregate
In the wind, in the cloud, and be their issue,

Things in a fall in a world of fall, and slip
Through the spiked branches and snapped joints of the evergreens,
White ants, white ants and the little ribs.

EQUATION

I open the phone book, and look for my adolescence.
How easy the past is—
Alphabetized, its picture taken,
It leans in the doorway, it fits in the back pocket.

The crime is invisible,
But it's there. Why else would I feel so guilty?
Why else would that one sorrow still walk through my sleep,
Looking away, dressed in its best suit?

I touch my palm. I touch it again and again.
I leave no fingerprint. I find no white scar.
It must have been something else,
Something enormous, something too big to see.

REUNION

Already one day has detached itself from all the rest up ahead.
It has my photograph in its soft pocket.
It wants to carry my breath into the past in its bag of wind.

I write poems to untie myself, to do penance and disappear
Through the upper right-hand corner of things, to say grace.

APRIL

The plum tree breaks out in bees.
A gull is locked like a ghost in the blue attic of heaven.
The wind goes nattering on,
Gossipy, ill at ease, in the damp rooms it will air.
I count off the grace and stays
My life has come to, and know I want less—

Divested of everything,
A downfall of light in the pine woods, motes in the rush,
Gold leaf through the undergrowth, and come back
As another name, water
Pooled in the black leaves and holding me there, to be
Released as a glint, as a flash, as a spark...

CHARLES WRIGHT

DRIVING THROUGH TENNESSEE

It's strange what the past brings back.
Our parents, for instance, how ardently they still loom
In the brief and flushed
Fleshtones of memory, one foot in front of the next
Even in retrospect, and so unimpeachable.

And towns that we lived in once,
And who we were then, the roads we went back and forth on
Returning ahead of us like rime
In the moonlight's fall, and Jesus returning, and Stephen Martyr
And St. Paul of the Sword . . .

—I am their music,
Mothers and fathers and places we hurried through in the night:
I put my mouth to the dust and sing their song.
Remember us, Galeoto, and whistle our tune, when the time comes,
For charity's sake.

THREE POEMS FOR THE NEW YEAR

1

I have nothing to say about the way the sky tilts
Toward the absolute,
                    or why I live at the edge
Of the black boundary,
                    a continent where the waves
Counsel my coming in and my going out.

I have nothing to say about the brightness and drear
Of any of that, or the vanity
                    of our separate consolations.
I have nothing to say about the companies of held breath.

All year I have sung in vain,
Like a face breaking up in the font of holy water,
                        not hungry, not pure of heart.
All year as my body, sweet pilgrimage,
                moved from the dark to the dark.

What true advice the cicada leaves.

2

How strange it is to awake
Into middle age, Rimbaud left blue and out cold
In the snow,
                the Alps wriggling away to a line
In the near distance,
                        someone you don't know
Coming to get your body, revive it, and arrange for the train.

How strange to awake to that,

The windows all fogged with breath,
The landscape outside in a flash,
                            and gone like a scarf
On the neck of someone else,
                    so white, so immaculate,
The deserts and caravans
Hanging like Christmas birds in the ice-dangled evergreens.

3

All day at the window seat
                    looking out, the red knots

Of winter hibiscus deep in the foregreen,
Slick globes of oranges in the next yard,
Many oranges,
                and slow winks in the lemon trees
Down the street, slow winks when the wind blows the leaves back.

The ache for fame is a thick dust and weariness in the heart.

All day with the knuckle of solitude
To gnaw on,
                the turkey buzzards and red-tailed hawk
Lifting and widening concentrically over the field,
Brush-tails of the pepper branches
                            writing invisibly on the sky . . .

The ache for anything is a thick dust in the heart.

CALIFORNIA DREAMING

We are not born yet, and everything's crystal under our feet.
We are not brethren, we are not underlings.
We are another nation,
                    living by voices that you will never hear,
Caught in the net of splendor
                        of time-to-come on the earth.
We shine in our distant chambers, we are golden.

Midmorning, and Darvon dustfall off the Pacific
Stuns us to ecstasy,
                  October sun
Stuck like a tack on the eastern drift of the sky,
The idea of God on the other,
                    body by body
Rinsed in the Sunday prayer-light, draining away
Into the undercoating and slow sparks of the west,
                        which is our solitude and our joy.

I've looked at this ridge of lights for six years now
                        and still don't like it,
Strung out like Good Friday along a cliff
That Easters down to the ocean,
A dark wing with ruffled feathers as far out as Catalina
Fallen from some sky,
                    ruffled and laid back by the wind,
Santa Ana that lisps its hot breath
                    on the neck of everything.

What if the soul indeed is outside the body,
                              a little rainfall of light
Moistening our every step, prismatic, apotheosizic?
What if inside the body another shape is waiting to come out,
White as a quilt, loose as a fever,
                              and sways in the easy tides there?
What other anagoge in this life but the self?
What other ladder to Paradise
                    but the smooth handholds of the rib cage?
High in the palm tree the orioles twitter and grieve.
We twitter and grieve, the spider twirls the honey bee,
Who twitters and grieves, around in her net,
                              then draws it by one leg
Up to the fishbone fern leaves inside the pepper tree
                              swaddled in silk
And turns it again and again until it is shining.

———————

Some nights, when the rock-and-roll band next door has quit playing,
And the last helicopter has thwonked back to the Marine base,
And the dark lets all its weight down
                    to within a half inch of the ground,
I sit outside in the gold lamé of the moon
                    as the town sleeps and the country sleeps
Like flung confetti around me,
And wonder just what in the hell I'm doing out here
So many thousands of miles away from what I know best.
And what I know best
                    has nothing to do with Point Conception
And Avalon and the long erasure of ocean
Out there where the landscape ends.
What I know best is a little thing.
It sits on the far side of the simile,
                    the like that's like the like.

———————

Today is sweet stuff on the tongue.
The question of how we should live our lives in this world
Will find no answer from us
                    this morning,
Sunflick, the ocean humping its back
Beneath us, shivering out
                    wave after wave we fall from

CHARLES WRIGHT

And cut through in a white scar of healed waters,
Our wet suits glossed slick as seals,
                              our boards grown sharp as cries.
We rise and fall like the sun.

———————

Ghost of the Muse and her dogsbody
Suspended above the beach, November 25,
Sun like a Valium disc, smog like rust in the trees.
White-hooded and friar-backed,
                      a gull choir eyeballs the wave reach.
Invisibly pistoned, the sea keeps it up,
                  plunges and draws back, plunges and draws back,
Yesterday hung like a porcelain cup behind the eyes,
Sonorous valves, insistent extremities,
                      the worm creeping out of the heart...

———————

Who are these people we pretend to be,
                      untouched by the setting sun?
They stand less stiffly than we do, and handsomer,
First on the left foot, and then the right.
Just for a moment we see ourselves inside them,
                                  peering out,
And then they go their own way and we go ours,
Back to the window seat above the driveway,
Christmas lights in the pepper tree,
                          black Madonna
Gazing out from the alicanthus.
Chalk eyes downcast, heavy with weeping and bitterness,
Her time has come round again.

———————

Piece by small piece the world falls away from us like spores
From a milkweed pod,
                      and everything we have known,
And everyone we have known,
Is taken away by the wind to forgetfulness,
Somebody always humming,
                      California dreaming...

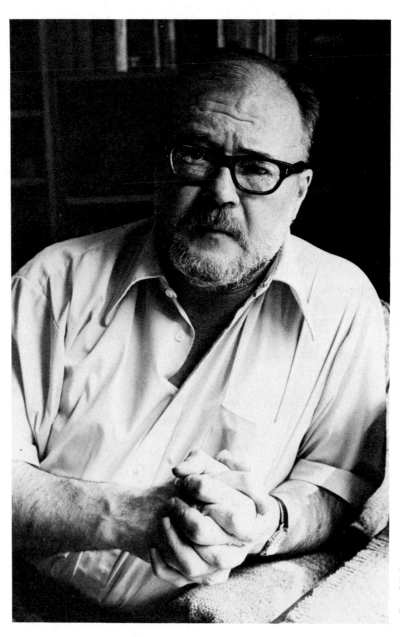

James Wright

GOODBYE TO THE POETRY OF CALCIUM

Dark cypresses—
The world is uneasily happy:
It will all be forgotten.

Theodor Storm

Mother of roots, you have not seeded
The tall ashes of loneliness
For me. Therefore,
Now I go.
If I knew the name,
Your name, all trellises of vineyards and old fire
Would quicken to shake terribly my
Earth, mother of spiralling searches, terrible
Fable of calcium, girl. I crept this afternoon
In weeds once more,
Casual, daydreaming you might not strike
Me down. Mother of window sills and journeys,
Hallower of scratching hands,
The sight of my blind man makes me want to weep.
Tiller of waves or whatever, woman or man,
Mother of roots or father of diamonds,
Look: I am nothing.
I do not even have ashes to rub into my eyes.

AS I STEP OVER A PUDDLE AT THE END OF WINTER, I THINK OF AN ANCIENT CHINESE GOVERNOR

And how can I, born in evil days
And fresh from failure, ask a kindness
of Fate?

Written A.D. *819*

Po Chu-i, balding old politician,
What's the use?
I think of you,

Uneasily entering the gorges of the Yang-Tze,
When you were being towed up the rapids
Toward some political job or other
In the city of Chungshou.
You made it, I guess,
By dark.

But it is 1960, it is almost spring again,
And the tall rocks of Minneapolis
Build me my own black twilight
Of bamboo ropes and waters.
Where is Yuan Chen, the friend you loved?
Where is the sea, that once solved the whole loneliness
Of the Midwest? Where is Minneapolis? I can see nothing
But the great terrible oak tree darkening with winter.
Did you find the city of isolated men beyond mountains?
Or have you been holding the end of a frayed rope
For a thousand years?

AUTUMN BEGINS IN MARTINS FERRY, OHIO

In the Shreve High football stadium,
I think of Polacks nursing long beers in Tiltonsville,
And gray faces of Negroes in the blast furnace at Benwood,
And the ruptured night watchman of Wheeling Steel,
Dreaming of heroes.

All the proud fathers are ashamed to go home.
Their women cluck like starved pullets,
Dying for love.

Therefore,
Their sons grow suicidally beautiful
At the beginning of October,
And gallop terribly against each other's bodies.

JAMES WRIGHT

LYING IN A HAMMOCK AT WILLIAM DUFFY'S FARM IN PINE ISLAND, MINNESOTA

Over my head, I see the bronze butterfly,
Asleep on the black trunk,
Blowing like a leaf in green shadow.
Down the ravine behind the empty house,
The cowbells follow one another
Into the distances of the afternoon.
To my right,
In a field of sunlight between two pines,
The droppings of last year's horses
Blaze up into golden stones.
I lean back, as the evening darkens and comes on.
A chicken hawk floats over, looking for home.
I have wasted my life.

THE JEWEL

There is this cave
In the air behind my body
That nobody is going to touch:
A cloister, a silence
Closing around a blossom of fire.
When I stand upright in the wind,
My bones turn to dark emeralds.

FEAR IS WHAT QUICKENS ME

1

Many animals that our fathers killed in America
Had quick eyes.
They stared about wildly,

When the moon went dark.
The new moon falls into the freight yards
Of cities in the south,
But the loss of the moon to the dark hands of Chicago
Does not matter to the deer
In this northern field.

2

What is that tall woman doing
There, in the trees?
I can hear rabbits and mourning doves whispering together
In the dark grass, there
Under the trees.

3

I look about wildly.

A BLESSING

Just off the highway to Rochester, Minnesota,
Twilight bounds softly forth on the grass.
And the eyes of those two Indian ponies
Darken with kindness.
They have come gladly out of the willows
To welcome my friend and me.
We step over the barbed wire into the pasture
Where they have been grazing all day, alone.
They ripple tensely, they can hardly contain their happiness
That we have come.
They bow shyly as wet swans. They love each other.
There is no loneliness like theirs.
At home once more,
They begin munching the young tufts of spring in the darkness.
I would like to hold the slenderer one in my arms,
For she has walked over to me
And nuzzled my left hand.

She is black and white,
Her mane falls wild on her forehead,
And the light breeze moves me to caress her long ear
That is delicate as the skin over a girl's wrist.
Suddenly I realize
That if I stepped out of my body I would break
Into blossom.

LATE NOVEMBER IN A FIELD

Today I am walking alone in a bare place,
And winter is here.
Two squirrels near a fence post
Are helping each other drag a branch
Toward a hiding place; it must be somewhere
Behind those ash trees.
They are still alive, they ought to save acorns
Against the cold.
Frail paws rifle the troughs between cornstalks when the moon
Is looking away.
The earth is hard now,
The soles of my shoes need repairs.
I have nothing to ask a blessing for,
Except these words.
I wish they were
Grass.

IN RESPONSE TO A RUMOR THAT THE OLDEST WHOREHOUSE IN WHEELING, WEST VIRGINIA, HAS BEEN CONDEMNED

I will grieve alone,
As I strolled alone, years ago, down along
The Ohio shore.
I hid in the hobo jungle weeds
Upstream from the sewer main,
Pondering, gazing.

I saw, down river,
At Twenty-third and Water Streets
By the vinegar works,
The doors open in early evening.
Swinging their purses, the women
Poured down the long street to the river
And into the river.

I do not know how it was
They could drown every evening.
What time near dawn did they climb up the other shore,
Drying their wings?
For the river at Wheeling, West Virginia,
Has only two shores:
The one in hell, the other
In Bridgeport, Ohio.

And nobody would commit suicide, only
To find beyond death
Bridgeport, Ohio.

A MORAL POEM FREELY ACCEPTED FROM SAPPHO

(For the marriage of Frances Seltzer and Philip Mendlow)

I would like to sleep with deer.
Then she emerges.
I sleep with both.
This poem is a deer with a dream in it.
I have stepped across its rock.
The three wings coiling out of that black stone in my breast
Jut up slashing the other two
Sides of the sky.
Let the dead rise.
Let us two die
Down with the two deer.
I believe that love among us
And those two animals
Has its place in the
Brilliance of the sun that is
More gold than gold,
And in virtue.

JAMES WRIGHT

A POEM OF TOWERS

I am becoming one
Of the old men.
I wonder about them,
And how they became
So happy. Tonight
The trees in the Carl Schurz
Park by the East River
Had no need of electricity
To light their boughs, for the moon
And my love were enough.
More than enough the garbage
Scow plunging, the front hoof
Of a mule gone so wild through the water,
No need to flee. Who pities
You tonight, white-haired
Lu Yu? Wise and foolish
Both are gone, and my love
Leans on my shoulder precise
As the flute notes
Of the snow, with songs
And poems scattered
Over Shu, over the East River
That loves them and drowns them.

BEAUTIFUL OHIO

Those old Winnebago men
Knew what they were singing.
All summer long and all alone,
I had found a way
To sit on a railroad tie
Above the sewer main.
It spilled a shining waterfall out of a pipe
Somebody had gouged through the slanted earth.
Sixteen thousand and five hundred more or less people
In Martins Ferry, my home, my native country,
Quickened the river
With the speed of light.

And the light caught there
The solid speed of their lives
In the instant of that waterfall.
I know what we call it
Most of the time.
But I have my own song for it,
And sometimes, even today,
I call it beauty.

YES, BUT

Even if it were true,
Even if I were dead and buried in Verona,
I believe I would come out and wash my face
In the chill spring.
I believe I would appear
Between noon and four, when nearly
Everybody else is asleep or making love,
And all the Germans turned down, the motorcycles
Muffled, chained, still.

Then the plump lizards along the Adige by San Giorgio
Come out and gaze,
Unpestered by temptation, across the water.
I would sit among them and join them in leaving
The golden mosquitoes alone.
Why should we sit by the Adige and destroy
Anything, even our enemies, even the prey
God caused to glitter for us
Defenseless in the sun?
We are not exhausted. We are not angry, or lonely,
Or sick at heart.
We are in love lightly, lightly. We know we are shining,
Though we cannot see one another.
The wind doesn't scatter us.
Because our very lungs have fallen and drifted
Away like leaves down the Adige,
Long ago.

We breathe light.

JAMES WRIGHT

THE JOURNEY

Anghiari is medieval, a sleeve sloping down
A steep hill, suddenly sweeping out
To the edge of a cliff, and dwindling.
But far up the mountain, behind the town,
We too were swept out, out by the wind,
Alone with the Tuscan grass.

Wind had been blowing across the hills
For days, and everything now was graying gold
With dust, everything we saw, even
Some small children scampering along a road,
Twittering Italian to a small caged bird.
We sat beside them to rest in some brushwood,
And I leaned down to rinse the dust from my face.

I found the spider web there, whose hinges
Reeled heavily and crazily with the dust,
Whole mounds and cemeteries of it, sagging
And scattering shadows among shells and wings.
And then she stepped into the center of air
Slender and fastidious, the golden hair
Of daylight along her shoulders, she poised there,
While ruins crumbled on every side of her.
Free of the dust, as though a moment before
She had stepped inside the earth, to bathe herself.

I gazed, close to her, till at last she stepped
Away in her own good time.

Many men
Have searched all over Tuscany and never found
What I found there, the heart of the light
Itself shelled and leaved, balancing
On filaments themselves falling. The secret
Of this journey is to let the wind
Blow its dust all over your body,
To let it go on blowing, to step lightly, lightly
All the way through your ruins, and not to lose
Any sleep over the dead, who surely
Will bury their own, don't worry.

Notes on the Poets

A. R. AMMONS (1926)

Born in Whiteville, North Carolina, A. R. Ammons was educated at Wake Forest College and the University of California at Berkeley. From 1952 to 1962, he was an executive of a biological glass company; since 1964 he has taught at Cornell University where he is presently Goldwin Smith Professor of Poetry. The recipient of fellowships from the Guggenheim Foundation and the American Academy of Arts and Letters, Ammons also was awarded the National Book Award in 1973 and the Bollingen Prize in 1975.

A. R. Ammons has been called an American Romantic. So he is—in more ways than one. To begin with, the surface of his poems bristles and blooms primarily with the flora of the natural world observed by a well-trained and informed sensibility. At times one senses that this poet has observed the ever-shifting vagaries of the natural world with the zeal of a professional bird watcher. At the same time, the world that Ammons perceives seems remarkably devoid of other humans and—perhaps as a consequence—devoid of that darker, painful, and seamier side of human life we've come to expect in the work of contemporary poets. Even when he turns his attention to an urban existence quite removed from nature, as in "The City Limits," or to the possibility of "the explosion or cataclysm," as in "The Eternal City," Ammons has a distinctive capacity for reaffirming the "gold skeined wings of flies swarming . . . / the coiled shit" and the manner in which even ruinage must "accept . . . into itself . . . all the old / perfect human visions, all the old perfect loves."

At the heart of Ammons's poetry and vision seems to be a profound philosophical belief that the radiant energy at the heart of the natural world—as perceived by the seer-poet—becomes the inward and organic energy of the poem itself, which in turn is transformed from within into an emblematic and musical affirmation of the cosmic energy at the heart of all life. In the presence of this radiance, even "fear lit by the breadth of such calmly turns to praise." And the more we hear Ammons's philosophical music, the more we see those "hues, shadings, rises, flowing bends and blends"; as we move further into the world of Ammons's poetry, the better we can understand his moral and aesthetic conviction: "I understand / and won't give assertion up."

NOTES ON THE POETS

Poetry

Ommateum, with Doxology. Philadelphia: Dorrance, 1955.   *Expressions of Sea Level.* Columbus: Ohio State University, 1964.   *Corsons Inlet.* Ithaca, N.Y.: Cornell University, 1965.   *Tape for the Turn of the Year.* Ithaca, N.Y.: Cornell University, 1965.   *Northfield Poems.* Ithaca, N.Y.: Cornell University, 1966. *Selected Poems.* Ithaca, N.Y.: Cornell University, 1968.   *Uplands.* New York: Norton, 1970.   *Briefings: Poems Small and Easy.* New York: Norton, 1971. *Collected Poems 1951–1971.* New York: Norton, 1972.   *Sphere: The Form of a Motion.* New York: Norton, 1974.   *Diversifications.* New York: Norton, 1975. *The Snow Poems.* New York: Norton, 1977.   *The Selected Poems 1951–1977.* New York: Norton, 1977.   *Selected Longer Poems.* New York: Norton, 1980.   *A Coast of Trees.* New York: Norton, 1981.   *Worldly Hopes.* New York: Norton, 1982. *Lake Effect Country.* New York: Norton, 1983.

JOHN ASHBERY (1927)

John Ashbery was born in Rochester, New York. A graduate of Harvard and Columbia, he was executive editor of *Art News* from 1965 to 1972; he currently teaches at Brooklyn College. His many honors include Fulbright Fellowships, grants from the Ingram Merrill and Guggenheim Foundations, and a National Institute of Arts and Letters award. In 1975 Ashbery's *Self-Portrait in a Convex Mirror* received the Pulitzer Prize, the National Book Award, and the National Book Critics Circle Award.

With the publication of *The Tennis Court Oath*, Ashbery was recognized as one of the most experimental and as, at times, one of the most exasperating poets of his generation: montages of words and unrelated, juxtaposed images threatened the reader to attention, but then these fragments slipped away like verbal hallucinations, leaving the atmosphere charged with an emotional haze. Critics recognized the possible influences of Wallace Stevens, the French symbolists, and New York action painters; however, even the most unorthodox tools of criticism were blunted by this enigmatic poetry whose syntax refused to yield a recognizable sense of development or sustained meaning. While Ashbery's recent poems have become ostensibly more accessible and translucent, most critics continue to be baffled and to venture complex interpretations that, by comparison, make Ashbery's poems sound utterly transparent.

One critic has observed that Ashbery's largest aesthetic principle is the discovery that the world consents, every day, to being shaped into a poem. Ashbery himself has modified this view by asserting that there are no traditional subjects or themes in his poetry: "Most of my poems," he has said in an interview, "are about the experience of experience . . . and the particular experience is of lesser interest to me than the way it filters through to me. I believe this is the way in which it happens with most people, and I'm trying to record a kind of generalized transcript of what's really going on in our minds all day long."

Before the publication of *Three Poems*—long prose poems that may be viewed, at least in part, as an extended statement of poetics—Ashbery offered a somewhat minimal key to his enigmatic poetics when he wrote: "the carnivorous / Way of these lines is to devour their own nature, leaving / Nothing but a bitter impression of absence, which as we know involves presence, but still. / Nevertheless these are fundamental absences, struggling to get up and be off themselves." And the more one reads Ashbery's work, the more it is clear that these "absences" in his poetry— as in the work of Rilke—are the consequences of the innocent eye confronting experience: the lingering pain of loss.

Poetry

Turandot and Other Poems. New York: Tibor de Nagy, 1953.   *Some Trees*. New Haven: Yale University, 1956; reprint, New York: Corinth, 1970.   *The Tennis Court Oath*. Middletown: Wesleyan, 1962.   *Rivers and Mountains*. New York: Holt, Rinehart and Winston, 1966; reprint, New York: Ecco, 1977.   *Sunrise in Suburbia*. New York: Phoenix Book Shop, 1968.   *Fragment*. Los Angeles: Black Sparrow, 1969.   *The Double Dream of Spring*. New York: Dutton, 1970; reprint, New York: Ecco, 1976.   *Three Poems*. New York: Viking, 1972; reprint, New York: Penguin, 1977.   *The Vermont Journal*. Los Angeles: Black Sparrow, 1975.   *Self-Portrait in a Convex Mirror*. New York: Viking, 1975; reprint, New York: Penguin, 1976. *Houseboat Days*. New York: Viking/Penguin, 1977.   *As We Know*. New York: Viking/Penguin, 1979.   *Shadow Train*. New York: Viking/Penguin, 1981.   *A Wave*. New York: Viking/Penguin, 1984.

Fiction and Drama

A Nest of Ninnies (novel, with James Schuyler). New York: Dutton, 1969; reprint, Calais, Vt.: Z Press, 1975.   *Three Plays*. Calais, Vt.: Z Press, 1978.

Bibliography

Kermani, David. *John Ashbery: A Comprehensive Bibliography*. New York: Garland, 1976.

Critical Studies

Lehman, David, ed. *Beyond Amazement: New Essays on John Ashbery*. Ithaca, N.Y.: Cornell University, 1980.   Shapiro, David. *John Ashbery: An Introduction to the Poetry*. New York: Columbia University, 1979.

MARVIN BELL (1937)

Marvin Bell was born in New York City. He attended Alfred University and Syracuse University; then he received his M.A. from the University of Chicago and his M.F.A. from the University of Iowa. In 1964–1965 he served as a foreign military training officer for the United States Army, and since 1965 he has been teaching at the University of Iowa, where he is now professor of English in the Writers' Workshop. Bell also has taught at the University of Hawaii and at Goddard College, as well as at many summer writers' conferences across the country, and in 1983 he was Senior Fulbright Scholar to Yugoslavia. He has served as editor of the magazine *Statements* and as poetry editor for *North American Review* and *Iowa Review,* and he has been a columnist for *American Poetry Review.* His many honors and distinctions include the Academy of American Poets' Lamont Prize for Poetry in 1969, nomination for the National Book Award in 1977, and fellowships from the National Endowment for the Arts and the Guggenheim Foundation.

Because of Bell's commitment to enlarging the experiment of American free verse, the surface quality of his poems can be deceptively laconic. But at their best they amply demonstrate the fact that the "freer" poetry seems to be, the more carefully crafted it is. (Of course, the obverse is equally true: the more carefully crafted a poem is, the freer it seems.) The effectiveness of his seemingly straightforward but somewhat strange love poem "To Dorothy," for example, is highly controlled by Bell's drawing on the centuries-old and rich tradition of love lyrics using gardens and flowers as metaphors for the loved one. The power of "Long Island," on the other hand, depends in part on a careful blending of concentric and intraconnecting images, rhythms, and syntactical repetitions.

On a philosophical level, Marvin Bell's subjects include love; desire; the nature of reality, knowledge, and belief; the existential nature of truth and of the human condition; courage and a pursuit of truths behind appearances that is peculiarly American. Those philosophical subjects, however, are rooted in the day-to-day human experiences of being a father and lover, remembering World War II or clover in moonlight, discovering a gingko plant on a New York City street or a potter's sponge in a foreign country, and, especially, trying to understand the inner nature of his vocation and his craft.

What is also remarkable about much of Marvin Bell's work is that, by fully *doing* what it says, a poem is not only "about" the immediate subject at hand but also is its own statement of poetics — just as Robert Frost's "Birches" is as much a poem about the nature of poetic craft as it is a poem about trees. A few other poets of this generation have written poems that are their own statement of poetics: Snyder's "Riprap," Creeley's "The Language," and Dickey's "In the Mountain Tent" come to mind. However, perhaps no poet has pursued the philosophical dimensions of aesthetics in so many individual poems as rigorously as Bell has. The rewards of that quest have been abundant, as much for us as readers as for Bell.

Although it isn't possible to devise a full-fledged system of aesthetics from Bell's poetry (that isn't what poetry does), it is possible to suggest a few of the touchstones that inform Marvin Bell's vibrant vision: a vigorous life of the imagination leads to much the same depth of knowledge as that offered by the pursuit of history, mathematics, and physics and the exploration of unknown frontiers ("Long Island"); commitment to one's art demands the same painful, self-effacing mortification and loneliness as any other quest for genuine excellence ("Homage to the Runner"); and human beings, born to be makers and lovers, realize that the ultimate source of meaningful loving and making is that ever-endless chain of honorable human labor—"because men and women had sown green grass, / and flowered to my eye in man-made light, / and to some would be as fire in the body / and to others a light in the mind. . . . "

Poetry

Things We Dreamt We Died For. Iowa City: Stone Wall, 1966.   *Poems for Nathan and Saul.* Mt. Vernon, Iowa: Hillside, 1966.   *A Probable Volume of Dreams.* New York: Atheneum, 1969.   *The Escape into You: A Sequence.* New York: Atheneum, 1971.   *Woo Havoc.* Somerville, Mass.: Barn Dream, 1971.   *Residue of Song.* New York: Atheneum, 1974.   *Stars Which See, Stars Which Do Not See.* New York: Atheneum, 1977.   *These Green-Going-to-Yellow.* New York: Atheneum, 1981. *Segues: A Correspondence in Poetry* (with William Stafford). Boston: Godine, 1983.   *Drawn by Stones, by Earth, by Things That Have Been in the Fire.* New York: Atheneum, 1984.

Criticism

Old Snow Just Melting: Essays and Interviews. Ann Arbor: University of Michigan, 1983.

Anthology

Iowa Workshop Poets 1963. Iowa City: Statements-Midwest Magazine, 1963.

JOHN BERRYMAN (1914–1972)

John Berryman graduated from Columbia and Clare College (Cambridge). He taught at Brown, Harvard, Princeton, and was, at the time of his death, professor of humanities at the University of Minnesota. A recipient of Rockefeller and Guggenheim fellowships and of a special grant from the National Arts Council, he also won the Pulitzer Prize (1965) and the National Book Award (1969). On January 7, 1972, John Berryman committed suicide.

In the course of his career, Berryman wrote not only a distinguished long poem in homage to Anne Bradstreet but also an equally notable sonnet sequence. However, his major work is his sequence of 385 "Dream Songs," for which he may well be recognized as one of the truly great poets of the century. The scope, depth, daring, and craftsmanship of these poems have caused critics to compare Berryman with Homer, Dante, and Whitman.

The Dream Songs constitute a loose narrative about a multidimensional figure most often called Henry Pussycat. Berryman wrote that Henry is "an imaginary character (not the poet . . .), a white American in early middle age sometimes in blackface, who has suffered an irreversible loss and talks to himself sometimes in the first person, sometimes in the third, sometimes even in the second; he has a friend, never named, who addresses him as Mr Bones and variants thereof." There are moments in the Dream Songs when Henry, Mr Bones, and the poet are barely distinguishable from one another—and are not meant to be distinguishable. Thus Berryman attempts and achieves a linear-multidimensional vision—maneuvered by a dazzling shift of pronouns—which is a verbal equivalent to what Picasso achieved in his cubist period.

Like Odysseus, Henry Pussycat undergoes a fantastic range of experience. He even dies and comes back to life. His emotions shift from incredible panic, horror, and self-pity to sheer joy and self-deprecating slapstick. If Henry gets out of hand, his friend and conscience, his side-kick and minstrel chorus are always there either to cut him down to size or to support him through despair. At the end of his journey, which takes him across spiritual as well as spatial and historical boundaries, Henry, the schizophrenic Odysseus of the atomic age, returns to his wife and child, scarred but bearing that most ancient and essential knowledge: to be human is to suffer.

Poetry

Poems. Norfolk, Conn.: New Directions, 1942.   *The Dispossessed.* New York: William Sloane, 1948.   *Homage to Mistress Bradstreet.* New York: Farrar, Straus & Giroux, 1956.   *His Thoughts Made Pockets & The Plane Buckt.* Pawlet, Vt.: C. Fredericks, 1958.   *Short Poems.* New York: Farrar, Straus & Giroux, 1964. *77 Dream Songs.* New York: Farrar, Straus & Giroux, 1967.   *His Toy, His Dream, His Rest.* New York: Farrar, Straus & Giroux, 1968.   *The Dream Songs.* New York: Farrar, Straus & Giroux, 1969.   *Love & Fame.* New York: Farrar, Straus & Giroux, 1970; revised edition, 1972.   *Delusions, Etc.* New York: Farrar, Straus & Giroux, 1972.   *Henry's Fate & Other Poems, 1967–1972.* New York: Farrar, Straus & Giroux, 1977.

Fiction and Criticism

Stephen Crane (biography). New York: William Sloane, 1950; reprint, Cleveland: World, 1962. *Recovery* (novel). New York: Farrar, Straus & Giroux, 1973. *The Freedom of the Poet* (essays and stories). New York: Farrar, Straus & Giroux, 1976.

Bibliographies

Arpin, Gary Q. *John Berryman: A Reference Guide*. Boston: G. K. Hall, 1976. Kelly, Richard J. *John Berryman: A Checklist*. Metuchen, N.J.: Scarecrow, 1972. Stefanik, Ernest C., Jr. *John Berryman: A Descriptive Bibliography*. Pittsburgh: University of Pittsburgh, 1972.

Biographical and Critical Studies

Conarroe, Joel. *John Berryman: An Introduction to the Poetry*. New York: Columbia University, 1977. Haffender, John. *The Life of John Berryman*. London: Routledge & Kegan, 1983. Linebarger, J. M. *John Berryman*. New York: Twayne, 1974. Martz, William J. *John Berryman*. Minneapolis: University of Minnesota, 1969.

ELIZABETH BISHOP (1911–1979)

A native of Worcester, Massachusetts, Elizabeth Bishop received her formal education at Vassar. She lived in Brazil for the better part of sixteen years; she taught at the University of Washington and at Harvard. She was Consultant in Poetry at the Library of Congress from 1949 to 1950 and was subsequently elected a chancellor of the Academy of American Poets and a member of the National Institute of Arts and Letters. Her many other honors include grants from the Guggenheim and Ingram Merrill Foundations, the Pulitzer Prize (1956), the National Book Award (1970), and the Order of Rio Branco (Brazil, 1971).

Although Elizabeth Bishop was far less prolific than most poets of her generation, she was one of the few poets about whom it could be said that each new book—indeed each new poem—was an "event." One reason may be that she was far less predictable than many of her contemporaries; that is, readers of poetry did not come to expect a particular kind of poem from Bishop the way that they had come to expect a certain kind of poem from Anne Sexton or Robert Lowell.

Another reason why Bishop's poems are rare moments of delight and epiphany stems from her stunning perceptions and reconstruction of the details of physical reality. As Randall Jarrell says in *Poetry and the Age*:

"all her poems have written underneath, *I have seen it.*" Whether the matter at hand is the exotic rainbow glow of a tremendous fish or the commonplace sheen of oil in a dingy filling station, Bishop knows that poetry and vision are rooted, first of all, in what Archibald MacLeish has called "the shine of the world." In her better poems, Bishop amply demonstrates that the perception of sensible objects and moral vision, for the poet, may be one and the same experience.

Ralph J. Mills, Jr., has rightfully noted another, more ambitious dimension of Bishop's achievement. In addition to her graceful use of fairly strict forms—and the unmistakable presence of a formalist approach even in the freer verse—Elizabeth Bishop's poems are distinguished by what Mills calls a "total accomplishment of language, technique, music, and imagery working simultaneously, or (in Eliot's phrase) 'the complete consort of dancing together.' "

Poetry

North and South. Boston: Houghton Mifflin, 1946.   *Poems: North and South — A Cold Spring.* Boston: Houghton Mifflin, 1955.   *Questions of Travel.* New York: Farrar, Straus & Giroux, 1965.   *The Ballad of the Burglar of Babylon.* New York: Farrar, Straus & Giroux, 1968.   *The Complete Poems.* New York: Farrar, Straus & Giroux, 1969; reprint, 1979.   *Geography III.* New York: Farrar, Straus & Giroux, 1976.   *The Complete Poems 1927–1979.* New York: Farrar, Straus & Giroux, 1983.

Prose

The Collected Prose. Edited and introduced by Robert Giroux. New York: Farrar, Straus & Giroux, 1984.

Translations: Prose and Poetry

The Diary of Helena Morley. New York: Farrar, Straus & Giroux, 1957.   *Anthology of Contemporary Brazilian Poetry* (editor and translator with others). Middletown: Wesleyan, 1972.

Bibliography

MacMahon, Candace W. *Elizabeth Bishop: A Bibliography, 1927–1979.* Charlottesville, Va.: University Press of Virginia, 1980.

NOTES ON THE POETS

Critical Studies

Schwartz, Lloyd, and Sybil Estess, eds. *Elizabeth Bishop and Her Art.* Ann Arbor: University of Michigan, 1982. Stevenson, Anne. *Elizabeth Bishop.* New York: Twayne, 1966.

ROBERT BLY (1923)

Robert Bly lives in rural Minnesota where he edits *The Eighties* (formerly *The Seventies, The Sixties, The Fifties*) and manages The Eighties Press (formerly The Seventies Press and The Sixties Press). For the 1975 edition of *Contemporary Poets*, Bly wrote: "I earn my living giving readings at American colleges and universities, and by translating." He graduated from Harvard and—though he hates to admit it—later did graduate work at the University of Iowa's Writers' Workshop. He has received Fulbright, Guggenheim, and Rockefeller fellowships; a grant from the National Institute of Arts and Letters; and the National Book Award in 1968.

Influenced by the thought of the seventeenth-century German theosophist, Jacob Boehme, and the techniques of such twentieth-century Spanish surrealists as Lorca and Neruda, Bly's poems tend to be almost purely phenomenological. Revolting against the rationalism and empiricism of his century, Boehme emphasized an intuitive perception of the outer tangible world of humans and things as a symbol of the corresponding and truer inner spiritual world. The outward man is asleep, Boehme wrote; he is only the husk of the real inner man. Like the American Romantic Transcendentalist Emerson, Boehme insisted that men neither see nor respond to that inner spiritual world: "the wise of this world . . . have shut and locked us up in their art and rationality, so that we have had to see with their eyes."

Bly himself has written that American poetry took a wrong turn, moving in "a destructive motion outward" rather than a "plunge inward, trying for a great (spiritual and imaginative) intensity." In his revolt against Eliot's theory of the "objective correlative" and against Pound's practice in the *Cantos* of "eating up more and more of the outer world, with less and less life at the center," Bly has fashioned his poems after the works of twentieth-century Spanish surrealists. In them, he seems to have found a poetics that corresponds to Boehme's mysticism, enabling him to plunge beneath the phenomenology of surfaces and find images and words to suggest the inner reality and spiritual intensity of experience. Moreover, many of Bly's poems continue to be implicit reaffirmations of a statement that appeared on the flyleaf of *The Lion's Tail and Eyes* (1962) in which he suggests that his poems come from "the part of the personality which is nourished by notice of things that are growing" and simultaneously that they "resist the Puritan insistence on being busy, the need to think of everything in terms of work."

Poetry

The Lion's Tail and Eyes: Poems Written Out of Laziness and Silence (with James Wright and William Duffy). Madison, Minn.: Sixties Press, 1962.   *Silence in the Snowy Fields.* Middletown: Wesleyan, 1962.   *The Light Around the Body.* New York: Harper & Row, 1967.   *The Morning Glory.* San Francisco: Kayak, 1969; expanded edition, New York: Harper & Row, 1975.   *The Teeth Mother Naked at Last.* San Francisco: City Lights, 1970.   *Jumping Out of Bed.* Barre, Mass.: Barre, 1973.   *Sleepers Joining Hands.* New York: Harper & Row, 1973.   *Point Reyes Poems.* Half Moon Bay, Calif.: Mudra, 1974.   *Old Man Rubbing His Eyes.* Greensboro, N.C.: Unicorn, 1975.   *This Body Is Made of Camphor and Gopherwood.* New York: Harper & Row, 1977.   *This Tree Will Be Here for a Thousand Years.* New York: Harper & Row, 1979.   *What the Fox Agreed To Do.* Athens, Ohio: Croissant, 1979.   *The Man in the Black Coat Turns.* New York: Dial, 1981.   *The Traveler Who Repeats His Cry: Seven Love Poems.* Madison, Wis.: Red Ozier, 1982.   *Out of the Rolling Ocean, and Other Love Poems.* St. Paul, Minn.: Ally Press, 1984.

Translations and Versions: Poetry

Twenty Poems of Georg Trakl (with James Wright). Madison, Minn.: Sixties Press, 1961.   *Twenty Poems of Cesar Vallejo* (with John Knoepfle and James Wright). Madison, Minn.: Sixties Press, 1962.   *Juan Ramón Jiménez: Forty Poems.* Madison, Minn.: Sixties Press, 1967.   *Pablo Neruda: Twenty Poems* (with James Wright). Madison, Minn.: Sixties Press, 1967.   *Tomas Transtromer: Twenty Poems.* Madison, Minn.: Seventies Press, 1970.   *Neruda and Vallejo: Selected Poems* (with John Knoepfle and James Wright). Boston: Beacon, 1971.   *Night Vision [Tomas Transtromer].* Northwood Narrows, N.H.: Lillabulero Press, 1971.   *Basho.* San Francisco: Mudra, 1972.   *Lorca and Jiménez: Selected Poems.* Boston: Beacon, 1973.   *Friends, You Drank Some Darkness: Three Swedish Poets, Martinson, Ekelof and Transtromer.* Boston: Beacon, 1976.   *The Kabir Book: Forty-Four of the Ecstatic Poems of Kabir.* Boston: Beacon, 1977.   *Vicente Aleixandre: Twenty Poems* (with Lewis Hyde). Madison, Minn.: Seventies Press, 1977.   *Rolf Jacobsen: Twenty Poems.* Madison, Minn.: Seventies Press, 1977.   *Rainer Maria Rilke: The Voices.* Denver: Ally Press, 1977.   *I Never Wanted Fame: Ten Poems and Proverbs* [Antonio Machado]. St. Paul, Minn.: Ally Press, 1979.   *Mirabai: Versions.* Madison, Wis.: Red Ozier, 1980.   *Rumi, Night and Sleep* (with Coleman Barks). Cambridge, Mass.: Yellow Moon, 1980.   *Canciones* [Antonio Machado]. Iowa City: Toothpaste Press, 1980.   *Truth Barriers: Poems by Tomas Transtromer.* San Francisco: Sierra Club

Books, 1980.   *October Day and Other Poems* [R. M. Rilke]. San Francisco: Calloipea, 1981.   *Selected Poems of Rainer Maria Rilke.* New York: Harper & Row, 1981.   *The Economy Spinning Faster and Faster.* New York: Sun, 1982.   *When Grapes Turn to Wine: Versions of Rumi.* Cambridge, Mass.: Firefly, 1983.   *Times Alone: Selected Poems of Antonio Machado.* Middletown: Wesleyan, 1983.

Criticism

Leaping Poetry: An Idea with Poems and Translations. Boston: Beacon 1975. *Talking All Morning: Collected Interviews and Conversations.* Ann Arbor: University of Michigan, 1979.   *The Eight Stages of Translation.* Boston: Rowan Press, 1983.

Anthologies

A Poetry Reading Against the Vietnam War (with David Ray). Madison, Minn.: American Writers Against the Vietnam War, 1960.   *Forty Poems Touching on Recent American History.* Madison, Minn.: Sixties Press, 1966; Boston: Beacon, 1970.   *The Sea and the Honeycomb: A Book of Tiny Poems.* Madison, Minn.: Sixties Press, 1966; Boston: Beacon, 1971.   *News of the Universe: Poems of Twofold Consciousness.* San Francisco: Sierra Club Books, 1980.

Critical Studies

Jones, Richard, and Kate Daniels, eds. *Of Solitude and Silence: Writings on Robert Bly.* Boston: Beacon, 1981.   Nelson, Howard. *Robert Bly: An Introduction to the Poetry.* New York: Columbia University, 1984.   Peseroff, Joyce. *Robert Bly: When Sleepers Awaken.* Ann Arbor: University of Michigan, 1984.

GWENDOLYN BROOKS (1917)

A graduate of Wilson Junior College in Chicago, Gwendolyn Brooks began her professional career in 1941 with Inez Stark Boulton's poetry workshop at the South Side Community Art Center in Chicago. She was awarded two Guggenheim Fellowships, a grant from the National Institute of Arts and Letters, and the Pulitzer Prize for her second book of poems in 1950. In 1969 Gwendolyn Brooks was named "Poet Laureate of the State of Illinois," an honor formerly held by Carl Sandburg.

Gwendolyn Brooks's poems are often marked by direct and bold social observation and by language which precedes — indeed foreshadows — much of the Black poetry written by younger poets today. Her Black hero's assertion, "I helped to save them. . . / Even if I had to kick their law into their teeth in order to do that for them," might well have been written in the sixties or seventies rather than in the forties. In those poems addressed specifically to the horror of the Black experience in America, she is also capable of a range of emotions: brutal anger, wry satire, and visionary serenity.

Informed by the spectrum of the Black experience and her own emotional objectivity, some of her poems are also marked by the simplicity, quiet, and gentility of a woman's sensibilities. Yet in a poem like "The Mother," she also demonstrates the kind of fierce emotion that other women poets like Anne Sexton and Adrienne Rich have displayed in more consciously personal or political poems. But gentle or fierce, personal or social, her poems consistently affirm the common denominator of human experience in poetry and in the human community.

Poetry

A Street in Bronzeville. New York: Harper & Brothers, 1945. *Annie Allen*. New York: Harper & Brothers, 1949. *Bronzeville Boys and Girls*. New York: Harper & Brothers, 1956. *Selected Poems*. New York: Harper & Row, 1963. *In the Mecca: Poems*. New York: Harper & Row, 1968. *Riot*. Detroit: Broadside, 1969. *The Wall*. Detroit: Broadside, n.d. *Family Pictures*. Detroit: Broadside, 1970. *Aloneness*. Detroit: Broadside, 1971. *Beckonings*. Detroit: Broadside, 1975. *To Disembark*. Chicago: Third World, 1981.

Prose and Poetry

Maud Martha (novel). New York: Harper & Brothers, 1953. *Report from Part One: An Autobiography*. Detroit: Broadside, 1972. *The World of Gwendolyn Brooks*. New York: Harper & Row, 1972.

Critical Study

Shaw, Harry B. *Gwendolyn Brooks*. Boston: Twayne, 1980.

LUCILLE CLIFTON (1936)

Lucille Clifton was born in Depew, New York, and educated at the State University of New York at Fredonia and Howard University. She has taught at Coppin State College, Goucher College, and the American University in Washington, D.C. Her other teaching experiences have included appointments as Elliston Poet at the University of Cincinnati, Jenny Moore Visiting Lecturer in Creative Writing at George Washington University, and Woodrow Wilson Scholar at Fisk University and at Trinity College. Clifton's awards and distinctions as a poet, fiction writer, and screenplay writer include the University of Massachusetts Press's Juniper Prize for poetry, a nomination for the Pulitzer Prize in poetry, an Emmy Award from the American Academy of Television Arts and Sciences, and creative writing fellowships from the National Endowment for the Arts.

Lucille Clifton's entire comment on her work in the third edition of *Contemporary Poets* (1980) consists of one brief sentence: "I am a Black woman poet, and I sound like one." And yet, after reading even a short selection of her poems, we quickly realize that Clifton's description of herself does not explain why she is one of the most unique voices of her generation. Of course, some of her subjects and themes share characteristics with those of certain other poets; like numerous other women writers, she explores the dimensions of her sexual identity and her role as daughter, as mother, as lover, as woman; like many other Black poets (men and women), she too addresses herself to the quality of the Black experience in America, just as she too makes full use of the Black idiom. But no other poet of her generation (regardless of gender or race) *sounds* quite like Lucille Clifton. Why that is, however, is rather difficult to identify in the standard language of literary criticism.

Clifton's subjects and themes run the gamut of contemporary — indeed of all — human experience. She laments the loss of an aborted child, but she also celebrates with wonderful verve her own mature body and sexuality. She admonishes children to "come home from the movies" and face the responsibilities of everyday life, but she also recalls the pain and terror of her own growth into adult responsibility. She engages in social criticism and in criticism of individual human beings, but she also affirms "the bond of live things everywhere." She feels religious doubts, but she is nonetheless a profoundly religious spirit whose sensibility encompasses both the Judaic-Christian tradition and a primal sense of spiritualism and magic. Despite the high seriousness of many of her poems, she also obviously revels in a vibrant sense of humor which she directs not only at others, but also at herself and her craft. She can poke gentle fun at herself because "she is a poet / she don't have no sense," but after the joy and celebration, after the anguish and despair, after the doubt and struggle to believe, she also can assert: "I am left with plain hands and / nothing to give you but poems."

One of the striking characteristics of Lucille Clifton's poems is their distilled brevity. Like Emily Dickinson, Clifton rarely offers any but the most essential elaborations on experience. However, for a clue to the sound of Lucille Clifton's poems, we have to turn elsewhere: Black spirituals and secular folksongs; the rich history of rhythm and blues; the rhythms and sounds of a Black fundamentalist revival meeting and of magical incantations; the phrasing and timing of classic Black humorists; an utterly physical sense of language (somehow we can *see* how these poems incorporate a range of bodily movements); a belief in the power of idiom to give voice to the human heart as much by transcending individual race and culture as by affirming it; a belief in the language of poetry, not as a threat of further social and human alienation but as a bridge of reconciliation; a belief in the power of song and in the impotency of slogans; a belief in tongues.

Poetry

Good Times. New York: Random House, 1969.   *Good News About the Earth.* New York: Random House, 1972.   *An Ordinary Woman.* New York: Random House, 1974. *Two-Headed Woman.* Amherst: University of Massachusetts, 1980.

Prose Memoir

Generations of Americans: A Memoir. New York: Random House, 1976.

Poetry and Fiction for Children

Some of the Days of Everett Anderson. New York: Holt, Rinehart and Winston, 1970. *The Black BC's.* New York: Dutton, 1970.   *Everett Anderson's Christmas Coming.* New York: Holt, Rinehart and Winston, 1972.   *All Us Come Cross the Water.* New York: Holt, Rinehart and Winston, 1973.   *Don't You Remember?* New York: Dutton, 1973.   *The Times They Used to Be.* New York: Holt, Rinehart and Winston, 1974. *My Brother Fine with Me.* New York: Holt, Rinehart and Winston, 1975.   *Three Wishes.* New York: Viking, 1976.   *Amifika.* New York: Dutton, 1977.   *The Boy Who Didn't Believe in Spring.* New York: Dutton, 1978.   *The Lucky Stone.* New York: Delacorte, 1979.   *Sonora.* New York: Dutton, 1981.

ROBERT CREELEY (1926)

A New Englander by birth and sensibility, Robert Creeley was born in Arlington, Massachusetts, and was educated at Harvard, Black Mountain College, and the University of New Mexico. He has traveled widely and has taught at the University of New Mexico and at Black Mountain College where he also edited the influential journal *Black Mountain Review*. In addition to his many books of poetry, fiction, and criticism, Creeley has edited a variety of other collections, including Charles Olson's letters. He is currently David Gray Professor of Poetry and Letters at the State University of New York at Buffalo.

Generally associated with the "Projectivists" and poets of the Black Mountain School, Creeley nevertheless is a Puritan at heart—Emily Dickinson's cool, hip, one-eyed, and unvirginal nephew. Like all good Puritans, Creeley is "hung up": "I think I grow tensions / like flowers..." Pain is central to his work—a sharp, stinging pain evoked in such images as "I can / feel my eye breaking." In more recent poems, like "Moment" and "On Vacation," a Puritan sensibility surfaces more explicitly, as it does in the very structure and substance of collections like *A Day Book* and *Hello*—sustained attempts at recording and discovering the "meaning" of diurnal events, an implicit quest for signs of salvation, especially love. "I love you. / Do you love me. / What to say / when you see me..." might be a summary of one of Creeley's central concerns.

No critical essay or explanatory statement reveals Creeley's poetics as precisely as his own poems, especially "The Language" and "The Window." In the former, he states simply: "Locate *I*..."; in the latter, he writes: "Position is where you / put it, where it is..." The position of the I—as locus, as viewer, and as speaker—largely determines the form and the direction of the poem. The position of words on the page results from the location of this I, who, by arranging the poem as it is, speaks not only in grammatical units but also in linear units. In other words, Creeley's poems evolve on both a sequential grammatical level and on a cumulative linear level, with each individual line reaffirming or modifying the sense of the sentence and of the poem. And such contrapuntal tension in the very structure of Creeley's poems—perhaps more than the sparse, occasionally hesitant language—reflects the contemporary struggle with those forces that would make us all inarticulate.

Poetry

Le Fou. Columbus, Ohio: Golden Goose, 1952.   *The Kind of Act Of.* Majorca: Divers, 1953.   *The Immoral Proposition.* Highlands, N. C.: Jonathan Williams, 1953.   *All That Is Lovely in Men.* Highlands, N. C.: Jargon, 1955.   *A Form of Women.* New York: Jargon-Corinth, 1959.   *For Love: Poems 1950–1960.* New York: Scribner's, 1962.   *Words.* New York: Scribner's, 1967.   *The Charm: Early and Uncollected Poems.* Madison, Wis.: Perishable Press, 1967; reprint, San Francisco: Four Seasons, 1969.   *The Finger* (with Bobbie Creeley). Los Angeles: Black Sparrow, 1968.   *Pieces.* Los Angeles: Black Sparrow, 1968.   *St. Martin's* (with Bobbie Creeley). Los Angeles: Black Sparrow, 1971.   *1–2–3–4–5–6–7–8–9–0* (with Arthur Okamura). Berkeley: Mudra, 1971.   *A Day Book.* New York: Scribner's, 1972.   *Thirty Things* (with Bobbie Creeley). Los Angeles: Black Sparrow, 1974.   *Away* (with Bobbie Creeley). Santa Barbara: Black Sparrow, 1976. *Presences* (with Marisol). Santa Barbara: Black Sparrow, 1976.   *Selected Poems.* New York: Scribner's, 1976.   *Hello.* New York: New Directions, 1978.   *Later.* New York: New Directions, 1979.   *Echoes.* West Branch, Iowa: Toothpaste Press, 1982.   *The Collected Poems of Robert Creeley 1945–1975.* Berkeley: University of California, 1982.   *Mirrors.* New York: New Directions, 1983.

Fiction and Criticism

The Island (novel). New York: Scribner's, 1963.   *The Gold Diggers and Other Stories.* New York: Scribner's, 1965.   *A Quick Graph: Collected Notes and Essays.* San Francisco: Four Seasons, 1970.   *Contexts of Poetry: Interviews 1961 – 1971.* Edited by Donald M. Allen. Bolinas, Calif.: Four Seasons, 1973.   *Was That a Real Poem & Other Essays.* Edited by Donald M. Allen. Bolinas, Calif.: Four Seasons, 1979. *Charles Olson & Robert Creeley: The Complete Correspondence.* Edited by George F. Butterick. Santa Barbara: Black Sparrow, 1983.   *The Collected Prose of Robert Creeley* (fiction). New York: Marion Boyars, 1984.

Bibliography

Novik, Mary. *Robert Creeley: An Inventory, 1945–1970.* Kent, Ohio: Kent State University, 1973.

Critical Studies

Edelberg, Cynthia. *Robert Creeley's Poetry: A Critical Introduction.* Albuquerque: University of New Mexico, 1978.   Ford, Arthur. *Robert Creeley.* Boston: G. K. Hall, 1978.   Paul, Sherman. *The Lost America of Love: Rereading Robert Creeley, Edward Dorn, and Robert Duncan.* Baton Rouge: Louisiana State University, 1981.

JAMES DICKEY (1923)

James Dickey received his bachelor's and master's degree from Vanderbilt University. He was a night fighter pilot during both World War II and the Korean War; as a civilian, he has worked as an advertising executive in Atlanta and New York; and he has taught at a variety of colleges and universities, including the University of South Carolina where he is presently poet-in-residence. In 1966 James Dickey received the National Book Award for poetry; from 1966 to 1968, he served as Consultant in Poetry at the Library of Congress.

One of the less ostensibly "academic" poets of his generation, Dickey's poems are often disarmingly frank in subject matter and in "moral tone." He has refused to assume those moral postures often expected of today's poets: during Vietnam, he did not write antiwar poetry but rather, in a poem like "The Firebombing," he confronted his own understanding of and sympathy with the pilot whose mission was to drop napalm on enemy villages without the luxury of questioning the morality of such an act. In several other poems, he has explored varieties of sexual experiences, including implicit and explicit sexual encounters between humans and animals, as in "The Sheep Child."

Dickey's poems are marked by an exuberant language and by a primal energy, passion, and ritual. Probing the most elemental in humankind, his poems often trace a human's mythic subconscious and paradoxical evolution to a primitive level where humans and animals become companions and mates in the same irrational but holy species. Moreover, in much of Dickey's work, poetry is the tongue articulating the consciousness of all creation on this planet, from the mute stone up the earthly chain of being to humankind. And in this way, his poems often recall Whitman's poetry and vision.

Simultaneously, many of Dickey's poems are also marked by a Southern Puritanism. His characters are grotesque—physically and spiritually wounded. They are violent creatures; their brutal sexuality is immersed in pain and death. And they move about in a world churning with violence and profound evil that is as much inherent in the human condition as it is man-made. Dickey's vision, then, includes the polarities of light and grace, darkness and sin. The total impact of his poems is often the drama of Adam, shimmering with primal light, awakening to guilt, and finding it magical.

Poetry

Into the Stone and Other Poems. In *Poets of Today VII.* New York: Scribner's, 1960. *Drowning with Others.* Middletown: Wesleyan, 1962. *Helmets.* Middletown: Wesleyan, 1964. *Buckdancer's Choice.* Middletown: Wesleyan, 1965. *Poems 1957–1967.* Middletown: Wesleyan, 1967; paper edition, New York: Collier, 1968; second paper edition, Middletown: Wesleyan, 1978. *The Eye-Beaters, Blood, Victory, Madness, Buckhead and Mercy.* New York: Doubleday, 1970. *Exchanges.* Bloomfield Hills, Mich.: Bruccoli-Clark, 1971. *The Zodiac.* New York: Doubleday, 1976. *The Strength of Fields* (for the Inauguration of Jimmy Carter). Bloomfield Hills, Mich.: Bruccoli-Clark, 1977. *The Enemy from Eden* (prose poems). Northridge, Calif.: Lord John, 1978. *The Strength of Fields.* New York: Doubleday, 1979. *The Early Motion: Drowning with Others and Helmets.* Middletown: Wesleyan, 1981. *Falling, May Day Sermon, and Other Poems.* Middletown: Wesleyan, 1981. *Puella.* New York: Doubleday, 1982.

Fiction and Other Prose

Deliverance (novel). Boston: Houghton Mifflin, 1970. *Jericho: The South Beheld* (with paintings by Hubert Shuptrine). Birmingham, Ala.: Oxmoor, 1974. *God's Images* (with photographs by Marvin Hayes). Birmingham, Ala.: Oxmoor, 1974. *In Pursuit of the Grey Soul.* Bloomfield Hills, Mich.: Bruccoli-Clark, 1979. *Night Hurdling.* Bloomfield Hills, Mich.: Bruccoli-Clark, 1983.

Criticism

The Suspect in Poetry. Madison, Minn.: Sixties Press, 1964.   *Babel to Byzantium: Poets & Poetry Now.* New York: Farrar, Straus & Giroux, 1968; paperback edition, New York: Ecco, 1981.   *Self-Interviews.* Edited by Barbara and James Reiss. New York: Doubleday, 1970; paperback edition, Baton Rouge: Louisiana State University, 1984.   *Sorties: Journals and New Essays.* New York: Doubleday, 1971; paperback edition, Baton Rouge: Louisiana State University, 1984.

Bibliographies

Ashley, Franklin. *James Dickey: A Checklist.* Detroit: Bruccoli-Clark/Gale Research, 1972.   Elledge, Jim. *James Dickey: A Bibliography, 1947–1974.* Metuchen, N.J.: Scarecrow, 1979.   Glancy, Eileen. *James Dickey, the Critic as Poet: An Annotated Bibliography with an Introductory Essay.* Troy, N.Y.: Whitston, 1971.

Critical Studies

Calhoun, Richard J., ed. *James Dickey: The Expansive Imagination.* Deland, Fla.: Everett Edwards, 1973.   Calhoun, Richard J., and Robert W. Hill. *James Dickey.* New York: Twayne, 1983.   Lieberman, Laurence. *The Achievement of James Dickey.* Glenview, Ill.: Scott, Foresman, 1968.   Weigl, Bruce, and T. R. Hummer. *The Imagination as Glory: Essays on the Poetry of James Dickey.* Champaign: University of Illinois, 1984.

ALAN DUGAN (1923)

Born in Brooklyn and a graduate of Mexico City College, Alan Dugan's first book of poems won the Yale Series of Younger Poets award, the Pulitzer Prize, and the National Book Award.

Although Dugan's most effective poems can be humorous, lyrical, or cerebral, his work also can be tough, brutal, and ugly. For William J. Martz's *The Distinctive Voice,* Dugan wrote about his voice as a poet: "I am trying to say what is hardest to say; that is, words wrung out of intense experience and not constructed." Moreover, as Richard Howard has observed, in Dugan's poetry one senses that "the act of writing poetry is, precisely, an invocation of destruction, a luring of language to its wreck ... He is too honest ... for the consolation of some visionary transcendence of language. ..."

In many of his poems, Dugan talks about the least public of experiences in a language still generally considered the least public—perhaps "unpoetic." Moreover, he refuses to burden his subject and language with any obviously stated mystical, magical, or "great social" impact. He tells it "like it is" and, rather than being offensive—as one might vaguely and uneasily wish they were—his poems emerge as the product of a fierce and fully American honesty and of a craftsmanship generating words that burn through all pretense like acid.

Poetry

Poems. New Haven: Yale University, 1961.   *Poems 2*. New Haven: Yale University, 1963.   *Poems 3*. New Haven: Yale University, 1967.   *Collected Poems*. New Haven: Yale University, 1969.   *Poems 4*. Boston: Atlantic-Little, Brown, 1974. *Sequence*. Cambridge, Mass.: Dolphin Editions, 1976.   *New and Collected Poems 1961−1983*. New York: Ecco, 1983.

ROBERT DUNCAN (1919)

A native of California, Robert Duncan was educated at the University of California, Berkeley. He has traveled extensively and has taught at San Francisco State, the University of British Columbia, and at Black Mountain College with Charles Olson. He has served as editor of *The Experimental Review* and *The Berkeley Miscellany*; in addition to poetry and criticism, he has been writing an extended study of H. D., parts of which have appeared in various journals. His awards include the Harriet Monroe Memorial Prize, two grants from the National Endowment for the Arts, and a Guggenheim Fellowship.

In *The Truth & Life of Myth*, Robert Duncan wrote: "The meaning and intent of what it is to be a man and, among men, to be a poet, I owe to the working of myth in my spirit, both the increment and associations gathered in my continuing study of mythological lore and my own apprehension of what my life is at work here." And in his statement reprinted in Donald Allen's anthology, *The New American Poetry* (1960), Duncan stated that "every moment of life is an attempt to come to life. Poetry is a 'participation,' a oneness." It is "the very life of the soul: the body's dreaming that it can dream. And perish into its own imagination." A poem, according to Duncan, is "a ritual referring to divine orders."

If not so much through his seemingly anachronistic use of classical and medieval mythology, then surely in his fundamental attitude toward his art, Duncan attempts to return poetry to its most profound roots in the rituals of the divine orders. Erudite, orphic, at times homoerotic (long before sexual preference was a political and aesthetic issue), lyrical, and often profoundly religious, the poems of Robert Duncan gather a momentum that is more, much more, than the "passages of moonlight upon the floor." Rather, they are human clues to what might conceivably be "the meaning of the music of the spheres."

Poetry

Heavenly City, Earthly City. Berkeley: Bern Porter, 1947.   *Poems 1948–1949.* Berkeley: Berkeley Miscellany, 1950.   *Medieval Scenes.* San Francisco: Centaur Press, 1950.   *The Song of the Border Guard.* Black Mountain, N.C.: Black Mountain College, 1952.   *Caesar's Gate: Poems 1949–1950.* Palma, Mallorca: Divers Press, 1955.   *Letters: Poems 1953–1956.* Highlands, N.C.: Jargon, 1958.   *Selected Poems.* San Francisco: City Lights, 1959.   *The Opening of the Field.* New York: Grove Press, 1960.   *Roots and Branches.* New York: Scribner, 1964.   *Writing, Writing: A New Composition Book of Madison 1953, Stein Imitations.* Albuquerque: Sumbooks, 1964.   *Wine.* Berkeley: Oyez, 1964.   *Uprising.* Berkeley: Oyez, 1965.   *A Book of Resemblances: Poems 1950–1953.* New Haven: Henry Wenning, 1966.   *Of the War: Passages 22–27.* Berkeley: Oyez, 1966.   *The Years as Catches: First Poems 1939–1946.* Berkeley: Oyez, 1966.   *Fragments of a Disordered Devotion.* San Francisco: Gnomon, 1966.   *Boob.* Privately printed, 1966.   *Epilogos.* Los Angeles: Black Sparrow, 1967.   *The Cat and the Blackbird.* San Francisco: White Rabbit, 1967.   *Christmas Present, Christmas Presence!* Los Angeles: Black Sparrow, 1967.   *Bending the Bow.* New York: New Directions, 1968.   *My Mother Would Be a Falconress.* Berkeley: Oyez, 1968.   *Names of People.* Los Angeles: Black Sparrow, 1968.   *The First Decade: Selected Poems 1940–1950.* London: Fulcrum, 1968.   *Derivations: Selected Poems 1950–1956.* London: Fulcrum, 1968.   *Play Time, Pseudo Stein.* New York: Poets Press, 1969. *Achilles' Song.* New York: Phoenix Book Shop, 1969.   *Poetic Disturbances.* San Francisco: Maya, 1970.   *Bring It Up from the Dark.* Berkeley: Cody's Books, 1970. *Tribunals: Passages 31–35.* Los Angeles: Black Sparrow, 1970.   *In Memoriam Wallace Stevens.* Storrs, Conn.: University of Connecticut, 1972.   *The Truth and Life of Myrtle.* Freemont, Mich.: Sumac, 1972.   *An Ode and Arcadia* (with Jack Spicer). Berkeley: Ark Press, 1974.   *Dante.* Canton, N.Y.: Institute of Further Studies, 1974.   *The Venice Poem.* Sydney, Australia: Prism, 1975. *Groundwork: Before the War.* New York: New Directions, 1984.

Criticism and Other Prose

The Artist's View. Privately printed, 1952.   *On Poetry.* New Haven: Yale University, 1964.   *As Testimony: The Poem and the Scene.* San Francisco: White Rabbit, 1964.   *The Sweetness and Greatness of Dante's "Divine Comedy," 1265–1965.* San Francisco: Open Spaces, 1965.   *Six Prose Pieces.* Rochester, Mich.: Perishable Press, 1966.   *The Truth and Life of Myth: An Essay in Essential Autobiography.* New York: House of Books, 1968; reprint, Fremont, Mich.: Sumac, 1968.   *Notes on Grossinger's "Solar Journal: Oecological Sections."* Los Angeles: Black Sparrow, 1970.

An Interview with George Bowering and Robert Hogg, April 19, 1969. Toronto: Coach House, 1971.   *Fictive Certainties: Five Essays in Essential Autobiography.* New York: New Directions, 1979.

Drama

Faust Foutou: Act One of Four Acts: A Comic Mask. San Francisco: White Rabbit, 1958; complete edition, *Faust Foutou: An Entertainment in Four Parts.* Stinson Beach, Calif.: Enkidu Surrogate, 1960.   *Medea at Kolchis: The Maiden Head.* Berkeley: Oyez, 1965.

Critical Studies

Bertholf, Robert J., and Ian W. Reid, eds. *Robert Duncan: Scales of the Marvellous.* New York: New Directions, 1979.   Faas, Ekbert. *Young Robert Duncan: A Portrait of the Poet as Homosexual in Society.* Santa Barbara: Black Sparrow, 1983.   Paul, Sherman. *The Lost America of Love: Rereading Robert Creeley, Edward Dorn, and Robert Duncan.* Baton Rouge: Louisiana State University, 1981.

LAWRENCE FERLINGHETTI (1919)

Born in Yonkers, New York, Lawrence Ferlinghetti received an A.B. from the University of North Carolina, an M.A. from Columbia, and a Doctorat de l'Université from the Sorbonne. He was a lieutenant-commander in the Naval Reserve during World War II and worked for *Time* magazine in the forties. He was cofounder of City Lights Books in 1952 and has been both owner and editor-in-chief since 1953. He is also generally recognized as having been one of the leading figures of what is known as the San Francisco Renaissance and the Beat Generation.

In a "Note on Poetry in San Francisco" (1955), Ferlinghetti wrote: "the kind of poetry which has been making the most noise here . . . is what should be called street poetry. For it amounts to getting the poet out of the inner esthetic sanctum where he has too long been contemplating his complicated navel. It amounts to getting poetry back into the street where it once was, out of the classroom, out of the speech department, and—in fact—off the printed page. The printed word has made poetry so silent."

Ferlinghetti's own poems, often conceived as "oral messages," are designed primarily for their oral impact and often share the characteristics of popular songs. In fact, Ferlinghetti's experiments with poetry and jazz in the early sixties may well have foreshadowed the later successful fusion of music and lyrics by such popular poets as Bob Dylan. Intended to be understood by the ear, not primarily by the eye, Ferlinghetti's poems often lack the density and complexity of the printed poem. For the same reason, they often depend on the literary cliché, which serves much the same function as the formula in ancient oral poetry.

Like Hart Crane, Ferlinghetti sees the poet as "a charleychaplin man," and with a measure of self-directed irony that Crane never could quite muster, he admits that the poet is "constantly risking absurdity." Thus in his poems, while engaging in slapstick and often corny humor aimed at sociocultural evils and absurdities, he pokes fun at the world and at himself, seeks moments of tenderness, sometimes succumbs to sentimentality, and occasionally discovers moments of terror.

Poetry

Pictures of the Gone World. San Francisco: City Lights, 1955.   *A Coney Island of the Mind.* New York: New Directions, 1958.   *Tentative Description of a Dinner Given to Promote the Impeachment of President Eisenhower.* San Francisco: Golden Mountain, 1958.   *One Thousand Fearful Words for Fidel Castro.* San Francisco: City Lights, 1961.   *Berlin.* San Francisco: Golden Mountain, 1961.   *Starting from San Francisco.* New York: New Directions, 1961; revised edition, 1967.   *Where Is Vietnam?* San Francisco: City Lights, 1965.   *The Secret Meaning of Things.* New York: New Directions, 1969.   *Tyrannus Nix?* New York: New Directions, 1969.   *Back Roads to Far Places.* New York: New Directions, 1971.   *Open Eye, Open Heart.* New York: New Directions, 1973.   *Who Are We Now?* New York: New Directions, 1976.   *Northwest Ecolog.* San Francisco: City Lights, 1978.   *Landscapes of Living & Dying.* New York: New Directions, 1979.   *Endless Life: Selected Poems.* New York: New Directions, 1981.   *The Populist Manifestos.* San Francisco: Grey Fox, 1981.   *Over All the Obscene Boundaries: European Poems and Transitions.* New York: New Directions, 1984.

Translations: Poetry

Selections from Paroles by Jacques Prévert. San Francisco: City Lights, 1963.

Drama, Prose, and Drawings

Her (fiction). New York: New Directions, 1960.   *Unfair Arguments with Existence* (drama). New York: New Directions, 1963.   *Routines* (drama). New York: New Directions, 1964.   *The Mexican Night: Travel Journal.* New York: New Directions, 1970.   *Leaves of Life: Fifty Drawings from the Model.* San Francisco: City Lights, 1983.

Bibliography

Morgan, Bill. *Lawrence Ferlinghetti: A Descriptive Bibliography.* New York: Garland, 1981.

Biographical and Critical Studies

Cherkovski, Neeli. *Ferlinghetti: A Biography.* New York: Doubleday, 1979.   Smith, Larry. *Lawrence Ferlinghetti: Poet-at-Large.* Carbondale: Southern Illinois University, 1983.

ISABELLA GARDNER (1915–1981)

A native of Newton, Massachusetts, a great-niece of Isabella Stewart Gardner (who bequeathed a museum to the city of Boston), and a cousin of Robert Lowell, Isabella Gardner insisted that she had received a minimal formal education. In fact, she attended the Foxcroft School, the Leighton Rollins School of Acting, and the Embassy School of Acting in London. She was a professional actress for several years and served as associate editor of *Poetry* from 1952 to 1956, while Karl Shapiro was editor. The last book Gardner published in her lifetime, *That Was Then: New and Selected Poems,* was nominated for the 1980 American Book Award for Poetry, and in 1981 Isabella Gardner was selected as the first recipient of the New York State Walt Whitman Citation of Merit for Poetry.

Having suffered a self-imposed silence during the last fifteen years of her life, Isabella Gardner published only four, relatively short, books of poetry during her tragic lifetime. And yet, what a remarkable artistic legacy she bequeathed to contemporary American poetry. The quality of that legacy no doubt is because of her utterly conscious commitment to her art as its own end. For example, despite the painfully dramatic events in her personal life, Gardner consistently eschewed the potential sensationalism of confessional poetry and the potential political stridency of feminist poetry. In "The Fellowship with Essence," the afterword she wrote for *That Was Then,* Gardner said: "I don't believe the poet should write with a cudgel, a lance or a crystal ball. A poet is no wiser nor more compassionate than anyone else; yet I feel that the poet is focused on a particularized participation in the most minute or enormous instants, as well as in incidents of hourly existence."

Ralph J. Mills, Jr., has rightfully noted that Gardner's own participation in the minute and enormous incidents of hourly existence resulted in a poetry characterized by an intense musical quality. That music, in turn, is the result of the richness of her language (reminiscent of that found in the work of Dylan Thomas, Edith Sitwell, and Gerard Manley Hopkins), coupled with her own innate rhythmic sense. Many of Gardner's poems, such as "The Widow's Yard" and "The Milkman," also reflect an acute precision of psychosexual observation like that found in the work of Emily Dickinson. No less important, her best poems are perfectly crafted gems whose sharply focused brilliance leaves us breathless. Short lyrics like "Lines to a Sea-Green Lover" are masterpieces of that genre, and the concluding stanzas of "Lines to a Sea-Green Lover" and "Letter from Slough Pond" achieve much the same kind of intense emotional catharsis as is found in the classic little poem of the sixteenth century, "Western Wind":

> Western wind, when will thou blow,
> The small rain down can rain?
> Christ, if my love were in my arms,
> And I in my bed again!

That many of Isabella Gardner's better poems are concerned with various dimensions of love is no accident. In "The Fellowship with Essence" she asserted: "If there is a theme with which I am particularly concerned, it is the contemporary failure of love. I don't mean romantic love or sexual passion, but the love which is the specific and particular recognition of one human being by another — the responses by eye and voice and touch of two solitudes. The democracy of universal vulnerability."

Poetry

Birthdays from the Ocean. Boston: Houghton Mifflin, 1955. *The Looking Glass: New Poems.* Chicago: University of Chicago, 1961. *West of Childhood: Poems 1960–1965.* Boston: Houghton Mifflin, 1965. *That Was Then: New and Selected Poems.* Brockport, N.Y.: BOA Editions, 1980. *Isabella Gardner: The Complete Poems.* Edited by Roland Flint. Brockport, N.Y.: BOA Editions, 1985.

ALLEN GINSBERG (1926)

Born in Newark, New Jersey, Allen Ginsberg attended Columbia University, was dismissed, but returned later to receive his B.A. in 1948. A leader of the Beat Movement and the San Francisco Renaissance, in 1954 he married Peter Orlovsky. He is the recipient of grants from the Guggenheim Foundation, the National Endowment for the Arts, and the National

Institute of Arts and Letters, of which he is a member. In 1974, with Adrienne Rich he was cowinner of the National Book Award for Poetry.

In his relatively recent poem "Ego Confession," Allen Ginsberg asserts: "I want to be known as the most brilliant man in America.../I want to be the spectacle of Poesy triumphant over trickery of the world..." Poet, guru, world traveler, prophet, and visionary Uncle Sam of the Flower-Acid-Rock Generation, Ginsberg may well be the planet's most renowned poet. And if Ginsberg's notoriety as a sociocultural *enfant terrible* has obscured his power as a poet, he is nevertheless recognized by his contemporaries as one of the most influential post-1945 poets. His first major poem, "Howl," is a milestone of the generation, perhaps as significant a poem and document as Eliot's "Waste Land"; moreover, Ginsberg's entire work eventually may achieve the stature of *Leaves of Grass*.

At once intimate and prophetic, hilarious and terrifying, profoundly religious and, at times, commensurately outrageous, Ginsberg's poetry encompasses a myriad of experiences, ranges over the full spectrum of human life on this planet, and — like the poetry of Whitman — is a combination of incredible power and drivel. Clearly, in technique, scope, and intent, Whitman is Ginsberg's model and mentor; like him, Ginsberg is attempting to re-create not only the world but also the full dimensions of a human's physical and spiritual odyssey through a given moment in history — with the crucial difference that Whitman's poems were hefty songs and Ginsberg's are often reverberating lamentations.

Part of Ginsberg's impact results from his prophetic stance as a man and as a poet, sustained by the vital spirit of William Blake and the prophets of the Old Testament. A modern-day Isaiah, whose public personality often betrays the range and depth of his erudition, Ginsberg is the public conscience of the nation — if not of the species — lamenting the imponderable evil humankind has perpetrated against life. But like Isaiah, Blake, and Whitman, he is also moved by a profound belief in the holiness of life and by a vision of a new Jerusalem, a new world.

Poetry

Howl and Other Poems. San Francisco: City Lights, 1956.   *Empty Mirror: Early Poems*. New York: Totem-Corinth, 1961.   *Kaddish and Other Poems*. San Francisco: City Lights, 1961.   *Reality Sandwiches*. San Francisco: City Lights, 1963.   *T. V. Baby Poems*. London: Cape Goliard, 1967; New York: Grossman, 1968.   *Airplane Dreams: Compositions from Journals*. Toronto: House of Anansi, 1968; San Francisco: City Lights, 1969.   *Ankor-Wat*. London: Fulcrum, 1968. *Planet News, 1961–1967*. San Francisco: City Lights, 1968.   *Bixby Canyon Ocean Path Word Breeze*. New York: Gotham Book Mart, 1972.   *The Gates of Wrath: Rhymed Poems, 1948–1952*. Bolinas, Calif.: Four Seasons, 1973.   *The Fall of America: Poems of These States, 1965–1971*. San Francisco: City Lights, 1973.

Iron Horse. Toronto: Coach House; San Francisco: City Lights, 1974.   *First Blues.*
New York: Full Court, 1975.   *Sad Dust Glories.* Berkeley: Workingman's Press,
1975.   *Mind Breaths: Poems 1972–1977.* San Francisco: City Lights, 1978.
Poems All Over the Place, Mostly 'Seventies. Cherry Valley, N.Y.: Cherry Valley
Editions, 1978.   *Mostly Sitting Haiku.* Patterson, N.J.: From Here Press,
1979.   *Plutonian Ode: Poems 1977–1980.* San Francisco: City Lights, 1982.
Collected Poems: 1947–1980. New York: Harper & Row, 1984.

Criticism and Other Prose

The Yage Letters (with William Burroughs). San Francisco: City Lights, 1963.
Indian Journals. San Francisco: Dave Haselwood, 1970.   *Improvised Poetics.* Edited
with an introduction by Mark Robinson. San Francisco: Anonym Books, 1971.
Gay Sunshine Interview. Bolinas, Calif.: Grey Fox, 1974.   *Allen Verbatim: Lectures
on Poetry, Politics, Consciousness.* Edited by Gordon Ball. New York: McGraw-Hill,
1974.   *The Visions of the Great Rememberer.* Amherst, Mass.: Mulch, 1974.
Chicago Trial Testimony. San Franscisco: City Lights, 1975.   *To Eberhart from
Ginsberg: A Letter About Howl 1956.* Lincoln, Mass.: Penmaen, 1976.   *As Ever: The
Collected Correspondence of Allen Ginsberg & Neal Cassady.* Edited with an
introduction by Barry Gifford. Berkeley: Creative Arts, 1977.   *Journals: Early
Fifties Early Sixties.* Edited by Gordon Ball. New York: Grove, 1977.   *Composed on
the Tongue.* Bolinas, Calif.: Grey Fox, 1980.

Bibliographies

Dowden, George, and Lawrence McGilvery. *A Bibliography of the Works of Allen
Ginsberg.* San Francisco: City Lights, 1971.   Kraus, M. *Allen Ginsberg Bibliography
1969–1978.* Metuchen, N.J.: Scarecrow Press, 1980.

Biographical and Critical Studies

Ehrlich, J. W. E. *Howl of the Censor.* San Francisco: Nourse, 1956.   Hyde, Lewis.
On the Poetry of Allen Ginsberg. Ann Arbor: University of Michigan, 1984.
Kramer, Jane. *Allen Ginsberg in America.* New York: Random House, 1969.
Merrill, Thomas F. *Allen Ginsberg.* New York: Twayne, 1969.   Portuges, Paul. *The
Visionary Poetics of Allen Ginsberg.* Santa Barbara: Ross-Erikson, 1979.   Simpson,
Louis. *A Revolution in Taste: Studies in Dylan Thomas, Allen Ginsberg, Sylvia Plath
and Robert Lowell.* New York: Morrow, 1978.

DONALD HALL (1928)

Born in New Haven, Connecticut, Donald Hall is a graduate of Phillips
Exeter Academy, Harvard University, Oxford University, and Stanford
University. In a way, he is also a "graduate" of the University of Michigan:

he taught there for some ten years before resigning to return to his family's farm in Danbury, New Hampshire, where he currently lives. Hall has been poetry editor for *The Paris Review*, a member of the editorial board for Wesleyan's Poetry Series, and literary consultant for Harper & Row. He is the recipient of the Lamont Award for Poetry and of Guggenheim Fellowships.

Donald Hall's many other accomplishments include monographs on Marianne Moore and Henry Moore and such noted textbooks as *Writing Well* (1973) and *The Pleasures of Poetry* (1971). He also has edited some thirteen anthologies, including *New Poets of England and America* (with Robert Pack and Louis Simpson, 1957; revised with Robert Pack, 1962) and, of course, *Contemporary American Poetry* (Penguin, 1962; revised, 1971), the introduction to which offers this editor a vital point of contention for his essay "The Radical Tradition," which appears later in this book.

In a variety of statements — and especially in his dazzling essay "Goatfoot, Milktongue, Twinbird: The Psychic Origins of Poetic Form" — Donald Hall has repeatedly affirmed that the essential beauty of poetry lies in the sensual body of the poem — the sheer physical pleasure that a poem offers. That physical pleasure, Hall observes, "reaches us through our mouths (Milktongue) . . . in the muscles of our legs (Goatfoot) . . . in the resolution of dance and noise (Twinbird)." Hall's quest for the sensual body of his own poems was originally in more traditional forms; later, his poems became less formal, more expansive, and more sensual — without losing the control and discipline learned in the atelier of formalism.

Moreover, Hall's quest for the sensual body of poetry hasn't been the aesthete's pursuit of pleasure found in the notions of Walter Pater or in the work of some of Hall's own contemporaries. For Hall knows all too well: "Milktongue also remembers hunger, and the cry without answer. Goatfoot remembers falling, and the ache that bent the night. Twinbird remembers the loss of the brother, so long he believed in abandonment forever." At the heart of Hall's own poetry are the ever-present ache and modulated cry of abandonment, of grief over loss that is also at the heart of human experience: the baby son who documents his father's bodily decay; the emblematic skeleton of the pilot in the lost airplane; the town buried under water.

More recently the acute sense of loss in Hall's poems has been complemented by a commensurate measure of a joyous reconciliation with personal history, a discovery of the redemptive power inherent in all cycles of existence. Thus twenty-five years after the grandfather's body has slid into the ground like snow melting on the roof of the saphouse, his grandchildren dip their fingers in the maple syrup the dead man preserved in his cellar. Thus Hall himself can exclaim: "Oh, this delicious falling into the arms of leaves, / into the soft laps of leaves! . . . / Now I leap and fall, exultant,

recovering / from death, on account of death, in accord with the dead . . ."
And thus he evokes still another ancient image of the sensual pleasure of
poetry in the myth of Philomel, magically transformed into a nightingale
whose torn tongue makes song, makes music, out of grief.

Poetry

(Poems). Oxford, England: Fantasy, 1952.   To the Loud Wind and Other Poems.
Cambridge, Mass.: Harvard Advocate, 1955.   Exiles and Marriages. New York:
Viking, 1955.   The Dark Houses. New York: Viking, 1958.   A Roof of Tiger
Lilies: Poems. New York: Viking, 1964.   The Alligator Bride: Poems New and
Selected. New York: Harper & Row, 1969.   The Yellow Room: Love Poems. New
York: Harper & Row, 1971.   The Town of Hill. Boston: David R. Godine,
1975.   Kicking the Leaves. New York: Harper & Row, 1978.   The Toy Bone.
Brockport, N.Y.: BOA Editions, 1979.

Criticism

Goatfoot Milktongue Twinbird: Interviews, Essays, and Notes on Poetry, 1970–76. Ann
Arbor: University of Michigan, 1978.   Remembering Poets: Reminiscences and
Opinions. New York: Harper & Row, 1978.   To Keep Moving: Essays 1959–69.
Clinton, N. Y.: Hobart and William Smith College, 1980.   Claims for Poetry (editor).
Ann Arbor: University of Michigan, 1982.   The Weather for Poetry: Essays, Reviews,
and Notes on Poetry 1977–81. Ann Arbor: University of Michigan, 1983.

Miscellaneous Prose

String Too Short To Be Saved: Childhood Reminiscences. New York: Viking, 1961;
reprint, Boston: Godine, 1979.   Henry Moore: The Life and Work of a Great
Sculptor. New York: Harper & Row, 1966.   Dock Ellis in the Country of Baseball.
New York: Coward, McCann & Geoghegan, 1976.   Fathers Playing Catch with
Sons. San Francisco: North Point, 1984.

MICHAEL S. HARPER (1938)

Michael S. Harper was born in Brooklyn and educated at California State
University–Los Angeles and the University of Iowa. In 1978 he was also a
postdoctoral fellow at the Center for Advanced Study at the University of
Illinois. He has taught at Lewis and Clark College, Reed College, Harvard,
and Yale. In 1979 he was Elliston Poet and Distinguished Professor at the
University of Cincinnati and Benedict Distinguished Professor at Carleton

College. Since 1970 he has taught at Brown University, where he is director of the Graduate Creative Writing Program and the I. J. Kapstein Professor of English. In addition to fellowships from the Guggenheim Foundation and the National Endowment for the Arts, Michael Harper's awards include the Black Academy of Arts and Letters Award, the Melville Cane Award from the Poetry Society of America, and a National Institute of Arts and Letters grant.

The titles of Michael S. Harper's books are genuine flags of his substantive and sustained concerns. Many of his poems are indeed "images of kin": the woman to whom he is married, their living children, their children who died as infants, his own parents and grandparents. But in Harper's poems kinship also expands in time and space to include historical figures, ranging from Frederick Douglass to Martin Luther King and Malcolm X, as well as members of the artistic community, jazz musicians like John Coltrane, Charlie Parker, Bessie Smith and Billie Holiday and writers like Richard Wright and, especially among his contemporaries, Robert Hayden.

Moreover, the focus of Harper's concern is a powerful sense of kinship as shared history. Such a vision, then, begins by asserting that "history is your own heartbeat," but it necessarily expands in ever-widening circles of kinship, generated by the pulse that is at the heart of the human family. Full and active participation in those human bonds, Harper knows, may often result in considerable pain and anguish, for to be fully human often necessitates recognizing the nightmare of our condition and accepting its necessary consequence: "nightmare begins responsibility."

Perhaps no other poet of his generation has been as influenced by the work and presence of the classic American jazz musicians as has Michael S. Harper. In his poems they assume the dimensions and implications of larger figures from ancient myths. But they are more than just mythical presences, for in their work Harper has searched for and learned what he calls "the cadence of street talk in the inner ear of the great musicians, the great blues singers." And as Ralph J. Mills, Jr., has noted, Harper's poetry is infused with "a complex jazz of sudden leaps, silences, long rides." No less important, Harper reflects that rich tradition of making music out of fundamental human suffering, whether it be personal, racial, or historical. The conscious transmutation of suffering into song is at once an assertion of our humanity and an affirmation of our freedom. But in a recent essay Harper also tells the story of how John Coltrane tried to find an especially soft reed that would alleviate his pain as he played his horn in search of a particular tone. Coltrane eventually gave up looking for such a reed, regardless of how painful it was for him to make music. "There was no easy way to get that sound," Harper concludes: "play through the pain to *a love supreme*"—the phrase that appears most frequently in Harper's work. No wonder Michael S. Harper's poems are such "healing songs."

Poetry

Dear John, Dear Coltrane. Pittsburgh: University of Pittsburgh, 1970.   *History Is Your Own Heartbeat.* Urbana: University of Illinois, 1971.   *Photographs: Negatives: History as Apple Tree.* San Francisco: Scarab, 1972.   *Song: I Want a Witness.* Pittsburgh: University of Pittsburgh, 1972.   *Debridement.* New York: Doubleday, 1973. *Nightmare Begins Responsibility.* Urbana: University of Illinois, 1974.   *Images of Kin: New and Selected Poems.* Urbana: University of Illinois, 1977.   *Healing Song for the Inner Ear.* Urbana: University of Illinois, 1984.

Anthologies

Heartblow: Black Veils. Urbana: University of Illinois, 1975.   *Chant of Saints: A Gathering of Afro-American Literature, Art, and Scholarship.* Urbana: University of Illinois, 1979.

ROBERT HAYDEN (1913–1980)

A native of Detroit, Robert Hayden received a B.A. from Wayne State University and an M.A. from the University of Michigan. He taught at Fisk, Louisville, and Washington, and he was professor of English at the University of Michigan. He was a staff member of the Breadloaf Writers Conference, and from 1976 to 1978 he served as Consultant in Poetry at the Library of Congress. His honors and awards include a Rosenwald Fellowship, a Ford Foundation grant, and the First World Festival of Negro Arts Prize for Poetry, Dakar, Senegal, in 1966.

Since the publication of his first book in 1940, Robert Hayden's poetry has consistently reflected a sensibility informed by a vital awareness of and participation in the broad spectrum of the Black experience. He has explored dimensions of his own childhood and personal life; he has focused on central historical and cultural figures and events; and he has recreated such immeasurable horrors as a Black man's castration at the hands of the Ku Klux Klan. No less important, while eschewing political rhetoric, he has recognized that much the same moral poison infected the air of both Selma and Saigon, that the ashes in the pits at Dachau resulted from a fire not unlike that which burned on lawns in innumerable American towns.

Hayden's moral vision is all the more powerful because his work reveals that he is equally conscious of the broader aesthetic traditions in the art of poetry and of the obvious — but often overlooked — fact that the wellsprings of poetry run more deeply and serendipitously than even the most active pools of political or racial experience. The impact of a poem like "Monet's 'Waterlilies'" emerges out of the fact that Hayden's vision is rooted specifically in such a seemingly apolitical and nonmoral work of art. The depths of horror in "Night, Death, Mississippi" are intensified by the delicate and exquisite lyrical qualities of "The Night-Blooming Cereus."

In short, whether writing about Frederick Douglass or Rilke or a diver, Robert Hayden's poems are themselves vibrant "lives grown out of his life, the lives / fleshing his dream of *the beautiful, needful thing.*"

Poetry

Heart-Shape in the Dust. Detroit: Falcon, 1940.   *The Lion and the Archer* (with Myron O'Higgins). Nashville: Counterpoise, 1948.   *Figures of Time: Poems.* Nashville: Hemphill, 1955.   *A Ballad of Remembrance.* London: Paul Breman, 1962.   *Selected Poems.* New York: October House, 1966.   *Words in the Mourning Time.* New York: October House, 1970.   *The Night-Blooming Cereus.* London: Paul Breman, 1972.   *Angle of Ascent: New and Selected Poems.* New York: Liveright, 1975.   *American Journal.* Taunton, Mass.: Effendi, 1978; expanded edition, New York: Liveright, 1980.

Prose

The Collected Prose of Robert Hayden. Edited by Frederick Glaysher. Foreword by William Meredith. Ann Arbor: University of Michigan, 1984.

Anthologies

Kaleidoscope: Poems by American Negro Poets. New York: Harcourt Brace, 1967. *Afro-American Literature: An Introduction.* New York: Harcourt Brace, 1971.

RICHARD HUGO (1923–1982)

Richard Hugo was born in Seattle and educated at the University of Washington. He was a bombardier in the U. S. Army Air Corps during World War II and subsequently worked for the Boeing Company for twelve years. From 1964 to 1982 he was a member of the English Department at the University of Montana (Missoula), where he was professor of English and director of the creative writing program. From 1977 to 1982 he also served as the editor of the Yale Younger Poets series. His awards include the Theodore Roethke Memorial Poetry Prize, a Rockefeller Fellowship, and a Guggenheim Fellowship.

Perhaps more than the work of any other poet of his generation, Richard Hugo's poetry is rooted in and mines a specific, identifiable landscape — the American Far West. However, Hugo's landscape isn't the breathtaking panorama of a Grand Canyon or spectacular hills and plains against a blazing sunset of romantic American western movies. The landscape in his poetry is suggested in Hugo's comment: "Usually I find a poem is triggered by something, a small town or an abandoned house, that I feel others would ignore." Thus the geographic, human, and moral landscape in Hugo's poems is a bleak and threatening panorama in which one finds those small, dry, and blistered towns where all life and human constructs decay too soon — and where perhaps nothing dies soon enough.

If, like Wallace Stevens, Richard Hugo understands the extent to which "the soil is man's intelligence," he nevertheless does not succumb to easy fatalism. In poems whose language and texture assert their own organic shapes and rhythms, as if in defiance of the odds of lunar dust, Hugo affirms the things of this earth and of his poetic landscape. Just as Rilke could assert: "Maybe we're here only to say: *house, / bridge, well, gate, jug, olive tree, window — / at most, pillar, tower* . . . but to say them, remember, / oh, to say them in a way that the things themselves / never dreamed of existing so intensely," so Hugo can assert: "To live good, keep your life and the scene. / Cow, brook, hay: these are names of coins."

"A part of the West belongs to Hugo," William Stafford has written. "By telling over and over again its places and people, he reclaims it from the very bleakness he confronts; and it all begins to loom as a great intense abode that we can't neglect, that we can't bear to let go." Thus Richard Hugo's intense love of the things of *his* earth keeps them and us alive at a level of intensity and joy we could not know without the melancholy and redemptive beauty of his poems.

Poetry

A Run of Jacks. Minneapolis: University of Minnesota, 1961.   *Death of the Kapowsin Tavern.* New York: Harcourt Brace, 1965.   *Good Luck in Cracked Italian.* Cleveland: World, 1969.   *The Lady in Kicking Horse Reservoir.* New York: Norton, 1973.   *Rain Five Days and I Love It.* Port Townsend, Wash.: Graywolf, 1975. *What Thou Lovest Well, Remains American.* New York: Norton, 1975.   *Duwamish Head.* Port Townsend, Wash.: Copperhead, 1976.   *31 Letters and 13 Dreams.* New York: Norton, 1977.   *Road Ends at Tahola.* Pittsburgh: Slow Loris, 1978. *Selected Poems.* New York: Norton, 1979.   *White Center.* New York: Norton, 1980. *The Right Madness on Skye.* New York: Norton, 1980.   *Making Certain It Goes On: The Collected Poems of Richard Hugo.* New York: Norton, 1983.   *Sea Lanes Out.* Story, Wyo.: Dooryard, 1983.

Fiction

Death and the Good Life. New York: Norton, 1981.

Criticism

The Triggering Town: Lectures and Essays on Poetry and Writing. New York: Norton, 1979.

Critical Studies

Allen, Michael S. *We Are Called Human: The Poetry of Richard Hugo.* Fayetteville: University of Arkansas, 1982.   Myers, Jack, ed. *A Trout in the Milk: A Composite Portrait of Richard Hugo.* Lewiston, Idaho: Confluence, 1982.

DAVID IGNATOW (1914)

A native of Brooklyn, David Ignatow has worked as a salesman, public relations writer, shipyard handyman—and treasurer and president of a bindery firm. He has taught at the New School for Social Research, Vassar, and Columbia; and from 1969 to 1983, he was poet-in-residence at York College. Coeditor of *Beloit Poetry Journal* from 1950 to 1959, he has also served as poetry editor for *The Nation* and as an associate editor of *American Poetry Review.* And since 1980 he has been president of the Poetry Society of America. In addition to awards from the National Institute of Arts and Letters and the National Endowment for the Arts, he has received a Rockefeller Fellowship and two Guggenheim Fellowships. In 1975 he was awarded the Bollingen Prize in poetry.

An avowed disciple of William Carlos Williams, who focuses primarily on the urban experience, Ignatow has written in his *Notebooks* that his role is to remind other poets—and, by implication, all readers of poetry—that "there is a world outside, the more decisive world that yet must be treated tragically by us in the highest intensity and sensuousness, though while it ignores us we must not run off into separate worlds of our own." Admitting that he is "antipoetic," he affirms that experience must be looked at and accepted just as it is and that "nothing should be taken for more than it says to you on its surface."

Ranging from comedy, through rage, to tragedy—and addressing himself to both his personal experiences as well as to our communal life—Ignatow constantly attempts to see life as it really is, without illusion or self-deception of any kind. And in so doing, he views himself as being at the opposite pole of Whitman's affirmative optimism. "My idea of being a moral leader," he writes, "is to point out the terrible deficiencies in man. Whitman spent his life boosting the good side. My life will be spent pointing out the bad." But he adds a most crucial phrase: if he is intent on pointing to human deficiencies, he says that he will do so "from the standpoint of forgiveness and peace."

A singular and powerful voice in contemporary poetry, eschewing all current modes of language to be himself first of all, David Ignatow's poetry is marked by a certain nontheatrical directness and is also charged with a unique strength of spirit, humanity, and wisdom.

Poetry

Poems. Prairie City, Ill.: Decker Press, 1948. *The Gentle Weight Lifter.* New York: Morris Gallery, 1955. *Say Pardon.* Middletown: Wesleyan, 1962. *Figures of the Human.* Middletown: Wesleyan, 1964. *Rescue the Dead.* Middletown: Wesleyan, 1968. *Poems: 1934–1969.* Middletown: Wesleyan, 1970. *Facing the Tree: New Poems.* Boston: Atlantic-Little, Brown, 1975. *Selected Poems.* Chosen with introductory notes and an afterword by Robert Bly. Middletown: Wesleyan, 1975. *The Animal in the Bush: Poems on Poetry.* Edited by Patrick Carey. Pittsburgh: Slow Loris, 1978. *Tread the Dark: New Poems.* Boston: Atlantic-Little, Brown, 1978. *Sunlight: A Sequence for My Daughter.* Brockport, N.Y.: BOA Editions, 1979. *Conversations.* New York: Survivors Manual Books, 1980. *Whisper to the Earth.* Boston: Atlantic-Little, Brown, 1981. *Ten Poems.* New York: The Silver Hands Press, 1983. *Leaving the Door Open.* New York: Sheep Meadow, 1984.

Criticism and Other Prose

The Notebooks of David Ignatow. Edited with an introduction by Ralph J. Mills, Jr. Chicago: Swallow, 1973; paperback edition, New York: Sheep Meadow, 1983. *Open Between Us: Essays, Reviews, and Interviews.* Edited by Ralph J. Mills, Jr. Ann Arbor: University of Michigan, 1980.

RANDALL JARRELL (1914–1965)

Randall Jarrell was born in Nashville and educated at Vanderbilt University where he received degrees in psychology and English. He served as a control tower operator in the U.S. Air Corps during World War II. Before and after the war, he taught at several colleges and universities, including Sarah Lawrence, Kenyon, the University of North Carolina, and Princeton. In addition, he was literary editor for *The Nation* and poetry critic for the *Partisan Review* and *Yale Review.* In 1956 he was appointed Consultant in Poetry at the Library of Congress and was elected a member of the National Institute of Arts and Letters and a chancellor of the Academy of American Poets. His many awards included a Guggenheim Fellowship, grants from the National Institute of Arts and Letters and from the Ingram Merrill Foundation, and the National Book Award.

Heralded for his translations, his criticism, and his poetry, Randall Jarrell seemed destined to be one of his generation's authentic men of letters before his untimely and enigmatic death. However, a measure of controversy continues to hound Jarrell's reputation as a poet. Some would argue that he was too much of a formalist, and yet a poem like "The Black Swan" certainly compares well to other formal poems written by someone like Richard Wilbur, while simultaneously calling to mind a coupling of Yeats's romantic and mythic concerns. Others would argue that too many of his poems succumbed to an excessive conversational and prosaic style, and yet Jarrell's successful nonformalist poems seem to presage the structural and lyrical quality of Robert Lowell's later work, especially the poems in *Day by Day*.

At the heart of Randall Jarrell's vision as a poet is an intense, Rilkean pursuit of transformation, if not transcendence. Jarrell was obsessed by the need to discover the possibility of *more* in the world around him and especially in himself. Like the speaker in "The Woman at the Washington Zoo," Jarrell repeatedly insists: "You know what I was, / You see what I am: change me, change me!" But the magnificent snow-leopard is "the heart of heartlessness"; the soul of the European emigrant to the new world "finds Europe waiting for it over every sea"; the ball turret gunner who dies for his country and topples from the sky like a modern-day Icarus isn't immortalized, rather his body is washed out of the turret with a hose. In short, "nothing comes from nothing ... / Pain comes from the darkness / And we call it wisdom. It is pain." Given such evidence, no wonder Robert Lowell said that Jarrell was "the most heartbreaking ... poet of his generation."

Poetry

Five Young American Poets (with others). New York: New Directions, 1940.   *Blood for a Stranger*. New York: Harcourt Brace, 1942.   *Little Friend, Little Friend*. New York: Dial, 1945.   *Losses*. New York: Harcourt Brace, 1948.   *The Seven-League Crutches*. New York: Harcourt Brace, 1951.   *Selected Poems*. New York: Knopf, 1955.   *The Woman at the Washington Zoo: Poems and Translations*. New York: Atheneum, 1960.   *Selected Poems*. New York: Atheneum, 1964.   *The Lost World: New Poems*. New York: Macmillan, 1965.   *The Complete Poems*. New York: Farrar, Straus & Giroux, 1969.

Translations: Prose and Poetic Drama

The Ghetto and the Jews of Rome [Ferdinand Gregorovius] (with Moses Hadas). New York: Schocken, 1948.   *The Rabbit Catcher and Other Fairy Tales of Ludwig Bechstein.* New York: Macmillan, 1962.   *The Golden Bird and Other Fairy Tales by the Brothers Grimm.* New York: Macmillan, 1962.   *Snow White and the Seven Dwarfs: A Tale from the Brothers Grimm.* New York: Farrar, Straus & Giroux, 1972. *The Juniper Tree and Other Tales by the Brothers Grimm.* New York: Farrar, Straus & Giroux, 1973.   *Goethe's Faust: Part One.* New York: Farrar, Straus & Giroux, 1974.

Criticism and Fiction

Poetry and the Age (essays). New York: Knopf, 1953.   *Pictures from an Institution: A Comedy* (novel). New York: Knopf, 1954.   *A Sad Heart at the Supermarket: Essays and Fables.* New York: Atheneum, 1962.   *The Third Book of Criticism* (essays). New York: Farrar, Straus & Giroux, 1969.   *Kipling, Auden & Co.* New York: Farrar, Straus & Giroux, 1980.

Bibliography

Adams, Charles M. *Randall Jarrell: A Bibliography.* Chapel Hill: University of North Carolina, 1958.

Critical Studies

Ferguson, Suzanne. *The Poetry of Randall Jarrell.* Baton Rouge: Louisiana State, 1971. Lowell, Robert, Peter Taylor, and Robert Penn Warren, eds. *Randall Jarrell 1914–1965.* New York: Farrar, Straus & Giroux, 1967.   Quinn, Sr. Bernetta. *Randall Jarrell.* Boston: Twayne, 1980.

DONALD JUSTICE (1925)

Donald Justice was born in Miami, Florida. He attended the University of Miami, the University of North Carolina — Chapel Hill, Stanford University, and the University of Iowa. He has taught at the University of Missouri — Columbia, Hamline University, Syracuse University, the University of California — Irvine, and the University of Iowa. He is currently professor of English at the University of Florida — Gainesville. Since winning the Academy of American Poets' Lamont prize for poetry in 1959, Donald Justice also has been the recipient of grants, awards, and fellowships from the Ford and

Guggenheim foundations, the National Endowment for the Arts, and the National Institute of Arts and Letters. In 1980 he was awarded the Pulitzer Prize for his *Selected Poems.*

Many of Donald Justice's poems generate much the same kind of emotional center and aura as Edward Hopper's well-known paintings (such as *Nighthawks*): the figures, landscapes, the dramatic situations reflect the depth of loneliness, the isolation, and the spiritual desolation at the heart of twentieth century experience. Any number of these people or situations could suddenly turn up in our own nightmares or in our living rooms. However, while Hopper achieves his effects by means of bold colors, thick strokes, and stark contrasts, the surface texture of Justice's poems is far more delicate and subtle — the restrained turn of a phrase (as in "Men at Forty"), the carefully controlled but haunting repetition of a line (as in "Bus Stop").

Given a list of some of Donald Justice's subjects — loneliness, isolation, madness, despair, terror — he might be wrongfully associated with some of the personal-confessional poets. His poems, however, do not suggest any of the verbal or emotional sensationalism that occasionally may be ascribed to some of those other poets. Rightfully celebrated for his formal qualities, as a craftsman Justice is a master of what might be called sparse elegance, with none of the pejorative connotations that may be clustered around those words. Justice's poems are not the result of emotional or technical self-indulgence; rather, they are moving because of his consummate linguistic, tonal, and formal exactitude.

If Donald Justice's commitment to the "well-made poem" suggests his formal schooling among the New Critics, he is also one of the obvious emotional-spiritual heirs of T. S. Eliot — i.e., that vision found in Eliot's earlier poems, before his conversion to Christianity. Like the work of other poets of his generation, Justice's poems flesh out in more intimate and sustained detail the figures and states of being that Eliot sketched only in poems like "The Love Song of J. Alfred Prufrock," "Preludes," and "The Waste Land." But what further distinguishes his work is not only Justice's unrelieved sense of loss ("Everything going away in the night again and again"), but also his profound acceptance of (*not* resignation to) the human condition as he finds it. But if Donald Justice's poems are elegies of loss, they are also unswerving and powerful affirmations that to be human is to make poetry of "the boredom, and the horror, and the glory."

Poetry

The Summer Anniversaries. Middletown: Wesleyan University, 1960.   *A Local Storm.* Iowa City: Stone Wall, 1963.   *Four Poets* (with others). Pella, Iowa: C.U.I., 1967. *Night Light.* Middletown: Wesleyan University, 1967.   *Sixteen Poems.* Iowa City:

Stone Wall, 1970.   *From a Notebook*. Iowa City: Seamark Press, 1972.
Departures. New York: Atheneum, 1973.   *Selected Poems*. New York, Atheneum,
1979.

Criticism

Platonic Scripts. Ann Arbor: University of Michigan, 1984.

Anthologies

The Collected Poems of Weldon Kees. Iowa City: Stone Wall, 1960; revised edition,
Lincoln: University of Nebraska, 1975.   *Midland: Twenty-Five Years of Fiction and
Poetry from the Writing Workshops of the State University of Iowa* (with Paul Engle and
Henri Coulette). New York: Random House, 1961.   *Contemporary French Poetry* (with
Alexander Aspel). Ann Arbor: University of Michigan Press, 1965.   *Syracuse Poems
1968*. Syracuse, N.Y.: Syracuse University Department of English, 1968.

GALWAY KINNELL (1927)

Galway Kinnell received an A.B. from Princeton and an M.A. from the
University of Rochester. He was a Fulbright Fellow in Paris, served in the
U. S. Navy and as a field worker for the Congress of Racial Equality, and has
traveled widely in the Middle East and Europe. Kinnell has taught at the
universities of Grenoble and Nice (France), California (Irvine), and
Pittsburgh, as well as at Sarah Lawrence, New York University, and the State
University of New York at Binghamton, where he is currently Director of
the Creative Writing Program. He has received the Brandeis University
Creative Arts Award as well as awards from the Rockefeller and
Guggenheim foundations and from the National Institute of Arts and
Letters, and he won the 1982 Pulitzer Prize for Poetry.

Galway Kinnell's earlier poems were both traditionally formal and
informed by a traditional Christian sensibility. However, while retaining an
essentially religious and sacramental dimension, his later work—as he has
said in an interview—has become an increasing "struggle against the desire
for heaven," as well as a movement away from competent, pleasing poetry
that risks being ornamental and toward a freer verse that takes more risks
and in which "there is the chance of finding that great thing you might be
after, of finding glory."

Confronted by a constant threat of extinction, in his poetry Kinnell
accepts all forms of death as part of the rhythm that produces life, but he

is capable of witnessing even the most elemental energy as an affirmation of life. Perhaps human life is a participation in the ultimate madness of a universe flinging itself into emptiness; the image of fire often reappearing in his poems may not be the flame of the phoenix. Thus Kinnell insists that for man, "as he goes up in flames, his own work / is / to open himself, to *be* / the flames."

In their language and substance, Kinnell's poems achieve that rhythm and solemnity often found in a shaman's chant. And yet his poems are also intensely personal, reflecting an attempt to strip away personality, to go deeper into the self "until," he says, "you're just a person. If you could keep going deeper and deeper, you'd finally not be a person either; you'd be an animal; and if you kept going deeper and deeper, you'd be a blade of grass or ultimately perhaps a stone. And if a stone could read, [poetry] would speak for it." For Kinnell, then, poetry is primal experience and myth, the most elemental kind of prayer, or a "paradigm of what people might wish to say in addressing the cosmos."

Poetry

What a Kingdom It Was. Boston: Houghton Mifflin, 1960.   *Flower Herding on Mount Monadnock.* Boston: Houghton Mifflin, 1964.   *Body Rags.* Boston: Houghton Mifflin, 1968.   *First Poems: 1946–54.* Mt. Horeb, Wis.: Perishable Press, 1970.   *The Book of Nightmares.* Boston: Houghton Mifflin, 1971.   *The Shoes of Wandering.* Mt. Horeb, Wis.: Perishable Press, 1971.   *The Avenue Bearing the Initial of Christ into the New World: Poems 1946–64.* Boston: Houghton Mifflin, 1974. *Three Poems.* New York: Phoenix Book Shop, 1976.   *Mortal Acts, Mortal Words.* Boston: Houghton Mifflin, 1980.   *Selected Poems.* Boston: Houghton Mifflin, 1982.

Translations: Poetry and Prose

Bitter Victory [a novel by René Hardy]. New York: Doubleday 1956.   *The Poems of François Villon.* New York: New American Library, 1965; revised edition, Boston: Houghton Mifflin, 1977; new edition, Hanover: University Press of New England, 1982.   *On the Motion and Immobility of Douve* [poems by Yves Bonnefoy]. Athens, Ohio: Ohio University, 1968.   *Lackawanna Elegy* [poems by Yvan Goll]. Fremont, Michigan: Sumac, 1970.

Criticism and Fiction

Black Light (novel). Boston: Houghton Mifflin, 1966; revised edition, San Francisco: North Point, 1981.   *Walking Down the Stairs: Selections from Interviews.* Ann Arbor: University of Michigan, 1978.   *How the Alligator Missed Breakfast* (fiction for children). Boston: Houghton Mifflin, 1982.

CAROLYN KIZER (1925)

Born in Spokane, Washington, Carolyn Kizer graduated from Sarah Lawrence College and was a fellow of the Chinese government in comparative literature at Columbia University, followed by a year of study in Nationalist China. The founder of the quarterly *Poetry Northwest,* in 1964–1965 she was a Specialist in Literature for the U.S. State Department in Pakistan, and from 1966 to 1970 she served as the first director of the Literature Program for the newly established National Endowment for the Arts. Since 1970 she has been professor, visiting professor, or poet-in-residence at universities throughout the United States, including the University of North Carolina at Chapel Hill, Washington University, Columbia University, Ohio University, the University of Iowa, the University of Cincinnati, the University of Hawaii, and the University of Louisville. She currently resides in Berkeley, California.

With the publication of her first book-length collection of poems, *The Ungrateful Garden* (1961), Carolyn Kizer staked out what were to be the diverse technical and thematic territories of her art. Whether she is working with free verse, with more formal verse, or with combinations of free verse and occasional slant rhymes, Kizer's poetry is always remarkable for its consummate grace and control. (She is one member of her generation who continues to explore the possibilities and power of strict form.) The intellectual credibility and emotional impact of her poems are further enhanced by her unique intellectual wit and hearty, often stinging, sense of humor. Indeed, Kizer was the first woman poet—and continues to be one of the few women poets—to approach feminist subjects and themes with a measure of healthy humor and sophisticated wit, which are an integral part of her sensibility rather than merely the device of poetic irony.

Kizer's concern for the cause of feminism has been at the heart of her poetry from the very start of her career—for the most fundamental of reasons: ". . . we are the custodians of the world's best-kept secret: / Merely the private lives of one-half of humanity." And it's important to note that the composition of "Pro Femina" dates back to the midfifties, before feminism was an issue of general consciousness. But Kizer's interest isn't limited to feminism as a sociopolitical cause; rather, what generally rivets her attention is the quality of representative women's diurnal experiences. "The Blessing," for example, is an exploration of the relationships of three generations of women. Similar in its subject matter to Isabella Gardner's "The Widow's Yard," Kizer's "A Widow in Wintertime" is a portrait of repressed sexuality, disciplined loneliness, and "metaphysic famines."

However, Kizer doesn't limit herself to the "famines" of experience either, for also at the heart of her poetry is her vision of the profound patterns of physical and metaphysical life: change, transformation, and transubstantiation in nature and in the spirit, for good or ill; birth, death, and rebirth of love, the self, the soul, as in "Semele Recycled," where "the inner parts remember . . . / the comfortable odor of dung, the animal incense, / and passion, its bloody labor, / its birth and rebirth and decay." In short, without sacrificing their feminist edge, Kizer's poems are powerful, myth-making hymns in celebration of "we who invented dying / And the whole alchemy of resurrection."

Poetry

Poems. Portland, Ore.: Portland Art Museum, 1959.   *The Ungrateful Garden.* Bloomington: Indiana University, 1961.   *Five Poets of the Pacific Northwest* (with others). Edited by Robin Skelton. Seattle: University of Washington, 1964.   *Knock Upon Silence.* New York: Doubleday, 1965; paperback edition, Seattle: University of Washington, 1966.   *Midnight Was My Cry: New and Selected Poems.* New York: Doubleday, 1971.   *Mermaids in the Basement: Poems for Women.* Port Townsend, Wash.: Copper Canyon, 1984.   *Yin.* Brockport, N.Y.: BOA Editions, 1984.

Translations: Poetry

Carrying Over: Poems from the Hebrew, Urdu, Chinese, and Macedonian. Laurinburg, N.C.: St. Andrews, 1985.

MAXINE KUMIN (1925)

Born in Philadelphia, Maxine Kumin received a bachelor's and master's degree from Radcliffe. The author of some twenty books for children (three of which she wrote with Anne Sexton), Maxine Kumin has served as a consultant for the Central Atlantic Regional Educational Laboratory and the Board of Coordinated Educational Services (Nassau County, New York). She also has taught at Tufts, the University of Massachusetts, Centre College (Kentucky), and at Princeton. An officer of the Radcliffe Institute's Society of Fellows and former chairperson of the Literature Panel of the National Endowment for the Arts, Maxine Kumin was awarded the Pulitzer Prize in 1973.

One of Maxine Kumin's critics has faulted her work for often being "the poetry of a special world, unmistakably upper middle-class, comfortable, urbane, safe in its place at the center of things." To suggest that such arenas of experience may not be legitimate or "worthy" concerns of poetry in this century and country is blatant nonsense, of course. Besides, when Eliot posited his dictum, "Redeem the time," he didn't specify that it had to be an urban and industrial time fraught with its unique sets of psychic and physical terrors. Moreover, if Kumin's poetry does focus on the middle-class experience, like Louis Simpson she too is "taking part in a great experiment— / whether writers can live peacefully in the suburbs / and not be bored to death."

Poetry

Halfway. New York: Holt, Rinehart and Winston, 1961. *The Privilege.* New York: Harper & Row, 1965. *The Nightmare Factory.* New York: Harper & Row, 1970. *Up Country.* New York: Harper & Row, 1972. *House, Bridge, Fountain, Gate.* New York: Viking, 1975. *The Retrieval System.* New York: Viking, 1978. *Our Ground Time Here Will Be Brief: New and Selected Poems.* New York: Viking, 1982.

Fiction

Through Dooms of Love. New York: Harper & Row, 1965. *The Passions of Uxport.* New York: Harper & Row, 1968. *The Abduction.* New York: Harper & Row, 1971. *The Designated Heir.* New York: Viking, 1974. *Why Can't We Live Together Like Civilized Human Beings?* New York: Viking, 1982.

Criticism

To Make a Prairie: Essays on Poets, Poetry, and Country Living. Ann Arbor: University of Michigan, 1979.

STANLEY KUNITZ (1905)

Born in Worcester, Massachusetts, and educated at Harvard, Stanley Kunitz has taught at Bennington, Brandeis, Columbia, and Yale. He also has been a Cultural Exchange Scholar in Russia and Poland. From 1969 to 1976, he was editor of the Yale Series of Younger Poets; from 1974 to 1976, he served as Consultant in Poetry at the Library of Congress. The recipient of grants from the Guggenheim and Ford Foundations, the Academy of American Poets, and the National Institute of Arts and Letters, he was also awarded the Pulitzer Prize in 1959 and elected a chancellor of the Academy of American Poets in 1970.

In addition to his moving translations of the poetry of Anna Akhmatova, Stanley Kunitz has been a major contributor to the many collections of translations of the poetry of Andrei Voznesensky and Yevgeny Yevtushenko that have appeared in this country. Moreover, since 1931, he has been one of the editors of eight major dictionaries of literary biographies.

After the publication of *The Testing-Tree* in 1971, Stanley Kunitz wrote: "I am no more reconciled than I ever was to the world's wrongs and the injustice of time." Among the wrongs and injustices present in Kunitz's poetry are: the memories of a painful childhood that seemingly cannot be redeemed or reshaped; inevitable participation in the outrageous scientific and technological violence against the human spirit; and—despite the moments of beauty's hope—the inescapable promise of "a dusty finger on my lip."

Throughout his career, Kunitz's measure of emotional and moral energy has been further intensified by his equally passionate reverence for and use of form. In his poems, more than in the work of most poets of his generation, one senses that any experience or vision—regardless of how intense it might have been in itself—has consistently been forged by the white heat of a metaphysical sensibility. Thus Kunitz's poems have a physical presence and quality that are verbal equivalents of graceful sculptures forged out of the toughest metal—just as the works of a contemporary metalsmith like Albert Paley are intricate sculptures of iron and steel that seem to be leaping toward pure sound.

Poetry

Intellectual Things. New York: Doubleday, 1930.   *Passport to the War: A Selection of Poems.* New York: Holt, Rinehart and Winston, 1944.   *Selected Poems 1928–1958.* Boston: Little, Brown, 1958.   *The Testing-Tree: Poems.* Boston: Atlantic-Little, Brown, 1971.   *The Lincoln Relics: A Poem.* Port Townsend, Wash.: Graywolf, 1978.   *The Poems of Stanley Kunitz 1928–1978.* Boston: Atlantic-Little, Brown, 1979.   *The Wellfleet Whale and Companion Poems.* New York: Sheep Meadow, 1983.   *Next-to-Last Things.* Boston: Atlantic-Little, Brown, 1985.

Translations

Poems of Akhmatova (with Max Hayward). Boston: Atlantic-Little, Brown, 1973.

Criticism

A Kind of Order, A Kind of Folly: Essays and Conversations. Boston: Atlantic-Little, Brown, 1975.

Critical Studies

Henault, Marie. *Stanley Kunitz.* Boston: Twayne, 1980.   Orr, Gregory. *Stanley Kunitz: An Introduction to the Poetry.* New York: Columbia University, 1985.

DENISE LEVERTOV (1923)

Born in Essex, England, Denise Levertov was privately educated, served as a nurse during World War II, and emigrated to the United States in 1948. She has taught at Vassar, Drew, City College of New York, M.I.T., and has recently retired from Tufts where she was a full professor. A scholar at the Radcliffe Institute for Independent Study, Levertov also has received the Morton Dauwen Zabel Prize for poetry, a Guggenheim Fellowship, and a grant from the National Institute of Arts and Letters.

Influenced by William Carlos Williams and the Black Mountain School—or simply their natural aesthetic compatriot—Denise Levertov's poems are nevertheless charged by an unmistakably distinctive voice. The following is a difficult statement to make these days, but clearly hers is also a woman's voice, capable of ranging from a tough to a tender lyricism that is proportionately intense. But her poems are not simply spoken by a woman; they fully explore and—with assurance, pleasure, or grief—celebrate the multifaceted experience of the contemporary woman. By so doing, they invite all of us into a celebration of the full range of human experience.

In an early interview Denise Levertov said: "I believe in writing about what lies under the hand, in a sense. . . . Not necessarily in the visual world—the external world—it can be an inner experience—but it must be something true." And in one of her poems Levertov writes: "The best work is made / from hard, strong materials, / obstinately precise. . . ." Her own poems repeatedly assert that the most obstinate and hard materials—even in that kind of natural lyrical poem she has mastered— are not onyx and steel, but rather the small, at times elusive, materials of daily human life.

An antiwar poem like "The Altars in the Street" affirms the inestimable power of the simple but sacred human gesture over "the frenzy of weapons, their impudent power." But so much of her work also reminds us that each new poem is that difficult and laborious Jacob's ladder between the facts of the diurnal and the bid for the eternal; each poem carves the physical details and quality of our daily communal experience in the unyielding onyx and steel of a cosmic history that would obliterate us.

Poetry

The Double Image. London: Cresset Books, 1946.　　*Here and Now.* San Francisco: City Lights, 1957.　　*Overland to the Islands.* Highlands, N.C.: Jargon, 1958. *With Eyes at the Back of Our Heads.* New York: New Directions, 1959.　　*The Jacob's Ladder.* New York: New Directions, 1961.　　*O Taste and See: New Poems.* New York: New Directions, 1964.　　*City Psalm.* Berkeley: Oyez, 1964.　　*The Sorrow*

Dance. New York: New Directions, 1967. *Three Poems.* Mt. Horeb, Wis.: Perishable Press, 1968. *A Tree Telling of Orpheus.* Los Angeles: Black Sparrow, 1968. *Embroideries.* Los Angeles: Black Sparrow, 1969. *Summer Poems / 1969.* Berkeley: Oyez, 1970. *Relearning the Alphabet.* New York: New Directions, 1970. *To Stay Alive.* New York: New Directions, 1971. *Footprints.* New York: New Directions, 1972. *The Freeing of the Dust.* New York: New Directions, 1975. *Life in the Forest.* New York: New Directions, 1978. *Collected Earlier Poems 1940–1960.* New York: New Directions, 1979. *Mass for the Day of St. Thomas Didymus.* Concord, N.H.: William Ewert, 1981. *Pig Dreams.* Woodstock, Vt.: Countryman, 1981. *Wanderer's Daysong.* Port Townsend, Wash.: Copper Canyon, 1981. *Candles in Babylon.* New York: New Directions, 1982. *Denise Levertov Poems 1960–1967.* New York: New Directions, 1983. *Two Poems.* Concord, N.H.: William Ewert, 1983. *Oblique Prayers.* New York: New Directions, 1984.

Translations: Poetry

In Praise of Krishna: Songs from the Bengali (with Edward C. Dimmock, Jr.). New York: Doubleday, 1968. *Selected Poems of Guillevic.* New York: New Directions, 1969.

Prose

The Poet in the World. New York: New Directions, 1973. *Light Up the Cave.* New York: New Directions, 1981.

Bibliography

Wilson, Robert. *A Bibliography of Denise Levertov.* New York: Phoenix Book Shop, 1972.

Critical Studies

Wagner, Linda Welshimer. *Denise Levertov.* New York: Twayne, 1967. Wagner, Linda Welshimer, ed. *Denise Levertov: In Her Own Province.* New York: New Directions, 1979.

PHILIP LEVINE (1928)

Philip Levine was born in Detroit. He received a B.A. and an M.A. from Wayne State University and an M.F.A. from the University of Iowa. Subsequently, he held a fellowship in poetry at Stanford University. Since

1958 he has taught at California State University, Fresno. He has received grants from the National Endowment for the Arts and the National Institute of Arts and Letters, as well as a Guggenheim Fellowship.

Critics can't seem to agree on what Philip Levine's central theme is. One says it's a "rogue's gallery" of drunks, draft-dodgers, boxers, Hell's Angels, midgets, poor neighbors." Another asserts that his themes include "Hiroshima, the torture of Algerian prisoners, soldiers in eye-to-eye combat, generalized and brutal bigotry . . . man's cruelty to man." Still another critic argues that Levine's "fields of exploration" include "experiences which manifest themselves in irrational, dreamlike, fantastic or visionary forms." In fact, all of these observations are true, for what is consistently striking about Levine's poetry is specifically his wide range of themes.

Levine himself has written: "I try to pay homage to the people who taught me my life was a holy thing, who convinced me that my formal education was a lie. . . . These people, both Black and white, were mainly rural people, and the horror of the modern world was clearer to them than to me, and the beauty and value of the world was something they knew in a way I did not, first hand." No less important in his poetry is the vital role of Levine's own sense of place—especially the bleak, dirty, and threatening industrial cityscape of Levine's childhood in Detroit; more recently one notes references to Levine's own personal life and background, especially members of his family.

Equally striking—although not immediately noticeable to the more casual reader—is Levine's mastery of a range of forms, from the most ostensible manipulation of tighter forms, through the freer lyric, to the more surrealistic and incantatory poems. One is also struck by Levine's seemingly contradictory range of emotional, moral, and often profoundly religious responses to the horror and beauty in the world around him and around us—as well as inside us all.

Reading the body of Philip Levine's work, one senses a fiercely honest exploration of the totality of a complex human life and a particular personality moving about the crucial arenas of our common experience. One also senses a complex, intense, and disciplined sensibility's response—in pity and in condemnation, in anger and in awe, in lamentation and in song—to the conflicting phenomena of contemporary life that offer us these choices: to sit on the father's shoulders and awaken in another world, to pray to become all we'll never be, or to offer ourselves as sacrificial animals in the slaughterhouse of a blasphemous industrial liturgy of annihilation. Philip Levine's answer to the last alternative continues to be a resounding, "No. Not this pig."

Poetry

On the Edge. Iowa City: Stone Wall Press, 1963. *Silent in America: Vivas for Those Who Failed.* Iowa City: Shaw Avenue Press, 1965. *Not This Pig.* Middletown: Wesleyan, 1968. *Five Detroits.* Santa Barbara: Unicorn, 1970. *Pili's Wall.* Santa Barbara: Unicorn, 1971. *Red Dust.* Santa Cruz, Calif.: Kayak, 1971. *They Feed They Lion.* New York: Atheneum, 1972. *1933.* New York: Atheneum, 1974. *The Names of the Lost.* New York: Atheneum, 1976. *Ashes: Poems Old and New.* New York: Atheneum, 1979. *7 Years from Somewhere.* New York: Atheneum, 1979. *One for the Rose.* New York: Atheneum, 1981. *Selected Poems.* New York: Atheneum, 1984.

Translations: Poetry

Tarumba: The Selected Poems of Jaime Sabines. Edited and translated with Ernesto Trejo. San Francisco: Twin Peaks Press, 1979. *Off the Map: The Selected Poems of Gloria Fuertes.* Edited and translated with Ada Long. Middletown: Wesleyan, 1984.

Criticism

Don't Ask. Ann Arbor: University of Michigan, 1981.

JOHN LOGAN (1923)

Born in Red Oak, Iowa, John Logan received a B.A. in zoology from Coe College, an M.A. in English from the University of Iowa, and did graduate work in philosophy at Georgetown, Notre Dame, and Berkeley. He has taught at Notre Dame, San Francisco State, the University of Hawaii, and the State University of New York at Buffalo, where he was a professor of English. Logan served as poetry editor for *The Nation;* he also founded and, with Aaron Siskind, edited *Choice*—a magazine of poetry and photography. He has been the recipient of a Rockefeller grant, a Morton Dauwen Zabel award for poetry from the National Institute of Arts and Letters, a Guggenheim Fellowship, a Fellowship in Poetry from the National Endowment for the Arts, and the Lenore Marshall Poetry Prize.

Perhaps because he began his career as a scientist, John Logan's poems are constructed out of the most minute details observed from the world around him. Such lines as "I let the rain / move its audible little hands /

gently on my skin" suggest the sensuousness of his language in response to the physical world. He lingers on things and the words for things, delighting in their sound and texture. In Logan's poetry suffering neither negates the fact of beauty nor the possibility of celebration. Pain and guilt do not negate the alternatives of joy and grace. His poems repeatedly affirm that "there is a freshness / nothing can destroy in us / not even we ourselves."

Moreover, what distinguishes the work of Logan from that of most personal-confessional poets is that his poems are far less confessional and less self-flagellating. He spares us the leprous details of individual incidents of failure, deterioration, and guilt. If he asks his readers to be confessors, as he openly does in "Three Moves," he doesn't seek absolution for any given act or general Manichean sense of sin. Rather, he offers an exchange of that more human and grace-giving embrace of an accepting forgiveness of the guilt that is in each of us. And thus each of us readers, as it were, becomes Logan's anonymous lover.

The full organic development and structure of his poems, as well as the careful orchestration of tone, further distinguish Logan's work. At his best, his poems are utterly personal and natural, determined neither by structural, thematic, nor tonal formula. His poems succeed in sounding as natural as breathing; they begin simply and grow in intensity out of their own emotional necessity, as the breath of a man in battle or in love. Through a harmonious counterpoint of tones that reflect the varied inner strains of a total personality, these poems rise to discoveries of — and are themselves — epiphanies. Rich mosaics of an integrated personality's experience of the human, illuminations of that range of music rising from the total self, the poems of John Logan are at once "unpredictable as grace" and "a ballet for the ear."

Poetry

Cycle for Mother Cabrini. New York: Grove, 1955; reprint, Berkeley: Cloud Marauder, 1972. *Ghosts of the Heart.* Chicago: University of Chicago, 1960. *Spring of the Thief: Poems 1960–1962.* New York: Knopf, 1963. *The Zig-Zag Walk: Poems 1963–1968.* New York: Dutton, 1969. *The Anonymous Lover.* New York: Liveright, 1973. *Poem in Progress.* Washington, D.C.: Dryad, 1975. *John Logan / Poems / Aaron Siskind / Photographs.* Rochester, N.Y.: Visual Studies Workshop, 1976. *The Bridge of Change* (pamphlet). Brockport, N.Y.: BOA Editions, 1978. *The Bridge of Change: Poems 1974–1979.* Brockport, N.Y.: BOA Editions, 1980. *Only the Dreamer Can Change the Dream: Selected Poems.* New York: Ecco, 1981. *The Transformation: Poems January to March 1981.* San Francisco: Pancake Press, 1983.

Fiction and Criticism

The House That Jack Built; or, A Portrait of the Artist as a Sad Sensualist. Omaha: Abbatoir, 1974; revised, trade edition, Pittsburgh: Slow Loris, 1984. *A Ballet for the Ear: Interviews, Essays, and Reviews.* Edited by A. Poulin, Jr. Ann Arbor: University of Michigan, 1983.

Critical Study

Waters, Michael, ed. *Dissolve to Island: On the Poetry of John Logan.* Houston: Ford-Brown & Co., 1984.

ROBERT LOWELL (1917–1978)

Born in Boston in 1917, Robert Lowell attended Harvard and graduated from Kenyon College in 1940. A conscientious objector during World War II, he spent several months in prison. During his career, he taught at various universities, including Harvard, the University of Iowa, and Boston University; in 1947–48, he served as Consultant in Poetry at the Library of Congress. His many awards include the Pulitzer Prize (1947), the National Book Award (1960), the Bollingen Poetry Translation Award (1964), the Copernicus Award (1974), and the National Book Critics Circle Award (posthumously, 1978).

Lowell's career seems to have evolved in three stages. His early poems, written under the tutelage of John Crowe Ransom and Allen Tate, were intricately wrought and complex, clearly reflecting the dictates of the New Criticism. Emerging out of a Christian spiritual tradition, an English poetic tradition influenced by the French symbolists, and a New England historical and ethical tradition, they were poems written by a young man whose sensibilities and talent began to mature at a time when T. S. Eliot was an overpowering presence in American poetry.

In *Life Studies,* perhaps his most brilliant and significant book—the result of an encounter with W. D. Snodgrass—Lowell implicitly renounced many of the New Critics' formal demands and Eliot's cultural and spiritual vision. His poems were less consciously wrought and extremely intimate. As M. L. Rosenthal has observed, the orchestration of *Life Studies* traced the deterioration of Western civilization, the United States republic, Lowell's own family, and his very self. In the powerful concluding poem, "Skunk Hour," Lowell asserted: "The season's ill . . . / My mind's not right." And in this cultural and personal wasteland, he found no kingfisher, no Christ diving in fire.

"I am tired. Everyone's tired of my turmoil," Lowell wrote in *For the Union Dead,* and this realization marked the start of a third phase in his career. The poems grew more serenely formal, less intricate, and surely less hysterical. In *Near the Ocean,* he turned to muted couplets; his *Notebook* and *History,* though tracing intimate aspects of his life, were sonnet sequences. Although their central theme of the desolation and deterioration of humans and their world remained, Lowell was able to view that drama with a measure of objectivity, distance, and—at times—profound detachment. In his last book, *Day by Day*, Lowell returned once again to the lyrical and personal modes; however, despite the intimacy of subject matter, the poems continued to be marked by a kind of intellectual detachment.

Poetry

Land of Unlikeness. Cummington, Mass.: Cummington Press, 1944.   *Lord Weary's Castle*. New York: Harcourt Brace, 1946.   *The Mills of the Kavanaughs*. New York: Harcourt Brace, 1951.   *Life Studies*. New York: Farrar, Straus & Giroux, 1959. *For the Union Dead*. New York: Farrar, Straus & Giroux, 1964.   *Near the Ocean*. New York: Farrar, Straus & Giroux, 1967.   *Notebook 1967–1968*. New York: Farrar, Straus & Giroux, 1969; augmented edition as *Notebook*, New York: Farrar, Straus & Giroux, 1970.   *For Lizzie and Harriet*. New York: Farrar, Straus & Giroux, 1973.   *History*. New York: Farrar, Straus & Giroux, 1973.   *The Dolphin*. New York: Farrar, Straus & Giroux, 1973.   *Selected Poems*. New York: Farrar, Straus & Giroux, 1976.   *Day by Day*. New York: Farrar, Straus & Giroux, 1977.

Imitations, Translations, Adaptations

Imitations. New York: Farrar, Straus & Giroux, 1961.   *Phaedra* [Racine]. New York: Farrar, Straus & Giroux, 1961.   *The Old Glory*. New York: Farrar, Straus & Giroux, 1965; expanded edition, New York: Farrar, Straus & Giroux, 1968.   *The Voyage and Other Versions of Poems by Baudelaire*. New York: Farrar, Straus & Giroux, 1968.   *Prometheus Bound*. [Aeschylus]. New York: Farrar, Straus & Giroux, 1969.   *The Oresteia of Aeschylus*. New York: Farrar, Straus & Giroux, 1979.

Bibliographies

Axelrod, Steven Gould, and Helen Deese. *Robert Lowell: A Reference Guide*. Boston: G. K. Hall, 1982.   Edelstein, J. M. *Robert Lowell: A Checklist*. Detroit: Gale Research, 1973.   Mazzaro, Jerome. *The Achievement of Robert Lowell, 1939–1959*. Detroit: University of Detroit, 1960.

Critical Studies

Cooper, Philip. *The Autobiographical Myth of Robert Lowell*. Chapel Hill: University of North Carolina, 1970.   Cosgrave, Patrick. *The Public Poetry of Robert Lowell*. London: Golancz, 1970.   Crick, John. *Robert Lowell*. Barnes & Noble, 1974. Fein, Richard J. *Robert Lowell*. New York: Twayne, 1970.   London, Michael, and Robert Boyers, eds. *Robert Lowell: A Portrait of the Artist in His Time*. New York: David Lewis, 1970.   Martin, Jay. *Robert Lowell*. Minneapolis: University of Minnesota, 1970.   Martz, William J. *The Achievement of Robert Lowell*. Glenview, Ill.: Scott, Foresman, 1966.   Mazzaro, Jerome. *The Poetic Themes of Robert Lowell*. Ann Arbor: University of Michigan, 1965.   Mazzaro, Jerome, ed. *Profile of Robert*

Lowell. Columbus, Ohio: Charles E. Merrill, 1971.   Parkinson, Thomas, ed. *Robert Lowell: A Collection of Critical Essays.* Englewood Cliffs, N.J.: Prentice-Hall, 1968. Perloff, Marjorie. *The Poetic Art of Robert Lowell.* Ithaca, N.Y.: Cornell University, 1973.   Price, Jonathan, ed. *Critics on Robert Lowell.* Miami: University of Miami, 1974.   Raffel, Burton. *Robert Lowell.* New York: Ungar, 1981.   Rudman, Mark. *Robert Lowell: An Introduction to the Poetry.* New York: Columbia University, 1984.   Simpson, Louis. *A Revolution in Taste: Studies of Dylan Thomas, Allen Ginsberg, Sylvia Plath and Robert Lowell.* New York: Morrow, 1978.   Staples, Hugh B. *Robert Lowell: The First Twenty Years.* New York: Farrar, Straus & Giroux, 1962.   Vereen, Bell M. *Robert Lowell: Nihilist as Hero.* Cambridge: Harvard University, 1983.   Williamson, Alan. *Pity the Monsters: The Political Poetry of Robert Lowell.* New Haven: Yale University Press, 1974.   Yenser, Stephen, *Circle to Circle: The Poetry of Robert Lowell.* Berkeley: University of California, 1975.

JAMES MERRILL (1926)

James Merrill was born in New York City, attended Lawrenceville School, served in the U.S. Army, and graduated from Amherst College in 1947. Merrill's several awards for his poetry include the Bollingen Prize (1973), the Pulitzer Prize (1977), and the National Book Award (1967, 1979). In 1971 he was elected a member of the National Institute of Arts and Letters. Unlike most of his contemporaries, Merrill has not sought a professional teaching career; he generally divides his time between living in Greece and in Connecticut.

Most critics would agree that James Merrill's poetry has consistently reflected the influence of New Criticism and that his mentor certainly would be W. H. Auden rather than William Carlos Williams. Indeed, in Merrill's new long trilogy, Auden's spirit is Merrill's "guide." Clearly, Merrill is a masterful formalist whose manipulation of metrics and of sound—especially end rhymes—reveals the range of startling and subtle nuances in language in much the same way as Rothko unveils the nuances of color in painting. Even in what seem to be more personal poems, one is never quite sure whether the speaker is Merrill or a persona. Most of his poems are marked by a tone edged with a measure of ironic detachment that, in some literary circles—where irony is blasphemy and guts rule—might be considered indicative of high, albeit elegant, decadence.

When so many poets of this generation lead their readers into the bedlam of their tortured souls and the bedrooms of their monstrous marriages—and, indeed, into their very own and much-used beds—one emerges from the surroundings of James Merrill's poetry with the heady sense of having lingered in a rather rarified atmosphere. This is the physical, moral, and aesthetic world as perceived by Proust rather than by Baudelaire, by Henry James rather than by Walt Whitman. This is the world where, in Merrill's words, "Light into the olive entered / And was oil," an arena of human experience where it does seem that "the world beneath the world is brightening."

And yet Merrill's Weltanschauung and aesthetic seemingly always lead him—and us—to the very edge of chaos. Merrill's persona in "Laboratory Poem" knows that the heart must climb "through violence into exquisite disciplines." The handsome young man in "Charles on Fire" must view his own hand gloved in fire before the mirror reassures his beauty. And whatever entrances into immortality that art may offer, it leaves us *and* the artist with that unnerving realization that "the life it asks of us is a dog's life." Thus, if poetry, if speech "is but a mouth pressed / Lightly and humbly against the angel's hand," in a Rilkean attempt to impress the angel with the things of this world, it's distinctly possible that this very angel "does not want even these few lines written." In short, in a society where "Art, Public Spirit / Ignorance, Economics, Love of Self / Hatred of Self" are earnestly dedicated to "*sparing* us the worst" and just as earnestly *inspire* the worst, Merrill's poems stand on the edge of chaos, radiant attempts to survive its meanings—and our own.

Poetry

The Black Swan. Athens: Icaros, 1946.   *First Poems.* New York: Knopf, 1951. *Short Stories.* Pawlet, Vt.: Banyan Press, 1954.   *The Country of a Thousand Years of Peace and Other Poems.* New York: Knopf, 1959; revised edition, New York: Atheneum, 1970.   *Water Street.* New York: Atheneum, 1962.   *Nights and Days.* New York: Atheneum, 1966.   *The Fire Screen.* New York: Atheneum, 1969. *Braving the Elements.* New York: Atheneum, 1972.   *The Yellow Pages.* Cambridge, Mass.: Temple Bar, 1974. *Divine Comedies.* New York: Atheneum, 1976. *Mirabell: Books of Number.* New York: Atheneum, 1978.   *Scripts for the Pageant. New York: Atheneum, 1980.   From the First Nine: Poems 1946–1976.* New York: Atheneum, 1982.   *The Changing Light at Sandover: Including the Whole of The Book of Ephraim, Mirabell's Books of Number, Scripts for the Pageant and a New Coda, The Higher Keys.* New York: Atheneum, 1982.   *Late Settings.* New York: Atheneum, 1985.

Fiction

The Seraglio. New York: Knopf, 1957.   *The (Diblos) Notebook.* New York: Atheneum, 1965.

Critical Studies

Berger, Charles, and David Lehman, eds.   *Merrill: Studies in Criticism.* Ithaca: Cornell University, 1982.   Labrie, Ross. *James Merrill.* New York: Twayne, 1982. Moffett, Judith. *James Merrill: An Introduction to the Poetry.* New York: Columbia University, 1984.

W. S. MERWIN (1927)

W. S. Merwin was born in New York City and educated at Princeton. He was tutor to Robert Graves's son for a year, but—unlike most of his contemporaries—he has not had a teaching career. Since 1951 he has devoted most of his time to writing and poetry readings and to translating from French, Spanish, Latin, Portuguese, Greek, Chinese, and Japanese originals. He has lived in the United States, England, Mexico, southern France, and currently resides in Hawaii. In addition to the Pulitzer Prize in 1971 and the Shelley Memorial Award in 1974, he has received grants from the National Endowment for the Arts, the Rockefeller Foundation, the Academy of American Poets, the National Institute of Arts and Letters, and the Arts Council of Great Britain.

W. S. Merwin is one of the most prolific poets and poet-translators of his generation; he is among those contemporary poets whose talents were originally shaped by New Criticism and whose style has undergone a radical change in the course of his career. His early poems were elegant, controlled, symmetrical, and often concerned with myth and archetype—as the recent republication of his early work, *The First Four Books of Poems*, makes eminently clear. However, the appearance of *The Drunk in the Furnace* (1960) suggested a dissatisfaction with old techniques: his forms were looser; his language appeared less contrived and closer to the spoken word. Like other poets of the period, he too turned to family history and individual human suffering in search of larger, more immediate patterns of human experience.

However, Merwin's most radical departure—and most exciting style—appeared later only in *The Moving Target* (1963). Open and terse, these surrealistic poems—and most of the poems that Merwin has published since—are controlled not as much by a craftsman's delicate hand as by a powerful imagination. And they rise out of the depths of a more personal, sometimes enigmatic necessity. Merwin's aesthetics are clear in the statement that he wrote for *Naked Poetry* (edited by Stephen Berg and Robert Mezey): "In an age when time and technique encroach hourly, or appear to, on the source itself of poetry, it seems as though what is needed for any particular nebulous hope that may become a poem is not a manipulable, more or less predictably recurring pattern, but an unduplicatable resonance, something that would be like an echo except that it is repeating no sound. Something that always belonged to it: its sense and its conformation before it entered words."

Throughout his career, one of Merwin's dominant concerns has been death—or perhaps more specifically, extinction. The journey motif that critics have recognized in Merwin's poetry is emblematic of all life's motion toward death. However, in later poems, this concern doesn't necessarily focus on any sudden or cataclysmic end of life. Rather, it is more manifest in powerful and menacing shadows surrounding frail light, in sound struggling against the tyranny of silence, in the slow but seemingly inevitable transformation of all organic life into inert matter. And if Merwin agrees with Berryman that the individual has undertaken the biggest job of all—*son fin*—Merwin has also erected a powerful emblem of his vision in his poetic prose piece, "Tergvinder's Stone." In the presence of a mysterious, almost mystical stone in the middle of his living room and his life, Merwin's central character kneels in the darkness of the stone, converses with the stone, and even in the silence of the stone "knows that it is peace."

Poetry

A Mask for Janus. New Haven: Yale University, 1952.   *The Dancing Bears*. New Haven: Yale University, 1954.   *Green with Beasts*. New York: Knopf, 1956.   *The Drunk in the Furnace*. New York: Macmillan, 1960.   *The Moving Target*. New York: Atheneum, 1963.   *The Lice*. New York: Atheneum, 1967.   *Animae: Poems*. San Francisco: Kayak, 1969.   *The Carrier of Ladders*. New York: Atheneum, 1970. *Writings to an Unfinished Accompaniment*. New York: Atheneum, 1973.   *The First Four Books of Poems (A Mask for Janus, The Dancing Bears, Green with Beasts, The Drunk in the Furnace)*. New York: Atheneum, 1975.   *The Compass Flower*. New York: Atheneum, 1977.   *Finding the Islands*. San Francisco: North Point Press, 1982.   *Opening the Hand*. New York: Atheneum, 1983.

Translations: Poetry and Prose

The Poem of the Cid. New York: New American Library, 1959.   *The Satires of Perseus*. Bloomington: Indiana University, 1961.   *Spanish Ballads*. New York: Doubleday, 1961.   *The Life of Lazarillo de Tormes: His Fortunes and Adversities*. New York: Doubleday, 1962.   *The Song of Roland*. New York: Modern Library, 1963.   *Selected Translations 1948–1968*. New York: Atheneum, 1968. *Transparence of the World: Poems of Jean Follain*. New York: Atheneum, 1969. *Products of the Perfected Civilization: Selected Writings* [Sebastian Chamfort]. New York: Macmillan, 1969.   *Voices: Selected Writings of Antonio Porchia*. Chicago: Follett, 1969.   *Twenty Love Poems and A Song of Despair* [Pablo Neruda]. London: Cape, 1969.   *Chinese Figures: Second Series*. Mt. Horeb, Wis.: Perishable Press, 1971.   *Japanese Figures*. Santa Barbara: Unicorn, 1971.   *Asian Figures*. New York: Atheneum, 1972.   *Selected Poems of Osip Mandestam* (with Clarence Brown). New York: Atheneum, 1974.   *Iphigenia at Aulis* [Euripedes] (with George E. Dimmock, Jr.). New York: Oxford University, 1977.   *Vertical Poetry: Poems by Roberto Juarroz*. Santa Cruz: Kayak, 1977.   *Selected Translations 1968–1978*. New York: Atheneum, 1979.   *The Peacock's Egg: Love Poems from Ancient India* (with J. Moussaieff Masson). San Francisco: North Point, 1981.   *Four French Plays*. New York: Atheneum, 1984.   *From the Spanish Morning*. New York: Atheneum, 1984.

Prose: Fiction and Autobiography

The Miner's Pale Children. New York: Atheneum, 1970.   *Houses and Travellers*.
New York: Atheneum, 1977.   *Unframed Originals* (Autobiography). New York:
Atheneum, 1982.

FRANK O'HARA (1926–1966)

Before his untimely, accidental death on Fire Island, Frank O'Hara was
associate curator and then curator of the international program at the
Museum of Modern Art in New York and an editorial associate for *Art News*.
Born in Baltimore, O'Hara was educated at the New England Conservatory
of Music, Harvard, and the University of Michigan. He collaborated in
various projects involving poetry and the visual arts, and in 1956 was
awarded a Ford Fellowship for drama.

Before the publication of his *Collected Poems* (and the companion
volume, *Poems Retrieved*), Frank O'Hara was almost a closet-poet, the
product and hero of a pop-camp imagination whose seeming antipoems
were light and chatty, marked by a spontaneity, exuberance, and wit that
were characteristic of his contemporaries in the visual arts. His most
memorable poems, like the paintings of Oldenburg and Warhol, focused on
the all-too-obvious things of our urban and suburban world: hamburgers,
malts, cigarettes, instant coffee. Looming above that world were its own
godly artifacts: Lichtenstein's suprahuman heroes of the comic strips and
Warhol's movie stars. Their mythic proportions were — and continue to be —
the dimensions of contemporary human fantasies and dreams of
redemption. Moreover, in O'Hara's poems there is the stinging, if somewhat
hysterical, crackle of a melancholy comment on the absurdity of such hollow
rites.

While it may still be too early to assess the full range of O'Hara's total opus,
it's eminently clear that his scope and power as a poet extend far beyond the
circumscribed world of a merely campy and gay subculture. One leaves the
body of O'Hara's poetry — and his sense of what constitutes the identifiable
substance and quality of our communal experience — with a verbal-
emotional equivalent of Kandinsky's acute perception of "the particular
spiritual perfume of the triangle." One also leaves the existential world of
O'Hara's poems with a fuller understanding of the truth of Cocteau's
rejection of history: "J'ai une très mauvaise mémoire de l'avenir."

NOTES ON THE POETS

Poetry

A City Winter and Other Poems. New York: Tibor de Nagy Gallery, 1952. *Meditations in an Emergency.* New York: Grove, 1957. *Hartigan and Rivers with O'Hara: An Exhibition of Pictures, with Poems.* New York: Tibor de Nagy Gallery, 1959. *Second Avenue.* New York: Totem-Corinth, 1960. *Odes.* New York: Tiber Press, 1960. *Lunch Poems.* San Francisco: City Lights, 1964. *Love Poems: Tentative Title.* New York: Tibor de Nagy Gallery, 1965. *In Memory of My Feelings: A Selection of Poems.* Edited by Bill Berkson. New York: Museum of Modern Art, 1967. *Odes.* New York: Poets Press, 1969. *The Collected Poems of Frank O'Hara.* Edited by Donald Allen. New York: Knopf, 1971. *The Selected Poems of Frank O'Hara.* Edited by Donald Allen. New York: Knopf, 1974. *Hymns of St. Bridget* (with Bill Berkson). New York: Boke Press, 1974. *Poems Retrieved.* Edited by Donald Allen. Bolinas, Calif.: Grey Fox, 1977.

Prose

Jackson Pollack. New York: George Braziller, 1959. *A Frank O'Hara Miscellany.* Bolinas, Calif.: Grey Fox, 1974. *Art Chronicles 1954—1966.* New York: George Braziller, 1975.

Critical Study

Perloff, Marjorie. *Frank O'Hara: Poet Among Painters.* Austin: University of Texas, 1968.

Bibliography

Smith, Alexander. *Frank O'Hara: A Comprehensive Bibliography.* New York: Garland, 1977.

MARY OLIVER (1935)

Born in Cleveland and educated at Ohio State University and Vassar College, Mary Oliver has been visiting professor in creative writing and poet-in-residence at Case Western Reserve. She is also a member of the writing staff at the Fine Arts Work Center in Provincetown, Massachusetts, where she lives. Her awards include the Achievement Award from the American Academy and Institute of Arts and Letters, a Guggenheim Fellowship, the Alice Fay di Castagnola Award from the Poetry Society of America, and a creative writing fellowship from the Literature Program of the National Endowment for the Arts. In 1984 she was awarded the Pulitzer Prize for poetry.

Reading Mary Oliver's poems is to immerse oneself in a world of intense physical sensation made doubly acute by the emotional transformation which Oliver achieves while registering the impact of the physical world on the world of her feelings: the "icy kick" of water, "the small kingdoms" of birds and insects breathing in the dark, the fish at spawning time following "the fragrance spilling / from her old birth pond," "the crows, plump / As black rocks in the cold trees" in winter. Reminiscent of the poetry of Theodore Roethke, James Wright, and Emily Dickinson in the precise observations of the things of this world, Oliver's poems have a physical impact like "the dark thorns of the wild grapes / on the unsuspecting tongue."

Although somewhat ambiguous, that image of pleasure and pain is also central to Oliver's hard-earned vision profoundly accepting an essential tension between the polarities that define the boundaries of all experience — whether in the physical world, in the realm of human relationships, or in the self. There is great pleasure and beauty and joy in the poems of Mary Oliver; but there is also a commensurate (though muted) measure of pain resulting from the recognition of one's full awareness of those elements of the natural and human world which transport and transform us, giving us a glimpse of eternity, perhaps, or of some kind of immortality — a recognition that also gives us a fuller awareness of the world's, and of our own, mortality.

The acceptance of the hard truths of mortal existence is at the heart and boundaries of Mary Oliver's poems. If thrown into the water and told to sink or swim, what we learn isn't necessarily how to swim, but "How to put off, one by one, / Dreams and pity, love and grace, — / How to survive in any place." Art in itself is no escape. While the beauty of music may be a "lick of flame" that transports and transforms the audience, for the artist it is only a momentary stay against a dreary and petty diurnal reality, against "the duties of flesh and home," perhaps against "the knife at the throat," and in fact, against that very "death in the metronome." "To live in this world," Oliver reminds us, requires three measures of acceptance: "to love what is mortal; / to hold it / against your bones knowing / your own life depends on it; / and, when the time comes to let it go, / to let it go." If life, love, and work do not negate our mortality, then our acceptance of it may allow us to view death as a "floating away into / The life of the snow," and our daily deaths as repeated vanishings "into something better." In Mary Oliver's poems, such acceptance is epiphany.

Poetry

No Voyage and Other Poems. Boston: Houghton Mifflin, 1965. *The River Styx, Ohio and Other Poems.* New York: Harcourt Brace, 1972. *The Night Traveler.* Cleveland: Bits Press, 1978. *Sleeping in the Forest.* Athens, Ohio: Ohio Review, 1979. *Twelve Moons.* Boston: Little, Brown, 1979. *American Primitive.* Boston: Atlantic-Little, Brown, 1983.

CHARLES OLSON (1910–1970)

Charles Olson was born in Worcester, Massachusetts, educated at Wesleyan and Yale universities, and received his doctorate from Harvard. From 1951 to 1956, he was an instructor and rector at Black Mountain College in North Carolina where he worked with other artists and writers like Robert Creeley and Merce Cunningham. For varying periods of time, he also taught at Harvard, the State University of New York at Buffalo, and other universities. The recipient of two Guggenhiem Fellowships, he also received a grant from the Gren Foundation to study Mayan hieroglyphics. During much of his life, he resided in Gloucester, Massachusetts, the setting for many of his "Maximus Poems."

Clearly the most substantial theoretician and one of the most influential of the postmodernist poets, Charles Olson's criticism and speculations concerning the nature and structure of verse have become the basis for what is generally known as the *Projectivist School* in contemporary poetry. Olson's celebrated essay, "Projective Verse," originally published in 1950, articulates some of his basic attitudes toward poetry and remains one of the central documents of the "revolution" that took place in American poetry after 1945.

Complex and often refusing to yield specific meaning, "Projective Verse" is no easy essay to summarize; but some of its central ideas are worth noting. Olson's premise is that if poetry "is to be of *essential* use," it must "catch up and put into itself certain laws and possibilities of the breath, of the breathing of the man who writes, as well as of his listenings." And he posits "open" or "field composition" as an alternative to non-Projective verse with its inherited line, its stanzas, and its overall traditional form. According to Olson, field or open composition includes (1) *kinetics*: "A poem is energy transferred from where the poet got it . . . by way of the poem itself to . . . the reader"; (2) *principle*: "Form is never more than an extension of content" (as rephrased by Robert Creeley); and (3) *process*: "One perception must immediately and directly lead to a further perception." Although various poets have cited Olson as their mentor, it may well be that he is the only genuine practitioner of his own theories.

Charles Olson's major work, no doubt, is his long series of "Maximus Poems," the first ten of which were originally published in 1953. As various critics have noted, one of the characteristics of this series is Olson's delicate and all-encompassing sense of place—the vibrant details of an ever-changing landscape. But equally present are Olson's sweeping sense of history and his vast range of knowledge, which have caused some critics to compare the Maximus Poems to Pound's Cantos. From an entirely different point of view, Olson's central character in the Maximus Poems also might be compared with Henry Pussycat in John Berryman's Dream Songs.

Poetry

Y & X. Washington, D.C.: Black Sun, 1948. *In Cold Hell, in Thicket.* Palma, Mallorca: Divers, 1953; reprint, San Francisco: Four Seasons, 1967. *The Maximus Poems 1–10.* Stuttgart, Germany: Jonathan Williams, 1953. *The Maximus Poems 11–22.* Stuttgart, Germany: Jonathan Williams, 1956. *O'Ryan 2 4 6 8 10.* San Francisco: White Rabbit, 1958; expanded edition as *O'Ryan 12345678910,* 1965. *The Maximus Poems.* New York: Jargon-Corinth, 1960. *The Distances: Poems.* New York: Grove, 1960. *West.* London: Cape Goliard, 1966. *The Maximus Poems IV, V, VI.* New York: Grossman, 1968. *Archaeologist of Morning: The Collected Poems Outside the Maximus Series.* New York: Grossman, 1971. *The Maximus Poems, Volume Three.* Edited by Charles Boer and George F. Butterick. New York: Grossman, 1975. *Spearmint and Rosemary.* Berkeley: Turtle Island, 1975. *Some Early Poems.* Iowa City: Windhover Press, 1978. *The Maximus Poems.* Edited by George F. Butterick. Berkeley: University of California, 1983.

Poetry and Prose

Charles Olson Reading at Berkeley. Transcribed by Zoe Brown. San Francisco: Coyote, 1966. *Selected Writings of Charles Olson.* Edited by Robert Creeley. New York: New Directions, 1967. *Causal Mythology.* San Francisco: Four Seasons, 1969. *Poetry & Truth: The Beloit Lectures and Poems.* Transcribed and edited by George F. Butterick. San Francisco: Four Seasons, 1971. *Mythologos: The Collected Lectures & Interviews.* Volume I. Edited by George F. Butterick. Bolinas, Calif.: Four Seasons, 1978. *Mythologos: The Collected Lectures & Interviews.* Volume II. Edited by George F. Butterick. Bolinas, Calif.: Four Seasons, 1979.

Criticism and Other Prose

Call Me Ishmael: A Study of Melville. New York: Reynal and Hitchcock, 1947; reprint, San Francisco: City Lights, 1967. *Projective Verse.* New York: Totem, 1959. *Proprioception.* San Francisco: Four Seasons, 1965. *The Human Universe and Other Essays.* Edited by Donald Allen. New York: Grove, 1967. *The Special View of History.* Edited by Ann Charters. Berkeley: Oyez, 1970. *Additional Prose: A Bibliography on America, Proprioception, and Other Notes and Essays.* Edited by George F. Butterick. Bolinas, Calif.: Four Seasons, 1974. *The Post Office: A Memoir to His Father.* Bolinas, Calif.: Grey Fox, 1974. *Charles Olson & Ezra Pound: An Encounter at St. Elizabeths.* Edited by Catherine Seelye. New York: Grossman, 1975. *The Fiery Hunt and Other Plays.* Bolinas, Calif.: Four Seasons, 1977.

Correspondence

The Mayan Letters. Edited by Robert Creeley. Palma, Mallorca: Divers Press, 1953; reprint, New York: Grossman, 1968.   *Letters for Origin 1950–1956.* Edited by Albert Glover. New York: Grossman, 1970.   *Charles Olson and Robert Creeley: The Complete Correspondence.* Volumes I–. Edited by George Butterick. Santa Barbara: Black Sparrow, 1980–.

Bibliography

Butterick, George F., and Albert Glover. *A Bibliography of Works by Charles Olson.* New York: Phoenix Book Shop, 1967.

Critical Studies

Boer, Charles. *Charles Olson in Connecticut.* Chicago: Swallow, 1975.   Butterick, George F. *Guide to The Maximus Poems of Charles Olson.* Berkeley: University of California, 1978.   Charters, Ann. *Olson/Melville: A Study in Affinity.* Berkeley: Oyez, 1968.   Christensen, Paul. *Charles Olson: Call Him Ishmael.* Austin: University of Texas, 1978.   Paul, Sherman. *Olson's Push: Origin, Black Mountain and Recent American Poetry.* Baton Rouge: Louisiana State University, 1978.   Von Hallberg, Robert. *Charles Olson: The Scholar's Work.* Cambridge: Harvard University, 1978.   Byrd, Don. *Charles Olson's "Maximus."* Urbana: University of Illinois, 1980. Cech, John. *Charles Olson and Edward Dahlberg: A Portrait of a Friendship.* Victoria, B.C.: University of Victoria, 1982.   Merrill, Thomas F. *The Poetry of Charles Olson: A Primer.* Newark: University of Delaware, 1982.

MARGE PIERCY (1936)

Marge Piercy was born in Detroit, Michigan. She received an A.B. from the University of Michigan and an M.A. from Northwestern University. One of the few writers of her generation who has chosen not to be a professional university teacher on a full-time basis, Piercy nevertheless has given readings and conducted workshops in more than 110 colleges and universities throughout the country. Periodically, she also has been visiting professor or poet-in-residence at such institutions as the University of Kansas, the Fine Arts Work Center (in Provincetown, Massachusetts), and the Women's Writers Conference at Cazenovia College, and she has held the Butler Chair of Letters at the State University of New York at Buffalo. Her awards include two Borestone Mountain Poetry Awards, a fellowship from the Literature Program of the National Endowment for the Arts, and the Literature Award from the (Massachusetts) Governor's Commission on the Status of Women.

That Marge Piercy works primarily with organic form, rather than with stricter and external traditional forms, is certainly no accident and perhaps not entirely a matter of conscious choice, either; rather, it is more probably the result of aesthetic necessity growing out of a deeply rooted philosophical vision. Thus, the form (and sometimes even the shape) of Piercy's successful poems is recognizably informed by their subject matter and theme. For example, on the surface "A Work of Artifice" is about the way in which the limbs of the traditional Japanese bonzai tree are repeatedly pruned so that a full-grown bonzai is only nine inches high (rather than achieving its natural height of eighty feet); the form and effectiveness of this poem also result in part from the manner in which the lines, syntax, and tone are appropriately "clipped."

The subjects of many of Marge Piercy's poems are objects and experiences in the natural world, as well as love, sex, and day-to-day human relationships. A central theme in her work is the powerful tension between one's inner identity and the force of outer (personal, social, and cultural) pressures. Such is the age-old tension between essence and existence as the determining factors of all life. And if one's essence is the primary determination of identity and growth, then the parameters within which one develops that identity and nurtures that growth are severely limited.

Piercy is especially concerned with the extent to which the sexual identity and individual personality of a woman in contemporary society is in conflict with those outer forces attempting to determine who and what she is. Of course, that dichotomy is at the heart of the feminist vision; but Piercy's work also attempts to reconcile even more powerful philosophical conflicts over whether *meaning* or *purpose* is the ultimate goal of human existence and activity. (Perhaps it is worth noting that in our culture the conflict between meaning and purpose is also at the root of the conflict between the sciences and the humanities.) In her poems Marge Piercy repeatedly affirms the necessity for the self to be in conflict with those outer forces intent on shaping it into something other than it is or wants to be. However, while recognizing the symbiotic relationship between the self and nature, in a variety of ways she also discovers the means to reaffirm the need for both meaning *and* purpose. In short, her poems repeatedly assert that the genuine meaning of the self and of all natural and human creation is "to be of use." She reminds us that Greek amphoras and Hopi vases are beautiful objects now kept in museums, "but you know they were made to be used. / The pitcher cries for water to carry / and a person for work that is real." Immersing herself and her readers in the physical substance and metaphysical serenity of such a reconciliation, Piercy also can periodically offer moments of enlightened discovery: "You are learning to live in circles / as well as straight lines."

Poetry

Breaking Camp. Middletown: Wesleyan, 1968. *Hard Loving*. Middletown: Wesleyan, 1969. *A Work of Artifice*. Detroit: Red Hanrahan, 1970. *4-Telling* (with others). Trumansburg, N.Y.: Crossing, 1971. *When the Drought Broke*. Santa Barbara: Unicorn, 1971. *To Be of Use*. New York: Doubleday, 1973. *Living in the Open*. New York: Knopf, 1976. *The Twelve-Spoked Wheel Flashing*. New York: Knopf, 1978. *The Moon Is Always Female*. New York: Knopf, 1980. *Circles on the Water: Selected Poems*. New York: Knopf, 1982. *Stone, Paper, Knife*. New York: Knopf, 1983.

Fiction

Going Down Fast. New York: Simon and Schuster, 1969. *Dance the Eagle to Sleep*. New York: Doubleday, 1970. *Small Changes*. New York: Doubleday, 1973. *Woman on the Edge of Time*. New York: Knopf, 1976. *The High Cost of Living*. New York: Harper and Row, 1978. *Vida*. New York: Summit, 1979. *Braided Lives*. New York: Knopf, 1983.

Drama

The Last White Class (with Ira Wood). Trumansburg, N.Y.: Crossing, 1979.

Criticism

Parti-Colored Blocks for a Quilt. Ann Arbor: University of Michigan, 1983.

SYLVIA PLATH (1932–1963)

A native of Boston and a graduate of Smith College, in 1955 Sylvia Plath won a Fulbright Scholarship to Newnham College, Cambridge. While in England, she met and married the British poet, Ted Hughes. After she taught for a year at Smith (1957–58), the couple returned to England where in 1960 she published her first book of poems and subsequently completed her novel, *The Bell Jar*. On February 11, 1963, Sylvia Plath committed suicide.

A friend of Anne Sexton and one of Robert Lowell's students, Sylvia Plath wrote poems that were intended to sound and to feel brutally personal, almost unbearably painful. Her poems are not merely *about* acute mental and emotional suffering; their very structure—the controlled flow of images, the insistent appositives—draws the reader fully into that suffering. Indeed, her later poems are so well crafted that some critics have argued, wrong-headedly, that she seemed engaged in "a murderous art"—that after writing such frighteningly honest and painfully personal poems, her suicide was virtually inevitable. As a *critical premise*, such an argument is utter nonsense, its absurdity manifestly clear when it is transferred to another artist and his or her work. If Sylvia Plath virtually had no choice but to commit suicide after writing the poems in *Ariel*, then what inevitable choice did someone like Melville have after writing *Moby Dick*?

What makes Sylvia Plath interesting as a poet is not primarily her ostensible subject matter and tone; rather, the success of the poems depends largely on her precision of observation, imagination, and language —as well as on the mastery of her craftsmanship. For example, the onion simile in "Cut" not only accurately describes the swirls of a thumb print but also serves as the entire poem's controlling metaphor. Moreover, in poems like "Cut" and "Lady Lazarus," or even in a celebrated poem like "Daddy," there is also a strong measure of wit and humor—albeit black—often conveyed through resuscitated clichés that manage to rescue the poems from pathos.

On more than one occasion, Sylvia Plath insisted that even the most personal poetry cannot be merely a *cri de coeur*; it has to be informed by and to participate in a greater historical drama. Her own poems participate fully in the vibrant Puritan tradition, not only through her preoccupation with evil (which is utterly distinct from personal suffering) but also through her metaphysical and emblematic technique. They also occur against a constant historical drama, especially the contemporary phenomenon of Nazi Germany out of which she fabricates a modern myth. In short, the pain, the suffering, the fine edge of madness—all are ultimately crafted and controlled by the poet's reasoned and careful hand flashing a measure of genius.

Poetry

The Colossus. New York: Knopf, 1962.   *Uncollected Poems.* London: Turret, 1965. *Ariel.* New York: Harper & Row, 1966.   *Crossing the Water: Transitional Poems.* New York: Harper & Row, 1971.   *Crystal Gazer and Other Poems.* London: Rainbow, 1971.   *Lyonesse: Poems.* London: Rainbow, 1971.   *Winter Trees.* New York: Harper & Row, 1972.   *The Collected Poems: Sylvia Plath.* Edited by Ted Hughes. New York: Harper & Row, 1981.   *Stings* (original drafts of the poem in facsimile with an essay by Susan R. Van Dyne). Northampton, Mass.: Smith College Library, 1982.

Fiction and Other Prose

The Bell Jar (novel written under pseudonym of Victoria Lucas). London: Heinneman, 1963; as Sylvia Plath, New York: Harper & Row, 1971.   *Letters Home*. Edited by Aurelia S. Plath. New York: Harper & Row, 1975.   *Johnny Panic and the Bible of Dreams: Short Stories, Prose, and Diary Excerpts*. Edited by Ted Hughes. New York: Harper & Row, 1979.   *The Journals of Sylvia Plath*. Edited by Frances McCullough. New York: Dial, 1982.

Bibliography

Land, Gary, and Maria Stevens. *Sylvia Plath*. Metuchen, N.J.: Scarecrow Press, 1978.

Critical and Biographical Studies

Aird, Eileen. *Sylvia Plath: Her Life and Work*. New York: Harper & Row, 1973. Bundtzen, Lydia K. *Plath's Incarnations: Woman and the Creative Process*. Ann Arbor: University of Michigan, 1983.   Butscher, Edward. *Sylvia Plath: Method and Madness*. New York: The Seabury, 1976.   Holbrook, David. *Sylvia Plath: Poetry and Existence*. New York: Humanities Press, 1976.   Kroll, Judith. *Chapters in a Mythology: The Poetry of Sylvia Plath*. New York: Harper & Row, 1976.   Lane, Gary, ed. *Sylvia Plath: New Views on the Poetry*. Baltimore: Johns Hopkins University, 1979.   Newman, Charles, ed. *The Art of Sylvia Plath*. Bloomington: Indiana University, 1971.   Rosenblatt, Jon. *Sylvia Plath: The Poetry of Initiation*. Durham: North Carolina University, 1979.   Simpson, Louis. *A Revolution in Taste: Studies of Dylan Thomas, Allen Ginsberg, Robert Lowell and Sylvia Plath*. New York: Morrow, 1978.   Steiner, Nancy Hunter. *A Closer Look at Ariel: A Memory of Sylvia Plath*. New York: Harper's, 1973.   Uroff, Margaret Dickie. *Sylvia Plath and Ted Hughes*. Urbana: University of Illinois, 1979.

ADRIENNE RICH (1929)

Adrienne Rich's first book of poems won the Yale Younger Poets competition while she was completing her undergraduate studies at Radcliffe. She has taught at Brandeis, Swarthmore, Columbia, Harvard, Rutgers, and City College of New York. Rich's many honors include awards from the American Institute of Arts and Letters, the Guggenheim and Ingram Merrill Foundations, and a commission from the Bollingen Foundation for the translation of Dutch poetry. In 1974 Adrienne Rich and Allen Ginsberg were cowinners of the National Book Award for Poetry. Rich rejected her share as a personal award, but in a statement written by herself and the two other women nominated that year, she accepted the award in the name of all women.

Adrienne Rich has described her more recent poems as "a coming-home to the darkest and richest source of my poetry: sex, sexuality, sexual wounds, sexual identity, sexual politics: many names for pieces of one whole. I feel [this poetry] continues the work I've been trying to do—breaking down the artificial barriers between private and public, between Vietnam and the lovers' bed, between the deepest images we carry out of our dreams and the most daylight events 'out in the world.' This is the intention and longing behind everything I write."

Sexual identity and its profound political implications are indeed among the substantial sources of Adrienne Rich's more recent work, especially in her courageous and beautiful sequence of love poems addressed to another woman—a theme that reappears in *The Dream of a Common Language*. Moreover, even as she speaks about and for women, her poetry is informed by a vigorous intelligence that transcends any unilateral sense of sexuality and politics. At its best, Rich's poetry reaches beyond the limited periphery of any "movement" to become at once a profoundly personal statement forged into a powerful description of our common condition.

If some of Adrienne Rich's poems can be read as a "diving into the wreck," it is crucial to realize that her purpose is not only "to see the damage that was done" but also to catch a glimpse of "the treasures that prevail." Like the astronomer in "Planetarium," she is "a woman trying to translate pulsations / into images," not only for their own sake, not only for her own sake, but "for the relief of the body / and the reconstruction of the mind." Meanwhile, having found the courage to utter, "I choose to love this time for once / with all my intelligence," she also can assert and demonstrate "*a whole new poetry beginning here.*"

Poetry

A Change of World. New Haven: Yale University, 1951.   The Diamond Cutters. New York: Harper & Brothers, 1955.   Snapshots of a Daughter-in-Law: Poems 1954–1962.   New York: Harper & Row, 1963; revised edition, New York: Norton, 1967.   Necessities of Life: Poems 1962–1965. New York: Norton, 1966.   Leaflets: Poems 1965–1968. New York: Norton, 1969.   The Will to Change: Poems 1968–1970. New York: Norton, 1971.   Diving into the Wreck: Poems 1971–1972. New York: Norton, 1973.   Poems: Selected and New, 1950–1974. New York: Norton, 1975.   Twenty-One Love Poems. Emeryville, Calif.: Effie's Press, 1976. The Dream of a Common Language: Poems 1974–1977. New York: Norton, 1978. A Wild Patience Has Taken Me This Far: Poems 1978–1981. New York: Norton, 1981. Sources. Woodside, Calif.: Heyeck, 1983.   The Fact of a Doorframe: Poems Selected and New, 1950–1984. New York: Norton, 1985.

Prose

Of Woman Born: Motherhood as Experience and Institution. New York: Norton, 1976. *On Lies, Secrets and Silence: Selected Prose 1966–1978.* New York: Norton, 1979. *Compulsory Heterosexuality and Lesbian Experience.* Denver: Antelope, 1982. *Women and Honor: Some Notes on Lying.* Pittsburgh: Motheroot, 1982.

Critical Edition

Adrienne Rich's Poetry. Selected and edited by Barbara Charlesworth Gelpi and Albert Gelpi. New York: Norton, 1975.

Critical Studies

Cooper, Jane Roberta. *Reading Adrienne Rich: Reviews and Re-visions, 1951–81.* Ann Arbor: University of Michigan, 1984. Martin, Wendy. *An American Triptych: Anne Bradstreet, Emily Dickinson, and Adrienne Rich.* Chapel Hill: University of North Carolina, 1983.

THEODORE ROETHKE (1908–1963)

Theodore Roethke was born in Saginaw, Michigan. The son of a florist, he received a bachelor's and a master's degree from the University of Michigan. He taught at Lafayette College (where he was also tennis coach and director of public relations), Michigan State, Pennsylvania State, Bennington, and the University of Washington where, after fifteen years of teaching and having received every major literary award in this country, he was eventually appointed poet-in-residence in 1962. Roethke's awards included two Guggenheim Fellowships, the Pulitzer Prize in 1954, both the National Book Award and the Bollingen Prize in 1958, and the National Book Award again in 1965, posthumously.

In his notebooks, Roethke repeatedly insisted on—and demonstrated with incredible brilliance—the crucial need for the poet to *look*, to be a good reporter, and to record even the most minute details of the physical world. His poems reflect not only attention to but also reverence for the glory and terror of the physical world: "Hair on a narrow wrist bone." But Roethke also insisted that it is not enough just to look and report; the poet also must learn: "It's the poet's business to be more, not less, than a man."

The range of Roethke's poems amply demonstrates his own dictum. In addition to his often masterful control of form, his poems are marked by a precise observation of natural phenomena and include a gentle, lilting humor or ironic eroticism, a quiet horror in the face of an inevitable annihilation, and a contrapuntal tension between existential despair and the hope for transcendence. If throughout much of his life Roethke was a man who walked the void, his poems are finally a prayer and an affirmation that, although the "dark comes down on what we do," the human spirit finally cannot be overwhelmed by time.

Poetry

Open House. New York: Knopf, 1941.   *The Lost Son and Other Poems.* New York: Doubleday, 1948.   *Praise to the End!* New York: Doubleday, 1951.   *The Waking: Poems 1933–1953.* New York: Doubleday, 1953.   *Words for the Wind: The Collected Verse of Theodore Roethke.* New York: Doubleday, 1958.   *Sequence, Sometimes Metaphysical.* Iowa City: Stonewall Press, 1963.   *The Far Field.* New York: Doubleday, 1964.   *The Collected Poems of Theodore Roethke.* New York: Doubleday, 1966.

Prose and Other Poetry

On the Poet and His Craft: Selected Prose of Theodore Roethke. Edited by Ralph J. Mills, Jr. Seattle: University of Washington, 1965.   *Selected Letters of Theodore Roethke.* Edited by Ralph J. Mills, Jr. Seattle: University of Washington, 1968.   *Straw for the Fire: From the Notebooks of Theodore Roethke.* Selected and arranged by David Wagoner. New York: Doubleday, 1972.

Bibliographies

Lane, Gary. *A Concordance to the Poems of Theodore Roethke.* Metuchen, N.J.: Scarecrow, 1972.   McLeod, James. *Roethke: A Manuscript Checklist.* Kent, Ohio: Kent State University, 1971.   McLeod, James. *Roethke: A Bibliography.* Kent, Ohio.: Kent State University, 1972.

Critical and Biographical Studies

Blessing, Richard. *Roethke's Dynamism: Vision and Technique.* Seattle: University of Washington, 1974.   Bowers, Neal. *Theodore Roethke: The Journey from I to Otherwise.* Columbia: University of Missouri, 1983.   Heyen, William, ed. *Profile of Theodore Roethke.* Columbus, Ohio: Charles E. Merrill, 1970.   LaBelle, Jennijoy. *The Echoing World of Theodore Roethke.* Princeton: Princeton University, 1976. Malkoff, Karl. *Theodore Roethke: An Introduction to the Poetry.* New York: Columbia

University, 1966. Martz, William J. *The Achievement of Theodore Roethke*. Glenview, Ill.: Scott, Foresman, 1966. Mills, Ralph J., Jr. *Theodore Roethke*. Minneapolis: University of Minnesota, 1963. Parini, Jay. *Theodore Roethke: An American Romantic*. Amherst: University of Massachusetts, 1979. Scott, Nathan A. *The Wild Prayer of Longing: Poetry and the Sacred*. New Haven: Yale University, 1971. Seager, Allan. *The Glass House: The Life of Theodore Roethke*. New York: McGraw-Hill, 1968. Stein, Arnold, ed. *Theodore Roethke: Essays on the Poetry*. Seattle: University of Washington, 1965. Sullivan, Rosemary. *Theodore Roethke: The Garden Master*. Seattle: University of Washington, 1974. Wolf, George. *Theodore Roethke*. Boston: Twayne, 1981.

ANNE SEXTON (1928–1974)

Anne Sexton was born in Newton, Massachusetts. According to the short autobiographical note she wrote for *A Controversy of Poets*, Anne Sexton received "no visible education." However, with Sylvia Plath and George Starbuck, she did attend seminars by Robert Lowell at Boston University; she participated in a summer seminar taught by W. D. Snodgrass at Antioch College; and from 1961 to 1963, she was a scholar at the Radcliffe Institute. In addition to her several books of poetry, she was coauthor with Maxine Kumin of three children's books. Her many awards included fellowships from the American Academy of Arts and Letters, the Radcliffe Institute, and the Ford Foundation. In 1967 she was awarded the Pulitzer Prize; in 1968 she was elected a fellow of the Royal Society of Literature in London. On October 4, 1974, Anne Sexton committed suicide.

Possibly the most famous of the personal-confessional poets, Anne Sexton also probably confessed to more than any of her contemporaries, recreating experiences with unabashed, almost embarrassing honesty. Indeed, it is also probable that she "confessed" to a number of events that she simply invented. In "With Mercy for the Greedy" she wrote: "I was born / doing reference work in sin, and born / confessing it." Like other confessional Puritans, she did just that. But in various interviews, she also insisted that poetry is as much fabrication as it is confession—that even the most brutal truth is shaped by imagination's energy and the artisan's hand. Moreover, doing research in sin, by necessity, must involve a commensurate search for grace, for God. That combination, for Sexton, was absolute—and as risky as a poker game.

Sexton also was a precursor of the now celebrated cause of women's liberation. When it wasn't fashionable for women to write poems about being a woman, she wrote them—openly, unashamedly, and without resorting to political rhetoric. She knew all along that the victimized woman is "misunderstood" and "not a woman, quite." But, like Hester Prynne, the first liberated woman in American literature, Sexton also knew that a relationship between a man and woman could make them gods. And she knew that she could be the ultimate survivor: "A woman like that is not ashamed to die."

Like Sylvia Plath and John Berryman, Anne Sexton chose the moment of her death. But before doing so—as Maxine Kumin has reported—she found the signs of grace and hope spelled out on her typewriter keys. Sexton knew full well that, regardless of how painful it might seem, each poem is an affirmation and celebration of life—as is all poetry.

Poetry

To Bedlam and Part Way Back. Boston: Houghton Mifflin, 1960.   *All My Pretty Ones.* Boston: Houghton Mifflin, 1962.   *Live or Die.* Boston: Houghton Mifflin, 1966.   *Love Poems.* Boston: Houghton Mifflin, 1969.   *Transformations.* Boston: Houghton Mifflin, 1971.   *The Book of Folly.* Boston: Houghton Mifflin, 1972. *The Death Notebooks.* Boston: Houghton Mifflin, 1974.   *The Awful Rowing Toward God.* Boston: Houghton Mifflin, 1975.   *45 Mercy Street.* Edited by Linda Gray Sexton. Boston: Houghton Mifflin, 1976.   *Words for Dr. Y: Uncollected Poems with Three Stories.* Edited by Linda Gray Sexton. Boston: Houghton Mifflin, 1978.   *Anne Sexton: The Complete Poems.* Edited by Linda Gray Sexton. With a Foreword by Maxine Kumin. Boston: Houghton Mifflin, 1981.

Prose

Anne Sexton: A Self-Portrait in Letters. Edited by Linda Gray Sexton and Lois Ames. Boston: Houghton Mifflin, 1977.

Critical Study

McClatchy, J. D., ed. *Anne Sexton: The Artist and Her Critics.* Bloomington: Indiana University, 1978.

LOUIS SIMPSON (1923)

Educated at Murro College (Jamaica, West Indies) and at Columbia where he received his doctorate, Louis Simpson has taught at Columbia and the University of California at Berkeley; he is currently professor of English at the State University of New York at Stony Brook. With

Donald Hall and Robert Pack, he edited the celebrated anthology *New Poets of England and America* (1957) and he is the author and editor of *An Introduction to Poetry* (St. Martin's Press, 1967). He has received the Rome Fellowship of the American Academy of Arts and Letters, a *Hudson Review* Fellowship, a Guggenheim Fellowship, and the Pulitzer Prize for poetry in 1964.

Like many other poets of his generation, Simpson began his poetic career as a formalist and gradually worked toward a verse in which content primarily determines form. In the process, his own language has become increasingly natural and closer to the colloquial idiom of American speech—a language "closely related to the language in which men actually think and speak." At the same time, both his language and his view of the American experience—the root source of much of his poetry —have retained an educated and literate edge that inform his poems with a fully conscious sense of history and tradition.

Reading Louis Simpson's poetry, one might be reminded of Robert Frost's famous aphorism about his lover's quarrel with the world. No less a lover, Simpson's quarrel is more specifically with America. It is an ongoing struggle to come to grips with the pathetic or tragic failure of the American dream and myth—especially as announced by Whitman. "Where are you, Walt? / The Open Road goes to the used-car lot," he says in "Walt Whitman at Bear Mountain." The open road also leads to the suburbs where, it seems, "You were born to waste your life." Simpson's grief is further intensified by his realization that the American dream has been perverted into a weapon capable of destroying not only supposed enemies but also America itself, which has become a foreign country where people speak a language that is strange even to themselves. "And yet there is also happiness. / Happiness . . ." A discovery of a music, even if it is "made entirely of silence."

Poetry

The Arrivistes: Poems 1940–1949. New York: Fine Editions Press, 1949. *Good News of Death and Other Poems.* In *Poets of Today II.* New York: Scribner's, 1955. *A Dream of Governors.* Middletown: Wesleyan, 1959. *At the End of the Open Road.* Middletown: Wesleyan, 1963. *Selected Poems.* New York: Harcourt, Brace & World, 1965. *Adventures of the Letter I.* New York: Harper & Row, 1971. *Searching for the Ox.* New York: Morrow, 1976. *Armidale.* Brockport, N.Y.: BOA Editions, 1980. *Caviare at the Funeral.* New York: Franklin Watts, 1980. *The Best Hour of the Night.* New York: Ticknor & Fields, 1983. *People Live Here: Selected Poems 1949–1983.* Brockport, N.Y.: BOA Editions, 1983.

Criticism and Other Prose

James Hogg: A Critical Study. New York: St. Martin's, 1962. *Riverside Drive* (novel). New York: Atheneum, 1962. *North of Jamaica* (autobiography). New York: Harper & Row, 1972. *Three on a Tower: The Lives and Works of Ezra Pound, T. S. Eliot and William Carlos Williams.* New York: Morrow, 1975. *A Revolution in Taste: Studies of Dylan Thomas, Allen Ginsberg, Sylvia Plath and Robert Lowell.* New York: Macmillan, 1978. *A Company of Poets.* Ann Arbor: University of Michigan, 1981.

Critical Studies

Lensing, George S., and Ronald Moran. *Four Poets and the Emotive Imagination: Robert Bly, James Wright, Louis Simpson and William Stafford.* Baton Rouge: Louisiana State University, 1976. Moran, Ronald. *Louis Simpson.* New York: Twayne, 1972. Roberson, William. *Louis Simpson: A Reference Guide.* Boston: G. K. Hall, 1982.

W. D. SNODGRASS (1926)

Born in Wilkinsburg, Pennsylvania, and educated at Geneva College and at the University of Iowa, W. D. Snodgrass has taught at the University of Rochester, Wayne State, Syracuse, and Old Dominion; he is currently a professor of English at the University of Delaware. He has received fellowships from the Guggenheim and Ingram Merrill foundations, the Academy of American Poets, and the National Institute of Arts and Letters, as well as from the National Endowment for the Arts. His first book of poems won the Pulitzer Prize in 1960.

Until recently W. D. Snodgrass has been known primarily as a personal-confessional poet; indeed, it's possible that he was primarily responsible for the emergence of that mode of poetry in the late fifties and early sixties. Unlike Lowell, Plath, and Sexton, Snodgrass made poetry not out of madness and sensationally violent suffering but rather out of the daily neuroses and everyday failures of a man—a husband, father, and teacher. Snodgrass also saw such domestic suffering as occurring against a backdrop of a more universal suffering inherent in the whole of human experience. In "Heart's Needle," he stated *and* demonstrated: "We need the landscape to repeat us." Snodgrass also shared that fundamental concern of his generation announced by Albert Camus: "There is but one truly serious philosophical problem, and that is suicide." In "April Inventory," he wrote:

"I have not learned how often I / Can win, can love, but choose to die."

Although noted for their candor, Snodgrass's early poems were also controlled by an unmistakable sense of irony, directed by a highly literate imagination shaped by the New Critics, and organized by a consciously formal craftsmanship. Consequently, Snodgrass achieves a good measure of distance between himself as subject and himself as poem; thus the speaker of a "personal" Snodgrass poem often sounds more like a personal-confessional "persona."

In any case, little in Snodgrass's early poetry foreshadowed the appearance of *The Führer Bunker*. A cycle of dramatic monologues, these poems are spoken by leading figures of the Nazi regime during the last days of the Third Reich—including Albert Speer, Martin Bormann, Joseph Goebbels, Magda Goebbels, Eva Braun, and Adolf Hitler. Displaying an even more powerful range of dazzling craftsmanship in *The Führer Bunker*—which unfolds like a modern-day *Inferno*—Snodgrass zeros in on the historical and moral landscape that modern humankind seems intent or fated to repeat. The power and the horror of this cycle do not depend on what Snodgrass has to say about the historical figures and events *per se*; he knows all too well that there is little that can be said. Rather, the emotional and moral impact of this cycle—that promises to be one of the truly great achievements of post-1945 American poetry—emerges out of the fact that, like the dark and suffering creatures Dante encountered in hell, the personages in this Nazi *Götterdämmerung* are not the monsters we have met in the history books. They are all too unmistakably recognizable, all too unmistakably human.

Poetry

Heart's Needle. New York: Knopf, 1959.   *After Experience*. New York: Harper & Row, 1968.   *Remains* [published under pseudonym, S. S. Gardons]. Mt. Horeb, Wis.: Perishable Press, 1970.   *The Führer Bunker: A Cycle of Poems in Progress*. Brockport, N.Y.: BOA Editions, 1977.   *If Birds Build with Your Hair*. New York: Nadja, 1979.   *Belladonna*. Cumberland, Iowa: Pterodactyl Press, 1984.   *Remains*. Revised, trade paperback edition. Brockport, N.Y.: BOA Editions, 1984.

Translations: Poetry

Gallows Songs [Christian Morgenstern] (translated with Lore Segal). Ann Arbor: University of Michigan, 1967.   *Six Troubadour Songs*. Providence, R.I.: Burning Deck, 1977.   *Traditional Hungarian Songs*. Newark, Vt.: Janus, 1978; printed for Charles Seluzicki, Poetry Bookseller, Baltimore, Md.   *Six Minnesinger Songs*. Providence, R.I.: Burning Deck, 1983.

Criticism

In Radical Pursuit: Critical Essays and Lectures. New York: Harper & Row, 1975.

Critical Study

Gaston, Paul. *W. D. Snodgrass.* New York: Twayne, 1978.

GARY SNYDER (1930)

Born in San Francisco, Gary Snyder received a bachelor's degree in literature and anthropology from Reed College. He did further study in oriental languages at Berkeley and later studied Zen Buddhism in a monastery in Kyoto, Japan. He has worked as a seaman, logger, and forester; and he has taught at Berkeley. The recipient of a Bollingen grant for Buddhist Studies, a grant from the National Institute of Arts and Letters, and a Guggenheim Fellowship, he was awarded the Pulitzer Prize in 1975.

In *Six San Francisco Poets*, David Kherdian quotes Snyder as saying: "As much as the books I've read, the jobs I've had have been significant in shaping me. My sense of body and language and the knowledge that intelligence and insight, sensitivity, awareness, and brilliance are not limited to educated people, or anything like it." Many of Snyder's poems are direct and simple, marked by an elemental reverence for life and salvaging poetry from the most basic human experience.

The simplicity, however, is not simplistic, for it reflects the profound influence of Zen on Snyder's sensibility and thought. As Snyder has said: "A poet faces two directions: one is the world of people and language and society, and the other is the nonhuman, nonverbal world, which is nature as nature is itself; and the world of human nature—the inner world, as it is itself, before language, before custom, before culture. There's no words in that realm."

Snyder's response to both the inner and outer worlds has resulted in the quest for a primitive identification with nature and a contemporary concern for the ecological consequences of progress and civilization. "As a poet," Snyder has said, "I hold the most archaic values on earth. They go back to the late Paleolithic: the fertility of the soil, the magic of animals, the power-vision in solitude, the terrifying initiation and rebirth, the love and ecstasy of the dance, the common work of the tribe. I try to hold history and wilderness in mind, that my poems may approach the true measure of things and stand against the unbalance and ignorance of our times."

Among the "archaic values" that Snyder has attempted to erect "against the unbalance and ignorance of our times" are a vital and sacred reintegration of human sexuality and a full celebration of the whole sexual self. Few poets of his generation have celebrated heterosexual love as vividly as Snyder has. Fewer poets have dared explore the precarious sensual and sexual dimensions of such a simple habit as eating, as Snyder has in "Song of the Taste." And Gary Snyder's "The Bath" marks the first time that any American poet perhaps since Whitman has celebrated the pleasurable glory of the male and female bodies with such unabashed and reverential joy.

Poetry

Riprap. Kyoto, Japan: Origin, 1959.   *Myths and Texts.* New York: Totem, 1960; reprint, New York: New Directions, 1978.   *Riprap and Cold Mountain Poems.* San Francisco: Four Seasons, 1965.   *Six Sections from Mountains and Rivers Without End.* San Francisco: Four Seasons, 1965.   *Three Worlds. Three Realms. Six Roads.* Marlboro, Vt.: Griffin, 1966.   *The Back Country.* New York: New Directions, 1968.   *The Blue Sky.* New York: Phoenix Book Shop, 1969.   *Regarding Wave.* New York: New Directions, 1970.   *Manzanita.* Bolinas, Calif.: Four Seasons, 1972.   *Turtle Island.* New York: New Directions, 1974.   *Axe Handles.* San Francisco: North Point, 1983.

Essays

Earth House Hold: Technical Notes and Queries to Fellow Dharma Revolutionaries. New York: New Directions, 1969.   *The Old Ways.* San Francisco: City Lights, 1977. *He Who Hunted Birds in His Father's Village: The Dimensions of a Haida Myth.* Bolinas, Calif: Grey Fox, 1979.   *The Real Work: Interviews & Talks 1964–1979.* Edited with an introduction by Scott McLean. New York: New Directions, 1980.   *Passage Through India.* San Francisco: Grey Fox, 1984.

Bibliography

MacNeil, Katherine. *Gary Snyder: A Bibliography.* New York: Phoenix Books, 1983.

Critical Studies

Almon, Bert. *Gary Snyder.* Boise: Boise State University, 1979.   McCord, Howard. *Some Notes to Gary Snyder's Myths & Texts.* Berkeley: Sand Dollar, 1971.

Molesworth, Charles. *Gary Snyder's Vision: Poetry and the Real Work*. Columbia: University of Missouri, 1983.   Steuding, Bob. *Gary Snyder*. New York: Twayne, 1976.

WILLIAM STAFFORD (1914)

William Stafford received his B.A. and his M.A. from the University of Kansas and his Ph.D from the University of Iowa where he was also a member of the Writers' Workshop. A conscientious objector during World War II and active in pacifist organizations, he has taught at Manchester College and San Jose State College. From 1956 to 1979, he taught at Lewis and Clark College where he is professor emeritus of English. From 1970 to 1971, he was Consultant in Poetry at the Library of Congress. In addition to a Guggenheim Fellowship, a grant from the National Endowment for the Arts, the Shelley Memorial Award, and the Melville Cane Award, he also has received the National Book Award (1963).

In a statement for William J. Martz's *The Distinctive Voice*, William Stafford wrote: "When you make a poem you merely speak or write the language of every day, capturing as many bonuses as possible and economizing on the losses; that is, you come awake to what always goes on in the language, and you use it to the limit of your ability and your power of attention at the moment." Part of what is truly distinctive about Stafford's poetry is his sustained ability to make each poem sound as though it were, in fact, the language of everyday. But it's clear that his power as a poet arises equally out of his ability to capture an extraordinary number of bonuses—the intensity of feeling that daily speech cannot maintain. By so doing, he achieves what he considers to be the meaningful opportunity in the social process of language: "to become more aware of what being alive means."

To a large extent, this awareness also may be the primary thematic focus of Stafford's work: "Your job is to find out what the world is trying to be," he writes in his poem "Vocation." Thus his poetry reflects his attempt not only to capture the possibilities of everyday language but also to maintain "the worth of local things": the plains and small towns of the midwestern and western landscape, the often overlooked experiences of everyday life, and his relationship with his family. Stafford's is also a highly personal poetry, but one which is neither self-torturing nor confessional; rather, it is calm and gentle while remaining honest and firm. Moreover, while neither ostensibly religious nor trailing remnants of the kind of Puritanism inherent in the work of many of his contemporaries, Stafford's poems—as Richard Howard notes in *Alone with*

America—occur within a *paysage moralisé* and are informed by an equally powerful moral vision.

Poetry

West of Your City. Los Gatos, Calif.: Talisman, 1961.   *Traveling Through the Dark.* New York: Harper & Row, 1962.   *The Rescued Year.* New York: Harper & Row, 1966. *Eleven Untitled Poems.* Mt. Horeb, Wis.: Perishable Press, 1968.   *Allegiances.* New York: Harper & Row, 1970.   *Temporary Facts.* Athens, Ohio: Duane Schneider, 1970.   *Someday, Maybe.* New York: Harper & Row, 1973.   *That Other Alone: Poems.* Mt. Horeb, Wis.: Perishable Press, 1973.   *Going Places.* Reno, Nev.: West Coast Poetry Review, 1974.   *Stories That Could Be True: New and Collected Poems.* New York: Harper & Row, 1977.   *All About Light.* Athens, Ohio: Croissant, 1978.   *Smoke's Way.* Port Townsend, Wash.: Graywolf, 1978.   *Things That Happen Where There Aren't Any People.* Brockport, N.Y.: BOA Editions, 1980.   *A Glass Face in the Rain.* New York: Harper & Row, 1982.   *Segues: A Conversation in Poetry* (with Marvin Bell). Boston: Godine, 1983.   *Smoke's Way: Poems from Limited Editions 1968–1981.* Port Townsend, Wash.: Graywolf, 1983.   *Roving Across Fields: A Conversation and Uncollected Poems 1942–1982.* Daleville, Ind.: Barnwood, 1983.

Criticism and Other Prose

Down in My Heart (memoir). Elgin, Ill.: Brethren Publishing, 1947; reprint, 1971. *The Achievement of Brother Antoninus.* Glenview, Ill.: Scott, Foresman, 1967. *Leftovers, A Care Package: Two Lectures.* Washington, D.C.: Library of Congress, 1973. *Writing the Australian Crawl: Views of the Writer's Vocation.* Ann Arbor: University of Michigan, 1978.

Critical Studies

Holden, Jonathan. *The Mark to Turn: A Reading of William Stafford's Poetry.* Lawrence, Kans.: University Press of Kansas, 1976.   Koontz, T., and T. Tammaro, eds. *The View from the Top of the Mountain.* Daleville, Ind.: Barnwood, 1981.   Lensing, George S., and Ronald Moran. *Four Poets and the Emotive Imagination: Robert Bly, James Wright, Louis Simpson and William Stafford.* Baton Rouge: Louisiana State University, 1976.

GERALD STERN (1925)

Born in Pittsburgh, Gerald Stern was educated at the University of Pittsburgh and Columbia University. He served in the United States Army Air Corps in 1949 and subsequently traveled widely in Europe, where he also tutored and taught high school English. In this country he has taught at various colleges and universities, including Sarah Lawrence, Somerset County College, Temple University, the University of Pittsburgh, and the University of Iowa, where he joined the faculty of the Writers' Workshop in 1982. In 1977 Stern received the Academy of American Poets' Lamont Poetry Award. He also has been the recipient of the Poetry Society of America's Melville Cane Award, a fellowship from the Guggenheim Foundation, and two creative writing grants from the National Endowment for the Arts.

Compared with many of today's poets, who publish their first books when they are in their early twenties, Gerald Stern came to poetry relatively late in life; he was forty-six when his first book was published. The wait, the years of seeming silence, the apprenticeship proved to be worthwhile, for in the past few years Stern has grown into a unique presence in contemporary poetry.

Reading Gerald Stern's poems and being moved by the persuasive rhythms of their exhilaration or by the resonating cadences of their sorrow, one may exclaim quite spontaneously, "Wonderful! Wonderful!" (At their best, Stern's poems seem to warrant such physical response.) But identification of the specific reasons for the poems' effectiveness or for our response may not be achieved quite so spontaneously. Clearly, the cultural and literary "influences" are all there: the biblical prophets and psalmists, William Blake and Walt Whitman, Allen Ginsberg and Frank O'Hara. Those influences, however, are more like translucent flags or crystalline signals, rather than prescriptive aesthetic or moral imperatives. Enigmatically, Stern seems to combine Ginsberg's visionary moral stance and O'Hara's chatty urban sophistication but in the process sounds entirely unique. In an interview published in *American Poetry Review* in early 1984, Stern offered a more personal explanation for his voice: "Everything depends on your signature, your breath, your person. Maybe your rhythm. Your peculiarity, your uniqueness. Your crankiness. That thumb print of yours."

Perhaps the seeming enigma lies more deeply in the expansiveness of Gerald Stern's imagination, for he is a poet whose work not only includes, but also attempts to reconcile, the emotional, moral, and existential polarities of experience into a more integrally human whole. Thus his poems encompass the urban experience as much as the rural experience; Cavafy's Alexandria as much as O'Hara's Bickford's; Dionysian joy as much as Judaic anguish. The poem "The Cemetery of Orange Trees in Crete" begins on a level of straightforward realism and suddenly blooms into a lovely surrealistic lyric, while the poem "Weeping and Wailing" begins with an Orphic figure making the trees, animals, and stars dance, moves progressively inward, and suddenly shifts from "I am singing / in harmony" to "I am weeping and wailing." In the same 1984 interview, Stern said: "Poets are witnesses, living proof of the uniqueness of the individual soul, of the unforgivable sadness of its perishing, of its immortality. . . . The more living the poet, the more unbearable the death; the greater the poem, the more it ransoms." To that end this poet understands the essential need for the reconciliation of polarities: "stretching my body and turning on my left side / for music, / humming to myself and turning on my right side / for words."

Poetry

The Pineys. New Brunswick, N.J.: Rutgers University Library Journal, 1971. *The Naming of the Beasts and Other Poems*. West Branch, Iowa: Cummington, 1972. *Rejoicings*. Fredericton, New Brunswick: Fiddlehead, 1973; reprinted as *Rejoicings: Poems 1966–1972*. Los Angeles: Metro Book, 1984. *Lucky Life*. Boston: Houghton Mifflin, 1977. *The Red Coal*. Boston: Houghton Mifflin, 1981. *Paradise Poems*. New York: Random House, 1984.

MARK STRAND (1934)

Mark Strand was born of American parents in Summerside, Prince Edward Island, Canada. He holds degrees from Antioch College, Yale University, and the University of Iowa, and he was a Fulbright Fellow at the University of Florence. Strand has taught in at least fifteen major universities in the United States, including Iowa, Columbia, Yale, Brooklyn, Princeton, Brandeis, Wesleyan, and Harvard. He is currently professor of English at the University of Utah. Mark Strand's grants and fellowships include a Fulbright lectureship in Brazil, an Ingram-Merrill fellowship, two National Endowment for the Arts fellowships, as well as Guggenheim and Rockefeller fellowships. His prizes include the Edgar Allan Poe Prize, the National Institute of Arts and Letters award, and the fellowship of the Academy of American Poets. In 1981 Mark Strand was elected a member of the American Academy and Institute of Arts and Letters.

The development and impact of Mark Strand's poems, like those of Elizabeth Bishop, depend in large part on the straightforward technique of reportage: a seemingly simple presentation of surface facts. What differentiates Strand's poetry from that of others who employ this technique, however, is that Strand doesn't report only the factual images of the perceived physical world, but especially the figures, contours, and dramatic configurations of dreams and of non-conscious states — what Jung termed the archetypal symbols of the collective unconscious. Even when they address themselves to recognizable figures and situations of the tangible world, Strand's poems continue to generate an aura of the dream-world.

The poems of Mark Strand are further differentiated — not only from other poets who use the technique of reportage but also from those who, like Robert Bly, use the unconscious as a source of imagery—by the measure of irony that suffuses so many of his poems. Given the dramatic situation of a Strand poem, the speaker seems to bring a very conscious intelligence to bear on his reporting; that conscious intelligence directs the development of the action and choreographs the emotional impact of the images, thereby harnessing the full surge of the subconscious—occasionally with an edge of humor. Thus, one of Strand's unique characteristics is that many of his poems reflect a controlling sensibility that might be termed ironic surrealism.

Another characteristic that is almost entirely unique to the poetry of Mark Strand is the extent to which the personality of the speaker of his poems seems to be the result of a conscious obliteration of all traces of the surface texture of personality. In other words, these poems offer us a personality of absence rather than of presence. It is this personality that suggests: "Wherever I am / I am what is missing." But such absence—the fact of absence, the threat of absence, the longing for absence—is also one of Mark Strand's central themes. And so there's a startling but also wonderful irony at work when Strand asserts: "More is less. / I long for more." Should some readers fault Strand's poems for personality of its speakers and theme of absence, it is important to note Strand's own realization that, confronted by such absence, it is possible to see "the blaze of promise everywhere."

Poetry

Sleeping with One Eye Open. Iowa City: Stone Wall, 1964.   *Reasons for Moving.* New York: Atheneum, 1968.   *Darker.* New York: Atheneum, 1970.   *The Sargentville Notebook.* Providence, R.I.: Burning Deck, 1973.   *The Story of Our Lives.* New York: Atheneum, 1973.   *The Late Hour.* New York: Atheneum, 1978.   *Elegy for My Father.* Iowa City: Windhover, 1973.   *Selected Poems.* New York: Atheneum, 1980.

Translations: Poetry and Prose

18 Poems from the Quechua. Cambridge: Halty Ferguson, 1971.   *The Owl's Insomnia: Selected Poems of Rafael Alberti.* New York: Atheneum, 1973.   *Texas* [Jorge Luis Borges]. Austin: University of Texas Humanities Research Center, 1975.   *Souvenir of the Ancient World: Selected Poems of Carlos Drummond de Andrade.* New York: Antaeus, 1976.   *The Selected Poems of Carlos Drummond de Andrade.* New York: Random House, 1983.

Prose and Fiction

The Monument. New York: Ecco, 1978.   *Mr. and Mrs. Baby.* New York: Knopf, 1985.

Anthologies

The Contemporary American Poets: American Poetry since 1940. Cleveland: World, 1969.
New Poetry of Mexico (with Octavio Paz). New York: Dutton, 1970.   *Another Republic:*
17 European and South American Writers (with Charles Simic). New York: Ecco Press,
1976.   *The Art of the Real: Nine American Figurative Painters.* New York: Clarkson
Potter, 1983.

LUCIEN STRYK (1924)

Born in Chicago, Lucien Stryk was educated at Indiana University, the Univer-
sity of London, the Sorbonne (Paris), and the University of Iowa. He has taught
at Niigata and Yamaguchi universities in Japan and he has been a Fulbright
lecturer and researcher in Iran and in Japan. Since 1953 he has taught at
Northern Illinois University (DeKalb), where he is professor of English and
Asian literatures. Stryk's many grants and awards for his poetry, translations,
and study of Oriental philosophy and literature include a National Endow-
ment for the Arts poetry fellowship, the Islands and Continents Translation
Award, a National Translation Center grant, fellowships from the Rockefeller
and Ford foundations, and a National Institute of Arts and Letters award.

One of the admirable qualities of Lucien Stryk's poetry is his recognizable
range and diversity of subjects. Since Stryk spent much of his career as a
scholar of Oriental thought and translator of Japanese poetry, it is natural
that that experience is also the focus of some of his poems, such as "Awaken-
ing" and "To a Japanese Poet." However, he is just as emotionally and
temperamentally comfortable writing about the effect of migrant workers in
a small town ("The Cannery"), the petty conflicts of suburbia ("Summer"), and
the yearly extermination of field mice ("Exterminator"). In the poem "Letter
to Jean-Paul Baudot, at Christmas," Stryk confronts, accepts, and forgives the
inhumanities of war's greater conflicts, just as in "Cherries" he recognizes and
accepts his own far more distant, though no less real, capacity for participa-
tion in the cycles of human annihilation.

Clearly, there is a dark edge to many of Stryk's poems; but that dark
assumes a more human opacity, because it is countered by at least a propor-
tionate measure of epiphany—a result of the aesthetic-moral vision inform-
ing Stryk's poetry. "A man's poems should reveal the full range of his life,
and hide nothing except the art behind them," Stryk wrote in his essay
"Making Poems" (in *American Poets in 1976*). One of the ways to "hide" that
art, he suggests, paraphrasing the Chinese Zen master Hui-neng, is to engage
in "pure seeing—not to look *at* things, but *as* things"—which, in Western
aesthetics, is similar to Keats's "negative capability." It is also a necessary cor-
ollary to Stryk's own pursuit of a seemingly unadorned and simple poetry that
"reveals . . . a quality of life . . . [and] takes on a moral grandeur."

The moral grandeur of Lucien Stryk's poetry emerges specifically from his ability to reveal, to accept, and to forgive (not in any Judeo-Christian sense of guilt) even the darker edges of human experience, because to do so is to awaken to, and to be fully aware of, our own most profound humanity. If that is akin to Whitman's assertion "Nothing human is alien to me," it also reflects the capacity to know that "near / books of tranquil Buddhas by the / screen. The war goes on and on"; to know "who will survive"; to know the possibility that "the book may jostle just a / bit, the paper bear a poem"; to know "Our lives depend on it"; to know that at this hour "the trees / are taken, one by one, / into the great wash of darkness"—and yet, to know, too, the epiphanal serenity that "At this hour I am always happy, / ready to be taken myself, / fully aware."

Poetry

Taproot. Oxford, England: Fantasy, 1953. *The Trespasser.* Oxford, England: Fantasy, 1956. *Notes for a Guidebook.* Denver: Swallow, 1965. *The Pit and Other Poems.* Chicago: Swallow, 1969. *Awakening.* Chicago: Swallow, 1973. *Selected Poems.* Chicago: Swallow, 1976. *The Duckpond.* London: J. Jay, 1978. *Cherries.* Bristol, R.I.: Ampersand, 1983. *Willows.* Cambridge, England: Embers, 1983. *Collected Poems, 1953–1983.* Chicago: Swallow/Ohio University, 1984.

Translations

Zen: Poems, Prayers, Sermons, Anecdotes, Interviews (with Takashi Ikemoto). New York: Doubleday, 1965; Chicago: Swallow/Ohio University, 1981. *Afterimages: Zen Poems of Shinkichi Takahashi* (with Takashi Ikemoto). Chicago: Swallow, 1971; New York: Doubleday, 1972. *Twelve Death Poems of the Chinese Zen Masters.* Providence, R.I.: Hellcoal, 1973. *Zen Poems of China and Japan: The Crane's Bill* (with Takashi Ikemoto and Taigan Takayama). New York: Doubleday, 1973; New York: Grove, 1981. *Three Zen Poems after Shinkichi Takahashi.* Knotting, England: Sceptre, 1976. *The Duckweed Way: Haiku of Issa.* Derry, Pa.: Rook, 1977. *Haiku of the Japanese Masters* (with Takashi Ikemoto). Derry, Pa.: Rook, 1977. *The Penguin Book of Zen Poetry* (with Takashi Ikemoto). London: Penguin, 1977; New York: Viking/Penguin, 1981. *On Love and Barley: Haiku of Basho* (with Takashi Ikemoto). New York: Viking/Penguin, 1984. *Triumph of the Sparrow: Zen Poems of Shinkichi Takahashi* (with Takashi Ikemoto). Urbana: University of Illinois, 1985.

Anthologies

Heartland: Poets of the Midwest. DeKalb: Northern Illinois University, 1967. *World of the Buddha: A Reader.* New York: Doubleday, 1968; New York: Grove, 1982. *Heartland II: Poets of the Midwest.* DeKalb: Northern Illinois University, 1975. *Encounter with Zen: Writings on Poetry and Zen.* Chicago: Swallow/Ohio University, 1982.

RICHARD WILBUR (1921)

A graduate of Amherst and Harvard, Richard Wilbur has taught at Harvard, Wellesley, and Wesleyan where he was an editor of the Wesleyan University Press poetry series; he is currently professor of English at Smith College. His many awards include Guggenheim and Ford Foundation fellowships, the Prix de Rome—as well as both the Pulitzer Prize and National Book Award in 1957.

In addition to his stunning poetry and translations, Wilbur's work includes an operetta, *Candide* (with Lillian Hellman, 1957); poetry for children, *Loudmouse* (1963) and *Opposites* (1973); and editions of the poems of Keats, Poe, and Shakespeare.

Among poets whose sensibilities were shaped by the New Critics, Wilbur continues to be the consummate artist. His poetry is marked by grace, wit, and a kind of masterful craftsmanship equaled by few of his contemporaries. In his statement for John Ciardi's *Mid-Century American Poets* (1950), Wilbur affirmed the poet's need for form, for "artistry," saying that "limitation makes for power: the strength of the genie comes of his being confined in a bottle." Elsewhere he has stated that the poet must move "to attempt a maximum range" and to do so "without apparent strain." At his best, Wilbur's mastery of language and form is not merely without strain—it is dazzling and breathtaking.

The precision of sensuous detail and the verbal *entrechats* in Wilbur's poems are formal affirmations of his profound humanism, his belief in humankind's potential natural grace in this "world of sensible objects." In an era when many other poets have loitered around the deterioration of social, psychic, and personal fabrics and have proclaimed us and our world to be absurd, Wilbur has consistently sought for "a reconciliation between joy and pleasure, between acceptance and transcendence"—often against strenuous odds. And he has succeeded. By so doing, his poems have found and continue to offer the possibility of human beauty and grace.

Poetry

The Beautiful Changes and Other Poems. New York: Reynal & Hitchcock, 1947. *Ceremony and Other Poems*. New York: Harcourt, Brace, 1950.   *Things of This World: Poems*. New York: Harcourt, Brace, 1956.   *Advice to a Prophet and Other Poems*. New York: Harcourt, Brace & World, 1961.   *The Poems of Richard Wilbur*. New York: Harcourt, Brace & World, 1963.   *Walking to Sleep: New Poems and Translations*. New York: Harcourt Brace Jovanovich, 1969.   *The Mind-Reader: New Poems*. New York: Harcourt Brace Jovanovich, 1976.   *Seven Poems*. Omaha: Abbatoir, 1981.

Translations: Poetry and Drama

The Misanthrope [Molière]. New York: Harcourt, Brace, 1955.   *Tartuffe* [Molière].
New York: Harcourt, Brace & World, 1963.   *The School for Wives* [Molière]. New
York: Harcourt Brace Jovanovich, 1971.   *The Learned Ladies* [Molière]. New York:
Harcourt Brace Jovanovich, 1978.   *The Whale and Other Uncollected Translations.*
Brockport, N.Y.: BOA Editions, 1982.   *Andromache* [Racine] . New York: Harcourt
Brace Jovanovich, 1982.   *Four Comedies: The Misanthrope, Tartuffe, The School for
Wives, The Learned Ladies* [Molière]. New York: Harcourt Brace Jovanovich, 1982.

Criticism

Responses: Prose Pieces, 1953–1976. New York: Harcourt Brace Jovanovich, 1976.

Bibliography

Field, John P. *Richard Wilbur: A Bibliographical Checklist.* Kent, Ohio: Kent State
University, 1971.

Critical Studies

Cummins, Paul F. *Richard Wilbur.* Grand Rapids: Eerdmans, 1971.   Hill, Donald.
Richard Wilbur. New York: Twayne, 1967.   Salinger, Wendy, ed. *Richard Wilbur's
Creation.* Ann Arbor: University of Michigan, 1983.

C. K. WILLIAMS (1936)

Born in Newark, New Jersey, and educated at Bucknell University and the
University of Pennsylvania, C. K. Williams has spanned a wide range of ac-
tivities during his professional career. He established a program of poetry-
therapy for emotionally disturbed patients at the Institute of the Pennsylvania
Hospital in Philadelphia, where he was also a group therapist in the treat-
ment of disturbed adolescents. He has been an editor and ghostwriter of ar-
ticles, booklets, and speeches in the fields of psychiatry and architecture. And
he has taught creative writing in various colleges and universities, including
Drexel University, the University of California at Irvine, Boston University,
Columbia University, and George Mason University, where he is currently
professor of English. C. K. Williams was awarded a Guggenheim Fellowship
in 1974 and the *Paris Review*'s Bernard F. Connor Prize in 1983.

Reading the poems of C. K. Williams, we are quickly struck by how much pain and grief are harbored in their stark lines. Perhaps no other postwar American poet has confronted so unswervingly and relentlessly the levels and dimensions of anguish as the fulcrum of human experience. Moreover, unlike many of his contemporaries, Williams has explored human suffering without the seeming intellectual comfort of a formal philosophical system like existentialism (W. D. Snodgrass), without even a precarious solace of faith or of a theological framework (John Berryman), and certainly without the emotional-aesthetic buffer of a strong ironic sense in the service of sustained artifice (Sylvia Plath). Whether confronting inner states of psychic pain in earlier poems or more external constructs of human anguish in later poems, C. K. Williams's poetry has as its heart the fundamental and essentially unconsoled vision announced in "It Is This Way with Men": "They are pounded into the earth / like nails; move an inch, / they are driven down again. / The earth is sore with them."

The anguish of our common condition, in an age that threatens annihilation on all sides, also seems to have rendered C. K. Williams commensurately unsympathetic to the kinds of artifices we have come to expect from poetry. Thus, in his earlier poems he seemed intent on stripping language down to its most essential syntax and then stripping it even further of most signs of syntax's own formal artifice. Consider the intense aesthetic and syntactical starkness of these lines: "if you told him god lived in his own penis / he'd bite into it / and tear like a carnivore / this is how men renounce / this is how we obliterate. . . . " Clearly, the visual aesthetic equivalent of such lines would be found more in Käthe Kollwitz's hauntingly sparse but blunt depictions of pain than in the more complex, inventive, and often witty depictions by Hieronymous Bosch.

In his more recent poems, C. K. Williams has introduced a long tonal line which may well be unique in postwar American poetry. While Williams's lines may look like Ginsberg's, they are not marked by the incantatory quality in many of Ginsberg's poems. While their tone is very conversational, like many of Simpson's recent poems, Williams's tone isn't marked by the crackling terseness found in Simpson's. Approaching the quality of a highly refined, sparse prose, Williams's new tonal lines continue to accommodate his dark vision but also enable him to be more experientially, intellectually, and aesthetically expansive, allowing the reader to participate in the poet's own thought processes. These new poems also reflect a maturation of Williams's vision: the pain, the anguish, the annihilation are still present and unconsoled, but that vision is also counterpointed by the recognition of the possibility of beauty in scenes such as "all the field pure white, / its surface glittering, the dawn, glancing from its glaze, oblique, relentless, unadorned."

Poetry

A Day for Anne Frank. Philadelphia: Falcon Press, 1968.   *Lies.* Boston: Houghton Mifflin, 1969.   *I Am the Bitter Name.* Boston: Houghton Mifflin, 1972.   *With Ignorance.* Boston: Houghton Mifflin, 1977.   *Tar.* New York: Random House, 1983.

Translations: Poetry and Drama

Women of Trachis [Sophocles] (with Gregory Dickerson). New York: Oxford University, 1978.   *The Lark. The Thrush. The Starling.* [Poems from Issa.] Providence, R.I.: Burning Deck, 1983.   *The Bacchae* [Euripides] (with H. Golder). New York: Oxford University, 1985.

CHARLES WRIGHT (1935)

Born in Pickwick Dam, Tennessee, Charles Wright was educated at Davidson College, the University of Iowa, and the University of Rome, where he was a Fulbright fellow. From 1957 to 1961 he served in the U.S. Army Intelligence Service, and since 1966 he has been teaching at various universities, including the University of Padua (Italy), where he was a Fulbright lecturer, as well as Iowa, Princeton, Columbia, and the University of California at Irvine. Currently he is professor of English at the University of Virginia in Charlottesville. Charles Wright's grants, awards, and prizes include fellowships from the National Endowment for the Arts, the Guggenheim Foundation, and the Ingram Merrill Foundation; the Poetry Society of America's Melville Cane Award; the Edgar Allan Poe Award of the Academy of American Poets; a grant from the American Academy and Institute of Arts and Letters; and the P.E.N. Translation Prize. In 1983 Wright also was cowinner of the American Book Award for poetry.

If Charles Wright's "The New Poem" were read as a statement of his poetics (in the way that Marvin Bell's "White Clover" or Robert Creeley's "The Window" may be read), we might rightfully conclude that Wright's sense of poetics — and the implicit broader vision from which it might issue — is desolate to the brink of barbarism. For the "new poem" would have nothing to do with the physical world, would reflect no characteristic inherent in the art of poetry, and would address no human concerns. It's no wonder that in 1979 one critic asserted that Wright's poetry struggles to render the connections between his life and his poems "tenuous, often invisible" and characterized Wright's poems as being "unanchored to incident," thus "resisting description" and "defying exposition."

In light of Charles Wright's full body of poetry, however, "The New Poem" is more rightly read as a statement of antipoetics, perhaps even as a parody of a certain modish aesthetic. That is, it is a poem suggesting what Wright hopes his own poems will *not* be, a nine-commandment tablet listing what poetry in general ought *not* to do, and, indeed, perhaps a kind of oxymoron repudiating that view in some literary circles which finds quality and worth in poetry that is seemingly not rooted in any recognizable human reality.

Because they are carefully, delicately crafted, and because, as other critics have noted, they often rely more on links of the imagination than on narrative and other surface connections, some of Wright's poems may seem less immediately accessible than the work of other poets. However, on closer examination it is clear that the range of Wright's concerns is fully rooted in the range of recognizable and shared human experience. His work includes poems of place energized by the spirit of that place, whether it is Blackwater Mountain in Tennessee or Laguna Beach, California; it includes poems emerging out of childhood, adolescent, and mature experience and the states of emotional feeling inherent in those stages of human development; and it includes poems of the natural/physical world with its splendors and horrors.

What is also striking about the work of Charles Wright is its strong and consistent religious nature; Wright is one of the few poets of his generation who continues to wrestle openly with the traditional values (if not the working tenets) of the Judaic-Christian tradition and to use the symbols, saints, and metaphors of that tradition as an integral part of his sensibility and vocabulary. The poem "Snow" uses as its launching point the biblical phrase "Dust thou art, and unto dust shalt thou return"; "Equation," in part, is an exploration of guilt *as guilt*, rather than as a symptom of neurosis; and the poems "Three Poems for the New Year" and "California Dreaming," whose very tone resonates with biblical rhythms and whose language incorporates traditional religious phrases and concepts, are profound explorations of the possibility of a tradition-oriented spirituality within the boundaries and texture of contemporary experience. What if, in his quest for transcendence, Wright recognizes that "The ache for anything is a thick dust in the heart," that transcendence may be no more than being "Released as a glint, as a flash, as a spark," and that the "other ladder to Paradise / [is] but the smooth handholds of the rib cage"? Of the people and places in his world, past and present, he asserts: "I am their music"; of his music, he ventures: "I write poems to untie myself, to do penance and disappear / Through the upper right-hand corner of things, to say grace."

Poetry

The Voyage. Iowa City: Patrician, 1963.   *6 Poems.* London: David Freed, 1965. *The Dream Animal.* Toronto: Anansi, 1968.   *Private Madrigals.* Madison, Wis.: Abraxas, 1969.   *The Grave of the Right Hand.* Middletown: Wesleyan, 1970.   *The Venice Notebook.* Boston: Barn Dream, 1971.   *Backwater.* Costa Mesa, Calif.: Golem, 1973. *Hard Freight.* Middletown: Wesleyan, 1973. *Bloodlines.* Middletown: Wesleyan, 1975. *China Trace.* Middletown: Wesleyan, 1977. *Colophons.* Iowa City: Windhover, 1977.   *The Southern Cross.* New York: Random House, 1981. *Country Music: Selected Early Poems.* Middletown: Wesleyan, 1982. *The Other Side of the River.* New York: Random House, 1984.

Translations: Poetry

The Storm and Other Poems [Eugenio Montale]. Oberlin, Ohio: Field, 1978.   *The Motets* [Eugenio Montale]. Iowa City: Windhover, 1981. *Orphic Songs* [Dino Campana]. Oberlin, Ohio: Field, 1984.

Critical Study

Wright: A Profile. Iowa City: Grilled Flowers, 1979.

JAMES WRIGHT (1927–1980)

James Wright was born in Martin's Ferry, Ohio—and he subsequently transformed it into a literary landmark in the contemporary imagination. He received his B.A. from Kenyon College, his M.A. and Ph.D. from the University of Washington, and attended the University of Vienna as a Fulbright Scholar. The recipient of several awards—including the Pulitzer Prize in 1972—he taught at Macalester College, the University of Minnesota, and Hunter College.

Like many other poets of his generation, James Wright's style underwent significant changes in the course of his career. With the publication of his first book, Wright stated that he "wanted to make [his] poems say something humanly important" and pointed to Robert Frost and E. A. Robinson as his models. Thus his early poems, such as "In Shame and Humiliation," are often concerned with his response to the life and suffering of others. After his second book, however, he asserted: "Whatever I write from now on will be entirely different."

According to Robert Bly, Wright's decision was largely the result of his having read—and translated—the work of the German poet Georg Trakl, a contemporary of Rilke. "In Trakl," Bly writes, "a series of images makes a series of events. Because these events appear out of their 'natural' order, without the connection we have learned to expect from reading newspapers, doors silently open to unused parts of the brain." In Wright's poems such as "The Jewel," "Lying in a Hammock. . .," and "A Blessing"—generally written between 1960 and 1970—the doors open to startling images, strange but emotionally precise. More personal than his earlier poems, these discover in his own subconscious and imagination the secret pools of human fear and joy. Moreover, the poems themselves seem to evolve quietly through layers of images until they surface with the quick thrust of a striking final image and epiphany.

In more recent poems (those written after the publication of his *Collected Poems* in 1971), Wright sought a vital integration of his earlier concern with others—"those old Winnebago men"—and the image of epiphany—"the instant in the waterfall." The results enable us to join Wright in his assertion: "I know what we call it / Most of the time. / But I have my own song for it, / And sometimes, even today, / I call it beauty."

Poetry

The Green Wall. New Haven: Yale University, 1957.   *Saint Judas.* Middletown: Wesleyan, 1959.   *The Lion's Tail and Eyes: Poems Written out of Laziness and Silence* (with Robert Bly and William Duffy). Madison, Minn.: Sixties Press, 1962. *The Branch Will Not Break.* Middletown: Wesleyan, 1963.   *Collected Poems.* Middletown: Wesleyan, 1971.   *Two Citizens.* New York: Farrar, Straus & Giroux, 1973.   *Moments of the Italian Summer.* Washington, D.C.: Dryad, 1976.   *To a Blossoming Pear Tree.* New York: Farrar, Straus & Giroux, 1977.   *Leave It to the Sunlight.* Edited by Anne Wright. Durango, Colo.: Logbridge-Rhodes, 1981.   *A Reply to Matthew Arnold.* Edited by Anne Wright. Durango, Colo.: Logbridge-Rhodes, 1981.   *This Journey.* Edited by Anne Wright. New York: Random House, 1982.

Translations: Poetry and Fiction

Twenty Poems of Georg Trakl (with Robert Bly). Madison, Minn.: Sixties Press, 1961. *Twenty Poems of Cesar Vallejo* (with Robert Bly). Madison, Minn.: Sixties Press, 1962.   *The Rider on the White Horse: Selected Short Fiction of Theodore Storm.* New York: New American Library, 1964.   *Pablo Neruda: Twenty Poems* (with Robert Bly). Madison, Minn.: Sixties Press, 1967.   *Poems by Hermann Hesse.* New York: Farrar, Straus & Giroux, 1970.   *Neruda and Vallejo: Selected Poems* (with Robert Bly and John Knoepfle). Boston: Beacon, 1971.   *Wandering: Notes and Sketches by Hermann Hesse* (with Franz Wright). New York: Farrar, Straus & Giroux, 1972.

Criticism

Collected Prose. Edited by Anne Wright. Ann Arbor: University of Michigan, 1982.

Critical Studies

Ironwood 10: James Wright: A Special Issue. Tucson: Ironwood Press, 1977. Lensing, George S., and Ronald Moran. *Four Poets and the Emotive Imagination: Robert Bly, James Wright, Louis Simpson and William Stafford.* Baton Rouge: Louisiana State University, 1976.   Smith, Dave, ed. *The Pure Clean Word: Essays on the Poetry of James Wright.* Champaign: University of Illinois, 1983.

Contemporary American Poetry: The Radical Tradition

American poetry since 1945 may be viewed as the product of the dialectics of generations. A recurrent phenomenon in literary as well as in much human history, the pattern of one generation's revolt against another is familiar—indeed, seemingly always close at hand. That rebellion, however, is usually not so much against the preceding generation's essential beliefs as against its excesses: principle atrophied into prejudice, freshness of thought and sensibility petrified into cliché, discipline forged into tyranny. Moreover, the revolution doesn't always realize a clean break with the immediate or distant past: the blood, the genes remain, camouflaged by a radical facade.

While emphasizing the freshness of contemporary poetry, some poets and critics have argued that it reflects a violent break with the first-generation modernist poetry of T. S. Eliot and Pound—if not with all tradition. In the introduction to his own important anthology of contemporary American poetry (1962), Donald Hall announced that the orthodoxy of T. S. Eliot and the New Critics had ceased: "In modern art anarchy has proved preferable to the restrictions of a benevolent tyranny." The contemporary artist, Hall wrote, "has acted as if restlessness were a conviction and has destroyed his own past in order to create a future." In *The Poem in Its Skin* (1968), Paul Carroll argued that contemporary poets have attempted "to write poems either alien or hostile to the poem as defined and explored by Eliot and leading writers dominating the scene ten or fifteen years ago." Later Carroll asserted: "This generation of American poets is on the high, happy adventure of creating and innovating a complex of new ways in which to view our common condition—an adventure which in its abundance, freshness, and originality is...as interesting as any since the Olympians of 1917."

That the adventure of today's poets has been somewhat anarchic but abundantly fresh is unquestionable. That it has produced poems entirely alien to the earlier modernist poetry is open to a good measure of debate. But the proposition that contemporary American poets have destroyed their own past as poets, for whatever reasons, is simply untenable. Admittedly, T. S. Eliot may have been aesthetically, temperamentally, and constitutionally incapable of writing such poems as Sylvia Plath's "Daddy," Maxine Kumin's "The Excrement Poem," Frank O'Hara's campy poem to Lana Turner, or Marge Piercy's "Barbie Doll." And such New Critics as Allen Tate, John Crowe Ransom, and William Empson, who transformed the experiments of modernist poets into a legislative critical system, would not have known what to make of certain kinds of poems. When confronted by the poems in Robert Lowell's

685

Life Studies, Allen Tate reportedly turned to Lowell, his former student —
known as Cal to friends — and agonizingly blurted: "But, *Cal,* it's not *poetry!*"

Although the dicta of the New Critics are no longer regarded as sacred
commandments by contemporary poets, much of their valid aesthetic
substance has been retained — as have some of the older and more profound
literary traditions. In *The New Poets* (1967), M. L. Rosenthal convincingly
traced the connections by which much of today's poetry may be considered
a continuation and expansion of a strong Romantic tradition. Hyatt H. Wag-
goner *(American Poetry from the Puritans to the Present,* 1968) and more recent-
ly Robert Pinsky *(The Situation of Poetry,* 1976) have explored the ways in
which the contemporary American poet actively participates in various other
traditions, especially the Emersonian tradition. No less important is the con-
tinuing presence of the equally profound Puritan and Whitman traditions:
they are both still active and vital, influencing the formal and thematic direc-
tions of much contemporary poetry. If today's poets have achieved a unique
vitality, they have done so by making full (if not always quite so obvious) use
of the past — immediate and distant, personal and communal, literary and
cultural — while simultaneously contributing new and energizing elements of
their own.

The characteristics of the first-generation modernist poem are obviously
vital elements in the work of such poets as Richard Wilbur, Robert Lowell,
John Berryman, and Stanley Kunitz, who in 1945 were the "younger" poets
of the modernist generation and whose sensibilities were shaped by the New
Critics. Commenting on his own work in *Poets on Poetry* (1961), Wilbur said:
"Most American poets of my generation were taught to admire the English
Metaphysical poets of the seventeenth century and such contemporary masters
of irony as John Crowe Ransom. We were led by our teachers and by the
critics whom we read to feel that the most adequate and convincing poetry
is that which accommodates mixed feelings, clashing ideas, and incongruous
images. Poetry could not be honest, we thought, unless it began by acknowledg-
ing the full discordancy of modern life and consciousness. I still believe that
to be a true view of poetry." Written under the tutelage of John Crowe Ran-
som and Allen Tate, Robert Lowell's early work, in particular, was immediately
hailed as a model of what the modernist poem could and should be. And John
Berryman's more recent monumental series of "Dream Songs" clearly employs
the essential techniques and assumptions of modernist poetry.

One of the major differences between modernist and contemporary poetry
is that the latter — at least seemingly — is more intimate and personal. The
elements of the modernist poem seemed consciously employed toward assuring
a certain artistic distance between the poets and their subjects, the poets and
their poems. From the purposeful use of persona to the conscious use of un-
mistakable "literary" tradition, each technique was a formal, emotional, and
intellectual device for the poets' objectification of subject, emotion, and
medium. The individual personality of the poets, their more intimate ex-

periences and emotions, were not just seemingly absent: indeed, in light of Eliot's misunderstood dictum that poetry was an escape from personality, what are now considered to be the personal elements in poetry were virtually taboo among modernist poets. And in the hands of lesser poets, such an attitude often resulted in a depersonalized and inhuman versification.

As Ralph J. Mills, Jr., has amply demonstrated in his brilliant essay "Creation's Very Self" (reprinted in *Cry of the Human*, 1974), what distinguishes the work of contemporary poets from that of their modernist predecessors is especially the presence and vitality of the personal element. Although possibilities for objectification remain, poetry is no longer considered an escape from personality by contemporary poets but rather a fuller cultivation and use of personality. The personality of the poet is seemingly more central and more vibrant than the poetic device of the persona: "he" or "she" is now frequently replaced by "I." The speaker of the poem and the poet often seem to be one and the same, an indivisible person; the subject of a poem often seems to be the poet's own — at times intimate — experiences, which the poet seemingly does not seek to present as anything other than personal experience. Consequently, the full appreciation of some contemporary poems sometimes seems to hinge on the reader's knowledge of biographical details of the poet's personal and intimate life. For example, Robert Lowell was, in fact, jailed as a conscientious objector — as he says he was in "Memories of West Street and Lepke"; Sylvia Plath did attempt suicide — as she says she did in "Lady Lazarus"; Lucien Stryk did confront firsthand those war experiences he speaks of in his poems. With the poet's private self as both subject and speaker of the poem, with the presence and use of the poet's own personality in the poem, the interaction between the work of art and the reader becomes proportionately more intimate: the poet seems to speak more directly to the reader, as if that reader were a confessor, psychiatrist, intimate friend, or lover.

The personalization of poetry has evolved in various other ways. In the work of Robert Bly, James Wright, and W. S. Merwin, for example, a personal poetry occurs as the result of the exploration of and response to the most inner reaches of the poet's self below the rational and conscious levels. Poems grow out of images discovered in the depths of human darkness, as it were, amidst the substrata of preconscious feeling and intuition. The personalization that occurs in Mark Strand's poetry is strangely the result of the extent to which he seems to consciously obliterate all traces of the surface textures of personality, thus offering a personality of absence rather than of presence. Particularly in Galway Kinnell's later work, one senses the poet's attempt to strip away formal, linguistic, and even surface emotional constructs that might filter or impede the poet's ongoing exploration of his inmost self and experience. Through shifts of emotion, language, and tone all within the same poem, one senses in the work of John Logan the vital interaction among the various facets of an individual personality: the harmonious counterpoint between intellectual irony and corny self-deprecating humor, between religious feeling and vulgarity, between commonplace banality and high lyrical excitement—in short, an integration of the individual parts of a multidimensional personality.

Although they contain moments of private joy and grief, the poems of Allen Ginsberg and Frank O'Hara take another direction: they depend primarily on the self's discovery of the outer world and response to it. In these poems one often senses the poet's self, his personality, being shaped by the "surround" in which he finds himself. The reader hears with O'Hara's ears or touches with Ginsberg's hands. In the poetry of others, the personal element seems to evolve primarily out of the relationship between the poet's private self and the social as well as geographical landscape he inhabits and with which he interacts: the sophisticated suburban landscape of Simpson's poems; the bleak and desolate western landscape of Hugo's poems; both the urban and suburban sources of grief and joy in Gerald Stern's poems; the stark, almost threatening, presence of the city in C. W. Williams's later work; and the range of both emotional and geographical landscape from the hills of Tennessee to Laguna Beach, California, in the work of Charles Wright.

The personalization of American poetry since 1945 is probably most obvious in the work of those poets who have chosen to incorporate in their poems elements of their personal histories—and events in their individual lives usually considered intimate, private, or confidential. Until recently the sexual preferences of some of this century's great poets were among the best-kept secrets in literary history—in large part because they were rightfully considered irrelevant to the poetry. Consequently, Allen Ginsberg's and Robert Duncan's poems about aspects of their homosexuality, as well as Adrienne Rich's open and moving explorations of her own sexual preference in some of her more recent poems, may be somewhat startling to some readers. Indeed, most Americans still feel somewhat threatened by such sexual honesty. It is worth noting, however, that even the much less intimate "Love Song of J. Alfred Prufrock" is probably as much an exploration of T. S. Eliot's feelings of sexual impotency as it is a record of Prufrock's frustrations. In any case, private revelations of personal illness, madness, failure, and self-destruction are some of the recurring subjects in the work of such personal-confessional poets as Lowell, Plath, Sexton, and Snodgrass.

Today's poets, then, have succeeded in making poetry that often resonates as being radically personal; however, under closer scrutiny, other factors come into focus to temper the reader's immediate response. Subject and voice paradoxically work toward making even the most intimate poetry less personal than it first seems and result in erecting another kind of persona—the part of the private self that the poet chooses to make public. Because they have been primarily concerned with physical and psychic limitations, the personal-confessional poets have written a poetry which, to a large extent, reveals *only* the deteriorating self speaking in a chosen voice, ranging from the modulated whine of W. D. Snodgrass to the near hysteria of Sylvia Plath. Moreover, in the work of some poets, the requirements of technique and craftsmanship raise further questions about just how personal and immediate a poem can be: by drawing attention to its formal qualities, even the poem ostensibly about the most intimate subject reminds the reader that the poem, any poem, is a fabrication and takes time and calculation to complete. Like any other art, personal poetry is a selective, calculated, and public gesture, a formal utterance for which the poet *selects* not only a language but also a voice, even if they are as approximate to his or her own as the poet can manage.

In his lecture entitled "The Inward Muse," Donald Hall may have been speaking for a number of his contemporaries when he said that while working on his early poems he "could sometimes hear the voice of Mr. Ransom" reminding him of irony and that "it took ten years to get rid of that voice." Nevertheless, irony and paradox continue to be vitally present in the work of today's poets. Confronted by the quality of our common condition, the sensitive and mature human being may not survive without a strong ironic sense: although irony may thwart much genuine emotion, its absence also makes genuine emotion virtually impossible. The uses of irony in contemporary poetry can be seen in the work of two rather different poets, Sylvia Plath and Frank O'Hara. In Sylvia Plath's poetry, the presence of irony serves to temper the intensity of suffering by undercutting the vehement and often near-Gothic imagery and the highly charged emotion. Indeed, many of Plath's more intense poems survive as *poems* specifically because her sharp ironic sense is also at play. For example "Lady Lazarus" is protected from bathos not only by the ironic sense of humor that views the would-be suicide as "the big strip tease" in a three-ring circus of Nazi-artistic-Christian horrors but also through intonation and line-break that begin the poem by suggesting that it could be spoken by some rich Jewish lady coming out of a beauty spa.

The irony in Frank O'Hara's poems may be more implicit—a pervasive impetus behind the total poem; nevertheless, it is present and crucial. In the poem to Lana Turner, for example, an ironic sensibility functions in a manner directly opposite to Plath's: it undercuts the humor by suggesting the emptiness—if not the decadence—of the emotion. In other words, in O'Hara's poems one recognizes the peculiar contemporary phenomenon of camp irony.

Because so much contemporary poetry seems so intensely personal, it also generally seems very direct and transparent; but the essential complexity of emotion, the richness of language, and the potential of form—not the least of which is the organic form of free verse—make ambiguity inescapable. On a rather basic level, for example, today's reader cannot avoid the rather obvious *double-entendre* in the opening lines of John Logan's "Love Poem": "Last night you would not come, / and you have been gone so long." John Ashbery's use of wide-open form and broken syntax in a poem like "Leaving the Atocha Station" often commands that the reader invent interpretation. The Proustian quality of James Merrill's later poems offers readers still another kind of complexity of language and texture. Robert Creeley's poems depend largely on structural ambiguity—the emotional and thematic tension between the linear unit and the syntactical unit—for their introverted effect. By eliminating punctuation in many of his poems since *The Moving Target,* W. S. Merwin succeeds in creating additional levels of ambiguity; and John Berryman achieves still another kind of ambiguity through a manipulation of pronouns referring to his schizoid persona.

Because many of today's poets have not been working in traditional poetic form in their pursuit of a more personal poetry, it would be a serious misunderstanding of the very nature of art in general and of poetry in particular if one were to assume that poets have discarded form altogether. In nature and in the world of things made by humans, form is virtually indistinguishable from essence. A tree is a tree, in part, because it has the general shape or form of a tree which differentiates it from that of a bush. A chair is a chair because its shape or form is what it is; there may be several variations of that form, but if one variation goes too far away from the essence of chairness, you have a stool; in the other direction, you have a chaise longue, which is one step removed from a couch or a bed. In poetry the line of demarkation may be somewhat subtle, as in the later poems of Louis Simpson and C. K. Williams, but it is nonetheless actively and recognizably real. While the language of those poems may sound like conversational prose, the energy that shapes the conversational tone is undoubtedly that of poetry and not that of conversation.

Clearly, a number of today's poets have continued to work with traditional forms throughout their career: Richard Wilbur, Carolyn Kizer, Isabella Gardner, and W. D. Snodgrass come to mind. Dissatisfied, unsympathetic, impatient, or simply uncomfortable with traditional form, John Berryman—by contrast—invented an entirely new form for his *Dream Songs.* For his poem sequence *History,* Robert Lowell modified the sonnet form. In "Counting the Mad" Donald Justice adopted and adapted the form of a nursery rhyme, "This Little Piggy Went to Market." In "Three Moves" John Logan made use of a musical structure somewhat like that of Mozart's "Eine Kleine Nacht Musik." And in "Long Island" Marvin Bell used syntactical repetitions and overlaid images as still another means of organizing and giving both internal and external shape to the poem.

One characteristic of the modernist poem that seems less prevalent in contemporary poetry is wit, especially as the word is used to refer to a kind of cerebral-aesthetic humor. A measure of this intellectual wit still can be found in a number of Carolyn Kizer's poems and, most obviously, in a poem like Richard Wilbur's "Praise in Summer," in which the genuine and vibrant wit controlling the thrust of the last line paradoxically negates *and* affirms the entire poem's thematic concern. However, much of today's poetry is generally marked by a much broader brand of humor, often a buffoonish or slapstick comedy. In "Pro Femina" Carolyn Kizer obviously relies on a broad, healthy humor to achieve her feminist theme effectively, and in many of her poems Lucille Clifton employs the kind of sharp and wry humor which is recognizably a part of the rich Black tradition of humor; in Clifton's poems humor is as much an engagement of the physical body as it is a matter of language. In his *Dream Songs* Berryman consciously uses minstrel comedy, situation comedy, and burlesque techniques, including a kind of verbal double take. In many of his poems, Lawrence Ferlinghetti is the literary Red Skelton of his generation, the innocent clown bumbling through an absurd, though sophisticated, universe where he, as poet and person, is constantly risking absurdity. As Paul Carroll has observed, Ferlinghetti—especially when he reads his poems—sounds like a hip Will Rogers. Moreover, in contemporary poetry, comedy often belies the poet's intent; humor verges on hysteria, laughter camouflages horror: Pagliacci facing a firing squad.

The reader of modernist poetry has come to expect allusion as part and parcel of a poem: T. S. Eliot's *The Waste Land* is the archetype of the poem as footnote. However, contemporary poets have consciously avoided the excesses of literary allusion that resulted in a "poetry about poetry." Although most post–World War II poets are university graduates and professional academicians, their poems do not obviously wear their erudition on their sleeves. The reasons are varied and complex. The scarcity of allusion, in part, is the result of the democratization of poetry under the strong influence of Walt Whitman and of William Carlos Williams, both of whom advocated the use of an American language and rhythm. Moreover, because much contemporary poetry is often intensely personal, the poet responds to experience in a visceral rather than in an intellectual fashion. Response is not filtered or controlled by knowledge or formal education, nor is it shaped by a conscious sense of the formal tradition. That this is an age when the individual, the self, is threatened by the dehumanization of a technocratic society and by the overwhelming sense of imminent atomic or ecological annihilation has long been a journalistic cliché—albeit one that has recently been infused with unequaled urgency. The energy we depend on for survival, just as surely as the fetus depends on the mother's blood for survival, is running out. Events at the nuclear power plant on Three Mile Island reminded us too acutely that our technology is as flawed and dangerous as the human intelligence that produced it. Despite the cliché of annihilation, the phenomenon is all too real and has resulted in the poet's vehement affirmation of the individual self and in an equally intense effort to respond fully to experience as a person and as an artist. This kind of Emersonian self-reliance—with absolute stakes—is an implicit repudiation of Eliot's theory of tradition and the individual talent, perhaps in large part because of the contemporary poet's profound fear of that history, culture, and tradition, which are ultimately responsible for the deterioration of the modern self.

Compared to Eliot and his followers, today's poet is noticeably less concerned with the use of allusion. However, as Susan Sontag has written: "Language is the most impure, the most contaminated, the most exhausted of all materials out of which art is made. . . . It's scarcely possible for the artist to write a word (or render an image or make a gesture) that doesn't remind him of something already achieved." Consequently, because language is contaminated, because history shackles, and because post–World War II poets simply cannot escape their own (and our) ruthless memory, allusion–conscious or not–persists and is found in both expected and unexpected places.

The more obvious examples of allusion can be found in the early work of Lowell, such as "Christmas Eve Under Hooker's Statue"; it can be found in such poems as Snodgrass's "April Inventory," which can be read as a retelling of an academic Prufrock's story, with intermittent references to Shakespeare's seventy-third sonnet, Hopkins's "God's Grandeur," Edward Taylor's "Meditation Six, First Series"–and with echoes of Thoreau and Camus. Ferlinghetti's "I Am Waiting," in spite of his renunciation of "poetry about poetry," relies heavily on obvious and well-known literary phrases. In Ashbery's "Leaving the Atocha Station," Paul Carroll has ferreted out mangled echoes of Pound, Eliot, Hopkins, and others. Certain critics have noted that James Dickey's famous "The Heaven of Animals" is derivative and perhaps consciously fashioned after Edwin Muir's "The Animals." A number of Louis Simpson's poems rely on the reader's being fully conversant with the work of Walt Whitman.

The burden of language and the grasp of memory result in the contemporary poet's using other kinds of allusion. For example, the presence of Rilke is clearly felt in the concluding line of James Wright's "Lying in a Hammock. . ." The position, tone, and emotional impact of Wright's line, "I have wasted my life," echoes the concluding line of Rilke's "Torso of an Archaic Apollo," which is generally translated as "You must change your life." Rilke's ninth "Duino Elegy" is present in the very title of Maxine Kumin's book, *House, Bridge, Fountain, Gate*–just as it is present in the concluding lines of Richard Hugo's poem "Montgomery Hollow." Moreover, in much of John Ashbery's more recent poetry, there is an even more all-pervasive *frisson* of Rilke's own elusive exploration of states of feeling; a specific poem like "Street Musicians" recalls the kind of vision and perspective found in Rilke's *Das Buch der Bilder* and *Neue Gedichte*. The imagery, tone, and effect of several of Robert Bly's poems reflect the more intense presence and influence of the Spanish surrealists Neruda and Vallejo. The imaginative and emotional lilt of Cavafy, the Greek master, is occasionally felt in Gerald Stern's poems, just as the influence of the Italian poet Eugenio Montale (whom Wright has translated) is occasionally felt in Charles Wright's poems.

Rather than relying on sometimes obscure literary allusions of the past, today's poet prefers to introduce more personal allusions to specific places, people, and experiences in the poet's personal life: Long Island, Missoula, Pine Island, William Duffy. The contemporary arts, especially the popular arts and popular performers, also become points of reference: movies, folk-rock, jazz, Lana Turner, Joan Baez, Bob Dylan, John Coltrane, and others. Contemporary poetry, then, is very much the poetry of today, requiring from the reader as much full consciousness of the present as of the past, of the banal as of the sublime.

Just as the contemporary poet is more drawn toward existential experience, he or she is also less inclined to use what Eliot understood to be "the mythical method" to organize and present experience. Indeed, except as a subconscious, elemental, and perhaps inevitable ritualistic pattern of human response, myth is virtually absent from the work of most post-1945 poets. However, if the traditional mythic method at this moment in history is not entirely viable, the mythical vision and the need for it remain an active force in contemporary poetry. During the past quarter of a century, American poets seem to have felt an increasing need to be not simply myth users, but myth makers. Even when poets feel the need to use traditional myth, as Carolyn Kizer does in "Semele Recycled," that need is accompanied by a commensurate need to modify the figures and configurations of the original. Both as persons and as poets, myth makers reflect "the instinct that their work-a-day world is interpenetrated with a super rational or extrarational activity in which they can and do share." If the pattern of such more-than-human activity is not immediately accessible as part of a formalized tradition, then poets must dig it out of the accumulation of their experience and create myths closer to the contemporary experience than those inherited from myth makers of the past. By so doing, contemporary poets are also returning poetry to one of its primal and sacred functions. Along with Carolyn Kizer, they trust that future generations will "concoct a scripture explaining this."

In the poetry of W. D. Snodgrass, a rather clear pattern of extrarational activity emerges, against which the action of the poem takes place and in which the speaker senses inevitable participation. As Snodgrass says in *Heart's Needle:* "We need the landscape to repeat us." This pattern is quite simply Darwin's theory of evolution subsequently transformed into the law of the survival of the fittest. Snodgrass may not be pleased to find himself participating in this brutal dialectic, but he recognizes its energy as one of the major determinants of human activity: in "After Experience...," he juxtaposes the rules of survival spoken softly by the gentle philosopher Spinoza with those shouted by a military instructor. The same concern for survival is also the energy generating "April Inventory," in which those who seem most fit to survive are the "solid scholars" who get "the degrees, the jobs, the dollars." In his more recent cycle of poems, *The Führer Bunker,* Snodgrass has coupled the myth of the survival of the fittest with the drama of Nazi Germany, and he has sought to reconstruct this contemporary myth without subjective or moral comment.

Other poets also have discovered myth in this and other contemporary dramas and figures. For an age of violence, Sylvia Plath has turned away from the ancient mythology found in her earlier poetry, such as the Colossus of Rhodes, and toward more recent history—Hiroshima, Hitler's concentration camps—for the mythic background against which her personal suffering occurs. For an age of media, Frank O'Hara has recognized the mythic dimensions of those "stars" whose personal and public lives determine the rhythm and quality of this civilization just as surely as the fabricated gods of other mythologies. Michael S. Harper has acknowledged much the same role which Black jazz musicians serve in his imagination and no doubt in the imagination of a great many other Americans who have had an intense emotional and aesthetic relationship with those musical artists. In the character of Henry Pussycat, Berryman has erected a myth out of, and for, the suffering, middle-aged, white "human American man." But throughout contemporary poetry, one also senses that the isolated self—the multifaceted and complex "I"—rises above communal, historical, and extrarational events and assumes mythic proportions of its own. Contemporary poets seem determined to accept Wallace Stevens's words at face value and "to make of their fate an instance of all fate." The collective impact of today's poetry, then, seems to say: I am my own myth.

The blood and genes inherited by contemporary poetry, however, are not merely the formal demands of New Criticism but the full tradition of American and British poetry. Muted, modified, transformed—nonetheless, the spirit and energy of this tradition continue as vital forces in today's poetry. And it is not simply an aesthetic heritage, but a complex of formal and thematic stances that constitute the polarities not only of our art but also probably of our psychic and mythic life.

The polarized stances—toward humankind, its history, the substance and quality of its individual and communal life, its art, and its destiny—constituting the mainstream of American poetry are the Puritan tradition and the Whitman tradition. Of course, other less powerful currents also have contributed to the evolution of American poetry. But the life and energy of American poetry, especially in the twentieth century, spring primarily from the tension, balance, and occasional reconciliation between the microcosmic and macrocosmic vision of the Puritan and Whitman traditions. What is vitally important about these two major traditions is specifically that each is a comprehensive vision of and response to the total human and cosmic experience. The significance of such a vision cannot be stressed enough, for it strongly influences (perhaps determines) what a poet sees and how a poet responds—influencing the subjects and the themes of poems—as well as the poet's mode of expression or style—shaping the language, rhythm, structure, and form of poems.

Whether written by Edward Taylor or Robert Lowell, Puritan poetry arises out of the fundamental view of humans as the heirs of the specific history of the fallen Adam. It views humans as essentially corrupt, as seeking the contours of their lives in an equally corrupt universe, and as incapable of personal salvation. Characteristically intellectual and highly personal, seeking the speaker's place in history, this poetry focuses primarily on the individual's spiritual and physical limitations and deterioration. Its structure is usually complex, emblematic, and metaphysical; the texture of its language is intricate. Because contemporary Puritan poets have rejected the possibility of the traditional concept of salvation—the one thread of light that sustained the original Puritan—in large part because the death of God is accepted as a premise of contemporary existence, sin is therefore symbolically replaced by mental and emotional imbalance. Lacking the hope of salvation while still believing in profound personal evil, the more recent Puritan poet is threatened by madness and is tempted to self-destruction, even though the very act of writing poetry is an affirmative one, a saying *no* to any force that would destroy the human spirit. The poetry of Robert Lowell, Sylvia Plath, and Anne Sexton probably best exemplifies the aesthetic and moral dimensions of the Puritan tradition in contemporary American poetry.

The Whitman tradition in contemporary poetry stands in stark contrast to the earlier Puritan tradition. Refusing to submit humans to the bonds of history, sacred or secular, this tradition asserts the holiness of the Adamic self, inside and out, and celebrates the grace of purely human and physical activity in a holy universe. Impatient with and often scornful of intellectualization, it focuses on the unique and separate self and points to the self's limitless potential for transcendence. Open, loose, often the product of emotion rather than of intellect or conspicuous craftsmanship, its language also tends to be more recognizably "American" and earthy. However, if poets in the contemporary Puritan tradition accept the death of God as a premise of existence, so too do poets in the contemporary Whitman tradition accept the rather tragic futility of the original Whitman vision. Thus Whitman's vision and his poems often serve as the basis for lament, and the contemporary poet decries the betrayal of history since Whitman's prophetic songs. Such a sense of betrayal is at the root of Allen Ginsberg's "Howl" and serves as the aesthetic and moral background against which so much of Louis Simpson's and David Ignatow's poetry evolves.

As critics have noted, American poetry also has continued to experience a large measure of internationalization and reflects the presence of other traditions. The influence of the French symbolists persists. Rilke's presence seems to loom larger and larger. Pound's "discovery" of the East can be traced to the next generation: one can observe the influence of Japanese poetry on the work of poets like Gary Snyder, W. S. Merwin, and, especially, Lucien Stryk; the influence of Chinese poetry on the work of James Wright is also unmistakable. And the work of Spanish surrealists has had a profound effect on the work of poets like Philip Levine and Robert Bly. That so many of today's American poets are also active and distinguished translators—as their bibliographies in this book make obvious—has also contributed to the internationalization of contemporary poetry in America.

Clearly, then, the vitality of contemporary American poetry depends in large part on its full participation in and transformation of a rich tradition of poetry. And yet, after having posited this participation, one must also recognize the contemporary poets' real measure of dissatisfaction and restlessness not only with that tradition but also with their specific art and medium—which also accounts for the vitality and diversity of today's poetry.

The poets' restlessness with their medium is largely evident in the number of those who, for various reasons, have changed their styles radically in the course of their careers. These stylistic transformations, in turn, reflect equally radical shifts in the poets' basic assumptions about the nature and function of their art. After having mastered the lyric rooted in the tenets of New Criticism, Robert Lowell discarded the lyric form in favor of a semi-sonnet form, which he subsequently discarded to return once again to the lyric in his last poems. From compact and trippingly anapestic poems dealing with somewhat private experience, James Dickey's poems have grown more expansive, looser, and more public—often charged by a kind of revivalist energy. On the other hand, W. S. Merwin's poems have moved from technical and structural complexity toward an imaginative and emotional density that is almost hermetic. At times savagely personal, some of Merwin's poems seemed to refuse all further human contact. Donald Hall's poems have evolved from a relatively strict formalism to a more expansive, Whitmanesque, and commensurately more human organic form. Both Charles Wright's and C. K. Williams's poems have moved from a certain tight and knotty intensity to a more accessible and serene expansiveness.

Other poets have shown a restlessness with their chosen medium by attempting the techniques of other media. Experiments with the prose poem by such writers as Robert Bly, David Ignatow, and James Wright are self-evident manifestations of discontent with the limits of more traditional poetic forms. In most of *The Anonymous Lover*, John Logan sought a closer, more obvious relationship between poetic and musical language. Some of John Ashbery's poems clearly reflect the influence of action painting; Lawrence Ferlinghetti's often explore the possibilities of poetry as a kind of verbal jazz. Underlying these stylistic transformations and experiments is not merely an obsession with originality but also a profound need to shape the structures and rhythms—as well as to explore the timbre—of the voice of the individual poet and of the times.

Each age discovers or fabricates one or two all-encompassing metaphors for the quality of human experience that it confronts or seeks. It was T. S. Eliot, of course, who fabricated the first encompassing metaphor for the twentieth century; the waste land was the image of human spiritual and cultural sterility—an image that, after Hiroshima and Nagasaki, proved to be frighteningly precise in its prophetic implications. To date, no single poet seems to have fabricated *the* central metaphor for the quality of our experience since World War II. Rather, this is what seems to have happened: although *The Waste Land* was a powerful *mise en scène* of the modern situation, to a large extent its characters were composite ghosts, unreal men and women in an unreal city. Eliot was describing the human condition, not the individual condition. In other words, Eliot set the scene, but contemporary poets have peopled that waste land, mostly with their individual selves. They have described the deterioration and sterility of the individual self, thereby fabricating a cumulative metaphor for our own age.

The language of this metaphor is as stark, brutal, and familiar as the experience. More often than not, it is the language of experience and emotion—and not recollected in tranquillity. The brutalized self responds neither in pentameters nor in euphemisms—nor, at times, even in metaphor. In the midst of unbearable suffering, Sylvia Plath, as do most of us, utters the most commonplace of clichés. In "Three Moves," at the peak of emotion and frustration, John Logan utters what in polite society would be considered vulgarities—but here transformed into lyrical epiphanies by their contextual power. The emotional and aesthetic impact of Lucille Clifton's poems relies especially on her use of a Black idiom which not only seeks to duplicate the rhythms of the street but is also deeply rooted in Black and African folk songs and tales. In differing ways, today's poets have followed the advice and example of Walt Whitman and of William Carlos Williams, who both sought to democratize the language of poetry; and they agree with George Starbuck's remark: "We've got language we haven't yet used." Above all, it is the language of today's poetry that immediately strikes us as vital, contemporary, and fresh. By making poetry out of the full range of everyday speech—including obscenity, vulgarity, and slang—contemporary poets have returned to poetry a richness of expression and experience that had been absent probably since the Renaissance.

Contemporary poets have managed to reinstate in poetry a directness and honesty toward the human tribe's sexual identity and experience, with all its ramifications. The range is virtually all-encompassing: menstruation, masturbation, love making, adultery, homosexuality, lesbianism, sodomy, abortion. Whether the cause for celebration or lamentation or both, sexuality in today's poetry is neither a programmatic metaphor, a consciously Freudian exploration, nor a pseudomystical Lawrencian Victorianism. Although clearly an essential element of the poet's theme, first and foremost it is an existential human experience, capable of being simultaneously ugly and the source of grace and, as John Berryman suggests, simultaneously lyrical and vulgar: "like the memory of a lovely fuck."

An imagination of commitment that responds directly, honestly, and morally to a broad spectrum of everyday political realities is also one of the distinguishing elements of today's poetry. The political climate has become a crucial arena within which contemporary poets have exercised their talents. This interest in politics reflects the contemporary poets' belief in a poetry *engagé* and thereby returns poetry to one of its long and vital traditions. The political tradition was all but ignored during the first half of the century, especially when the notion of art for art's sake virtually prohibited poetry from being anything but hermetic and when political concern had to be masked with myth, clothed with wit, and moved by indirection. Some reactionary critics still haven't forgiven Archibald MacLeish for his political involvements and concerns. But the contemporary poet agrees with Sartre and Camus that art must be committed if it is to survive. As Ferlinghetti said: "Only the dead are disengaged."

Commitment, however, does not necessitate blatant "headline" poetry. In a statement for *The London Magazine* (1962), Sylvia Plath suggested what an imagination of commitment really implies: "the issues of our time which preoccupy me at the moment are the incalculable genetic effects of fallout and...the terrifying, mad, omnipotent marriage of big business and the military in America...[But] my poems do not turn out to be about Hiroshima, but about a child forming itself finger by finger in the dark. They are not about the terrors of mass extinction, but about the bleakness of the moon over a yew tree in a neighborhood graveyard."

The imagination of commitment is reflected in at least three obvious, though by no means exclusive, ways in today's poetry. The first includes poems informed by a general and sometimes indirect sociopolitical consciousness. Plath's preoccupation with the "incalculable genetic effects of fallout" is reflected in "Nick and the Candlestick"; addressing her young—perhaps unborn—child, she suggests the end of the world and of the universe in two stanzas that also reflect the scientific quality of her imagination:

> Let the stars
> Plummet to their dark address.
>
> Let the mercuric
> Atoms that cripple drip
> Into the terrible well....

The possible destruction of the world through a nuclear holocaust is also the immediate occasion for Wilbur's "Advice to a Prophet." In "After Experience Taught Me...," Snodgrass suggests not only the inherent horror in any system of ideas or values carried to its logical conclusion but also that terrifying brotherhood of men—the seeming inevitability of the military-industrial-university complex. The extent to which most Americans live their conscious or subconscious lives in the constant threat of nuclear annihilation is eminently clear in Kinnell's "Vapor Trail Reflected in the Frog Pond," in Snyder's "Vapor Trails," in Stafford's "At the Bomb Testing Site," and in C. K. Williams's "Tar." Clearly it is an active sociopolitical consciousness that informs Gwendolyn Brooks's "The Lovers of the Poor," as well as so many of Louis Simpson's and David Ignatow's poems. Moreover, a poem like Ginsberg's "Howl" is a full-scale indictment of the quality of American life and the recent history that has contributed to such an experience.

In the second group, specific historical events inform the poets' imaginations. The poems from W. D. Snodgrass's *The Führer Bunker* are obvious examples, since Snodgrass uses specific historical personages and events to

reconstruct that Nazi *Götterdämmerung*. Meanwhile, other poets are respond-
ing to the Nazi experience in other ways—such as Bell, in "The Extermina-
tion of the Jews," and Stern, in "The War Against the Jews"—and to other
specific historical events, recalled in Justice's poem "The Assassination" and
in Hayden's "Frederick Douglass" and "Night, Death, Mississippi." These are
only a few of the poems that suggest the imagination of commitment in con-
temporary poetry has not been challenged exclusively by the war in Vietnam.

However, Vietnam probably did occasion the largest number of overtly
political poems, perhaps more than any other single event since World War
I. Of course, World War II had generated poetry about war: Wilbur's "On the
Eyes of an SS Officer," Stryk's "Letter to Jean-Paul Baudot, at Christmas,"
and Jarrell's "The Death of the Ball Turret Gunner" are only a few examples.
Despite the fact that many of today's poets were active participants in World
War II—or perhaps because they were—that experience did not seem to grip
their imaginations as much as the conflict in Vietnam did. The poets' opposi-
tion to the war and to the political figures responsible for it was eminently
clear—in their poetry as well as in their active political lives. Poems like Bly's
"Counting Small-Boned Bodies," Levertov's "The Altars in the Street," and
Merwin's "Some Last Questions" reflect a profound moral outrage against this
nation's participation in and support of the war in Vietnam, as well as the
depth of frustration that the continued involvement in this war generated.
At the root of much antiwar poetry, moreover, was not only moral outrage
at the atrocities but also a kind of implicit belief that the war might be stopped
with the language of poetry.

Political or moral questions aside, contemporary antiwar poetry does raise
important questions—the most obvious of which is where does poetry leave
off and propaganda begin? And this question raises the equally important ques-
tion: can propagandistic poetry be good? (Dryden's "Mac Flecknoe" probably
sets a precedent, and many of today's feminist poems raise the same ques-
tions.) Moreover, contemporary antiwar poetry is the result of a peculiar set
of circumstances, for, unlike the poetry that emerged out of World War I and
World War II, the poetry generated by the war in Vietnam was written by
individuals who were noncombatants, most of whom had never been in the
embattled country. (One is reminded of the shocking contrast between Wilfred
Owen's poems written in the trenches and Rupert Brooke's chauvinistic son-
nets written in the comfort of his precious university circle.) Thus the anti-
war poetry of the sixties and seventies was based not on the reality of direct
experience but on the removed reality of the media: the atrocities were not
witnessed, they were "viewed." Often this was a poetry not about the victims
of war but about the perpetrators of war; not about the blood of war but about
the language of war; not about the pity of war but about the policy of war.
Nevertheless, if it was imperfect as poetry, as it sometimes was—an increas-
ing number of those poems now strain our willing suspension of aesthetic

disbelief—it did testify to the contemporary poets' full and human commitment to the quality of their fellow creatures' lives.

Moreover, if the political climate has become a crucial arena within which today's poets have exercised their talents, so too their work has generated an aesthetic and critical climate in which the imagination of commitment is more fully understood as a vital element in contemporary poetry. It is difficult to read much of the poetry of David Ignatow or of Philip Levine without being aware of the strong sociopolitical consciousness the work reflects. The poetry of Denise Levertov continues to reflect a refined revolutionary commitment that was so much part of the poetry she wrote during the late sixties and early seventies. In many of her recent poems, Adrienne Rich has brought her enviable powers as a poet to bear on the question of sexual identity and sexual politics. The strong, though differing, feminist sensibilities informing the work of Carolyn Kizer and Marge Piercy are clearly a direct response to an identifiable sociopolitical and cultural situation which was all but ignored by generations of poets. In his poetry and prose, Robert Bly has repeatedly sought to come to grips with a fuller reintegration of the feminine and masculine principles, as have Gary Snyder and John Logan. Of course, at the heart of much of Snyder's poetry is also a profound concern for this planet's ecological balance. In short, the imagination of commitment is not only a vital element in much of today's poetry but also seems to have become an essential attitude of the reader as well as of the poet.

The poets' moral stance toward sociopolitical events is only part of their more inclusive aesthetic, ethical, and spiritual concerns. It is important to note that many poets have been just as much concerned in their poems with the nature of poetry itself as with political phenomena. Indeed, the radical tradition in contemporary poetry and the poetics governing American poetry since 1945 might well be approached simply by a reading of poems that are either explicitly or implicitly about the art of poetry. Ashbery's "Leaving the Atocha Station" may well be an articulation of the need for a revolutionary poetic technique and a new poetic sensibility. Many of Ammons's poems are as much about the nature of poetry as they are ostensibly about natural phenomena. Snyder's "Riprap," Ferlinghetti's "Constantly risking absurdity," Creeley's "The Language," Charles Wright's "The New Poem," Bell's "White Clover," Clifton's humorous "Admonitions," Kunitz' "Single Vision," and many of Duncan's and Olson's poems—these are all statements of contemporary poetics, reflecting the contemporary poets' acute and ongoing concern about the nature of their art. In a less explicit manner, it is conceivable that James Dickey's "The Heaven of Animals," Robert Hayden's "The Night-Blooming Cereus," and Donald Hall's "Ox Cart Man" are as much explorations of the poetic process as they are observations of animals, flowers, and a shrewd old man. If the past few decades have been called an "age of poetry" rather than an "age of criticism"—because poets have only infrequently engaged in the writing of poetic theory in critical essays—they nevertheless have wrestled with the elusive nature of their art in the poems themselves, which may offer a more essential understanding of today's poetics than any analytical essay.

When confronting contemporary American poetry, it is also essential to realize that what may seem to be political issues, what may seem to be linguistic devices, and what may seem to be shockingly intimate experiences of the bedroom are, in fact, profoundly moral and spiritual explorations. Moreover, the issues of the day ought not be imposed on poems in order to reduce them to the equivalent of buzz words or slogans. It is clear, for example, that a poem like Mary Oliver's "The Fish" is not merely a statement of ecological concern any more than Elizabeth Bishop's "The Fish," Maxine Kumin's "The Grace of Geldings in Ripe Pastures," or Randall Jarrell's "The Black Swan" are merely poems about the animals mentioned in the titles. The preponderance of poems about animals in contemporary poetry suggests far more than a mere fascination with fauna, far more than a concern for ecological balance; rather, it suggests a moral and spiritual vision of the animal kingdom as an emblematic, if not always totemic, kingdom. In an age noticeably lacking in angels, saints, and heroes, certain poets seem to be returning to more primal symbols of hierarchy in the natural world.

Meanwhile, the concern of contemporary poets for various aspects of human sexuality is far more important than a seemingly adolescent fascination with bedroom antics or sex and its range of dirty words; indeed, it's more important than sexual politics. In a technocratic age that would obliterate all identity, one's sexuality is at the physical and psychic root of individual identity. Carolyn Kizer's "A Widow in Wintertime" and Isabella Gardner's "The Milkman" explore the profound psychological and emotional consequences of repressed sexuality, while Marge Piercy's "You Ask Why Sometimes I Say Stop" unearths the polarity of masculine-feminine sexual experience. The celebration of the male torso in Robert Duncan's poem by that name is as essential to the poet's homosexual identity as Anne Sexton's celebration of her uterus is essential to her female identity. Moreover, a poem like Gary Snyder's "The Bath" not only celebrates the glory of the sexual human body but also attempts to redeem that physical glory from this society's more prevalent attitude, described in James Wright's "Autumn Begins in Martins Ferry, Ohio," where "sons grow suicidally beautiful" and therefore "gallop terribly against each other's bodies." The sexual concerns of today's poets thus constitute an attempt to redeem the sexual self in a society that has traditionally suppressed it, distorted it, and indeed transformed it into a weapon.

These same sexual concerns extend far beyond social mores, practices, and weaponry. Since an explicit or implicit belief in the death of God necessarily posits the end of belief in a supernatural life or life force, it simultaneously necessitates a greater understanding of what is ostensibly the most powerful manifestation of the human life force, sexuality. In the past, the spiritual and cultural heritage of the West has been such that the traditional affirmation of the supernatural life force has been at the expense of the natural life force.

Indeed, we have no comfortable language for our sexuality except for precise scientific terms or the more graphic language of the street. And so in a language that may sometimes be awkward or fumbling, the contemporary poets' celebration of sexuality may well be equivalent to a celebration of the god within as well as an implicit affirmation of the sexual nature of poetry itself—thereby suggesting a double measure of the sacred. Clearly, the sexual concerns in a poem like James Dickey's "The Sheep Child" extend far beyond the level of the dirty joke, far beyond the matter of sexual politics; they reach into the very heart of the god and of the creator within.

Although none of these poets has publicly proclaimed allegiance to any formal ethical or religious system to date, and although some have been members of the Catholic church, for example, and later quietly left it, one can point to a diversity of profound religious experiences in the work of most contemporary poets. In some of Richard Wilbur's poems—"A Dubious Night," for example—the existence of God is at best irrelevant, at worst a handicap to the discovery of that more profound salvation discovered in purely human activity. The ending of Lawrence Ferlinghetti's "Sometime during eternity" affirms—but implicitly laments—the contemporary theological stance that God is dead; his "I Am Waiting" humorously reveals the poet's quest for and anticipation of salvation. A profound mystical sense is clearly at the heart of Allen Ginsberg's "Wales Visitation," just as it is at the heart of much of Roethke's poetry. In "Mary's Song" Sylvia Plath sees the cycle of Christian salvation reflected in contemporary history's need for sacrificial victims. Moreover, in much of her poetry one senses the ancient mysticism that affirms salvation through suffering: "The fire makes it precious."

To a large extent, most contemporary poets—like many of their modernist predecessors—view traditional, formal, and established religious belief as impossible. Rather, they affirm a personal and vital religious or mystical, spiritual sense. John Berryman is one of the few who uses the traditional Judaic-Christian mythology—complete with God, Saint Peter, and Satan—as a potentially legitimate framework for religious experience. However, the work of John Logan, perhaps one of the most truly religious poets of the generation, is a clearer example of the contemporary poet's movement from a formal and established religious belief to a more personal one. Logan's early work relied primarily on what James Dickey called an "orthodox symbology" and a religious sense. His later work, having shed the formal accouterments of religion, also has gained in intensity—tempered by a greater human complexity. The mystery of salvation is seen in its human incarnation. Grace is discovered and given and received specifically through human and incarnate acts.

Politics, sex, and religion in all their complex ramifications—the outdated taboos of so-called civilized society and polite conversation—are only a few of the primary concerns to which today's poets have addressed themselves. They are also only a few of the themes that contribute to the freshness, and especially to the relevance, of contemporary poetry. Alive with the blood and genes of the immediate and distant tradition of poetry, rebelling against all that is petrified and dead in that heritage, and asserting their fierce personal response to all that is demanded of a human being at this moment in history, contemporary American poets repeatedly affirm, with Louis Simpson, that American poetry:

> Whatever it is...must have
> A stomach that can digest
> Rubber, coal, uranium, moons, poems....
>
> It must swim for miles through the desert
> Uttering cries that are almost human.

Criticism: A Selected Bibliography

Most of the following books and pamphlets contain substantial discussions of the work of individual American poets, especially those represented in this book; some also include critical essays or statements of poetics by these poets. A few books in this bibliography, however, are primarily concerned with American poetry before 1945; still others focus on various aspects of the art of American poetry in the twentieth century. Book-length critical studies written by individual poets generally appear both in this bibliography and in the "Notes on the Poets"; book-length critical studies devoted *to* individual poets appear only in the "Notes."

With the exception of Norman Friedman's unique study of the "Wesleyan Poets" and Stanley Plumly's provocative two-part essay, "Chapter and Verse," on language and tone in the work of more recent American poets, individual critical essays aren't listed here, since most bibliographies of critical essays become outdated too quickly.

I trust that serious readers of poetry will turn to book-length bibliographies devoted to individual poets and to such standard bibliographical sources as *Contemporary Poets* (St. Martin's Press); *Contemporary Authors* (Gale Research Co.); the annual bibliographies published in *PMLA, American Literature,* and *Journal of Modern Literature;* the regular bibliographies in *Twentieth Century Literature;* and *Contemporary Literary Criticism* (Gale Research Co.), an annual volume of critical excerpts. Of course, many of the books listed on the pages that follow also include their own individual bibliographies of varying lengths.

Lastly, readers should be aware that even some of the seminal books of criticism devoted to post-1945 American poetry listed on the following pages are presently out of print and therefore available only in some of the larger libraries.

I am grateful to Jerome Mazzaro, Ralph J. Mills, Jr., Peter Stitt, and Michael Waters for their assistance in the preparation of this bibliography.

Allen, Donald M., and Warren Tallman, eds. *The Poetics of the New American Poetry.* New York: Grove, 1973.

Altieri, Charles. *Enlarging the Temple: New Directions in American Poetry During the 1960's.* Lewisburg: Bucknell University, 1979.

Bell, Marvin. *Old Snow Just Melting: Essays and Interviews.* Ann Arbor: University of Michigan, 1983.

Bellamy, Joe David, ed. *American Poetry Observed: Poets on Their Work.* Urbana: University of Illinois, 1984.

Berke, Roberta. *Bounds out of Bounds: A Compass for Recent American and British Poetry.* New York: Oxford University, 1981.

Bloom, Harold. *The Anxiety of Influence: A Theory of Poetry.* New York: Oxford University, 1973.

Bloom, Harold. *A Map of Misreading.* New York: Oxford University, 1975.

Bogan, Louise. *Achievement in American Poetry.* Chicago: Gateway, 1951.

Bogan, Louise. *A Poet's Alphabet: Reflections on the Literary Art and Vocation.* Robert Phelps and Ruth Lummer, eds. New York: McGraw-Hill, 1970.

Boyers, Robert, ed. *Excursions: Selected Literary Essays.* Port Washington, N.Y.: Kennikat, 1977.

Breslin, James E. B. *From Modern to Contemporary: American Poetry, 1945–1965.* Chicago: University of Chicago, 1984.

Bunge, Nancy, ed. *Finding the Words: Interviews with Writers Who Teach.* Athens, Ohio: Swallow/University of Ohio, 1984.

Cambon, Glauco. *Recent American Poetry.* Minneapolis: University of Minnesota, 1962.

Carroll, Paul. *The Poem in Its Skin.* Chicago: Follett, 1968.

Carruth, Hayden. *Effluences from the Sacred Caves: More Selected Essays and Reviews.* Ann Arbor: University of Michigan, 1983.

Charters, Samuel. *Some Poems/Poets: Poets and Poetry Now.* Berkeley: Oyez, 1971.

Clausen, Christopher. *The Place of Poetry: Two Centuries of an Art in Crisis.* Lexington: University Press of Kentucky, 1981.

Clausen, Jan. *A Movement of Poets: Thoughts on Poetry & Feminism.* Brooklyn: Long Haul Press, 1983.

Davie, Donald. *Trying to Explain.* Ann Arbor: University of Michigan, 1983.

Dickey, James. *Babel to Byzantium: Poets and Poetry Now.* New York: Farrar, Straus & Giroux, 1968; paperback edition, New York: Ecco, 1981.

Duberman, Martin. *Black Mountain: An Exploration in Community.* New York: Dutton, 1972.

Ehrenpreis, Irvin. *American Poetry.* Stratford-on-Avon Studies 7. New York: St. Martin's, 1965.

Faas, Ekbert, ed. *Towards a New American Poetics: Essays and Interviews.* Santa Barbara: Black Sparrow, 1978.

Francis, Robert. *Pot Shots at Poetry.* Ann Arbor: University of Michigan, 1980.

Friebert, Stuart, and David Young, eds. *A Field Guide to Contemporary Poetry and Poetics.* New York: Longman, 1980.

Friedman, Norman. "*The Wesleyan Poets I-IV,*" *Chicago Review,* vol. 18, nos. 3-4; vol. 19, nos 1, 2, 3, 1966–1967.

Goodman, Paul. *Speaking and Language: A Defence of Poetry.* New York: Random House, 1971.

Gould, Jean. *Modern American Women Poets.* New York: Dodd, Mead, 1984.

Gross, Harvey. *Sound and Form in Modern Poetry: A Study of Prosody from Thomas Hardy to Robert Lowell.* Ann Arbor: University of Michigan, 1964.

Haines, John. *Living Off the Country: Essays on Poetry and Place.* Ann Arbor: University of Michigan, 1981.

Hall, Donald. *Claims for Poetry*. Ann Arbor: University of Michigan, 1982.

Hass, Robert. *Twentieth Century Pleasures: Prose on Poetry*. New York: Ecco, 1984.

Henderson, Stephen, ed. *Understanding the New Black Poetry: Black Speech and Black Music as Poetic Reference*. New York: Morrow, 1973.

Heyen, William, ed. *American Poets in 1976*. Indianapolis: Bobbs-Merrill, 1975.

Holden, Jonathan. *The Rhetoric of the Contemporary Lyric*. Bloomington: Indiana University, 1980.

Homberger, Eric. *The Art of the Real: Poetry in England and America Since 1939*. London: J. M. Dent, 1977.

Howard, Richard. *Alone with America: Essays on the Art of Poetry in the United States Since 1950*. New York: Atheneum, 1969; enlarged edition, 1980.

Hungerford, Edward B., ed. *Poets in Progress: Critical Prefaces to Thirteen Modern American Poets*. Evanston: Northwestern University, 1967.

Kalstone, David. *Five Temperaments: Elizabeth Bishop, Robert Lowell, James Merrill, Adrienne Rich, John Ashbery*. New York: Oxford University, 1977.

Kherdian, David. *Six San Francisco Poets*. Fresno: Giligia, 1969.

Kostelanetz, Richard. *The Old Poetries and the New*. Ann Arbor: University of Michigan, 1981.

Kostelanetz, Richard, ed. *On Contemporary Literature*. New York: Avon, 1964.

Kuzma, Greg, ed. *A Book of Rereadings in Recent American Poetry*. Lincoln, Nebraska: Pebble and The Best Cellar Press, 1980.

Lensing, George S., and Ronald Moran. *Four Poets and the Emotive Imagination: Robert Bly, James Wright, Louis Simpson and William Stafford*. Baton Rouge: Louisiana State University, 1976.

Lieberman, Laurence. *Unassigned Frequencies: American Poetry in Review*. Urbana: University of Illinois, 1977.

Lifshin, Lyn, ed. *Ariadne's Thread: A Collection of Contemporary Women's Journals*. New York: Harper & Row, 1982.

Malkoff, Karl. *Crowell's Handbook of Contemporary American Poetry: A Critical Handbook of American Poetry Since 1940*. New York: Crowell, 1973.

Malkoff, Karl. *Escape from the Self*. New York: Columbia University, 1977.

Mariani, Paul. *A Usable Past: Essays on Modern and Contemporary Poetry*. Amherst: University of Massachusetts, 1984.

Martin, Robert K. *The Homosexual Tradition in American Poetry*. Austin: University of Texas, 1979.

Mazzaro, Jerome, ed. *Modern American Poetry: Essays in Criticism*. New York: David McKay, 1970.

Mazzaro, Jerome. *Postmodern American Poetry*. Urbana: University of Illinois, 1980.

Meltzer, David, ed. *The San Francisco Poets*. New York: Ballantine, 1971.

Mersmann, James F. *Out of the Vietnam Vortex: A Study of Poets and Poetry Against the War*. Lawrence: University Press of Kansas, 1974.

Mills, Ralph J., Jr. *Contemporary American Poetry*. New York: Random House, 1965.

Mills, Ralph J., Jr. *Creation's Very Self: On the Personal Element in Recent American Poetry*. Fort Worth: Texas Christian University, 1969.

Mills, Ralph J., Jr. *Cry of the Human: Essays on Contemporary American Poetry*. Urbana: University of Illinois, 1974.

Molesworth, Charles. *The Fierce Embrace: A Study of Contemporary American Poetry*. Columbia: University of Missouri, 1979.

Moss, Howard. *Whatever Is Moving*. Boston: Little, Brown, 1981.

Nelson, Cary. *Our Last First Poets: Vision and History in Contemporary American Poetry*. Urbana: University of Illinois, 1981.

Nemerov, Howard, ed. *Poets on Poetry*. New York: Basic Books, 1961.

Nemerov, Howard. *Reflexions on Poetry & Poets*. New Brunswick, N.J.: Rutgers University, 1972.

Oberg, Arthur. *Modern American Lyric*. New Brunswick, N.J.: Rutgers University, 1978.

Ossman, David. *The Sullen Art: Interviews by David Ossman with Modern American Poets*. New York: Corinth, 1963.

Ostriker, Alicia. *Writing Like a Woman*. Ann Arbor: University of Michigan, 1983.

Ostroff, Anthony, ed. *The Contemporary Poet as Artist and Critic*. Boston: Little, Brown, 1964.

Owen, Guy, ed. *Modern American Poetry: Essays in Criticism*. Deland, Fla.: Everett/Edwards, 1972.

Packard, William, ed. *The Craft of Poetry: Interviews from the New York Quarterly*. New York: Doubleday, 1974.

Parkinson, Thomas, ed. *A Casebook on the Beat*. New York: Crowell, 1961.

Paul, Sherman. *The Lost America of Love: Rereading Robert Creeley, Edward Dorn, and Robert Duncan*. Baton Rouge: Louisiana State University, 1981.

Peters, Robert. *The Great American Poetry Bake-Off*. Metuchen, N.J.: Scarecrow, 1979.

Peters, Robert. *The Great American Poetry Bake-Off, Second Series*. Metuchen, N.J.: Scarecrow, 1982.

Phillips, Robert. *The Confessional Poets*. Carbondale: Southern Illinois University, 1973.

Pierce, Roy Harvey. *The Continuity of American Poetry*. Princeton: Princeton University, 1973.

Piercy, Marge. *Parti-Colored Blocks for a Quilt*. Ann Arbor: University of Michigan, 1982.

Pinsky, Robert. *The Situation of Poetry: Contemporary Poetry and Its Traditions*. Princeton: Princeton University, 1977.

Plumly, Stanley. "Chapter and Verse," *American Poetry Review*, Vol. 7 (January—February), 1978; "Chapter and Verse, Part II," *American Poetry Review*, Vol. 7 (May—June), 1978.

Quinn, Sr. Bernetta. *The Metamorphic Tradition in Modern Poetry*. New Brunswick, N.J.: Rutgers University, 1955.

Rexroth, Kenneth. *American Poetry in the Twentieth Century*. New York: Seabury, 1973.

Rodman, Selden. *Tongues of Fallen Angels* [Interviews]. New York: New Directions, 1984.

Rosenthal, M. L. *The Modern Poetic Sequence: The Genius of Modern Poetry*. New York: Oxford University, 1983.

Rosenthal, M. L. *The Modern Poets: A Critical Introduction*. New York: Oxford University, 1962.

Rosenthal, M. L. *The New Poets: American and British Poetry Since World War II*. New York: Oxford University, 1967.

Rosenthal, M. L. *Poetry and the Common Life*. New York: Oxford University, 1974; revised edition, New York: Schocken, 1984.

Shaw, Robert B., ed. *American Poetry Since 1960: Some Critical Perspectives*. Chester Springs, Pa.: Dufour, 1974.

Simpson, Eileen. *Poets in Their Youth: A Memoir*. New York: Random House, 1982.

Simpson, Louis. *A Revolution in Taste: Studies of Dylan Thomas, Allen Ginsberg, Sylvia Plath and Robert Lowell*. New York: Macmillan, 1978.

Stepanchev, Stephen. *American Poetry Since 1945: A Critical Survey*. New York: Harper & Row, 1965.

Sternberg, Janet, ed. *The Writer on Her Work*. New York: Norton, 1980.

Tomlinson, Charles. *Some Americans: A Personal Record*. Berkeley: University of California, 1981.

Vendler, Helen. *Part of Nature, Part of Us*. Cambridge: Harvard University, 1980.

Vinson, James, ed. *Contemporary Poets*. Fourth Edition. New York: St. Martin's, 1985.

Waggoner, Hyatt H. *American Poetry from the Puritans to the Present*. Boston: Houghton Mifflin, 1968; paperback edition, New York: Dell, 1970; revised edition, Baton Rouge: Louisiana State University, 1984.

Wagner, Linda. *American Literature: The New England Heritage*. New York: Garland, 1981.

Wakoski, Diane. *Toward a New Poetry*. Ann Arbor: University of Michigan, 1979.

Writers at Work: The Paris Review Interviews. First Series. New York: Viking, 1958; Second Series, 1963; Third Series, 1967; Fourth Series, 1976; Fifth Series, 1981.

Index of Poets and Their Publishers

Intended to encourage and to help readers to buy and read books of poetry by individual poets represented in *Contemporary American Poetry*, this index is divided into two parts. The first part is an index of individual poets and many of the publishers that have published their books. The second part is an index of the names and addresses of commercial publishers, university presses, and small presses that have published work by poets represented in this anthology. These indexes do not include publishers of limited editions intended only for collectors of rare books; nor do they include the many other fine poets—not included in this anthology—whom these publishers represent.

For a more comprehensive list of commercial publishers and university presses, readers should turn to the annual *Literary Market Place: The Directory of American Book Publishing*, R. R. Bowker Company, 205 East 42nd Street, New York, New York 10017. For a more comprehensive list of small presses, readers should turn to *The International Directory of Little Magazines and Small Presses*, Dustbooks, P.O. Box 100, Paradise, California 95969.

Teachers, students, and organizations interested in inviting poets to give public readings of their work will find the names and addresses of most American poets in *A Directory of American Poets and Fiction Writers*, Poets & Writers, Inc., 201 West 54th Street, New York, New York 10019.

Many state arts councils have funds to help sponsor public readings by poets and fiction writers, as does the Literature Program, National Endowment for the Arts, 1100 Pennsylvania Avenue NW, Washington, D.C. 20506.

INDEX OF POETS

(And Their Publishers)

INDEX OF POETS AND THEIR PUBLISHERS

INDEX OF PUBLISHERS

(And Poets They Publish)

Ampersand Press, Department of English, Roger Williams College, Bristol, Rhode Island 02809 *Lucien Stryk*

Atheneum Publishers, 597 Fifth Avenue, New York, New York 10017 *Marvin Bell, Randall Jarrell, Donald Justice, James Merrill, W. S. Merwin, Mark Strand*

Beacon Press, 25 Beacon Street, Boston, Massachusetts 02108 *Robert Bly*

Black Sparrow Press, Box 3993, Santa Barbara, California 93130 *John Ashbery, Robert Creeley, Robert Duncan, Denise Levertov*

BOA Editions, Ltd., 92 Park Avenue, Brockport, New York 14420. (Books distributed by Writer & Books, Inc., 892 South Clinton Street, Rochester, New York 14620) *Isabella Gardner, Donald Hall, David Ignatow, Carolyn Kizer, John Logan, Louis Simpson, W. D. Snodgrass, William Stafford, Richard Wilbur*

Broadside Press, 74 Glendale Avenue, Highland Park, Michigan 48203 *Gwendolyn Brooks*

Burning Deck Press, 71 Elmgrove Avenue, Providence, Rhode Island 02906 *W. D. Snodgrass, Mark Strand, C. K. Williams*

City Lights Books, Inc., 261 Columbus Avenue, San Francisco, California 94133 *Lawrence Ferlinghetti, Allen Ginsberg, Frank O'Hara*

Copper Canyon Press, P.O. Box 271, Port Townsend, Washington 98368 *Carolyn Kizer*

The Dial Press, 245 Park Avenue, New York, New York 10167. (Books distributed by Doubleday Publishing Co.) *Robert Bly*

Doubleday Publishing Co., 245 Park Avenue, New York, New York 10167 *James Dickey, Theodore Roethke, Lucien Stryk*

The Ecco Press, 18 West 30th Street, New York, New York 10001. (Books distributed by W. W. Norton & Co., Inc.) *John Ashbery, Alan Dugan, John Logan*

Farrar, Straus & Giroux, Inc., 19 Union Square West, New York, New York 10003 *John Berryman, Elizabeth Bishop, Randall Jarrell, Robert Lowell, James Wright*

Field, Rice Hall, Oberlin College, Oberlin, Ohio 44074 *Charles Wright*

Four Seasons Foundation, Box 31190, San Francisco, California 94131 *Allen Ginsberg, Gary Snyder*

David R. Godine Publisher, Inc., 306 Dartmouth Street, Boston, Massachusetts 02116. (Books distributed by Harper & Row, Publishers, Inc.) *Marvin Bell, Donald Hall, William Stafford*

Graywolf Press, P.O. Box 142, Port Townsend, Washington 98368 *Richard Hugo, Stanley Kunitz, Philip Levine, William Stafford*

Grove Press, Inc., 196 West Houston Street, New York, New York 10014. (Books distributed by Random House, Inc.) *Frank O'Hara*

Harcourt Brace Jovanovich, Inc., 757 Third Avenue, New York, New York 10017 *Robert Lowell, Richard Wilbur*

Harper & Row, Publishers, Inc., 10 East 53rd Street, New York, New York 10022 *Robert Bly, Gwendolyn Brooks, Allen Ginsberg, Donald Hall, Sylvia Plath, W. D. Snodgrass, William Stafford*

Houghton Mifflin Co., Two Park Street, Boston, Massachusetts 02108 *Galway Kinnell, Anne Sexton, Gerald Stern*

Alfred A. Knopf, Inc., 201 East 50th Street, New York, New York 10022 *Frank O'Hara, Marge Piercy, Sylvia Plath, W. D. Snodgrass*

Little, Brown & Co., 34 Beacon Street, Boston, Massachusetts 02106 *David Ignatow, Stanley Kunitz, Mary Oliver*

Liveright Publishing Corp., 500 Fifth Avenue, New York, New York 10110. (Books distributed by W. W. Norton & Co., Inc.) *Robert Hayden*

Metro Book Co., 3208 Cahuenga Boulevard, West, Los Angeles, California 90068 *Gerald Stern*

William Morrow & Co., Inc., 105 Madison Avenue, New York, New York 10016 *Louis Simpson*

New Directions Publishing Corp., 80 Eighth Avenue, New York, New York 10011. (Books distributed by W. W. Norton & Co., Inc.) *Robert Creeley, Robert Duncan, Lawrence Ferlinghetti, Denise Levertov, Gary Snyder*

North Point Press, 850 Talbot Avenue, Berkeley, California 94706 *W. S. Merwin, Gary Snyder*

W. W. Norton & Co., Inc., 500 Fifth Avenue, New York, New York 10110 *A. R. Ammons, Richard Hugo, Adrienne Rich*

Ohio University Press, Scott Hall 143, Athens, Ohio 45701 *Lucien Stryk*

Pancake Press, 163 Galewood Circle, San Francisco, California 94131 *John Logan*

Random House, Inc., 201 East 50th Street, New York, New York 10022 *Lucille Clifton, Gerald Stern, C. K. Williams, Charles Wright, James Wright*

Charles Scribner's Sons, 597 Fifth Avenue, New York, New York 10017 *Robert Creeley, Robert Duncan*

The Sheep Meadow Press, 5247 Independence Avenue, Riverdale-on-Hudson, New York 10471. (Books distributed by Persea Books, 225 Lafayette Street, New York, New York 10012) *David Ignatow, Stanley Kunitz*

Slow Loris Press, 923 Highview Street, Pittsburgh, Pennsylvania 15206 *Richard Hugo, David Ignatow*

The Swallow Press, Inc., 811 West Junior Terrace, Chicago, Illinois 60613. (Books distributed by Ohio University Press) *Lucien Stryk*

Ticknor & Fields, 52 Vanderbilt Avenue, New York, New York 10017. (Books distributed by Houghton Mifflin Co.) *Louis Simpson*

University of California Press, 2120 Berkeley Way, Berkeley, California 94720 *Robert Creeley, Charles Olson*

University of Illinois Press, 54 East Gregory Drive, Champaign, Illinois 61820. (Books distributed by Harper & Row, Publishers, Inc.) *Michael S. Harper*

University of Massachusetts Press, Box 429, Amherst, Massachusetts 01004 *Lucille Clifton*

University of Pittsburgh Press, 127 North Bellefield Avenue, Pittsburgh, Pennsylvania 15260 *Michael S. Harper*

The Viking Press (Viking/Penguin), 40 West 23rd Street, New York, New York 10010 *John Ashbery, Maxine Kumin, Lucien Stryk*

Franklin Watts, Inc., 387 Park Avenue South, New York, New York 10016 *Louis Simpson*

Wesleyan University Press, 110 Mt. Vernon Street, Middletown, Connecticut 06457. (Books distributed by Harper & Row, Publishers, Inc.) *John Ashbery, Robert Bly, James Dickey, David Ignatow, Donald Justice, Marge Piercy, Louis Simpson, Charles Wright, James Wright*

A Note on the Editor

A. Poulin, Jr., was born of immigrant Québecois parents in Lisbon, Maine. He received a B.A. from St. Francis College, an M.A. from Loyola University (Chicago), and an M.F.A. from the University of Iowa; he did postgraduate work at the State University of New York at Buffalo. He has taught for the European Division of the University of Maryland, at the University of New Hampshire, and at St. Francis College, where he was chairman of the Division of Humanities and assistant to the president for curriculum planning and development. Since 1971 Poulin has taught at the State University of New York, College at Brockport, where he is professor of English and Faculty Exchange Scholar, and in 1980 he was Visiting Fulbright Lecturer in Contemporary American Poetry at the universities of Athens and Thessaloniki in Greece.

Poulin also has been director of the Brockport Writers Forum and has recorded videotaped interviews with more than twenty contemporary poets, including John Ashbery, Robert Bly, Robert Creeley, Lawrence Ferlinghetti, Allen Ginsberg, Robert Hayden, David Ignatow, Galway Kinnell, Carolyn Kizer, Stanley Kunitz, John Logan, Adrienne Rich, Anne Sexton, Louis Simpson, Gary Snyder, William Stafford, and Mark Strand—some of the poets represented in this edition of *Contemporary American Poetry*.

A poet, translator, and editor, Poulin has written the following books and chapbooks of poetry: *In Advent* (1972); *Catawba: Omens, Prayers & Songs* (1977); *The Widow's Taboo: Poems After the Catawba* (1977); *The Nameless Garden* (1978); *The Slaughter of Pigs* (1981); *Makers and Lovers* (1984); and *Begin Again* (1985). His books of translations include *Duino Elegies and The Sonnets to Orpheus* by Rainer Maria Rilke (1977); five collections of French poems by Rilke: *Saltimbanques* (1978), *The Roses & The Windows* (1980), *The Astonishment of Origins* (1982), *Orchards* (1982), and *The Migration of Powers* (1984); and *Poems* by the Québecois poet Anne Hébert (1980). Besides the four editions of *Contemporary American Poetry* (1971, 1975, 1980, 1985), Poulin is also coeditor with David A. DeTurk of *The American Folk Scene: Dimensions of the Folksong Revival* (1967) and editor of *A Ballet for the Ear: Interviews, Essays, and Reviews* by John Logan (1983).

For his poetry and translations, Poulin has received both a creative writing fellowship and a translator's grant from the National Endowment for the Arts, a translation award from Columbia University's Translation Center, a Faculty Enrichment Programme grant for research and translation from the Embassy of Canada, and several fellowships and grants-in-aid from the Research Foundation of the State University of New York; twice he has been a fellow at Yaddo. He also has received several program grants from the National Endowment for the Arts, the New York State Council on the Arts, and the Ford Foundation.

In addition to teaching and writing, Poulin has served as a member of the State University of New York's University-Wide Committee on the Arts and as a member of the Literature Panel of the New York State Council on the Arts. Moreover, he was founding executive director of the New York State Literary Center and is the founding editor and publisher of BOA Editions, Ltd., a nonprofit organization devoted to the publication of poetry and of poetry in translation.

A. Poulin, Jr., currently resides in Brockport, New York, with the metalsmith and jeweler B. H. Poulin and their daughter, Daphne.

Acknowledgments

A.R. Ammons: "Apologia Pro Vita Sua," "Laser," "He Held Radical Light," "Working with Tools," "The Unifying Principle," "Cut the Grass," "The City Limits," and "The Eternal City" are reprinted from COLLECTED POEMS, 1951–1971, by A.R. Ammons. Copyright © 1972 by A.R. Ammons. "White Dwarf" "Distraction," "Neighbors," and "Breaking Out" are reprinted from A COAST OF TREES, by A.R. Ammons. Copyright © 1981 by A.R. Ammons. "Extrication" and "Volitions" are reprinted from WORLDLY HOPES, Poems by A.R. Ammons. Copyright © 1982 by A.R. Ammons. All by permission of W.W. Norton & Company, Inc.

John Ashbery: "As You Came from the Holy Land" from *Self-Portrait in a Convex Mirror* by John Ashbery. Copyright © 1972, 1973, 1974, 1975 by John Ashbery. "The Ice-Cream Wars" and "Street Musicians" from *Houseboat Days* by John Ashbery. Copyright © 1975, 1976, 1977 by John Ashbery. "Paradoxes and Oxymorons" from *Shadow Train* by John Ashbery. Copyright © 1980, 1981 by John Ashbery. "Introduction" from *A Wave* by John Ashbery. Copyright © 1984 by John Ashbery. All reprinted by permission of Viking Penguin Inc. "They Dream Only of America" copyright © 1959 and "Leaving the Atocha Station" copyright © 1961 by John Ashbery reprinted from *The Tennis Court Oath* by permission of Wesleyan University Press. "Definition of Blue" from *The Double Dream of Spring* copyright © 1970 by John Ashbery. "Picture of Little J.A. in a Prospect of Flowers" from *Some Trees* copyright © 1956 by John Ashbery. Both reprinted by permission of Georges Borchardt, Inc. and the author.

Marvin Bell: "Drawn by Stones, by Earth, by Things That Have Been in the Fire," "White Clover," "They," and "The Nest" from *Drawn by Stones, by Earth, by Things That Have Been in the Fire.* Copyright © 1984 by Marvin Bell. "During the War," "The Last Thing I Say," and "These Green-Going-to-Yellow" from *These Green-Going-to-Yellow.* Copyright © 1981 by Marvin Bell. "The Mystery of Emily Dickinson" and "To Dorothy" from *Stars Which Do Not See.* Copyright © 1977 by Marvin Bell. "Homage to the Runner" from *The Escape into You.* Copyright © 1971 by Marvin Bell. "The Extermination of the Jews" from *A Probable Volume of Dreams.* Copyright © 1969 by Marvin Bell. All reprinted with the permission of Atheneum Publishers. "Long Island" copyright © 1984 by Marvin Bell. Reprinted with the permission of Marvin Bell.

John Berryman: "Song of the Tortured Girl" from *Short Poems* by John Berryman. Copyright 1948 by John Berryman. Selections from *The Dream Songs* by John Berryman. Copyright © 1959, 1962, 1963, 1964, 1965, 1966, 1967, 1968, 1969 by John Berryman. Selection from "Eleven Addresses to the Lord" from *Love and Fame* by John Berryman. Copyright © 1970 by John Berryman. "Henry's Understanding" from *Delusions, Etc.* by John Berryman. Copyright © 1969, 1971 by John Berryman. Copyright © 1972 by the Estate of John Berryman. All reprinted with the permission of Farrar, Straus & Giroux, Inc.

Elizabeth Bishop: "The Man-Moth," "The Fish," "Letter to N.Y.," and "The Armadillo" from *The Complete Poems* by Elizabeth Bishop. Copyright © 1935, 1936, 1940, 1946, 1955, 1956, 1957, 1969 by Elizabeth Bishop. Renewed copyright © 1968, 1973 by Elizabeth Bishop. "One Art" from *Geography III* by Elizabeth Bishop. Copyright © 1976 by Elizabeth Bishop. "One Art" originally appeared in *The New Yorker.* "North Haven" by Elizabeth Bishop. Copyright © 1978 by Elizabeth Bishop.

ACKNOWLEDGMENTS

"North Haven" appeared originally in *The New Yorker.* "In the Waiting Room" from *Elizabeth Bishop: The Complete Poems 1927-1979.* Copyright © 1983 by Alice Helen Methfessel. Copyright © 1971 by Elizabeth Bishop. All reprinted by permission of Farrar, Straus & Giroux, Inc.

Robert Bly: "Surprised by Evening," "Waking from Sleep," "Poem in Three Parts," "Snowfall in the Afternoon," "In a Train," "Driving to Town Late to Mail a Letter," and "Watering the Horse" copyright © 1962 by Robert Bly. Reprinted from *Silence in the Snowy Fields,* as published by Wesleyan University Press. "At Midocean" and "In Rainy September" copyright © 1984 by Robert Bly. "After Long Busyness" copyright © 1973 by Robert Bly. Reprinted from *Jumping Out of Bed,* as published by The Barre Press. "Looking into a Tide Pool" copyright © 1971 by Robert Bly. Reprinted from *The Morning Glory,* as published by Kayak Books. All reprinted with the permission of Robert Bly. "For My Son Noah, Ten Years Old," "Visiting Emily Dickinson's Grave with Robert Francis," and "My Father's Wedding" from *The Man in the Black Coat Turns.* Copyright © 1981 by Robert Bly. A Dial Press book. Reprinted by permission of Doubleday & Company, Inc. "Driving My Parents Home at Christmas," "Insect Heads," and "Passing an Orchard by Train" from *This Tree Will Be Here for a Thousand Years* by Robert Bly. Copyright © 1979 by Robert Bly. From *Light Around the Body* by Robert Bly: "Counting Small-Boned Bodies," copyright © 1967 by Robert Bly. "The Hermit" copyright © 1967 by Robert Bly. "Looking Into a Face" copyright © 1965 by Robert Bly. From *Sleepers Joining Hands* by Robert Bly: "Shack Poem" copyright © 1971 by Robert Bly. All reprinted by permission of Harper & Row, Publishers, Inc.

Gwendolyn Brooks: From *The World of Gwendolyn Brooks* by Gwendolyn Brooks: "kitchenette building," "the mother," "a song in the front yard," "of De Witt Williams on his way to Lincoln Cemetery," and "Negro Hero" copyright 1945 by Gwendolyn Brooks Blakely. "We Real Cool" copyright © 1959 by Gwendolyn Brooks. "The Lovers of the Poor" copyright © 1960 by Gwendolyn Brooks. All reprinted by permission of Harper & Row, Publishers, Inc. "An Aspect of Love, Alive in the Ice and Fire" from *Riot* and "To Don at Salaam" from *Family Pictures,* both by Gwendolyn Brooks, by permission of Broadside Press. Both © 1970 by Gwendolyn Brooks Blakely.

Lucille Clifton: "Admonitions," "If I Stand in My Window," and "Miss Rosie" from *Good Times* copyright © 1969 by Lucille Clifton. "The Lost Baby Poem" from *Good News about the Earth* copyright © 1972 by Lucille Clifton. "God's Mood," "Roots," "To a Dark Moses," "She Understands Me," "Cutting Greens," "At Last We Killed the Roaches," "Breaklight," "The Carver," and "Come Home from the Movies" from *An Ordinary Woman* copyright © 1974 by Lucille Clifton. All by permission of Curtis Brown, Ltd. Poems from *Two-Headed Woman* by Lucille Clifton reprinted by permission of The University of Massachusetts Press.

Robert Creeley: "The Business," "I Know a Man," "A Form of Women," "A Wicker Basket," "The Flower," "The Rain," "The Memory," and "The Rescue" from *For Love Poems 1950 – 1960* by Robert Creeley. Copyright © 1962 by Robert Creeley. Reprinted by permission of Charles Scribner's Sons. "The Language," "The Window," "Moment," and "On Vacation" from *The Collected Poems of Robert Creeley.* © 1982 by The Regents of the University of California, reprinted by Permissions of the University of California Press. "First Rain," "Mother's Voice," "Outside," and "The Movie Run Backward" from Robert Creeley, *Mirrors.* Copyright © 1983 by Robert Creeley. Reprinted by permission of New Directions Publishing Corporation.

James Dickey: "The Heaven of Animals," "The Performance," "The Hospital Window," "In the Mountain Tent," "Sled Burial, Dream Ceremony," "The Sheep Child," "Adultery," and "Deer Among Cattle" reprinted from *Poems 1957 – 1967* by James Dickey. Copyright © 1960, 1961, 1962, 1965, 1966. All by permission of Wesleyan University

Press. "The Heaven of Animals," "The Hospital Window," and "In the Mountain Tent" first appeared in *The New Yorker*. "False Youth: Autumn: Clothes of the Age" from *The Strength of Fields* by James Dickey. Copyright © 1977 by James Dickey. "Doorstep, Lightning, Waif-Dreaming" copyright © 1982 by The Kenyon Review. From *Puella* by James Dickey. All reprinted by permission of Doubleday & Company, Inc.

Alan Dugan: "Love Song: I and Thou," "Tribute to Kafka for Someone Taken," "Elegy," "To a Redheaded Do-Good Waitress," "For Masturbation," "Fabrication of Ancestors," "Poem (What's the balm)," "Elegy for a Puritan Conscience," "Prayer," "On Leaving Town," " 'Space Is Not Merely a Background...,' " "Untitled Poem (Once, one of my students read a book we had.)," "On Finding the Tree of Life," "Last Statement for a Last Oracle" copyright © 1961, 1963, 1967, 1974, 1981 by Alan Dugan. From *New and Collected Poems, 1961 – 1983* by Alan Dugan, published by The Ecco Press in 1983. Reprinted by permission.

Robert Duncan: "Often I Am Permitted to Return to a Meadow," "Poetry, A Natural Thing," and "Ingmar Bergman's *Seventh Seal*" from Robert Duncan, *The Opening of the Field*. Copyright © 1960 by Robert Duncan. "Such Is the Sickness of Many a Good Thing," "Bending the Bow," "The Torso," and "My Mother Would Be a Falconress" from Robert Duncan, *Bending the Bow*. Copyright © 1963, 1966, 1968 by Robert Duncan. "The Work" from Robert Duncan, *Ground Work*. Copyright © 1984 by Robert Duncan. All reprinted by permission of New Directions Publishing Corp.

Lawrence Ferlinghetti: "Sometime during eternity," "Constantly risking absurdity and death," "The pennycandystore beyond the El," and "I Am Waiting" from Lawrence Ferlinghetti, *A Coney Island of the Mind*. Copyright 1955, © 1957 by Lawrence Ferlinghetti. "Monet's Lilies Shuddering" from Lawrence Ferlinghetti, *Who Are We Now?* Copyright © 1976 by Lawrence Ferlinghetti. "The Photo of Emily" from Lawrence Ferlinghetti, *Over All the Obscene Boundaries*. Copyright © 1984 by Lawrence Ferlinghetti. All by permission of New Directions Publishing Corp.

Isabella Gardner: "Summers Ago," "Lines to a Seagreen Lover," "In the Museum," "The Widow's Yard," "The Milkman," "Letter from Slough Pond," "Part of the Darkness," "On Looking in the Looking Glass," "To Thoreau on Rereading Walden," and "That Was Then" copyright 1980 by Isabella Gardner. Copyright © 1984 by The Estate of Isabella Gardner. Reprinted from *That Was Then: New and Selected Poems* by Isabella Gardner with the permission of BOA Editions, Ltd.

Allen Ginsberg: From *Collected Poems: 1947 – 1980* by Allen Ginsberg: "Howl" copyright © 1956, 1959 by Allen Ginsberg. "America" copyright © 1956, 1959 by Allen Ginsberg. "Love Poem on Theme by Whitman" copyright © 1978 by Allen Ginsberg. "Psalm III" copyright © 1978 by Allen Ginsberg. "Wales Visitation" copyright © 1968 by Allen Ginsberg. "On Neal's Ashes" copyright © 1972 by Allen Ginsberg. "Fourth Floor, Dawn, Up All Night Writing Letters" copyright © 1980 by Allen Ginsberg. "Ode to Failure" copyright © 1982 by Allen Ginsberg. All reprinted by permission of Harper & Row, Publishers, Inc.

Donald Hall: "My Son, My Executioner," "Digging," and "The Man in the Dead Machine" copyright © 1969 by Donald Hall. Reprinted from *The Alligator Bride: Poems New and Selected*, as published by Harper & Row, with the permission of Donald Hall. "The Town of Hill" from *The Town of Hill* by Donald Hall. Copyright 1971, 1972, 1973, 1974, 1975 by Donald Hall. Reprinted by permission of David R. Godine, Publisher, Boston. "The Toy Bone" copyright © 1979 by Donald Hall. Reprinted from *The Toy Bone* by Donald Hall with the permission of BOA Editions, Ltd. "Names of Horses" and "Ox Cart Man" reprinted by permission; © 1977 The New Yorker Magazine, Inc. From *Kicking the Leaves* by Donald Hall. "Maple Syrup" copyright © 1976 by Donald Hall. "Kicking the Leaves" copyright © 1975 by Donald Hall. Both reprinted by permission of Harper & Row, Publishers, Inc.

Michael S. Harper: "Healing Song," "Grandfather," "Buck," "Nightmare Begins Responsibility," and "Here Where Coltrane Is" From *Images of Kin: New and Selected Poems* by Michael S. Harper reprinted by permission of The University of Illinois Press. Copyright © 1977 by The University of Illinois Press. "The Borning Room" and "Song" reprinted from *Song: I Want a Witness* by Michael Harper by permission of The University of Pittsburgh Press. © 1972 by Michael Harper. "Black Study" and "New Season" reprinted from *Dear John, Dear Coltrane* by Michael Harper, as published by The University of Pittsburgh Press. Copyright © 1970, 1984 by Michael Harper and reprinted with the permission of Michael Harper. "New Season" originally appeared in *Poetry*.

Robert Hayden: "The Tattooed Man" is reprinted from AMERICAN JOURNAL, Poems by Robert Hayden with the permission of Liveright Publishing Corporation. Copyright © 1978 by Robert Hayden. Copyright © 1982 by Erma Hayden. Selections are reprinted from ANGLE OF ASCENT, New and Selected Poems by Robert Hayden, with the permission of Liveright Publishing Corporation. Copyright © 1975, 1972, 1970, 1966 by Robert Hayden. "The Prisoners" from *American Journal* copyright c 1978 by Robert Hayden copyright c 1982 by Erma Hayden, reprinted with the permission of Michael S. Harper and the Estate of Robert Hayden.

Richard Hugo: Poetry selections are reprinted from MAKING CERTAIN IT GOES ON, The Collected Poems of Richard Hugo, by permission of W.W. Norton & Company. Copyright © 1984 by The Estate of Richard Hugo.

David Ignatow: "My Place" copyright © 1965 by David Ignatow "Sunday at the State Hospital" copyright © 1960 by David Ignatow "Epitaph," "The Bagel," "Rescue the Dead," and "Against the Evidence" copyright © 1968 by David Ignatow "First Coffin Poem" copyright © 1969 by David Ignatow "Communion" and "Waiting Inside" copyright © 1970 by David Ignatow. All from *Poems 1934–1969*, reprinted by permission of Wesleyan University Press. "The Question" copyright © 1978 by David Ignatow; reprinted from *Tread the Dark* as printed by Atlantic – Little, Brown & Co., with the permission of David Ignatow. "He got his friends . . .," "Lying quietly on the bed," and "In the spaces . . ." Reprinted from *Leaving the Door Open* by David Ignatow by permission of The Sheep Meadow Press. "[I am proud]" and "[My infinite child]" copyright © 1979 by David Ignatow. Reprinted from *Sunlight: A Sequence for My Daughter* by David Ignatow with the permission of BOA Editions, Ltd.

Randall Jarrell: Selections from *The Complete Poems* by Randall Jarrell. Copyright 1936, 1941, 1945, 1951, 1969 by Mrs. Randall Jarrell. Copyright renewed © 1968, 1969, 1972 by Mrs. Randall Jarrell. "A Camp in the Prussian Forest" from *The Complete Poems* by Randall Jarrell. Copyright 1946 by Mrs. Randall Jarrell. Copyright renewed © 1973 by Mrs. Randall Jarrell. All reprinted with the permission of Farrar, Straus and Giroux, Inc. Randall Jarrell, "The Woman at the Washington Zoo" from *The Woman at the Washington Zoo*. Copyright © 1960 by Randall Jarrell. Reprinted with the permission of Atheneum Publishers.

Donald Justice: "Landscape with Little Figures" and "Counting the Mad" copyright © 1981 by Donald Justice. Reprinted from *The Summer Anniversaries*. "Men at Forty," "The Missing Person," "The Tourist from Syracuse," and "Bus Stop" copyright 1965, 1966 by Donald Justice. Reprinted from *Night Light*. All by permission of Wesleyan University Press. Poems from *Selected Poems*. Copyright © 1979 by Donald Justice. Reprinted with the permission of Atheneum Publishers. "Complaint of the Grandparents" reprinted by permission of Gramercy Review. "In Memory of the Unknown Poet Robert Boardman Vaughn" copyright © 1984 by Donald Justice. Reprinted as originally published by *Antaeus* with the permission of Donald Justice.

Galway Kinnell: "First Song" from *What a Kingdom It Was* by Galway Kinnell. Copyright © 1960 by Galway Kinnell. "How Many Nights," "Vapor Trail Reflected in the Frog Pond," "The Bear," and "Last Songs" from *Body Rags* by Galway Kinnell.

Copyright © 1967 by Galway Kinnell. "Saint Francis and the Sow" from *Mortal Acts, Mortal Words* by Galway Kinnell. Copyright © 1960 by Galway Kinnell. "On Frozen Fields" from *Flower Herding on Mount Monadnock* by Galway Kinnell. Copyright © 1964 by Galway Kinnell. "Under the Maud Moon" from *The Book of Nightmares* by Galway Kinnell. Copyright © 1971 by Galway Kinnell. All reprinted by permission of Houghton Mifflin Company. "The Fundamental Project of Technology" copyright © 1984 by Galway Kinnell. Reprinted with the permission of Galway Kinnell.

Carolyn Kizer: "I will speak about women of letters..." from "Pro Femina" copyright © 1965 by Carolyn Kizer. Reprinted from *Knock Upon Silence* as published by Doubleday. "A Widow in Wintertime" and "The Ungrateful Garden" copyright © 1971 by Carolyn Kizer. Reprinted from *Midnight Was My Cry: New and Selected Poems* as published by Doubleday. All by permission of Carolyn Kizer. "Semele Recycled," "The Copulating Gods," and "The Blessing" copyright © 1984 by Carolyn Kizer. Reprinted from *Yin* by Carolyn Kizer with the permission of BOA Editions, Ltd.

Maxine Kumin: Poems from *Our Ground Time Here Will Be Brief* by Maxine Kumin. Copyright © 1965, 1971, 1972, 1975, 1976, 1978, 1979, 1980, 1981 by Maxine Kumin. "How It Is" and "The Longing To Be Saved" originally appeared in *The New Yorker*. Reprinted by permission of Viking Penguin Inc.

Stanley Kunitz: Poems from *The Poems of Stanley Kunitz: 1928 – 1978* copyright 1930, 1944, 1953, © 1957, 1971, 1978, 1979 by Stanley Kunitz. By permission of Little, Brown and Company in association with the Atlantic Monthly Press. "The Wellfleet Whale" copyright © 1983 by Stanley Kunitz. Reprinted from *The Wellfleet Whale and Companion Poems,* as published by The Sheep Meadow Press, with the permission of Stanley Kunitz. "The Abduction" copyright © 1984 by Stanley Kunitz. Reprinted with the permission of Stanley Kunitz.

Denise Levertov: "The Jacob's Ladder," "Hypocrite Women," "A Psalm Praising the Hair of Man's Body," "The Wings," Stepping Westward," and "The Altars in the Street" from Denise Levertov, *Poems 1960-1967.* Copyright © 1961, 1964, 1966 by Denise Levertov. "Intrusion" and "The Poem Unwritten" from Denise Levertov, *Footprints.* Copyright © 1970, 1972 by Denise Levertov. "Ways of Conquest" from Denise Levertov, *The Freeing of the Dust.* Copyright © 1975 by Denise Levertov. "Wedding-Ring" from Denise Levertov, *Life in the Forest.* Copyright © 1975 by Denise Levertov. "Seeing for a Moment" and "Passage" from Denise Levertov, *Oblique Prayers.* Copyright © 1984 by Denise Levertov. "Man Alone" from Denise Levertov, *Footprints.* Copyright © 1972 by Denise Levertov. All reprinted by permission of New Directions Publishing Corporation.

Philip Levine: "Animals Are Passing from Our Lives" copyright © 1968 by Philip Levine and "To a Child Trapped in a Barber Shop" copyright © 1966 by Philip Levine reprinted from *Not This Pig* by permission of Wesleyan University Press. Philip Levine, "You Can Have It" and "Let Me Begin Again" from *7 Years from Somewhere.* Copyright © 1979 by Philip Levine. Philip Levine, "Starlight" from *Ashes.* Copyright © 1979 by Philip Levine. Philip Levine, "Zaydee" from *1933.* Copyright © 1974 by Philip Levine. Philip Levine, "Coming Home" and "They Feed They Lion" from *They Feed They Lion.* Copyright © 1972 by Philip Levine. All reprinted by permission of Atheneum Publishers. "The House" copyright © 1983 by Philip Levine. Reprinted with the permission of Philip Levine. (Previously published in the now defunct *Midwestern Poetry Review.*)

John Logan: "To a Young Poet Who Fled," "Spring of the Thief," "Three Moves," "Suzanne," and "Love Poem" copyright c 1963, 1969 by John Logan. From *Only the Dreamer Can Change the Dream* by John Logan, published by The Ecco Press in 1981. Reprinted by permission. "Avocado" from *The Transformation: Poems January to March 1981* by John Logan. Reprinted by permission of Pancake Press. "Poem for

ACKNOWLEDGMENTS

My Brother," "Believe It," and "Poem in Progress: Second Prelude. Reality in Albuquerque: The Son" copyright © 1981 by John Logan. Reprinted from *The Bridge of Change: Poems 1974–1980* by John Logan with the permission of BOA Editions, Ltd. "Happening on Aegina" from *Two Poems of Greece* by John Logan reprinted by permission of *The American Poetry Review*.

Robert Lowell: "Colloquy in Black Rock" and "Christmas Eve Under Hooker's Statue" from *Lord Weary's Castle*, copyright 1946, 1974 by Robert Lowell. Reprinted by permission of Harcourt Brace Jovanovich, Inc. "Memories of West Street and Lepke," "Man and Wife," "To Speak of Woe That Is in Marriage," and "Skunk Hour" from *Life Studies* by Robert Lowell. Copyright c 1956, 1959 by Robert Lowell. "Eye and Tooth" from *For the Union Dead* by Robert Lowell. Copyright © 1962, 1964 by Robert Lowell. "Homecoming" and "Epilogue" from *Day by Day* by Robert Lowell. Copyright © 1975, 1976, 1977 by Robert Lowell. "History" from *History* by Robert Lowell. Copyright © 1967, 1968, 1969, 1970, 1973 by Robert Lowell. All by permission of Farrar, Straus & Giroux, Inc.

James Merrill: Poems from *From the First Nine: Poems 1946–1976*. Copyright © 1981, 1982 James Merrill. Reprinted with the permission of Atheneum Publishers. "Waterspout" copyright © 1984 by James Merrill. Originally appeared in *The Boston Review*. Reprinted with the permission of James Merrill.

W.S. Merwin: W.S. Merwin, "The Drunk in the Furnace" from *The First Four Books of Poems*. Copyright © 1975 by W.S. Merwin. W.S. Merwin, "Dead Hand," "Air," and "We Continue" from *The Moving Target*. Copyright © 1963 by W.S. Merwin. W.S. Merwin, "Some Last Questions," "December Night," and "For the Anniversary of My Death" from *The Lice*. Copyright © 1967 by W.S. Merwin. W.S. Merwin, "Tergvinder's Stone" from *The Miner's Pale Children*. Copyright © 1970 by W.S. Merwin. W.S. Merwin, "Do Not Die" and "Animula" from *The Carrier of Ladders*. Copyright © 1970 by W.S. Merwin. W.S. Merwin, "A Door" from *Writing to an Unfinished Accompaniment*. Copyright © 1973 by W.S. Merwin. W.S. Merwin, "The Falcons" from *The Compass Flower*. Copyright © 1977 by W.S. Merwin. W.S. Merwin, "The Waving of a Hand," "Son," "A Family," "The Fields," and "The Black Jewel" from *Opening the Hand*. Copyright © 1983 by W.S. Merwin. All reprinted with the permission of Atheneum Publishers.

Frank O'Hara: "Poem [The eager note]" and "Meditations in an Emergency" from *Meditations in an Emergency* by Frank O'Hara used by permission of Grove Press. "The Day Lady Died," "Steps," "Yesterday Down at the Canal," and "Poem [Lana Turner has collapsed!]" from *Lunch Poems* by Frank O'Hara. Copyright © 1964 by Frank O'Hara. Reprinted by permission of City Lights Books. "Autobiographia Literaria," "All the Mirrors," "To My Dead Father," "To John Ashbery," and "Why I am Not a Painter" copyright © 1958, 1967, 1971 by Maureen Granville-Smith, Administratrix of the Estate of Frank O'Hara. Reprinted from *The Collected Poems of Frank O'Hara*, Edited by Donald Allen, by permission of Alfred A. Knopf, Inc.

Mary Oliver: "The Swimming Lesson" copyright © 1965 by Mary Oliver. Reprinted from *No Voyage and Other Poems*, as published by Houghton Mifflin Company, with the permission of Mary Oliver. "Sleeping in the Forest," "The Fish," "Music Lessons," "The Black Walnut Tree," and "Storm" from *Twelve Moons: Poems* by Mary Oliver. Copyright © 1979 by Mary Oliver. "The Kitten," "Tasting the Wild Grapes," "An Old Whorehouse," "University Hospital, Boston," and "In Blackwater Woods" from *American Primitive: Poems* by Mary Oliver. Copyright © 1983 by Mary Oliver. All by permission of Little, Brown and Company in association with the Atlantic Monthly Press.

Charles Olson: "The Librarian" and "Moonset, Gloucester . . ." reprinted from *The Distances* by Charles Olson by permission of George F. Butterick, Literary Executor, Estate of Charles Olson. "Maximus, to Himself," "I, Maximus of Gloucester, to You,"

"Maximus to Gloucester, Letter 27 [Withheld]," and "A Later Note on Letter #15" from Charles Olson, *The Maximus Poems of Charles Olson* (1983). Used by permission of The University of California Press.

Marge Piercy: "The Skyscrapers of the Financial District..." copyright © 1967 by Marge Piercy. Reprinted from *Breaking Camp*. "The Friend" copyright © 1969 by Marge Piercy. Reprinted from *Hard Loving*. Both by permission of Wesleyan University Press. "A Work of Artifice," "Barbie Doll," "To Be of Use," "The Love of Lettuce," "You Ask Why Sometimes I Say Stop," "Crows," "Cats Like Angels," and "Digging In" from *Circles on the Water*, by Marge Piercy. Copyright © 1969, 1971, 1973, 1977, 1978, 1979, 1982 by Marge Piercy. Reprinted by permission of Alfred A. Knopf, Inc.

Sylvia Plath: "The Colossus" copyright c 1961 by Sylvia Plath. Reprinted from *The Colossus and Other Poems*, by Sylvia Plath, by permission of Alfred A. Knopf, Inc. From *The Collected Poems of Sylvia Plath* edited by Ted Hughes: "Daddy," "Mary's Song," "Cut," "Lady Lazarus," and "Winter Trees" all copyright © 1963 by Ted Hughes. "Witch Burning" copyright © 1960 by Ted Hughes. "Crossing the Water" copyright © 1962 by Ted Hughes. "Brasília" copyright © 1964 by Ted Hughes. "Nick and the Candlestick" and "The Munich Mannequins" copyright © 1965 by Ted Hughes. All selections reprinted by permission of Harper & Row, Publishers, Inc., and Olwyn Hughes. British publisher: Faber & Faber, London.

Adrienne Rich: Selections are reprinted from Poems, Selected and New, 1950–1974, by Adrienne Rich with permission of W. W. Norton & Company, Inc. Copyright © 1975, 1973, 1971, 1969, 1966 by W. W. Norton & Company, Inc. Copyright © 1967, 1963, 1962, 1960, 1959, 1961, 1958, 1957, 1956, 1955, 1954, 1953, 1952, 1951 by Adrienne Rich. "Splittings" is reprinted from THE DREAM OF A COMMON LANGUAGE, Poems 1975–1977, by Adrienne Rich, by permission of W. W. Norton & Company, Inc. Copyright © 1978 by W. W. Norton & Company, Inc. Selections are reprinted from THE FACT OF A DOORFRAME, Poems Selected and New, 1950–1984, by Adrienne Rich, by permission of W. W. Norton & Company, Inc. Copyright© 1984 by Adrienne Rich. Copyright ©1975, 1978 by W. W. Norton & Company, Inc. Copyright ©1981 by Adrienne Rich.

Theodore Roethke: "The Premonition," "Cuttings (later)," "Forcing House," "Elegy for Jane," "The Waking," "I Knew a Woman" copyright 1941, 1948, 1946, 1950, 1953, 1954 by Theodore Roethke. "My Papa's Waltz" copyright 1942 by Hearst Magazines, Inc. "Meditation at Oyster River," "In a Dark Time," "In Evening Air" copyright © 1960 by Beatrice Roethke, Administratrix of the Estate of Theodore Roethke. From the book *The Collected Poems of Theodore Roethke*. Reprinted by permission of Doubleday & Company, Inc.

Anne Sexton: "Her Kind" from *To Bedlam and Part Way Back* by Anne Sexton. Copyright © 1960 by Anne Sexton. "Man and Wife" from *Live or Die* by Anne Sexton. Copyright © 1966 by Anne Sexton. "With Mercy for the Greedy" and "The Abortion" from *All My Pretty Ones* by Anne Sexton. Copyright © 1962 by Anne Sexton. "In Celebration of My Uterus" and "Us" from *Love Poems* by Anne Sexton. Copyright © 1967, 1968, 1969 by Anne Sexton. "The Fury of Cocks" from *The Death Notebooks* by Anne Sexton. Copyright © 1974 by Anne Sexton. "Rowing" and "Two Hands" from *The Awful Rowing Toward God* by Anne Sexton. Copyright © 1975 by Loring Conant, Jr., Executor of the Estate of Anne Sexton. All reprinted by permission of Houghton Mifflin Company.

Louis Simpson: "To the Western World" and "Hot Night on Water Street" copyright © 1957 by Louis Simpson. Reprinted from *A Dream of Governors*. "American Poetry" and "In the Suburbs," copyright © 1963 by Louis Simpson, and "Walt Whitman at Bear Mountain" copyright © 1960 by Louis Simpson. Reprinted from *At the End of the Open Road* by permission of Wesleyan University Press. "Physical Universe" from

The Best Hour of the Night by Louis Simpson. Copyright © 1983 by Louis Simpson. Reprinted by permission of Ticknor & Fields, a Houghton Mifflin Company. "After Midnight," "Luminous Night," "American Dreams," "Port Jefferson," "The Silent Piano," "Sacred Objects," and "As a Man Walks" copyright ©1965, 1971, 1979, 1983 by Louis Simpson. Reprinted from *People Live Here: Selected Poems 1949–1983* by Louis Simpson with the permission of BOA Editions, Ltd.

W. D. Snodgrass: "April Inventory" and "Heart's Needle #6" copyright © 1957, 1959 by W. D. Snodgrass. Reprinted from *Heart's Needle*, by W. D. Snodgrass, by permission of Alfred A. Knopf, Inc. "The Mother," "Disposal," and "Viewing the Body" copyright © 1984 by W. D. Snodgrass. Reprinted from *Remains* by W. D. Snodgrass. "Eva Braun, 22 April" and "Dr. Josef Goebbels, 1 May" copyright © 1977 by W. D. Snodgrass. Reprinted from *The Führer Bunker: A Cycle of Poems in Progress* by W. D. Snodgrass. All with the permission of BOA Editions, Ltd. "After Experience Taught Me . . ." and "A Flat One" copyright © 1968 by W. D. Snodgrass. Reprinted from *After Experience,* as published by Harper & Row, with the permission of W. D. Snodgrass. "Old Apple Trees" from *If Birds Build with Your Hair* by W. D. Snodgrass, reprinted by permission of Nadja Press.

Gary Snyder: "Vapor Trails" from Gary Snyder, *The Back Country.* Copyright © 1968 by Gary Snyder. "I Went into the Maverick Bar," "The Bath," and "As for Poets" from Gary Snyder, *Turtle Island.* Copyright © 1972, 1974 by Gary Snyder. "Song of the Taste" from Gary Snyder, *Regarding Wave.* Copyright © 1970 by Gary Snyder. First published in *Poetry.* All reprinted by permission of New Directions Publishing Corporation. "Axe Handles" and "Soy Sauce" excerpted from *Axe Handles:* Poems by Gary Snyder, © 1983 by Gary Snyder. Published by North Point Press and reprinted by permission. All rights reserved. "Riprap," "Hay for the Horses," and "Milton by Firelight" copyright ©1969 by Gary Snyder. Reprinted from *Riprap, & Cold Mountain Poems,* as published by Four Seasons Foundation, with the permission of Gary Snyder.

William Stafford: "Temporary Facts" and "Assurance" from *Smoke's Way* by William Stafford by permission of Graywolf Press. "Answers," "The Early Ones," and "Things That Happen Where There Aren't Any People" copyright © 1980 by William Stafford. Reprinted from *Things That Happen Where There Aren't Any People* by William Stafford with the permission of BOA Editions, Ltd. "A Certain Bend" and "Ode to Garlic" copyright © 1984 by William Stafford. Reprinted with the permission of William Stafford. *From Stories That Could Be True:* New and Collected Poems by William Stafford: "At the Bomb Testing Site" and "Traveling Through the Dark" copyright © 1960 by William E. Stafford; "Vocation" copyright © 1962 by William E. Stafford; "My Father: October 1942" and "Across Kansas" copyright © 1963 by William E. Stafford; "A Family Turn," copyright © 1966 by William E. Stafford; "An Introduction to Some Poems" copyright © 1968 by William E. Stafford; "Report from a Far Place" copyright © 1970 by William E. Stafford; and "The Stick in the Forest" copyright © 1969 by William E. Stafford. All selections reprinted by permission of Harper & Row, Publishers, Inc.

Gerald Stern: "In Carpenter's Woods," from *Rejoicings: Poems 1966–1972,* copyright © 1973 by Gerald Stern, Metro Book Co., 3208 Cahuenga Blvd., W., Los Angeles. "The War Against the Jews," "Lord, Forgive a Spirit," "The Shirt Poem," and "Days of 1978" from *The Red Coal* by Gerald Stern. Copyright © 1981 by Gerald Stern. Reprinted by permission of Houghton Mifflin Company. "Song" ("There's Nothing in This Gardenous World"), "Weeping and Wailing," and "Romance" from *Paradise Poems,* by Gerald Stern. Copyright © 1982, 1983, 1984 by Gerald Stern. Reprinted by permission of Random House, Inc. "At Bickford's" and "The Cemetery of Orange Trees in Crete" copyright © 1977 by Gerald Stern. Reprinted from *Lucky Life,* as published by Houghton Mifflin Company, with the permission of Gerald Stern.

Mark Strand: Specified poems from *Selected Poems.* Copyright © 1980 by Mark

Strand. Reprinted with the permission of Atheneum Publishers. "Always" copyright © 1983 by Mark Strand. Reprinted from the broadside published by Palaemon Press Ltd. (as amended by Mark Strand) with the permission of Mark Strand.

Lucien Stryk: "Awakening," "To a Japanese Poet," "The Cannery," "Summer," "Letter to Jean-Paul Baudot, at Christmas," and "Farmer" from *Selected Poems*, by Lucien Stryk, Swallow Press Edition. Used with permission of Ohio University Press. "Cherries," "Exterminator," "Juggler," "Watching War Movies," and "Dawn" from *Cherries* by Lucien Stryk. Used with the permission of Ampersand Press.

Richard Wilbur: "Advice to a Prophet" copyright © 1959 by The New Yorker Magazine, Inc. Reprinted from *Advice to a Prophet and Other Poems* by Richard Wilbur. "Love Calls Us to the Things of This World" and "A Baroque Wall-Fountain in the Villa Sciarra" from *Things of This World*, copyright © 1956 by Richard Wilbur. "Year's End" copyright 1949 by The New Yorker Magazine, Inc.; renewed 1977 by Richard Wilbur. Reprinted from *Ceremony and Other Poems* by Richard Wilbur. "On the Eyes of an SS Officer," "Potato," "A Dubious Night," and "Praise in Summer" from *The Beautiful Changes and Other Poems*, copyright 1947, 1975 by Richard Wilbur. "The Writer" copyright © 1971 by Richard Wilbur and "Cottage Street, 1953" copyright © 1972 by Richard Wilbur reprinted from his volume *The Mind-Reader*. All by permission of Harcourt Brace Jovanovich, Inc. "Hamlen Brook" reprinted from *Poetry*, October 1982, by permission of the Editor of *Poetry*. Copyright 1982 by The Modern Poetry Association.

C. K. Williams: "From My Window," "The Gas Station," and "Tar" from *Tar: Poems by C. K. Williams.* Copyright © 1980, 1981, 1982, 1983 by C. K. Williams. Reprinted by permission of Random House, Inc. "It Is This Way with Men" and "Patience Is When You Stop Waiting" copyright © 1969 by C. K. Williams. Reprinted from *Lies*, as published by Houghton Mifflin Company. "Then the Brother of the Wind" and "They Warned Him Then They Threw Him Away" copyright © 1972 by C. K. Williams. Reprinted from *I Am the Bitter Name*, as published by Houghton Mifflin Company. "Spit" copyright © 1977 by C. K. Williams. Reprinted from *With Ignorance*, as published by Houghton Mifflin Company. All used with the permission of C. K. Williams.

Charles Wright: "The New Poem" copyright © 1971 by Charles Wright. "Blackwater Mountain" copyright © 1972 by Charles Wright and first appeared in *Poetry*. "Nightdream" copyright © 1973 by Charles Wright and first appeared in *Poetry*. "Snow" copyright © 1975 by Charles Wright. "Equation," "Reunion," and "April" copyright © 1977 by Charles Wright. All reprinted from *Country Music: Selected Early Poems* by permission of Wesleyan University Press. "Driving Through Tennessee," "Three Poems for the New Year," and "California Dreaming" from *The Southern Cross*, by Charles Wright. Copyright © 1981 by Charles Wright. Reprinted by permission of Random House, Inc.

James Wright: "As I Step Over a Puddle...," "Lying in a Hammock...," "Fear Is What Quickens Me," and "A Blessing" copyright © 1961 by James Wright. "Goodbye to the Poetry of Calcium" copyright © 1959 by James Wright. "Autumn Begins in Martins Ferry, Ohio" and "The Jewel" copyright © 1962 by James Wright. "Late November in a Field" copyright © 1969 by James Wright. "In Response to a Rumor..." copyright © 1966 by James Wright. "A Moral Poem..." copyright © 1971 by James Wright. All reprinted from *Collected Poems* by James Wright by permission of Wesleyan University Press. "The Journey" and "Yes, But" from *This Journey* by James Wright. Copyright © 1982 by Anne Wright, Executrix of the Estate of James Wright. Reprinted by permission of Random House, Inc. "A Poem of Towers" from *Two Citizens* by James Wright, copyright © 1970, 1971, 1972, 1973 by James Wright. "Beautiful Ohio" from *To a Blossoming Pear Tree* by James Wright, copyright © 1973, 1974, 1975, 1976, 1977 by James Wright. Reprinted by permission of Farrar, Straus & Giroux, Inc.

To the Student

Will you take the time to write your reactions to *Contemporary American Poetry*? Your comments will help us to plan future editions of the work. Please fill out the questionnaire and mail it to:

Marketing Services
College Division
Houghton Mifflin Company
One Beacon Street
Boston, MA 02108

1. Please give the name and number of the course for which you used this textbook. Indicate whether the course is one or two semesters.

   _____

   Name of your college or university

   _____

   Which year did you take the course?
   ____ Freshman   ____ Sophomore   ____ Junior   ____ Senior

2. Please check the name of each poet below whose works you read for the course.

__ Ammons	__ Gardner	__ Levertov	__ Sexton
__ Ashbery	__ Ginsberg	__ Levine	__ Simpson
__ Bell	__ Hall	__ Logan	__ Snodgrass
__ Berryman	__ Harper	__ Lowell	__ Snyder
__ Bishop	__ Hayden	__ Merrill	__ Stafford
__ Bly	__ Hugo	__ Merwin	__ Stern
__ Brooks	__ Ignatow	__ O'Hara	__ Strand
__ Clifton	__ Jarrell	__ Oliver	__ Stryk
__ Creeley	__ Justice	__ Olson	__ Wilbur
__ Dickey	__ Kinnell	__ Piercy	__ Williams
__ Dugan	__ Kizer	__ Plath	__ C. Wright
__ Duncan	__ Kumin	__ Rich	__ J. Wright
__ Ferlinghetti	__ Kunitz	__ Roethke	

3. Of the poets you read, please list the five or so who made the strongest impression on you. _____

   _____

4. Of the poets you read, please list any whose works you feel you did not understand or appreciate. _____

   _____

5. When you studied a given poet, did you read all of his or her works in the anthology?   ____ Usually   ____ Sometimes   ____ Rarely

6. Did your course include poets who are not represented in this textbook? ___Yes ___ No   If you read additional poets, please list as many as you can recall. _____

_____

7. Do you plan to keep this textbook for your own library?
___Yes   ___ No

8. How much did you use the Poet Notes at the back of the book?
___ Very often ___ Often ___ Occasionally ___ Rarely ___ Never

9. Did you read the essay about contemporary poetry at the back of the book? ___Yes ___ No   If yes; please comment on its usefulness. _____

_____

10. Did you use the selected bibliography of critical works?
___ Yes   ___ No

11. Please make any additional comments that you care to about the anthology.

_____

_____

_____

_____

_____

_____

_____

_____

_____

_____

_____

_____

_____

_____

_____

_____

_____

_____

Thank you for your help.